The Train-Watcher's Guide to North American Railroads

SECOND EDITION

RAILROAD REFERENCE SERIES NO. 11

COMPILED BY GEORGE H. DRURY

Editor: Bob Hayden   Copy Editors: Terrence Spohn, Christine Reel   Art Director: Lawrence Luser

On the cover: An eastbound Santa Fe freight train with auto racks and piggy-back flats in the consist rolls through Darling, Arizona, 329 miles west of Albuquerque, New Mexico, on April 19, 1990. Photo by Mike Danneman.

KALMBACH BOOKS

Library of Congress Cataloging-in-Publication Data

Drury, George H.
    Train-watcher's guide to North American railroads / by
George H. Drury. — 2nd ed.
       p.   cm. — (Railroad reference series: no. 11)
    ISBN 0-89024-131-7: $14.95
    1. Railroads—United States—Directories. 2. Railroads—Canada—
Directories. 3. Railroads—Mexico—Directories. I. Title. II. Series
TF23.D75 1993   92-35627
385'.025'7—dc20   CIP

To order additional copies of this book or other
Kalmbach books, call toll free at (800) 533-6644.

INTRODUCTION

Some industries are more satisfying to watch than others. Transportation is close to the top of the list — when did you last see someone enthralled by a librarian reshelving books or encounter a collection of photos of insurance agencies? In the transportation world, trains have an advantage over boats and planes in that they can be viewed easily in their habitat. About the only place you can see a ship cruising across the ocean is from the deck of another ship; you see a plane either nosed up to the gate at the airport or as a tiny speck leading a vapor trail across the sky. Trains are easier. The tracks run through cities and towns and cross the streets you use. To see a train doing its job — carrying goods or people — you go to the tracks and wait.

Train-watching as a hobby begins when you feel curiosity: Where is the train going? Where did it come from? What is it carrying? Whose is it? How does it work? How do you find the answers?

Back in olden days you found out about railroads first by reading all the railroad books in the public library (there were three, one of them by Lucius Beebe) and then by hanging around the depot, the latter at some cost in parental disapproval and undone homework.

It was a bright day when the agent in the ticket office gave you a system timetable. In it were schedules and equipment lists for the passenger trains of the railroad, perhaps an ad for the road's freight service, and a map. On the map, which usually occupied the center spread, the railroad's own lines were straight and thick. Friendly connections were narrower, and competing roads, even the four-track main line of the New York Central, were squiggly hairlines.

Then came a day when the agent gave you an old copy of *The Official Guide of the Railways* — a pulp paper monthly, 7 inches by 10 and a couple of inches thick. After perusing it for a few minutes you knew how Keats felt, standing silent on that peak in Darien, looking into his copy of Chapman's Homer.

The *Guide* contained timetables for every railroad in North and Central America and maps for most of them — the same maps that were in the railroads' timetables, but you could average the straight and crooked lines.

The *Guide* showed you where each railroad went and which connected with which. It gave substance to the freight cars you saw at trackside and on hobby shop shelves. You could pinpoint those decrepit short lines Beebe admired. You could read yourself to sleep at night planning trips. It was great stuff.

Now it's different. The depot has been torn down, the agent sits next to a telephone with an 800 number, and kids hang around shopping malls. The *Guide* is a pair of books: a freight edition that's mostly piggyback schedules and lists of officials — and it no longer includes all the railroads — and a passenger edition with timetables for Amtrak, VIA Rail Canada, and a few of Europe's principal trains.

The *Guide* wasn't a complete reader's companion — it couldn't tell you how many freight cars Santa Fe owned, or where Union Pacific's major classification yards were, or what the initials "DWP" stood for. Some of those questions were answered in the *Handbook of American Railroads* by Robert G. Lewis, published by Simmons-Boardman in 1951 and 1956, but now long out of date and even longer out of print. Today's railroad enthusiast needs some sort of unofficial guide, a combination field guide, modeler's bluebook, reader's companion, and friendly station agent — in other words, a good quick source of short answers and a pointer to longer ones. This book should satisfy that need.

What is a railroad?

It is useful to remember that a railroad consists of four elements: fixed plant (track, right of way, and buildings), rolling stock (locomotives and cars), human organization, and financial structure. Not all railroads have all four. For years the Buffalo, Rochester & Pittsburgh had only financial structure and fixed plant; it was operated by the Baltimore & Ohio with B&O cars and locomotives. The Clinchfield was an unincorporated company — employees and rolling stock — that operated the fixed plant of the Carolina, Clinchfield & Ohio Railway. Amtrak began operations with only financial structure and a few employees.

In the first edition of this book, published in 1984, I predicted that the railroad scene would continue to change and that soon we would have a very few large railroad systems, a lot of short lines, and very little in the way of medium-size roads. Publishing such a prediction, of course, virtually ensured the proliferation of medium-size regional railroads, which has been the most significant trend in railroading of the past decade.

Today's railroad scene

The railroad scene is not a static one. The 1970s and 1980s saw the disappearance of many well-known railroads. Some were merged by other railroads; other companies simply went out of existence. At the same time rail passenger service became almost exclusively a government business. The formation of Conrail in 1976 was the end of several of the oldest railroads in the United States (and one of the newest, Penn Central), but it also marked the beginning of a large number of short lines, as Conrail sold off many of its branches and secondary lines. In 1980 the bankrupt Rock Island shut down and the Milwaukee Road pulled back from Puget Sound to eastern Montana. Between 1981 and 1986 Western Pacific, Missouri Pacific, and Missouri-Kansas-Texas disappeared into Union Pacific.

During that period the national railroad map changed significantly. Years ago most pairs of major cities were connected by several railroad lines, each owned by a different company. Mergers had the effect of putting two or three or more of those lines under the same ownership. To reduce taxes and maintenance costs, the railroads concentrated their traffic on one of the lines and abandoned or pruned back the others. The effect is that the railroad network has much less connectivity today; the map has fewer through routes and more stub-end branches.

Another important factor is the shift in traffic emphasis to bulk commodities. Years ago it was important to offer merchandise and less-than-carload service to towns along the route; now much of that traffic moves by truck — and often those trucks move between major terminals on piggyback flat cars and to and from smaller towns by highway.

Classification of railroads

It used to be simple to classify railroads. As late as 1950, you could group them as major railroads, short lines, and switching and terminal roads, and pretty much match the Interstate Commerce Commission classification: Class 1, Class 2, and Class 3. (The ICC used and still uses Roman numerals; I'll stick with Arabic for clarity.) A Class 1 railroad was one with annual gross operating revenues of $1 million or more. There were well over 100 of them, and they ran the gamut from the Pennsylvania and the Southern Pacific down to the Charleston & Western Carolina and the Montour — from trunk lines to what the late David P. Morgan, editor of TRAINS, called "welterweights." In 1955 the Class 1 threshold was moved up to $3 million, knocking a dozen or so railroads off the list.

The entry fee for the Class 1 Club kept climbing, and it was not all due to inflation. By 1992 Class 1 meant annual operating revenue of $90 million or more (and it was raised later in the year to $250 million); Class 2 was $17.6 million to $87.9 million (the gap between 87.9 and 90 was undefined territory), and Class 3 was below $17.6 million.

The definitions don't include the word "freight," but it is implied. Some recent lists of Class 1 railroads have included Amtrak, perhaps grudgingly. Wisconsin Central and Montana Rail Link, which qualify on the basis of revenue, petitioned to remain a Class 2 railroad because of the extra paperwork required of Class 1 railroads.

Most passenger trains today, both commuter and intercity, are the responsibility of a government agency or a government-backed company. A train of electric commuter cars owned by the Connecticut Department of Transportation and a Boston-Washington Amtrak train stand adjacent at New Haven, Conn., in this 1982 scene. Photo by Tom Nelligan.

The Association of American Railroads also has three classes: Class 1, Regional, and Local. The AAR agrees with the ICC on what constitutes a Class 1 railroad. A regional railroad is a line-haul railroad with revenues between $40 million and $90 million or with more than 350 miles of track. A local railroad is a line-haul railroad falling below those criteria or a switching or terminal railroad.

There is no official or legal definition of "short line," but the railroad industry as a whole and the American Short Line Railroad Association apply the term to railroads with less than 100 miles of mainline track. For the railroad enthusiast perhaps the touchstone is the locomotive roster. Short lines tend to buy locomotives one at a time (Burlington Northern and Union Pacific order them by the hundred) and often secondhand. A railroad with no more than two examples of any locomotive model (except GE 44-tonners and 70-tonners in the past and now CF7s) is a short line.

Further confusing the classification systems are the commuter railroads, transit authorities, and tourist and museum railroads. How necessary to the railroad enthusiast is a classification system? It may be adequate to divide the railroads into three groups: the 11 major railroad systems (Amtrak, Burlington Northern, Canadian National, Conrail, CP Rail, CSX Transportation, National Railways of Mexico, Norfolk Southern, Santa Fe, Southern Pacific, and Union Pacific); the president is also the accountant and the engineer, and everything between. Simpler still is the binary classification used by some enthusiasts: My Favorite Railroad and Others.

What is in this book?

I have included all railroads more than 200 miles long or with more than 1,000 freight cars in interchange service (or some compromise between those two criteria), and all the commuter operating authorities. A few roads in the book don't meet these criteria; I included them because they are interesting in one way or another.

The definition of railroad has been left loose enough to include operating companies such as VIA Rail Canada that own cars and locomotives but no track, but I have excluded "invisible railroads" — those that are leased to or operated by other railroads, either singly or jointly, and have no rolling stock of their own. I have not included museum and tourist railroads nor have I included full descriptions of rail transit operations.

Information sources:
• Company name (using an ampersand for "and," whether or not the railroad does) — *Pocket List of Railroad Officials.*
• Brief history and description — drawn from several sources: *Moody's Transportation Manual*, books, TRAINS Magazine, and other periodicals. Here I chose to stick to the basics of where and when the railroad began and how it became what it is rather than detail each corporate change.
• Mailing address of general offices — *Pocket List of Railroad Officials.*
• Miles of road operated — In some cases this is ambiguous or hard to determine. For example, consider the former Milwaukee Road main line between Techny and Rondout, Illinois. The track is owned by Metra, which operates Chicago-Fox Lake commuter trains on it. On that stretch of track you can also find Soo Line freight trains (which serve local industries), Wisconsin & Calumet freight trains (which are running through between Chicago and WICT's own track at Fox Lake), and Amtrak's Chicago-Milwaukee trains and Chicago-Seattle-Portland *Empire Builder* (and it's uncertain whether Amtrak's mileage figures count Chicago-Milwaukee once or twice). The figure cited is taken from either *The Official Railway Equipment Register* or *The Pocket List of Railroad Officials.*
• Reporting marks, the initials with which each railroad marks its freight cars. These may include initials of predecessor railroads and initials used on cars assigned to special services. I have included only those reporting marks in current use. *The Official Railway Equipment Register*, April 1992.
• Number of locomotives — *Diesel Locomotive Rosters: U. S., Canada, Mexico* (Third Edition).
• Number of freight cars in revenue interchange service (that is, omitting cabooses, maintenance of way equipment, and other items not usually found off home rails) — *The Official Railway Equipment Register.*
• Principal commodities carried — annual reports of the railroads and *Moody's Transportation Manual*, but omitted if no item was predominant.
• Location and name of major yards and shops (for large railroads) — various sources.
• Junctions with other railroads (for small railroads) — *The Official Railway Equipment Register*, April 1992. I have omitted junctions not used for interchange and connections made through another railroad.

5

• Passenger routes, lines of the railroad you can ride as a paying passenger — Amtrak, VIA, and commuter-operator timetables.
• Radio frequencies — *Compendium of American Railroad Radio Frequencies*. Unless the entry is noted otherwise, the frequencies given are channel 1, channel 2, and yard or other.
• Historical and technical society — the criterion for inclusion is receipt of some publication from the group within the past year by the Kalmbach Publishing Co. library. MODEL RAILROADER magazine carries a current list of these groups in its February issue; the list also appears annually in TRAINS magazine.
• Recommended reading — in my opinion the best books for general information on the railroad and also recent magazine articles. I have tried to cite books that are in print. Often on library shelves you'll find older books, such as the corporate histories that many railroads commissioned in the 1940s and 1950s. I have given the most recent name and address of the publisher, and I have cited the International Standard Book Number for those books that have one. With that number, a bookstore should be able to track down a copy of any book still in print. For a few books I have provided instead the Library of Congress Catalog Card Number.
• Map — the purpose of the map is to cast the railroad in its geographic setting, not show every line in full detail. The maps are not drawn to a uniform scale. Maps for two or more railroads have been combined where appropriate. For a few small railroads the map is omitted, and the descriptive paragraph should suffice. Railroad lines are shown on some highway maps, in particular those published by the American Automobile Association and some state highway departments, and in the state atlases published by DeLorme Mapping Company, P. O. Box 298, Freeport, ME 04032.

The individual railroad entries were submitted to the railroads for review and correction; I have taken their word as the best authority.

For further information: Since a book the size of this one can't begin to tell everything, turn to:
• *The Official Railway Equipment Register* (quarterly list of all the freight cars in North America).
• *The Pocket List of Railroad Officials* (quarterly).

Both are published by the K-III Information Company, 424 W. 33rd Street, New York, NY 10001.

• *The Railroad — What It Is, What It Does*, by John H. Armstrong, published by Simmons-Boardman Publishing Corporation, 1809 Capitol Avenue, Omaha, NE 68102.
• *Handy Railroad Atlas of the United States* (revised every few years), published by Rand McNally & Co. (railroad maps for each state). Publication was discontinued after the 1988 edition.
• *1948 Handy Railroad Atlas of the United States*, published by Kalmbach Publishing Co., 21027 Crossroads Circle, P. O. Box 1612, Waukesha, WI 53187.
• *Compendium of American Railroad Radio Frequencies*, compiled by Gary L. Sturm and Mark J. Landgraf, published by Gary L. Sturm, P. O. Box 80041, Fort Wayne, IN 46898.
• *Railroad Names*, by William D. Edson, published in 1984 by William D. Edson, 10820 Gainsborough Road, Potomac, MD 20854
• *Canadian Trackside Guide*, published annually by Bytown Railway Society, P. O. Box 141, Station A, Ottawa, ON K1N 8V1
• Other useful references on the railroad scene are TRAINS Magazine, which has been exploring the new regional railroads in depth; my *Historical Guide to North American Railroads*, which documents the major railroads that have disappeared through merger or abandonment since 1930; Edward A. Lewis's *American Shortline Railway Guide*; and Charles W. McDonald's *Diesel Locomotive Rosters: United States, Canada, Mexico*, all published by Kalmbach Publishing Co., 21027 Crossroads Circle, P. O. Box 1612, Waukesha, WI 53187.

Acknowledgments

There are more than a hundred persons working for railroads in the U. S., Canada, and Mexico who reviewed copy and made corrections and additions. Several photographers responded quickly and generously to my request for current photos. Christine Reel and Terrence Spohn made sure I commited no crimes against the language. Bob Hayden added clarity and conciseness with his blue pencil. I thank them all.

GEORGE H. DRURY

Waukesha, Wisconsin
September 1992

THE HARDWARE OF TODAY'S RAILROADING

The fundamental hardware of modern railroading has been in use long enough that few people question why it was chosen or how it works. The answers to those questions reveal a great deal about how railroad technology developed.

Steel wheels, steel rails

Railroads rely on the principle that hard things roll better than soft things. A tin can rolls across a vinyl kitchen floor far more easily than a sponge-rubber ball rolls across the carpet in the living room. A bicycle with hard tires rolls more easily than a bicycle with soft tires. A steel wheel rolls on a steel rail far more easily than a rubber tire rolls on pavement — and it takes less energy to make it roll.

There's a catch. It is difficult to change the direction of a hard wheel rolling on a hard surface. While steel-wheeled automobiles would roll almost effortlessly over steel highways, they would slide off the road at the first curve. A steel wheel-steel surface system needs something to keep the wheel from moving sideways (and a benefit of that is that the running surface needs to be only as wide as the wheels). Ridges to guide the wheels might be a logical choice, but debris could collect in the angle between the ridge and the running surface. Flanges on the wheels work better. A single flange per wheel is sufficient, since the wheels come in pairs. Flanges on the inside of the rails work better — centrifugal force will tend to lift the wheel on the inside of the curve and force the outside wheel into firmer contact with the rail.

What is a train?

You'd think that any string of locomotives and cars is a train. No. Quantity isn't involved. The official definition, found in every railroad's rule book, is: "An engine or more than one engine coupled, with or without cars, displaying markers." A marker is a light or flag at the rear of the train, and generally one is sufficient to satisfy the rule. Another rule requires that a headlight be displayed at the front of every train. A train

Markers, such as the two oil-burning lanterns hung on the rear of this Boston & Maine train of decades ago, are part of the definition of a train. Photo by S. K. Bolton Jr.

therefore requires a means of propulsion, something indicating the rear of the train, and something indicating the front.

Locomotives

The first railroads used horses for motive power. Even if the best-known contest between horse and steam — horse versus Baltimore & Ohio's *Tom Thumb* in 1830 — went to the horse, steam ultimately won. The steam locomotive proved simple and durable, but it required a great deal of service and maintenance.

The electric locomotive appeared on the scene in the 1890s, offering many advantages and one major drawback: the apparatus required to get electricity to the locomotive. Internal combustion engines appeared soon afterward. Experience soon showed that an electric transmission was the best means to harness such an engine for railroad use, in effect creating an electric locomotive that carried its own power plant, and that the diesel

Typical of today's diesels are Conrail 8217, a 2000-h.p. GP38-2, and 6460, a 3000-h.p. SD40-2, both products of the Electro-Motive Division of General Motors. Model Railroader **Magazine photo by Jim Hediger.**

engine was better suited to railroad work than the gasoline engine.

Diesel-electric locomotives began to take over switching duties in the 1920s, and in the 1930s they found their way into passenger service, usually on lightweight streamlined trains. In 1939 Electro-Motive Corporation, a subsidiary of General Motors, produced a four-unit, 5400-h.p. diesel locomotive for freight service. That locomotive changed the course of railroading. By the mid-1950s steam was uncommon on North American railroads, and by 1960 dieselization was virtually complete.

Most of North America's diesel locomotives today are of a standard design: a 12- or 16-cylinder engine driving an alternator which produces current for series-wound nose-hung traction motors on each axle. Electro-Motive diesels are of the two-stroke cycle type; General Electric, four-stroke cycle. Some locomotives ride on two 4-wheel trucks; others on two 6-wheel trucks. Construction is the same: the machinery is carried on a frame and covered by a removable hood with walkways on each side or by a removable full-width cowl. A cab is located at or near one end of the locomotive. The diversity of diesels elsewhere in the world — hydraulic transmission, a single motor driving two or more axles, a cab at each end — is not found in North America.

Freight cars

Freight cars are of two basic types, open and closed. Open cars are used for cargos that aren't affected by weather. The most basic open car is the flat car, simply a platform supported by a pair of trucks. Any load shipped on a flat car will require restraint — even a 100-ton block of granite can shift as the car starts and stops and turns and jounces. Among the specialized kinds of flat cars are piggyback flats with fifth-wheel hitches and tie-downs for highway trailers, container flats with sockets and latches, and center-beam flat cars for lumber, plywood, and wallboard. An auto rack flat car has a superstructure with one or two additional decks for carrying cars and trucks; nowadays most also have sides, end doors, and a roof to protect the vehicles.

Put sides around a flat car and you have a gondola car, good for carrying anything that can be dumped in and lifted out: steel shapes, rail, scrap, and the like. A special type of gondola is used for coal; it is unloaded by tipping it over in a rotary car dumper, and a swiveling coupler at one end permits that to be done without uncoupling it from a train.

Add unloading doors to the floor of a gondola and a sloping floor at each end, and you have a hopper car. Without the sloping end sheets you have a drop-bottom gondola, and you'll have to shovel some of the cargo over to the doors; a hopper car is self-clearing by definition.

The covered hopper car was developed from the hopper car in the late 1930s. Originally it looked like a hopper car fitted with a roof and loading hatches; later designs have curved sides or roofs that make maximum use of the cross section. The first covered hoppers were for bulk cement; now they carry grain, plastic pellets, sugar — just about any dry commodity that will flow but requires protection from the weather. Covered hoppers are now the most numerous type of freight car. About 40 percent of those in service are owned by shippers and car leasing companies.

The most common closed car is the box car, which is just what its name implies: a box with a sliding door on each side. Modifications for special duties include wide doors, various types of load-restraining devices, cushion underframes, and insulation.

Refrigerator cars used to be box cars with insulation, tight-fitting hinged doors, and bunkers to hold ice to keep the load cool. In the 1950s refrigeration units powered by small diesel engines began to supersede ice-cooled cars. The diesel engines in these mechanical refrigerators could run for two weeks without refueling or other attention; "icers" had to be re-iced every day or so and could not attain temperatures low enough for frozen foods.

Tank cars carry liquids and gases and exist with a variety of features: special linings, heater coils, sloping bottoms, and multiple compartments. Often the tank itself constitutes the center sill of the car. Almost all tank cars are owned by shippers or car leasing companies rather than railroads.

The conductor and the rear brakeman used to ride in the caboose at the rear of the train. Now the entire crew (most often two persons rather than the four or five it used to be) usually rides in the locomotive cab, where communication is easier and they aren't battered about by slack action. Sophisticated telemetering devices known as FREDs (Flashing Rear End Devices) hung on the rear coupler serve as a marker and keep the crew apprised of pressure in the brake line and continuity of the train.

Passenger cars are discussed in the articles on Amtrak (Amtrak's passenger cars), Metra (commuter cars), and Private Cars.

Couplers and brakes

The first trains were held together by chains. At the first stop, when the cars came bumping together, passengers and railroaders alike immediately recognized the need for a coupler that could handle both tension and compression. Early North American railroads adopted the link and pin coupler, which satisfied that requirement. It was completely manual. As cars were pushed together, a man stood between them to guide a link protruding from a socket on one car into the socket on the other, then dropped a pin through the socket and the link at the right instant. The link and pin coupler was the principal reason that advertisements for artificial hands and legs were a staple in early volumes of *The Official Guide*.

There were many proposals for automatic couplers. Eli Janney's 1873 design, which had a swinging knuckle, was adopted by the Master Car Builders' Association in 1887. The knuckle coupler has been refined during

Replacing oil-burning markers and the caboose that carried them is today's end-of-train device, which incorporates a red warning light and radio telemetry. Photo by Douglas N. Koontz.

the past century, but it is still not fully automatic: brake hoses and other air and electrical connections between cars must be joined manually. Fully automatic couplers can be found today on transit systems, where equipment is captive and not interchanged with other railroads.

Brakes were something of an afterthought on the earliest locomotives and cars. The railroads settled on steam operated locomotive brakes and hand brakes on the cars; stopping a train required that brakemen move from car to car setting the brakes on each. This was almost as dangerous as the link and pin coupler, and there were numerous proposals for automatic brakes. George Westinghouse's air brake of 1869 was the one adopted. Still in use today, it has a fail-safe feature: a reduction of air pressure in the train line, whether caused by the engineer's brake valve or by air hoses coming apart, applies the brakes. Brakes, too, have been refined over the years; as with couplers, the refinements have been constrained by the requirement for compatibility with existing systems.

Track

The first rails were wood beams with iron running surfaces. Solid iron rails were in common use by 1845. Steel rails appeared in 1865 and by the 1890s had replaced iron. The characteristic cross-section of rail appeared early: a wide base to spread the weight on the tie, a vertical web to resist bending under the weight of a train, and a more-or-less rectangular head to serve as the running surface. Rail is measured by weight per yard. Mainline rail nowdays ranges from 112 to 145 pounds per yard. Lighter rail can be found on branch lines and in yards.

For years rail came in 39-foot lengths (because it was shipped in standard 40-foot freight cars) that were bolted together, with a little space between rails to allow for expansion in the summer and contraction in the winter. The joints are the least rigid and the weakest part of the track; most problems occur there. About 1930 welding technology improved to the point that welded rail joints were possible, creating continuous rails and eliminating most of the problems at rail joints.

How does continuous welded rail deal with temperature differences that make it expand and contract? It is laid during hot weather so that it will be at its maximum length. When the temperature falls, the rail will try to contract. Steel is quite elastic, and if the rail is restrained longitudinally (rail anchors keep it from sliding along the ties; ballast holds the ties in place), the rail will be forced to stretch. In practice the contraction takes place only in the cross section of the rail, not in the length.

On the first railroads the rails were fastened to large stone blocks, creating a rigid, immovable structure. In 1832 a shipment of stone blocks to

Track consists of rail, spikes, tie plates, ties, and ballast, all resting on a roadbed. This photo shows a rail joint. Six bolts and nuts through the splice bars (one on each side of the rail) and the web of the rail hold the two rails together. The wire between the two rails is for the signal circuit. Photo by H. Reid.

the Camden & Amboy Railroad was delayed, holding up construction. The superintendent ordered the temporary use of wood crossties. They were far easier to handle and they formed a track structure that was more flexible and easier on the rolling stock. Fastening the rail was much easier; spikes with an offset head could be driven into the tie next to the base of the rail. Wood ties quickly became standard. Later, steel tie plates were developed to spread the weight over a wider area of the tie.

Steel ties have been used occasionally for special purposes or where wood was scarce. Precast concrete ties have come into common use in the past decade. They are heavier than wood ties and create a firmer track structure.

The track is not anchored in place vertically; indeed, it flexes up and down as a train passes over it. Ballast transmits the weight of the track and train to the roadbed, holds the track in place laterally, and allows water to drain away from the rail and ties. The best material for ballast is crushed rock, with sharp edges that lock into each other and into the ties. Gravel, cinders, and other softer material are sufficient for light duty and low speeds.

Operating the trains

The need for train control arose with the frightening possibility that two trains could occupy the same piece of track at the same time. One of the earliest forms of train control was the timetable (the operating or employee timetable), which specified where each train should be — on the main track or in a siding — at any time. Any variation from the schedule had to be authorized by a train order, which was issued by the dispatcher and telegraphed to operators at stations, who wrote or typed it and gave it to the conductor and the engineer of each train affected by the order.

The train order system initially required trains to stop the train to ascertain if there were orders. Signals were soon developed to tell the engineer in advance that there were orders, and whether they could be picked up on the fly or a stop was necessary.

Another form of train control was (and is) the block system. The track is divided into sections or blocks, and only one train may occupy a block. Signals indicating block occupancy were operated manually at first. The invention of the track circuit, which uses an electric current through the rails to detect a train, permitted them to be operated automatically.

Signals at junctions indicate the status of track switches and the permissible speed through the junction. The signals and switches are interlocked so that conflicting routes cannot be given clear signals.

The earliest signals consisted of a ball or a flag hoisted to the top of a pole. They were superseded by semaphores, which conveyed their indication by means of a moving blade. Night operation required signal lights in addition to semaphore blades, and as technology progressed, lights were found sufficient for daytime use too.

Signals are usually mounted on masts to the right of the track they govern; on multiple-track lines they are on bridges or gantries over the tracks. In yards and terminals where speeds are low and clearances are tight, dwarf signals are placed at track level.

Semaphore signals remain in use on a few railroads. They are of two types: lower quadrant, in which the blade pivots between horizontal and 60 degrees below horizontal, and upper quadrant, in which the blade swings upward from horizontal to 45 degrees for caution and vertical for proceed. Color light signals have a lamp and lens for each color; the lenses can be arrayed in a vertical row (most common), a triangle, or a horizontal row (primarily Chicago & North Western). The searchlight signal has a single lamp and lens with a moving spectacle plate inside the housing providing the colors. The position light signal, developed by the Pennsylvania Railroad, uses horizontal, vertical, and diagonal rows of three amber lights (two white lights for dwarf signals). The Baltimore & Ohio developed the color position light signal, which uses pairs of colored lights in a central signal head and supplemental white lights above and below.

Signal aspects — the arrangement and colors of the lights and semaphore blades — vary from one railroad to the next, but basic indications are the same: red means stop, green means proceed, and yellow means the next signal is red. Indications such as "proceed at medium speed through interlocking" and "approach second signal prepared to stop" call for two

or three lights. A good rule of thumb is that the position of the yellow or green lights — high, middle, or low — in a column of red lights indicates the permissible speed.

Whistles used to be practically the sole means of communication between the engine crew, the train crew, and operators in signal towers. Passenger trains were equipped with signal lines that enabled the conductor to sound a small air-operated whistle in the engine cab to signal such messages as "Proceed," "Stop at the next station," and "Turn off the train heat." (Freight train crews had to rely on hand and lantern signals.) The engineer used the locomotive whistle or horn to answer those signals and to warn of the train's approach. There is a long list of standard whistle signals conveying such messages as "Flagman protect rear of train" and "Release brakes," but radios have taken over the job of communication, and practically the only whistle signal used nowadays is the long-long-short-long highway-crossing warning.

The searchlight signal is the most prevalent type. It has a single lamp and lens. An internal moving spectacle plate provides the color. Photo by C. R. Yungkurth.

Recommended reading: *The Railroad — What It Is, What It Does*, by John H. Armstrong, published in 1990 (Third Edition) by Simmons-Boardman Publishing Corporation, 1809 Capitol Avenue, Omaha, NE 68102 (ISBN 0-911382-04-6)

ABERDEEN, CAROLINA & WESTERN RAILWAY

Aberdeen, Carolina & Western operates the "old" Norfolk Southern main line from Charlotte to Gulf, North Carolina, 105 miles, and the former Aberdeen & Briar Patch from Aberdeen to Star, N. C.

The old Norfolk Southern Railway was a 933-mile railroad (in 1930) with a main line that ran south from Norfolk, Virginia, crossed Albemarle Sound on a long trestle, then turned west through Raleigh to Charlotte. Branches reached Morehead City, Fayetteville, Durham, Asheboro, and Aberdeen. The NS had several narrow-gauge predecessors, and it spent much of its life in receivership.

The Southern Railway purchased the Norfolk Southern in 1974 — perhaps more for the name than anything else, in the light of later events. SR merged the Norfolk Southern into the Carolina & Northwestern Railway (another Southern subsidiary) under the Norfolk Southern name; then restored the Carolina & Northwestern name in 1981 so the Norfolk Southern name could be used for a newly formed holding company as part of the process of merging the Southern and the Norfolk & Western.

In 1983 the Carolina & Northwestern sold the 34-mile branch from Star to Aberdeen to the Aberdeen & Briar Patch Railway. The Aberdeen, Carolina & Western purchased the A&BP in June 1987. In May 1989 the AC&W leased from the "new" Norfolk Southern 105 miles of the old Norfolk Southern main line, from Charlotte east to through Star to Gulf, a junction northwest of Sanford.

Address of general offices: P. O. Box 646, Aberdeen, NC 28315
Miles of road operated: 289
Reporting marks: ACWR
Number of locomotives: 7
Number of freight cars: 12
Principal commodities carried: Grain, aggregate, brick, lumber, pulpwood, wood chips
Shops: Star, N. C.
Junctions with other railroads:
Aberdeen & Rockfish: Aberdeen, N. C.
CSX: Aberdeen, N. C.
Norfolk Southern: Charlotte, N. C.; Gulf, N. C.
Radio frequency: 160.680

Aberdeen, Carolina & Western GP9 No. 900, handsomely repainted, stands at Star, North Carolina with a GP7 still wearing Bangor & Aroostook colors. Photo by Jim Shaw.

ALASKA RAILROAD

The Alaska Railroad is descended from two short lines: the Alaska Northern Railway and the Tanana Valley Railroad. The Alaska Northern was reorganized in 1909 from the Alaska Central Railroad, a standard gauge line incorporated in 1902. It had a 72-mile line extending inland from Seward when it was purchased by the U. S. goverment in 1915.

The Tanana Valley was a narrow gauge line connecting Fairbanks to the head of navigation on the Tanana River and to a gold-mining area 35 miles to the northeast. It began operation in 1904, was purchased by the

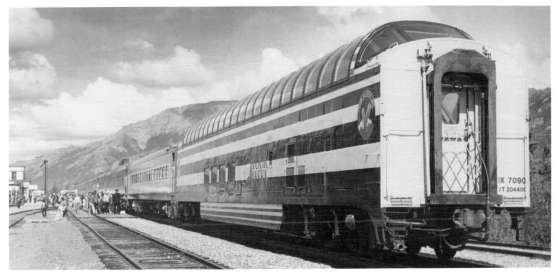

Alaska Railroad train 2 from Anchorage to Fairbanks pauses for passengers at Denali Park. On the rear of the train is a Tour Alaska dome car. Photo by John C. Illman.

U. S. government in 1917, and was converted to standard gauge in 1923.

There was pressure to build a tidewater-to-interior railroad to unlock the treasure chest which Alaska was considered at the time, but the lack of population in the territory made it clear that such a line would have to be built by the government. In 1912 President Taft asked Congress for such a measure; Congress provided it later that year as a rider on a bill granting Alaska self-government. The Alaska Central and the Tanana Valley were taken over by the Alaska Engineering Commission, which then built a railroad connecting the two lines, no small task. The line was renamed the Alaska Railroad in 1923, the year of its completion. The last spike was driven by President Harding.

The railroad was operated by the Department of the Interior until 1967, when it came under the Federal Railroad Administration, part of the new Department of Transportation. Ownership of the railroad was transferred to the State of Alaska on January 6, 1985.

The main line extends from Anchorage to Fairbanks, 356 miles. Other routes reach south from Anchorage to Seward and Whittier. All main routes have passenger service. Privately operated tour cars supplement regular equipment on the Anchorage-Fairbanks run. Auto-ferry trains operate on the Portage-Whittier branch because there are no highways.

Address of general offices: Pouch 7-2111, Anchorage, AK 99510
Miles of road operated: 526
Reporting marks: ARR
Number of locomotives: 49
Number of freight cars: 456
Number of passenger cars: 17
Principal commodities carried: Sand and gravel, coal, chemicals, petroleum, manufactured goods
Shops: Anchorage, Alaska
Junctions with other railroads:
Alaska Hydro-Train barges from Seattle): Whittier, Alaska
Canadian National barges from Prince Rupert, B. C.): Whittier, Alaska
Radio frequencies: 161.355, 161.385, 161.415
Passenger routes: Anchorage-Fairbanks, Anchorage-Seward, Portage-Whittier
Recommended reading: *Rails Across the Tundra*, by Stan Cohen, published in 1984 by Pictorial Histories Publishing Co., 713 South Third West, Missoula, MT 59801 (ISBN 0-933126-43-4)

ALGOMA CENTRAL CORPORATION

The Algoma Central was chartered in 1899 to build into the Ontario wilderness north of Sault Ste. Marie to bring out pulpwood and iron ore. In 1901 the ambitions of its founder added "& Hudson Bay" to the corporate title. It was 1912 before the road reached Hawk Junction; construction north to Hearst took another two years. The name reverted to Algoma Central in 1965.

The railroad has developed an excursion train business carrying tourists north from Sault Ste. Marie to the Agawa River canyon, where the railroad has developed a park. In 1990 the company was renamed Algoma Central Corporation, with the railway as a subsidiary. The company also has shipping, trucking, real estate, and land and forest subsidiaries.

Address of general offices: P. O. Box 7000, Sault Ste. Marie, ON, Canada P6A 5P6
Miles of road operated: 322
Reporting marks: AC, ACIS
Number of locomotives: 22
Number of freight cars: 953
Number of passenger cars: 40
Principal commodities carried: Iron ore, forest products
Shops: Sault Ste. Marie, Ont.
Junctions with other railroads:
Canadian National: Hearst, Ont.; Oba, Ont.
CP Rail: Franz, Ont.; Sault Ste. Marie, Ont.
Wisconsin Central: Sault Ste. Marie, Ont.

Algoma Central train 1 offers its passengers a last look at industrial scenery at Steelton, a few minutes from the train's origin at Sault Ste. Marie. From here the train heads into the forests of Ontario. MODEL RAILROADER Magazine photo by Jim Hediger.

Radio frequencies: 160.530 (road), 160.650 (dispatcher), 160.605 (dispatcher)
Passenger routes: Sault Ste. Marie-Hearst, Ont.
Recommended reading:
Algoma Central Railway, by O. S. Nock, published in 1975 by A & C Black Limited, London (ISBN 0-7136-1571-0)
The Algoma Central Story, by Dale Wilson, published in 1984 by Nickel Belt Rails, P. O. Box 483, Station B, Sudbury, ON P3E 4P6 (ISBN 0-920356-05-2)

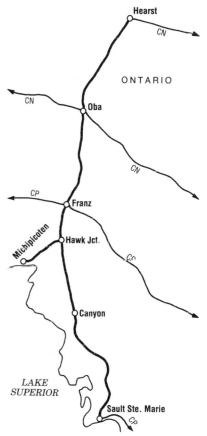

ALLEGHENY RAILROAD

The Sunbury & Erie Railroad was chartered in 1837 as part of a link between Lake Erie at Erie, Pennsylvania, and Philadelphia. Construction began in 1852; it was completed in 1864 by a successor company, the Philadelphia & Erie Railroad. The promoters of the railroad favored a direct route across the mountains of northwestern Pennsylvania — 88 miles shorter than a more southerly route that followed river valleys, but characterized by steep grades and sharp curves. The Pennsylvania Railroad leased the line before it was completed and purchased it in 1907.

For decades a mainstay of traffic on the line was iron ore moving east from Erie. In the 1950s the Pennsy shifted its ore facilities to Ashtabula, Ohio, and heavy ore trains disappeared from the Erie line.

Through freight trains disappeared from the line during Penn Central days, and the segment between Warren and Kane was considered unprofitable and excluded from Conrail. The Pennsylvania Department of Transportation purchased the Warren-Kane portion and subsidized Conrail service in order to preserve the route, but traffic continued to dwindle. In 1982 Conrail discontinued service between Erie and St. Marys, Pa.

A group of local shippers formed the Irvine, Warren, Kane & Johnsonburg Railroad, bought the Irvine-Warren and Kane-Johnsonburg segments, and contracted with Sloan Cornell, the owner and operator of the Gettysburg Railroad to operate them and the state's Warren-Kane segment from 1982 until 1985 as the Johnsonburg, Kane, Warren & Irvine.

The Hammermill Paper Co. needed a way to transport pulpwood to its mill in Erie and to transfer pulp between mills at Erie and Lock Haven. It evaluated the rail line between Erie and Emporium. In May 1985 Hammermill agreed to purchase the Erie-Irvine and Johnsonburg-St. Marys segments from Conrail; later that year it acquired the St. Marys-Emporium segment and the portions that the IWK&J and the state owned.

The Allegheny Railroad began operation in September 1985. Since much of the line had lain dormant after several years of little maintenance, an extensive rehabilitation program was necessary to bring the track back up to operating condition. The road is now owned by International Paper Company, which purchased Hammermill in 1986. Allegheny's traffic is equally divided between traffic destined to or from the mills

Allegheny GP40 No. 101 moves a train of oil at Waterford, Pennsylvania, on June 3, 1988. Photo by Jim Shaw.

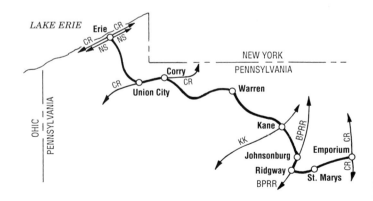

of its owner (including a run-through wood and pulp train between Erie and Lock Haven operated by Conrail), and movements to and from other customers along the line, which have increased markedly since the Allegheny began operation.

Address of general offices: 316 Pine Street, Warren, PA 16365
Miles of road operated: 154
Reporting marks: ALY
Number of locomotives: 6
Principal commodities carried: Pulpwood, wood pulp, lumber, steel, chemicals, petroleum products

Shops: Warren, Pa.
Junctions with other railroads:
Conrail: Erie, Pa.; Emporium, Pa.
Buffalo & Pittsburgh: Johnsonburg, Pa.
Knox & Kane: Kane, Pa.
Radio frequencies: 161.460, 160.290, 160.425
Recommended reading: "Allegheny: the phoenix of northwestern Pennsylvania," by John S. Murray, in TRAINS Magazine, September 1988, pages 22-29

ALTON & SOUTHERN RAILWAY

The Alton & Southern is a belt line serving East St. Louis, Illinois, and connecting with all the railroads entering the area. Its Gateway Yard is used by several other roads.

The road was incorporated in 1913 and was controlled for many years by the Aluminum Corporation of America (Alcoa). In 1966 Missouri Pacific petitioned the ICC for permission to buy the A&S, offering to match a previous bid by the St. Louis Southwestern (Cotton Belt). The ICC recom-

An Alton & Southern transfer run from Madison and Mitchell heads south on the causeway across Horseshoe Lake on March 16, 1975. Photo by Clyde L. Anderson.

mended joint ownership by Missouri Pacific, Cotton Belt, and Chicago & North Western; MP and C&NW purchased the road in 1968. In 1973 Cotton Belt purchased C&NW's half interest in the road. Union Pacific succeeded to Missouri Pacific's share of the ownership in 1982.

Address of general offices: 1000 S. 22nd Street, East St. Louis, IL 62207

Miles of road operated: 32

Reporting marks: ALS

Number of locomotives: 19

Major yards: Gateway Yard

Shops: East St. Louis, Ill.

Connects with:
Burlington Northern
Chicago & North Western
Conrail
CSX
Gateway Western
Illinois Central
Manufacturers Railway
Norfolk Southern
Southern Pacific (SPCSL)
St. Louis Southwestern
Terminal Railroad Association of St. Louis
Union Pacific
all within the St. Louis-East St. Louis Switching Districts

Radio frequencies: 160.770, 160.355

AMERICAN SHORT LINE RAILROAD ASSOCIATION

From the beginning, the dominant trend in the railroad industry was for companies to expand and merge. It made travel and the shipment of goods easier for the public, and it brought economies of scale to the railroads. Consider the situation across upstate New York in 1841. A trip from the Hudson River to the shore of Lake Erie at Buffalo involved seven railroads: Mohawk & Hudson, Utica & Schenectady, Syracuse & Utica, Auburn & Syracuse, Auburn & Rochester, Tonawanda (which ran from Rochester to Attica), and Attica & Buffalo. Those railroads early recognized the difficulties travelers faced both in booking passage on seven railroads and in changing trains. They first coordinated their train service, then, in 1853, consolidated as the New York Central Railroad.

The usual pattern was for large railroads to absorb connecting small railroads. Occasionally a small railroad wasn't absorbed for any of several reasons: the owners were making a good return on their investment; shippers and passengers were served well by local control; the small railroad connected with only one large railroad and there was no need to secure its business; or the small railroad wasn't especially .

Short lines developed a different way of doing business — flexible, quick to respond to their customers, and, because they were not usually covered by union agreements, relaxed in the matter of who does what job: the owner of the road might serve as the salesperson, the engineer might also supervise maintenance of the locomotive. Where a large railroad might say to a shipper, "One car of grain? Do you think you might have six by the end of the week?" the short line would be likely to say, "Call me when it's loaded, and Ralph and I will take it over to the junction."

For years the dividing point between short lines and big railroads was 100 route miles — any more than that and the Richmond, Fredericksburg & Potomac would have been a short line. The 100-mile criterion still holds, but "short line" is no longer synonymous (if it ever was) with Class 3 in the ICC classification or with the AAR's "local railroad."

Early in the 20th century the short lines recognized that they needed an organization to deal with legislative matters. The Short Line Railroad Association of the South was established in 1913, and in 1918 it changed its name to American Short Line Railroad Association, at the same time open-

ing its membership to shortline railroads across the country. In 1920 it absorbed the Western Association of Short Line Railroads. The ASLRA provides legal, traffic, and management assistance, information on statutory agencies, and liaison with government agencies.
Address of general offices: 2000 Massachusetts Avenue, N.W., P. O. Box 19026, Washington, DC 20036

Recommended reading: *American Shortline Railway Guide*, by Edward A. Lewis, published in 1991 (Fourth Edition) by Kalmbach Publishing Co., 21027 Crossroads Circle, P. O. Box 1612, Waukesha, WI 53187 (ISBN 0-89024-109-8)

AMTRAK
(National Railroad Passenger Corporation)

Amtrak is America's most visible railroad. It stretches from Boston to San Diego and from Miami to Seattle — none of the freight railroads covers that much territory. It advertises extensively on television, on billboards, and in newspapers and magazines, and its trains are eyecatching. Significantly, Amtrak is virtually the only railroad which large numbers of people have any contact with as a customer.

In the decade after World War II, the railroads invested heavily in their passenger business, streamlining and dieselizing trains and accelerating schedules. They offered all kinds of enticements to the passenger: Vista-Domes, private-room sleepers, and food and lounge service of every description. However, passenger traffic declined and passenger deficits increased. Chief among the many reasons were the postwar prosperity that put a new car in every garage, and construction of the federally financed Interstate highway system that made auto travel speedy and comfortable.

Railroads began to discontinue passenger trains. It was a cumbersome process, involving hearings before the Interstate Commerce Commission and state commissions. The ICC was capricious in the matter of approval, requiring one railroad to continue running a local train on a route covered by four other trains while allowing another to discontinue a well-patronized train that was the only direct Chicago-Atlanta service. Railroads dropped sleeping and dining cars on long-distance trains, then testified before the ICC that ridership had dropped; others discontinued short segments of long-distance trains within a single state, leaving orphan trains with no riders.

By the late 1960s it was clear that the railroads were no longer willing to provide passenger service at a loss. There was still some need for such service, so a government corporation was formed to take over the business. Railroads could either join and discontinue their passenger trains or not join and continue running them. Most joined.

On May 1, 1971, the National Railroad Passenger Corporation — using the name Amtrak — took over supervision of the operation of most remaining intercity passenger trains in the U. S. At first the railroads continued to operate the trains for Amtrak's account as they had on their own; gradually Amtrak hired the on-board service people, station staff, train crews, and so on.

Shortly after it began operation Amtrak purchased secondhand passenger cars and locomotives from the railroads, but in succeeding years the corporation began to purchase new locomotives and cars and to rebuild the best old equipment. A major achievement was the replacement of steam for car heating and generators and batteries on each car for lighting and air conditioning with electricity furnished by the locomotive.

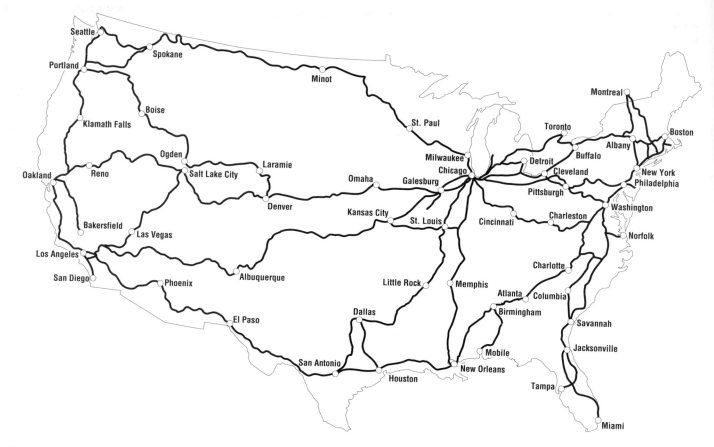

Amtrak also established a nationwide computerized reservation and ticketing system, which was available not only to Amtrak ticket sellers but also to travel agents. Soon "We'll have to wire Los Angeles for that space — we should know by this time next week" gave way to "(click click blink blink) It's all available. Which credit card would you like to use?" Amtrak's most significant achievement, however, was the reversal of the long decline in passenger train ridership. By 1979, Amtrak was carrying more passengers per year than the railroads had carried in 1970.

Most Amtrak trains operate over the track of other railroads, but Amtrak owns much of its own right of way in the Northeast Corridor — lines that were part of the New Haven and Pennsylvania railroads between Boston and Washington, Springfield and New Haven, and Philadelphia and Harrisburg. State agencies own the right of way and track from Boston to the Rhode Island state line and from New Haven to New Rochelle, N. Y. Several railroads operate freight service through trackage rights on various portions of this route. Amtrak also owns the former New York Central line between Kalamazoo, Mich., and Porter, Ind.

Amtrak's early years were characterized by what could only be called government interference. Its routes and operations are established by Congress, and the corporation is subsidized by the federal government. In addition, states can request and subsidize the operation of trains, so-called "403-b" trains. Amtrak was required to operate trains through the districts of influential legislators, regardless of the need for the service. In October 1979 Amtrak was required to discontinue four relatively well-patronized trains. Soon afterward, Congress decreed that Amtrak at least break even on dining car service, traditionally a loss leader for the railroads. Various administrations in Washington proposed dismantling Amtrak, eliminating its funding, and selling it off piece by piece. Amtrak managed to survive, though, and improve its offerings. Congested highways, crowded air space, and energy crises have helped. Each year Amtrak comes closer to its goal of covering its expenses entirely with fares.

Success stories: In December 1971 the Auto-Train Corporation began operating a daily train between Lorton, Virginia, a few miles south of Washington, and Sanford, Florida, carrying passengers and their automobiles. The train was successful, but three years of operating a poorly patronized Louisville, Kentucky-Sanford service and several derailments

A Rohr-built Turboliner skims alongside the Hudson River between Stuyvesant and Hudson, N. Y. Photo by William D. Middleton.

strained the company financially — then a proliferation of discount airline fares finished the job of pushing the company into bankruptcy. Auto-Train's last trains arrived at their terminals on May 1, 1981, and the equipment was soon auctioned off. Amtrak began operating a tri-weekly service labeled "Auto Train" between Lorton and Sanford on October 30, 1983; the frequency has since increased to daily.

In California, the state that years ago gave its heart to the automobile, Amtrak has increased the frequency of service on two short-distance routes and added short-distance service to a third route. In 1971 Amtrak offered two daily trains and one tri-weekly train between Los Angeles and San Diego. At the end of 1991 there were eight daily *San Diegans* each way, two of them extended beyond Los Angeles to Santa Barbara, plus a Monday-through-Friday train between Los Angeles and San Juan Capistrano. In 1974 Amtrak inaugurated a single daily train between Oakland and Bakersfield. It was not an overwhelming success the first few years of its life. What made it a success was connecting bus service under the sponsorship of the California Department of Transportation. The buses in effect extend the *San Joaquins* (there were four by the end of 1992) as far north

W. GRAHAM CLAYTOR JR. (1912-) was born in Roanoke, Virginia. He received a Bachelor of Arts degree from the University of Virginia in 1933 and the Juris Doctor degree (summa cum laude) from Harvard in 1936. He worked as a law clerk for Judge Learned Hand and Justice Louis Brandeis, then joined the Washington law firm of Covington & Burling in 1938. He served in the Navy from 1941 to 1946. In 1948 he married Frances Hammond, also an officer in the naval reserve.

Claytor became vice president-law of the Southern Railway in 1963 and president and chief executive officer of the Southern in 1967. The Southern was a well-run, profitable railroad and it continued so under Claytor's leadership.

Claytor, who was well known for his collection of antique toy trains, proved also to be a railroad enthusiast. Shortly after Claytor joined the Southern, Paul Merriman asked permission to move his newly acquired steam locomotive, Kentucky & Tennessee 12 (formerly Southern 4501), from Stearns, Kentucky, to Chattanooga, Tennessee. Southern had dieselized completely and efficiently in 1953 and gave its approval reluctantly. It very quickly recognized the publicity value of the steam locomotive. Under Claytor's direction the Southern developed a steam locomotive program that grew to encompass 9 steam locomotives running excursion trains nearly every weekend from March through November.

When Amtrak was formed, the Southern elected to continue running its own passenger trains: three more-or-less local trains and the Washington-New Orleans *Southern Crescent*. The Southern had offices in

Washington and Atlanta, and the train was as valuable for shuttling company staff between the two offices as it was for transportation for the general public. During years when Amtrak was struggling with a diverse fleet of secondhand cars, the *Southern Crescent* acquired a reputation for well-maintained equipment, courteous staff, and precise operation, and Claytor took a personal interest in it. Not until after his retirement did it become an Amtrak train — and soon after that it became his train again.

In 1977 Claytor reached the Southern's mandatory retirement age. He entered government service during the Carter administration as Secretary of the Navy from 1977 to 1979, Acting Secretary of Transportation in 1979, and Deputy Secretary of Defense from 1979 to 1981. He returned to Covington & Burling in 1981.

In 1982 he returned to railroading as president and chairman of the board of Amtrak. The company had nearly completed a much-needed rebuilding of the Boston-New York-Washington corridor and most of its passenger cars and locomotives fleet were less than 10 years old. However, Amtrak was being targeted for elimination by the Reagan administration's Director of Management and Budget David Stockman, which meant it would be impossible to get financing of any kind. Claytor set as his goal profitability — no more operating subsidies — by the year 2000, and a decade after that enough income to cover capital needs as well. His tactics have included cost controls, updating of work rules, modest expansion of the system if it can be done without major subsidy, and other sources of revenue such as mail and express traffic and development of real estate — all while increasing the quality of Amtrak's service.

as Willits and Redding, as far southeast as Indio, and to numerous towns and cities not on the route of the train, in addition to connecting the *San Joaquins* and the *San Diegans*. Two noteworthy features of the service are guaranteed trainside connections and through fares and ticketing. In

1991 Amtrak inaugurated three San Jose-Sacramento trains, the *Capitols*, on a route previously served only by long-distance trains. The new trains were an immediate success.

In the 1970s Washington Union Station was the victim of a misguided attempt by the federal government to create a visitor center, with rail passengers banished to a shed behind the building. Eventually it was recognized as a national disgrace, and Amtrak undertook restoration. It reopened in 1988 as an elegant shopping and restaurant center *and* railroad station. Amtrak has also restored many other stations, including Chicago Union Station, Amtrak's hub.

On April 7, 1991, Amtrak moved from New York's Grand Central Terminal to Penn Station, facilitating connections between Empire Service trains (New York-Albany-Buffalo) and the rest of the Amtrak system and consolidating Amtrak's operations in New York at one station (as it did in Chicago in 1972). The move necessitated reactivating the former New York Central West Side freight line, unused since 1983, and constructing a short, steep connection from that line down into Penn Station.

Aware of the proliferation of private railroad cars, dinner trains, and luxury services such as the American European Express, Amtrak tried its hand at luxury service by operating a deluxe parlor-dining car twice week-ly on the *Keystone*, a daytime train between New York and Pittsburgh, from August 1, 1991, through June 30, 1992.

Other operations: In 1983 Amtrak took over operation of the twice-daily Baltimore-Washington commuter trains that Conrail had been operating for the Maryland Department of Transportation; the frequency has since increased. In 1987 Amtrak began operating the commuter services of Massachusetts Bay Transportation Authority, and in 1992 Amtrak began operating Virginia Railway Express commuter trains and was awarded the contract to operate CalTrans' San Francisco commuter service. Amtrak has used excess shop capacity to assemble rapid-transit cars, and has found purchasers overseas for its computerized reservation system.

Address of general offices: 60 Massachusetts Avenue, N.E., Washington, DC 20002

Miles of road operated: 24,596

Reporting marks: AMTK

Number of diesel locomotives: 334

A Chicago-Milwaukee train speeds toward downtown Milwaukee on August 22, 1992, with a former Metroliner converted to a control coach leading and two Horizon coaches following. Photo by George H. Drury.

Amtrak's Superliner fleet includes coach-baggage cars with high-density seating upstairs for passengers only going short distances and a baggage room downstairs. Three are shown on the *Michigan Executive* (since discontinued) at Dearborn, Mich. The entrance vestibule and the baggage door are at platform level; passage between cars is on the upper level. Photo by J. David Ingles.

Number of electric locomotives: 65
Number of freight cars: 863 (for maintenance-of-way service)
Number of passenger cars: 1,919
Number of Turboliner power units: 26
Principal shops: Beech Grove, Ind. (cars and diesel locomotives); Wilmington, Del. (electric locomotives)
Radio frequencies: 160.800 (road — Northeast Corridor)
Railroads over which Amtrak operates:
Amtrak: Boston-New Haven; Springfield-New Haven; New Rochelle, N. Y.-Washington; Philadelphia-Atlantic City; Philadelphia-Harrisburg; Battle Creek, Mich.-Michigan City, Ind.
Atchison, Topeka & Santa Fe: Chicago-Albuquerque-San Bernardino-Pasadena-Los Angeles; San Bernardino-Fullerton, Calif.; Los Angeles-San Diego; Bakersfield-Port Chicago, Calif.; Fort Worth-Temple, Texas
Burlington Northern: Chicago-Denver; Galesburg-West Quincy, Ill.; St.
Paul-Havre-Spokane-Wenatchee-Seattle; Spokane-Pasco-Portland; Seattle-Portland
Canadian National: East Alburgh, Vt.-Montreal; Rouses Point, N. Y.-Montreal; Niagara Falls-Toronto, Ont. (operated by VIA Rail Canada); Toronto-Sarnia, Ont. (operated by VIA Rail Canada)
Central Vermont: New London, Conn.-East Alburgh, Vt.
Conrail: Boston-Albany; Buffalo-Niagara Falls, Ont.; Poughkeepsie-Albany-Buffalo-Cleveland-Chicago; Toledo-Detroit-Battle Creek, Mich.; Harrisburg-Pittsburgh-Alliance-Cleveland; Indianapolis-Crawfordsville, Ind.; Dyer, Ind.-Chicago
CP Rail System (Delaware & Hudson): Schenectady-Rouses Point, N. Y.
CP Rail System (Soo Line): Chicago-Milwaukee-St. Paul
CSX: Washington-Cumberland-Pittsburgh-Willard-Garrett-Chicago; Washington-Charlottesville-Huntington-Cincinnati-Indianapolis; Washington-Selma-Charleston-Jacksonville-Orlando-Tampa; Richmond-New-

AMTRAK'S LOCOMOTIVES AND CARS

Amtrak started with Electro-Motive Es and Fs that more or less came with the passenger cars. The company then bought 150 SDP40Fs, the least successful of various adaptations of the six-axle freight unit for passenger service. Amtrak switched its allegiance to Electro-Motive's F40PH, a four-axle cowl unit, which has proved to be an excellent locomotive for both short and long-haul service. Amtrak purchased 216 F40PHs (six of them secondhand from GO Transit) and at this writing has 212 on its roster.

In 1992 Amtrak took delivery of 20 3200-h.p. P32BHs from GE. These safety-cab hood units introduced a new multi-stripe paint scheme. They are assigned to short-distance corridor trains in California and long-distance trains operating out of Los Angeles.

Electric locomotives

Amtrak inherited 40 GG1s for Northeast Corridor service. The newest of them were built in 1943, and their cast-steel frames were beginning to show the effects of metal fatigue. Even though the GG1s were still performing admirably, they were incapable of the higher speeds Amtrak was planning for the Northeast Corridor — and

Amtrak's P32BHs wear a unique multi-striped paint scheme. Two are shown bringing the eastbound *Southwest Chief* around the horseshoe curves at Blanchard, New Mexico, the scene of numerous Santa Fe publicity pictures. Photo by Wesley Fox.

Amtrak's experience was that sustained speeds above 90 mph were destructive to them. After purchasing E60Cs from General Electric, Amtrak saw it needed something faster and lighter. It tested two elec-

port News; Raleigh-Columbia-Savannah; Jacksonville-Ocala-Miami; Birmingham-Mobile; Crawfordsville-Dyer, Ind.; Grand Rapids-New Buffalo, Mich.
Grand Trunk Western: Sarnia, Ont.-Battle Creek, Mich.
Illinois Central: Chicago-New Orleans; Chicago-Joliet
Metro-North: New Haven, Conn.-New Rochelle, N. Y.; Spuyten Duyvil-Poughkeepsie, N. Y.
Norfolk Southern: Washington-New Orleans; Selma-Raleigh-Greensboro, N. C.; Centralia, Ill.-St. Louis
Southern Pacific Lines: Joliet-St. Louis; Dallas-Houston; New Orleans-El Paso-Los Angeles; Denver-Salt Lake City; Winnemucca, Nev.-Oakland, Calif.; Port Chicago Martinez, Calif.; Portland, Ore.-Roseville, Calif., Los Angeles-San Jose-Oakland
Union Pacific: St. Louis-Kansas City; St. Louis-Fort Worth; Temple, Texas San Antonio; Denver-Cheyenne-Ogden-Boise-Portland; Salt Lake City-Winnemucca, Nev.; Salt Lake City-Las Vegas-Barstow, Calif.
Recommended reading: *All Aboard Amtrak*, by Mike Schafer, published in 1991 by Railpace Publications, P. O. Box 927, Piscataway, NJ 08855-0927 (ISBN 0-9621541-4-8)

tric locomotives from Europe: a six-axle French locomotive with a single motor on each truck, and a four-axle Swedish locomotive. The latter became the prototype for the AEM7, an ASEA design built by EMD with a Budd body (recently built AEM7s have bodies built in Austria).

Self-propelled equipment

Amtrak's experience with self-propelled cars has been mixed. The Budd RDCs which Amtrak used mostly for New Haven-Springfield and Chicago-Dubuque trains (the latter long since discontinued) were already 20 years old when Amtrak got them. Amtrak and the Connecticut Department of Transportation have both tried to forget the Budd-built SPV-2000s that CDOT purchased for local service in Connecticut. The electric-powered Metroliner cars are described below in the section on Amfleet.

Most of Amtrak's self-propelled passenger cars have been turbine-powered trainsets. The two United Aircraft TurboTrains spent their lives (1967-1975) demonstrating the variety of jobs they were unsuited for. The ANF-Frangeco Turboliners, built in 1973 to French National Railways' specifications, had an insatiable appetite for fuel and either too much or too little passenger capacity. They were stored in 1981; a few were rebuilt for New York-Albany-Niagara Falls service.

Amtrak's greatest success with turbine power has been with the Turboliners built by Rohr for service from New York to Albany, Niagara Falls, and Montreal. They are equipped with third-rail shoes and electric motors for operation in Grand Central Terminal and Penn Station in New York.

Passenger cars

In 1971 Amtrak purchased a fleet of secondhand passenger cars ranging from 6 to 34 years old. Amtrak tried to choose the best of the 3,000 or so intercity passenger cars available. The ideal car was of all-stainless-steel construction with outside-swing-hanger trucks, disk brakes, and electromechanical air conditioning, but there were far fewer of those than Amtrak needed. Many of the 1,190 cars Amtrak purchased initially were characterized by ordinary steel construction,

inside-swing-hanger trucks, shoe brakes, and Waukesha (propane engine) or steam-ejector air conditioning. Amtrak continued to purchase and lease used cars and soon had a fleet of astounding diversity.

Most cars received at least cosmetic refurbishing, but Amtrak's efforts to renovate and rejuvenate the mechanical components were often less than successful. Once Amtrak appeared to have a future — and in the beginning many believed it didn't— it ordered new cars, first the French Turboliners and then the Amfleet cars.

Amfleet

In 1966 the Pennsylvania Railroad ordered a fleet of 61 self-propelled electric cars from the Budd Company for high-speed service between New York and Washington (the cars weren't dubbed Metroliners until just before they entered service; they had been referred to briefly as Speedliners). They were delivered to the Pennsylvania Railroad, but debugging and testing took so long that they entered service in early 1969 under Penn Central's aegis, initially making a single daily round trip between New York and Washington. They were mechanically and electrically complex, and were not successful in the service for which they were intended. In recent years about half of them were rebuilt into control coaches for push-pull trains, and Metroliner service was taken over by AEM7 locomotives and Amfleet cars.

Amtrak urgently needed new cars for the Northeast Corridor between Boston, New York, and Washington. The Budd Company used the Metroliner design as the basis for locomotive-hauled cars. Originally they were called Metroshell cars, but later Amfleet — Amcoach, Amcafe, Amdinette, Amclub, and Amlounge.

Amfleet cars have an almost tubular cross-section and inboard-bearing trucks. The biggest difference between the Amfleet cars and previous equipment was that all power for heating, lighting, and air conditioning was to be supplied by the locomotive — head-end power (HEP). To get through the transition period from axle generators and steam heat to HEP without leaving the passengers in the dark or freezing them, Amtrak acquired a number of steam generator cars to use

Amfleet II coaches trail behind AEM7 No. 904 at Elkton, Maryland, on a test run in 1981. They can be distinguished from earlier Amfleet coaches by the larger windows and the vestibule at only one end. Photo by William W. Kratville.

with HEP-equipped locomotives and HEP generator cars to use with locomotives that still had steam generators.

Amcoaches seat 84 passengers in the regular version and 60 or 68 in the long-distance and Metroliner versions. Food-service cars have a windowless snack-counter area at the center of the car (close inspection of the exterior reveals four square openings in the window panel, though); in some of those cars, one or both ends are given over to dining tables, a lounge, or club (first-class) seats.

Amtrak ordered 492 Amfleet cars between 1973 and 1975; Budd delivered them between 1975 and 1977. They were initially assigned to Northeast Corridor trains but soon appeared on short-haul trains across the Amtrak system.

The initial orders were followed by 150 Amfleet II coaches and lounges constructed between 1981 and 1983 for long-distance service on trains east of Chicago. Their principal external differences are taller windows and only one vestibule.

The Superliners

Amtrak's next new cars were the Superliners, bilevel cars for trains west of Chicago, where clearances were greater. They were inspired by Santa Fe's Hi-Level cars built by Budd in 1956 and 1964. The Superliners stand 16 feet 1½ inches tall. The main floor is 8 feet 9 inches above the rails and extends the full length of the car (85 feet over couplers). The lower floor is 14 inches above the rails and lies between the trucks. Air conditioning equipment, air reservoirs, and water tanks are above the trucks at each end of the car. Superliner coaches and sleeping cars have an entrance vestibule at the center of the lower level; a stairway to the upper level is adjacent. The cars ride on German-built trucks.

There are five configurations:
- Coach: 62 leg-rest seats upstairs; 15 seats and toilet rooms downstairs (102 cars).
- Coach-baggage: 78 seats upstairs (some have 62 leg-rest seats); baggage room and toilet rooms downstairs (48 cars).
- Sleeping car: 5 deluxe rooms and 10 economy rooms upstairs; 4 economy rooms, a family bedroom, a handicapped-accessible bedroom, and toilet rooms downstairs. The deluxe and handicapped bedrooms have their own toilets; some cars have been rebuilt with a toilet room upstairs (70 cars).
- Dining car: 18 four-place tables upstairs; kitchen downstairs (39 cars).
- Sightseer lounge: full-length lounge upstairs; lounge and snack counter downstairs. The upper level has large windows that curve into the roof (25 cars).

Built between 1979 and 1981, they were the last passenger cars Pullman-Standard built. In 1991 Amtrak ordered 140 Superliner cars from Bombardier.

Heritage Fleet

Amtrak was quick to repaint and reupholster the secondhand cars it purchased, but recognized that something more was necessary. The mechanical, electrical, and heating systems of those cars were not only widely different but also obsolete — and in many cases worn out. The Amfleet and Superliner cars were equipped for head-end power. Amtrak needed single-level sleeping and dining cars. New ones would require a long period of design and testing, and money was in short supply.

Amtrak's roster of secondhand cars included several hundred built by Budd. The chief virtue of Budd-built passenger cars was (and still is) that they are entirely stainless steel, which doesn't rust or corrode.

Amtrak rounded up the best of its Budd cars and sent them to its shops at Beech Grove, Indiana, where they were overhauled and given new head-end-powered heating, lighting, and air conditioning systems.

The Heritage Fleet includes former Union Pacific coaches built by St. Louis Car Co. in 1960 and 1964, among the last long-distance passenger cars built before Amtrak began operation, and the Budd-built Santa Fe Hi-Level cars. Some of the Hi-Level coaches that were built as transition cars, with low-level train doors at one end, have been rebuilt as coach–crew-dormitory cars for use with Superliners.

Horizon Fleet

In 1989 and 1990 Amtrak received 104 Horizon Fleet cars, 86 coaches and 18 cafe coaches, from Bombardier. Rather than develop a new design, Amtrak and Bombardier modified the commuter coach Pullman-Standard and Bombardier (which bought PS's designs) have been building since 1970 with such necessary items for long-distance service as reclining seats, toilets, and high-speed trucks.

The Viewliners

In 1987 Budd delivered three experimental carbodies designsd by Amtrak. Beech Grove shops outfitted two as sleeping cars and the third as a dining car, and they entered revenue service for testing. They are the prototypes for single-level cars that will eventually replace Heritage Fleet sleepers and diners on most trains east of Chicago. They have angled flat sides rather than the curved sides of the Amfleet, and a row of small windows above the regular ones, reducing the closed-in feel of the upper berths in the sleeping cars and giving a more open feel to the dining car.

Baggage and Material Handling Cars and Auto-Carriers

Checked baggage is only a minor portion of the cargo in the cars at the front of the train, but Amtrak has a healthy mail and express business. To augment aging baggage cars, between 1986 and 1988 Amtrak took delivery of 145 Material Handling Cars from Thrall. They are plug-door box cars with high-speed trucks. In earlier decades they'd have been called express box cars or mail storage cars.

Amtrak's bilevel auto carriers were built by Canadian Car & Foundry for Canadian National in 1956. They operated briefly for Auto-Train. The trilevel auto carriers were originally Santa Fe auto-rack cars.

APALACHICOLA NORTHERN RAILROAD

The Apalachicola Northern was incorporated in 1903. It entered brief receiverships in 1907 and 1914 and was purchased by the St. Joe Paper Co., its present owner, in 1936. In addition to the wood and paper products that have traditionally been its principal items of traffic, AN operates unit coal trains from Port St. Joe, deepest natural harbor on the Gulf of Mexico, to a connection with CSX at Chattahoochee for forwarding to a power plant near Palatka, Florida.

Address of general offices: P. O. Box 250, Port St. Joe, FL 32456
Miles of road operated: 96
Reporting marks: AN
Number of locomotives: 14
Number of freight cars: 1,044
Principal commodities carried: Coal, pulpboard, wood chips, chemicals, scrap paper
Shops: Port St. Joe, Fla.
Junctions with other railroads: CSX: Chattahoochee, Fla.
Radio frequencies: 160.380 (road), 160.500 (yard)

An Apalachicola Northern freight moves northward behind a GP15T and three SW1500s at Fort Gadsden, Florida, on May 26, 1986. The boxy structures on the cab roofs house air conditioners. Photo by Jim Shaw.

ARIZONA & CALIFORNIA RAILROAD

Between 1907 and 1910 the Arizona & California Railway, a subsidiary of the Santa Fe, opened a line from Matthie, Arizona, a junction 5 miles northwest of Wickenburg, west to the Colorado River at Parker, then to Cadiz, California, on the Santa Fe main line. The new line gave Santa Fe a shortcut between California and southern Arizona, 224miles shorter than the route through Ash Fork and without the climb to northern Arizona. The line was built for through traffic rather than local business. It passed through a few small towns in Arizona and practically nothing in California. In 1930 it could boast a name train, the *Phoenix*, trains 17 and 18, between Los Angeles and Phoenix. The service, if not the name and the numbers (which were given to the *Super Chief*), lasted until 1954.

In 1991 Santa Fe sold the line and the Rice-Blythe-Ripley branch along

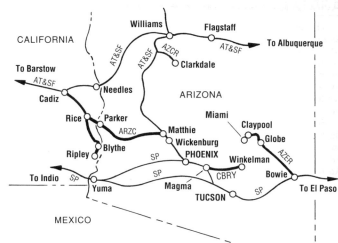

Arizona & California 3802 is a GP40d. It wears a handsome paint scheme of green and cream with yellow striping. Photo by William R. May.

the Colorado River to the Arizona & California Railroad. Arizona & California has trackage rights over Santa Fe from Matthie to Phoenix, 60 miles.

Address of general offices: P. O. Box AF, Parker, AZ 85344
Miles of road operated: 257
Reporting marks: ARZC
Number of locomotives: 9
Principal commodities carried: Lumber, LP gas, agricultural products, intermodal trailers and containers
Shops: Parker, Ariz.
Junctions with other railroads: Atchison, Topeka & Santa Fe: Cadiz, Calif.; Matthie, Ariz.
Radio frequencies: 160.860

ARIZONA EASTERN RAILWAY

The Gila Valley, Globe & Northern Railway built a line from Bowie, Arizona, northwest to the copper-mining town of Globe between 1895 and 1899. (An interesting bit of trivia: GVG&N locomotive No. 1 was former Central Pacific *Jupiter*, one of the two locomotives at the golden spike ceremony at Promontory, Utah, on May 10, 1869.) By 1905 the GVG&N was owned by Southern Pacific and was operated as part of the Arizona Eastern Railroad, an SP subsidiary. The line was extended a few miles farther west to Miami in 1909. Passenger service on the line ended in 1953.

Southern Pacific sold the Bowie-Miami branch in 1988 to the Arizona Eastern Railway, a unit of Kyle Railways. Arizona Eastern's principal business is carrying copper and copper byproducts to a connection with SP at Bowie.

Address of general offices: P. O. Box Y, Claypool, AZ 85532

Miles of road operated: 134
Reporting marks: AZER
Number of locomotives: 10
Number of freight cars: 20
Principal commodities carried: Copper
Shops: Miami, Ariz.
Junctions with other railroads: Southern Pacific: Bowie, Ariz.
Radio frequencies: 160.935
Recommended reading:
Railroads of Arizona, Volume II, by David F. Myrick, published in 1980 by Howell-North Books, 850 North Hollywood Way, Burbank, CA 91505 (ISBN 0-8310-7118-3)
"Espee's sandy satellites, by James W. Terrell, in TRAINS Magazine, July 1986, pages 18-19
Map: See Arizona & California, opposite

Four of Arizona Eastern's five GP9s have hopper cars rolling at Peridot, Arizona, on March 31, 1992. Photo by Jim Shaw.

ARKANSAS & MISSOURI RAILROAD

Arkansas & Missouri's route from Monett, Missouri, south to Fort Smith, Arkansas, was built between 1880 and 1882 by the St. Louis, Arkansas & Texas Railway, an affiliate of the St. Louis-San Francisco. The route served as the Frisco's principal route to and from Texas from its completion to Paris, Texas, in 1887, until 1902, when Frisco opened a route through Tulsa. The Frisco became part of Burlington Northern on November 21, 1980.

Not long afterward, a segment of the Monett-Fort Smith-Paris route in southeast Oklahoma was abandoned. What had been a secondary through route was now two stub branches, from Monett to Fort Smith and from Antlers, Okla., to Paris, Texas (the latter is now part of the Kiamichi Railroad).

In 1986 the group of investors that had developed the Maryland & Delaware Railroad looked west. They purchased the Monett-Fort Smith line from BN, and formed the Arkansas & Missouri Railroad. Most of the Arkansas & Missouri's traffic is inbound, destined for customers located along the portion of the line between Bentonville and Fayetteville, Ark.

Address of general offices: 107 North Commercial Street, Springdale, AR 72764
Miles of road operated: 139
Reporting marks: AM
Number of locomotives: 16
Number of freight cars: 88
Principal commodities carried: Grain, paper products, sand, gravel
Shops: Springdale, Ark.

Arkansas & Missouri's diesel roster is all-Alco. Two of those Alcos, C420s 52 and 46, bring a southbound local freight through the road's headquarters town, Springdale, Arkansas. Photo by Jim Shaw.

Junctions with other railroads:
Burlington Northern: Monett, Mo.
Fort Smith Railroad: Fort Smith, Ark.
Kansas City Southern: Fort Smith, Ark.
Union Pacific: Fort Smith, Ark.; Van Buren, Ark.

Radio frequencies: 160.440, 160.785
Passenger routes: Rogers-Van Buren, Ark. — Boston Mountain Rail Excursions
Recommended reading: "Alcos in Arkansas," by Frank W. Bryan, in TRAINS Magazine, November 1987, pages 32-39

ARKANSAS MIDLAND RAILROAD

The Arkansas Midland began operation in February 1992 on four separate ex-Union Pacific (formerly Missouri Pacific) lines in Arkansas. Three of the routes branch from UP's St. Louis-Little Rock-Texarkana main line: North Little Rock to Carlisle, 33 miles (originally part of Rock Island's Memphis-Little Rock main line); Malvern to Mountain Pine, 34 miles; and Gurdon to Birds Mill, 53 miles. The fourth is a 12-mile line from Lexa to Helena, on the Mississippi River. The Arkansas Midland is part of the Pinsly Railroad Company. Other railroads in the Pinsly group are Pioneer Valley, Greenville & Northern, Florida Central, Florida Midland, and Florida Northern.

Address of general offices: P. O. Box 183, Lake Hamilton Branch, Hot Springs, AR 71951
Miles of road operated: 131
Reporting marks: AKMD
Number of locomotives: 10
Principal commodities carried: Lumber, wood products
Junctions with other railroads:
Union Pacific: Gurdon, Lexa, Malvern, and North Little Rock, Ark.
St. Louis Southwestern: North Little Rock, Ark.
Radio frequencies: 160.275, 161.460

ASHLEY, DREW & NORTHERN RAILWAY
ARKANSAS LOUISIANA & MISSISSIPPI RAILWAY
FORDYCE & PRINCETON RAILROAD

Georgia Pacific Corporation, a nationwide producer of building materials, owns three railroads in southeast Arkansas: the Ashley, Drew & Northern Railway, the Arkansas, Louisiana & Mississippi Railroad, and the Fordyce & Princeton Railroad. They serve the largest interrelated mill complex in the world — 12 plants making paper, building products, and chemicals derived from the southern pine tree. Because they operate as a unit and pool equipment, they are described together.

Ashley, Drew, & Northern

In 1905 the Crossett Railway was chartered to serve the Crossett Lumber Co. of Crossett, Ark. In 1912 the 10-mile line was sold to the Crossett, Monticello & Northern, which planned to extend the line north to a junction with the St. Louis, Iron Mountain & Southern (later Missouri Pacific) at Monticello. The line got partway there, ran out of money, and was resold to a new company, the Ashley, Drew & Northern. The line reached Monticello in 1913. The railroad was leased to the Arkansas, Louisiana & Gulf

in 1914 and regained its independence in 1920. The Georgia Pacific Corporation purchased the AD&N and the Crossett Lumber Co. in 1963.

Arkansas Louisiana & Mississippi

The Arkansas, Louisiana & Gulf Railway was chartered in 1906 to build a line from Monroe, Louisiana, to Pine Bluff, Ark. In 1908 the line was

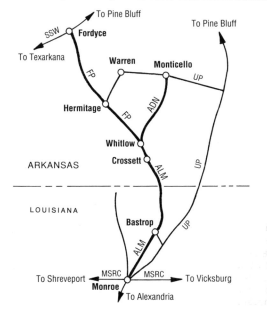

34

opened from Monroe to Hamburg and Crossett, Ark., a little more than one-third of the distance to Pine Bluff. The company entered receivership in 1913; in 1915 the railroad was sold to the Arkansas & Louisiana Midland Railway. That same year the Arkansas & Louisiana Midland leased the Ashley, Drew & Northern. The lease of the AD&N was cancelled and the Arkansas & Louisiana Midland was sold by its receiver in 1920.

The Arkansas & Louisiana Missouri was incorporated in 1920 to take over the Arkansas & Louisiana Midland. It runs from Crossett, Ark., to Monroe, La. (the Rolfe Junction-Hamburg portion was abandoned in the 1920s). For a time around 1930 the A&LM was under the same management as the Nacogdoches & Southeastern Railroad, the Louisiana & Pine Bluff Railway, and the Mansfield Railway and Transportation Co. — all were listed in the *Official Guide* as the Huttig, Mansfield & Nacogdoches Railroads.

The Arkansas & Louisiana Missouri was owned by Olinkraft, Inc., a division of Olin Mathieson. In 1991 the A&LM was acquired by Georgia Pacific, renamed the Arkansas Louisiana & Mississippi Railway, and placed under the same management as the Ashley, Drew & Northern.

Ashley, Drew & Northern 1810, a GP10, and 1206, an SW1200, both painted in the green and white used by Georgia Pacific railroads, lead loaded woodchip hopper cars and pulpwood racks on the Fordyce & Princeton in 1983. Photo by Jim Shaw.

Fordyce & Princeton

The Fordyce & Princeton was incorporated in 1890 and built a 9-mile narrow-gauge line north from Fordyce, Arkansas, to Toan. It was standard-gauged in 1907. By 1916 it reached to Bryants Spur and Trigg, a total of 17 miles; in 1930 it was still 17 miles long and had acquired a second connection with the Rock Island at Ivan (Rock Island and Cotton Belt routes crossed at Fordyce). The road never reached Princeton, northwest of Fordyce. Between 1940 and 1950 the railroad was gradually pruned back to a switching operation at Fordyce. Through much of its history the Crossett name appears on the Fordyce & Princeton's list of officers; it is possible there was some link with the Crossett Lumber Co.

The Fordyce & Princeton was purchased by the Georgia Pacific Corporation in 1963. In 1981 the railroad acquired the Fordyce-Crossett portion of the former Rock Island between Little Rock, Ark., and Eunice, Lousiana, to provide a connection to the St. Louis Southwestern (at Fordyce) for the Ashley, Drew & Northern and for the Georgia Pacific mills in the Crossett area.

Address of general offices: P. O. Box 757, Crossett, AR 71635

Miles of road operated: ALM, 54; ADN, 41; FP, 57
Reporting marks: ALM; ADN; FP
Number of locomotives: ALM, 1; ADN, 7; FP, 3
Number of freight cars: ALM, 255; ADN, 1500; FP, 137
Principal commodities carried: Pulpwood, paper products, chemicals
Shops: Fordyce, Ark.
Junctions with other railroads:
MidSouth: Monroe, La.
St. Louis Southwestern: Fordyce, Ark.
Union Pacific: Bastrop, La.; Monroe, La.; Monticello, Ark.
Warren & Saline River: Hermitage, Ark.
Radio frequencies:
ALM: 160.980
ADN: 160.770, 160.710, 161.535
FP: 160.770, 161.535
Recommended reading: *Short Line Railroads of Arkansas*, by Clifton E. Hull, published in 1969 by the University of Oklahoma Press, Norman, OK 73069

ASSOCIATION OF AMERICAN RAILROADS

As North America's railroads developed into a transcontinental network, mechanical standardization became necessary. The interchange of cars among railroads raised the problem of repairs. Why should a Southern Pacific shop foreman in California fix a broken truck frame on a New Haven boxcar? What kept a car man on the East Coast from tipping an Espee gondola into the dump as unserviceable for some minor fault? The answer was an industry-wide reciprocal agreement for repairs; without it, North America's rail system might have evolved quite differently.

The Master Car Builders' Association was founded in 1867. The initial purpose of the organization was to facilitate the interchange of cars among railroads. In 1876 it established rules for prompt interchange of cars, repairs to damaged and defective cars, and billing and payment for the repairs. The association established standards for car parts, with the result that from 1882 to 1918 the number of different axles and journal bearings

in use was reduced from more than 50 to 5. The MCB adopted automatic couplers in 1887 and automatic air brakes in 1888.

The association also attacked the problem of confusion in part names. In 1871 it appointed a committee to prepare a dictionary of car-building terms. Published in 1879 by *The Railroad Gazette*, the dictionary defined everything from "adjustable-globe lamp" to "yoke" in words and pictures. The book evolved into today's *Car and Locomotive Cyclopedia of American Practice*.

In 1918 the United States Railroad Administration, which managed the nation's railroads for 26 months from the end of 1917 to the beginning of 1920, asked that the various railroad associations be amalgamated. The American Railway Master Mechanics' Association and the Master Car Builders' Association were consolidated as Section III, Mechanical, of the American Railroad Association, which was a reorganization of the American Railway Association (by mid-1920 the "R" in "ARA" again stood for "Railway"). One immediate difference was that where MCB's rules had been recommendatory, ARA's were mandatory. In 1934 the Association of American Railroads was formed by the consolidation of the American Railway Association; the Association of Railway Executives; the Railway Accounting Officers Association; the Railway Treasury Officers Association; and the Bureau of Railway Economics. Eight other associations were brough into the AAR by the end of 1934.

For years the AAR was the public relations and educational agency of the railroad industry. Grade-school teachers could write to the AAR for material that could be the basis of a unit on railroads. The packet always included *Quiz*, a booklet of questions and answers about trains, and a set of pictures. (When the unit was done and the class turned its attention to dairy farming or fire prevention, the teacher usually gave the material to the class railfan, who by the sixth grade could identify most of the railroads in the pictures, even though the AAR's retoucher had carefully airbrushed out the road names.) The AAR's library has served since 1910 as a mjor resource to the industry.

One of the AAR's many purposes — obvious from the location of its headquarters in Washington — is legislative. The AAR lobbies for the passage of legislation favorable to the railroads. It continues to coordinate interchange among the railroads, dealing not only with wheels and couplers but also with bits and bauds: every car interchanged by two railroads has a parallel exchange of digital data.

The AAR operates the Transportation Test Center at Pueblo, Colorado. Opened by the U. S. Department of Transportation in May 1971 for the development of high-speed ground transportation, the center was taken over in 1982 by the AAR, which shifted its emphasis to the improvement of existing rail and intermodal technology and emergency response training. The AAR also operates a research center in Chicago.

The major freight railroads of the United States are members of the AAR. Amtrak and the major Canadian and Mexican railroads are special members.

Address of general offices: 50 F Street, N.W., Washington, DC 20001

ATCHISON, TOPEKA & SANTA FE RAILWAY

The Santa Fe was chartered in 1859 to join Atchison and Topeka, Kansas, with Santa Fe, New Mexico. In its early years the railroad opened Kansas to settlement. Much of its revenue came from wheat grown there and from cattle driven north from Texas to Wichita and Dodge City.

Rather than turn its survey southward at Dodge City, the railroad chose to head southwest over Raton Pass because of coal deposits near Trinidad, Colorado, and Raton, New Mexico. The Denver & Rio Grande was also aiming at Raton Pass, but the Santa Fe crews arose early one morning in 1878 and were hard at work with picks and shovels when the Rio Grande crews showed up after breakfast. At the same time the two railroads had a series of skirmishes over occupancy of the Royal Gorge west of Canon City, Colo.; the Rio Grande won that right of way.

The Santa Fe reached Albuquerque in 1880 (Santa Fe, the original destination of the railroad, found itself at the end of a short branch from Lamy, N. M.) and connected with the Southern Pacific at Deming, N. M.,

in 1881. The road then built southwest from Benson, Arizona, to Nogales, on the Mexican border. There it connected with the Sonora Railway, which the Santa Fe had constructed north from the Mexican port of Guaymas.

The Atlantic & Pacific Railroad was chartered in 1866 to build west from Springfield, Missouri, along the 35th parallel of latitude (approximately through Amarillo, Texas, and Albuquerque, New Mexico) to a junction with the Southern Pacific at the Colorado River. The infant A&P had no rail connections. The line that was to become the St. Louis-San Francisco Railway (the Frisco) wouldn't reach Springfield for another 4 years, and SP didn't build east from Mojave to the Colorado River until 1883. The A&P started construction in 1868, built southwest into what would become Oklahoma, and promptly entered receivership.

In 1879 the A&P struck a deal with the Santa Fe and the Frisco. Those railroads would jointly build and own the A&P west of Albuquerque. In 1883 the A&P reached Needles, California, where it connected with the SP, but the Tulsa-Albuquerque portion of the A&P was still unbuilt.

The Santa Fe began to expand: a line from Barstow, Calif., to San Diego in 1885 and to Los Angeles in 1887; control of the Gulf, Colorado & Santa Fe (Galveston to Fort Worth) in 1886 and a line between Wichita and Fort Worth in 1887; lines from Kansas City to Chicago, from Kiowa, Kansas to Amarillo, Texas, and from Pueblo to Denver (paralleling the Denver & Rio Grande) in 1888; and purchase of the Frisco and the Colorado Midland in 1890.

The depression of 1893 had the same effect on the Santa Fe that it had on many other railroads: financial problems and subsequent reorganization. In 1895 Santa Fe sold the Frisco and the Colorado Midland and wrote off the losses, but it retained control of the Atlantic & Pacific.

The Santa Fe still wanted to reach California on its own rails (it leased Southern Pacific line from Needles through Barstow to Mojave), and the state of California eagerly courted the Santa Fe in order to break SP's monopoly. In 1897 the railroad traded the Sonora Railway to Southern Pacific for the SP line between Barstow and Mojave, giving the Santa Fe its own line all the way from Chicago to the Pacific. It was unique in that regard until the Milwaukee Road completed its extension to Puget Sound in 1909. (The Sonora Railway is now part of National Railways of Mexico.)

Subsequent expansion of the Santa Fe encompassed lines from Amarillo to Pecos (1899); from Ash Fork, Ariz., to Phoenix (1901); the Belen Cutoff from the Pecos line at Texico to Isleta, south of Albuquerque, bypassing the grades of Raton Pass (1907); and the Coleman Cutoff, from Texico to Coleman, Texas, near Brownwood (1912).

In 1907 Santa Fe and Southern Pacific jointly formed the Northwestern

Pacific Railroad, which took over several short railroads and built new lines connecting them to form a route from San Francisco north to Eureka. In 1928 Santa Fe sold its half of the NWP to Southern Pacific. Also in 1928 the Santa Fe purchased the U. S. portion of the Kansas City, Mexico & Orient (the Mexican portion of the line became the Chihuahua-Pacific Railway, now part of National Railways of Mexico). Post-World War II construction projects included an entrance to Dallas from the north and relocation of the main line across northern Arizona.

Because long stretches of its main line traverse areas without water,

The Santa Fe scene on the cover of this book typifies the road's fast Chicago-California main line. Quite different in character is this grain train passing between two semaphores north of Wagon Mound, New Mexico. Photo by Wesley Fox.

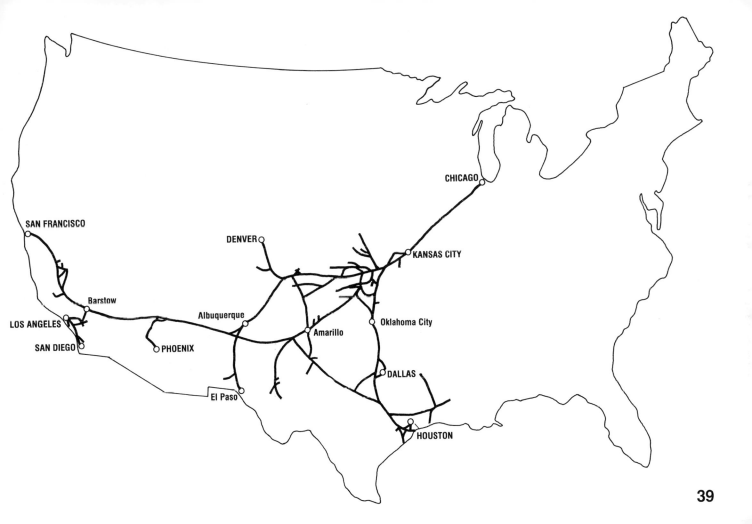

SAN FRANCISCO

CHICAGO

DENVER

KANSAS CITY

Barstow

Albuquerque

Oklahoma City

LOS ANGELES

Amarillo

SAN DIEGO

PHOENIX

DALLAS

El Paso

HOUSTON

39

Santa Fe's newest power, GP60s in both cab and booster form, wearing the revived red-and-silver warbonnet livery, lead a piggyback train around a curve at Cajon, California. Photo by Jim Shaw.

Santa Fe was one of the first purchasers of diesel locomotives for road freight service. The road was known for its passenger trains, notably the Chicago-Los Angeles *Super Chief,* and for the on-line eating houses and dining cars that were operated by Fred Harvey.

In 1960 the Santa Fe bought the Toledo, Peoria & Western Railroad, then sold a half interest to the Pennsylvania Railroad. The TP&W cut straight east across Illinois from near Fort Madison, Iowa, to a connection with the Pennsy at Effner, Indiana, forming a bypass around Chicago for traffic moving between the two lines. The TP&W route didn't mesh with the traffic pattern Conrail developed after 1976, so Santa Fe bought back the other half, merged the TP&W in 1983, then sold it back into independence in 1989.

Today's Santa Fe is one of America's Super Seven freight railroads — the smallest of that group. It derives a much higher portion of its revenue from intermodal traffic — containers and trailers — than other railroads of its size, and it has a reputation for speed.

Address of general offices: 80 E. Jackson Boulevard, Chicago, IL 60604

Miles of road operated: 12,056

Reporting marks: ATSF, SFLC, SFRC

Number of locomotives: 1,997

Number of freight cars: 32,126

Major yards: Barstow, Calif.; Chicago (Corwith); Kansas City, Kans. (Argentine)

Principal shops: Barstow, Calif.; Cleburne, Texas; Kansas City, Kans. (Argentine); San Bernardino, Calif.; Topeka, Kans.

Radio frequencies: 160.650, 161.370 (yard)

Passenger routes:

Amtrak — Chicago-Albuquerque-Pasadena-Los Angeles (*Southwest Chief*), Barstow-Fullerton-Los Angeles (*Desert Wind*), Los Angeles-San Diego (*San Diegans*), Fort Worth-Temple, Tex. (*Eagle*), Port Chicago, Calif.-Bakersfield (*San Joaquins*)

Historical and technical societies:

Santa Fe Modelers Association, 1704 Valley Ridge, Norman, OK 73072

Santa Fe Railway Historical Society, P. O. Box 92887, Long Beach, CA 90809-2887

Recommended reading:

History of the Atchison, Topeka and Santa Fe Railway, by Keith L. Bryant, Jr., published in 1974 by Macmillan Publishing Co., New York (ISBN 0-02-517920-9)

THE MEGA-MERGER THAT DIDN'T HAPPEN

In the 1960s the Santa Fe talked merger with the Frisco and the Missouri Pacific, and Mopac acquired a large block of Santa Fe stock. The Frisco became part of Burlington Northern in 1980, and Mopac became part of Union Pacific in 1982. Santa Fe, which had been the top road in the U. S. in route mileage in the 1950s, was no longer the biggest kid on the block. It looked around and discovered the only other unattached major railroad was Southern Pacific — No. 2 railroad in mileage in the 1950s and a longtime rival. (Contemporary accounts of the Prosperity Special, an order of 20 Southern Pacific freight locomotives delivered en masse in 1922, refer to the locomotives as 2-10-2s rather than by the common name of the type, Santa Fe.)

Santa Fe and Southern Pacific announced a proposed merger in May 1980; four months later they called it off. In mid-1983 they were talking merger again, to create the third longest railroad in the United States (after Burlington Northern and CSX). On December 23, 1983, Santa Fe Industries and Southern Pacific Company, the parent companies of the two railroads, were merged by Santa Fe Southern Pacific Corporation. The railroads remained separate pending Interstate Commerce Commission approval of the Southern Pacific & Santa Fe Railway. SP and Santa Fe painted many locomotives red and yellow and lettered them SP__ or __SF, leaving room for the other letters.

The reaction of other railroads was predictable. Union Pacific wanted trackage rights from El Paso, Texas, west to Colton, California, and from Los Angeles up the San Joaquin Valley to Oakland. Denver & Rio Grande Western asked for trackage rights from Ogden, Utah, to Oakland and to Klamath Falls, Oregon, then petitioned to purchase the route from Ogden to Roseville, Calif., and get trackage rights south to Bakersfield and north to Portland (which it did, and more, but that's getting ahead of the story). The U.S. Department of Justice vehemently opposed the merger; the Department of Transportation endorsed it.

The ICC had a history of approving mergers of parallel railroads, and Southern Pacific & Santa Fe seemed a sure thing. On July 24, 1986, the ICC said "No," because it would create a monopoly that would outweigh public benefits. SFSP had to divest itself of one railroad.

SFSP made peace with UP and D&RGW and appealed the case. On June 30, 1987, the ICC voted by the same 4-1 margin to turn down the merger. Offers to buy SP came from Kansas City Southern; Rio Grande Industries, parent of the Denver & Rio Grande Western; Guilford Transportation Industries; and SP management. On August 9, 1988, the ICC approval sale of the SP to Rio Grande Industries. The sale was completed on October 13, 1988.

Repainted Southern Pacific and Santa Fe hood units meet at Woodford, California, in October 1986. Disapproval of the merger by the ICC changed SPSF from "Southern Pacific Santa Fe" to "Shouldn't Paint So Fast." Photo by Ted Benson.

SANTA FE SPINOFFS

In recent years the Santa Fe has spun off some branch lines to become short lines, including its lines to Atchison and Santa Fe, leaving only one city in the railroad's name still on the railroad. Among the major segments are:

• American Railway Corporation: all branches west of Topeka, north of Oklahoma City, and east of Dodge City, except Strong City to Superior and Salina, 830 miles (1992)

• Arizona & California Railroad: Matthie, Arizona-Cadiz, California, and Rice-Ripley, Calif., 240 miles (May 9, 1991)

• Arizona Central Railroad: Drake-Clarksdale, Arizona, 38 miles (April 14, 1989)

• Chapparal Railroad: Paris-Farmerville, Texas, 60 miles (April 6, 1990)

• Floydada & Plainview Railroad: Plainview to Floydada, Texas, 27 miles (May 7, 1990)

• Garden City Northern Railway: Garden City-Shallowater, Kansas, 31 miles (September 7, 1989)

• Gulf, Colorado & San Saba Railroad: Lometa-Brady, Texas, 67 miles

• Santa Fe Southern Railroad: Lamy-Santa Fe, New Mexico, 18 miles (March 13, 1992)

• Seagraves, Whiteface & Lubbock Railroad: Lubbock to Seagraves and Whiteface, Texas, 111 miles (April 2, 1990)

• South Kansas & Oklahoma Railroad: Tulsa, Oklahoma-Iola, Kansas, 147 miles; Chanute-Wellington, Kan., 139 miles; and Cherryvale-Coffeyville, Kan, 18 miles (December 28, 1990)

• South Orient: San Angelo Junction-Presidio, Texas, 385 miles (December 31, 1991)

• Southwestern Railroad: Whitewater to Tyrone, Fierro, and Santa Rita, New Mexico, 37 miles; and Shattuck, Oklahoma-Morse, Texas, 102 miles

• T&P Railway: Topeka-Parnell, Kansas, 43 miles

• Texas & Oklahoma Railroad: Cherokee, Oklahoma-Maryneal, Texas, 359 miles (1991)

ATLANTA & ST. ANDREWS BAY RAILWAY

The Atlanta & St. Andrews Bay was incorporated in 1906 and completed in 1908. It was conceived as a logging line but its name reflected a grander notion, that of a railroad linking Atlanta to the Gulf of Mexico. The railroad did reach the shores of St. Andrews Bay at Panama City, Fla., but penetrated no farther north than Dothan, Ala. The line was owned for a while by the United Fruit Co., which intended to make Panama City the nation's banana port, and in 1931 it was sold to International Paper Co. The railroad has been owned by Stone Container Corp. since 1987.

The Atlanta & St. Andrews Bay operates the Abbeville-Grimes Railway, also owned by Stone Container. The line is a former CSX branch (ex-Atlantic Coast Line) from Grimes to Abbeville, Ala., 27 miles; 6 miles of trackage rights on CSX from Grimes to Dothan connect it with the Atlanta & St. Andrews Bay.

Address of general offices: P. O. Box 2775, Panama City, FL 32402
Miles of road operated: 89
Reporting marks: ASAB

Number of locomotives: 11
Number of freight cars: 768
Principal commodities carried: Pulpwood, paper products, chemicals, grain
Junctions with other railroads:
Abbeville-Grimes Railway: Dothan, Ala.
Norfolk Southern: Dothan, Ala.
Hartford & Slocomb: Dothan, Ala.
CSX: Cottondale, Fla.; Dothan, Ala.
Radio frequencies: 160.770, 161.295
Map: See Apalachicola Northern, page 29

Five units are lined up to move a Bay Line freight north out of Panama City, Florida, in 1986. Photo by Jim Shaw.

ATLANTIC & WESTERN RAILWAY

The Atlantic & Western Railway was incorporated in 1927 to take over the Atlantic & Western Railroad. It had been incorporated in 1899 to build from Sanford, North Carolina, east to Goldsboro, and was constructed as far as Lillington, 26 miles. In 1962 the line was abandoned between Lillington and Jonesboro, its present terminus. The road was acquired by K. E. Durden in 1988.

Address of general offices: P. O. Box 1208, Sanford, NC 27330
Miles of road operated: 3
Reporting marks: ATW
Number of locomotives: 2
Number of freight cars: 1,417
Principal commodities carried: Scrap iron, sand and gravel, mineral wool, furniture
Junctions with other railroads:
CSX: Sanford, N. C.
Norfolk Southern: Jonesboro, N. C.; Sanford, N. C.
Radio frequencies: 160.275

Red-and-yellow GE 70-tonner No. 100, half of Atlantic & Western's locomotive fleet, has one of the road's gondolas and a Conrail covered hopper in tow near the east end of the line in Sanford, North Carolina, on May 23, 1986. Photo by Jim Shaw.

AUSTIN & NORTHWESTERN RAILROAD

Austin & Northwestern Railroad operates the former Southern Pacific line from Giddings, Texas, west to Austin, the state capital, then north and west to Llano, with a branch from Fairland to Marble Falls. The Giddings-Austin line was opened by the Houston & Texas Central in 1871. The Austin-Llano line was opened in 1882 by a previous Austin & Northwestern Railroad, which was merged in 1901 by the Houston & Texas Central, by then a Southern Pacific subsidiary.

The rail line is owned by the city of Austin. The Austin & Northwestern is part of the Rail-Tex group.

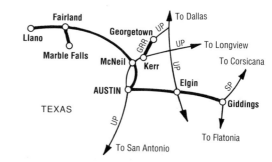

Address of general offices: 500 Robert T. Martinez Jr. Street, Austin, TX 78702

Miles of road operated: 163

Reporting marks: AUNW

Number of locomotives: 8

Principal commodities carried: Stone, lumber, beer, paper

Shops: Austin, Texas

Junctions with other railroads:

Southern Pacific: Giddings, Texas

Union Pacific: McNeil, Texas; Elgin, Texas

Radio frequencies: 161.520, 160.305

Three red-and-black GP9s depart Austin, Texas, on December 11, 1987. Photo by Michael W. Blaszak.

Two GP38s and a GP 7 in Bangor & Aroostook's orange, gray, and black livery head a southbound freight at Chapman. Photo by Jim Shaw.

BANGOR & AROOSTOOK RAILROAD

Maine's northernmost county is Aroostook. In area it is somewhat larger than Connecticut and Rhode Island combined; the population even today is less than 100,000. Much of the county is forested wilderness, and the region is best known for growing potatoes.

As late as 1891 Aroostook County was connected to the rest of the state only by some primitive wagon roads. In 1871 a rail route had been opened from Bangor, Maine, north and east to the Canadian border at Vanceboro, forming part of a route from Boston through Portland and Bangor to Saint John, New Brunswick. In 1889 Canadian Pacific completed a line east from Montreal that cut across the state, meeting the Boston-Saint John route at Mattawamkeag, Maine. CPR had branches that penetrated the state of Maine from the east as far as Houlton and Presque Isle, but otherwise northern Maine was devoid of railroads.

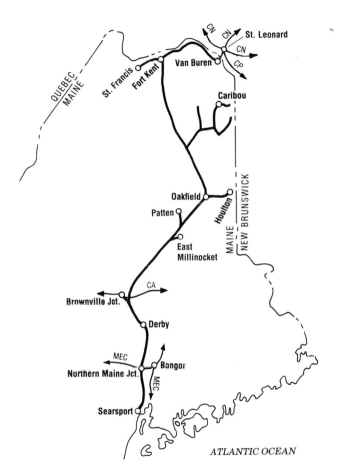

The Bangor & Aroostook Railroad was incorporated in 1891 to build north from Brownville, Maine, on the CPR line, to Caribou, Ashland, and Fort Fairfield. In 1892 it purchased the Bangor & Piscataquis Railroad and the Bangor & Katahdin Iron Works Railway to achieve a connection with the U. S. railroad network. The first BAR train rolled into Houlton in December 1893; in December 1894 the road reached Caribou. The railroad continued to extend lines through much of Aroostook County. In 1905 the BAR built a line south from South LaGrange to a new connection with the Maine Central at Northern Maine Junction, 6 miles west of Bangor, and on south to tidewater at Searsport. By 1910 the road had reached its greatest extent, except for a bridge opened in 1915 between Van Buren, Maine, and St. Leonard, N. B.

In 1922 the first abandonment took place, and since then a number of branches and duplicate lines have been trimmed. BAR discontinued rail passenger service in 1961 but operated buses between Bangor and Aroostook County points until 1983.

In the 1950s the railroad achieved recognition out of proportion to its size and remoteness: for a fleet of red, white, and blue boxcars blazoned "State of Maine Products;" for purchasing sufficient diesels to cover peak traffic and then leasing them during most of the year to the Pennsylvania Railroad; and for working a similar arrangement with Pacific Fruit Express to keep its fleet of potato-carrying refrigerator cars moving and thus earning money.

More than 99 percent of the outstanding stock of the Bangor & Aroostook is owned by the Amoskeag Co.

Address of general offices: Northern Maine Junction Park, R. R. 2, Bangor, ME 04401
Miles of road operated: 422
Reporting marks: BAR
Number of locomotives: 38
Number of freight cars: 2,835
Principal commodities carried: Forest products
Shops: Northern Maine Junction, Maine
Junctions with other railroads:
Canadian National: St. Leonard, N. B.
CP Rail System: Brownville Jct., Maine; St. Leonard, N. B.
Maine Central (Guilford Transportation Industries): Northern Maine Jct., Maine
Radio frequencies: 160.440, 160.920, 160.740
Recommended reading: *Bangor and Aroostook*, by Jerry Angier and Herb Cleaves, published in 1986 by Flying Yankee Enterprises, P. O. Box 595, Littleton, MA 01460 (ISBN 0-9615574-3-5)

BAY COLONY RAILROAD

Bay Colony Railroad Corporation was formed in 1982 to operate freight service on several state-owned ex-Conrail, ex-New Haven branch lines in eastern Massachusetts:
• Middleboro to Hyannis with branches to Falmouth and South Dennis
• Braintree to North Plymouth
• Medfield Junction to Newton Highlands, and a branch to West Roxbury
• Weir Junction to Dean Street (all within Taunton)
• Westport Factory to Watuppa
• West Concord to Acton
• Braintree to Hingham

One of the major commodities carried by the Bay Colony is trash, moving from a truck-to-rail transfer facility to a power plant at Rochester, Mass. Bay Colony's lines include a notable feat of engineering, the vertical lift bridge over the Cape Cod Canal at Buzzards Bay, built by the U. S. Army Corps of Engineers between 1933 and 1935.

Amtrak's seasonal trains to Cape Cod operate over Bay Colony lines between Middleboro and Hyannis, and a Bay Colony subsidiary, Cape Cod Scenic Railroad, operates summer passenger service between Hyannis and Buzzards Bay.

Address of general offices: 420 Washington St., Braintree, MA 02184

Miles of road operated: 124
Reporting marks: BCLR
Number of locomotives: 10
Number of freight cars: 66
Principal commodities carried: Trash, building materials, LP gas, food products, packaging products, salt, grain, coal
Junctions with other railroads:
Guilford Transportation Industries (Boston & Maine): West Concord, Mass.

Conrail: Braintree, Medfield Junction, Middleboro, North Dartmouth, and Weir Junction (Taunton), Mass.
Radio frequencies: 160.305, 161.355
Passenger routes: (state-owned track carrying passenger trains and Bay Colony freight trains)
Middleboro-Hyannis — Amtrak, seasonal
Buzzards Bay-Hyannis — Cape Cod Scenic Railroad, seasonal
Needham Heights-Needham Junction-West Roxbury: Massachusetts Bay Transportation Authority

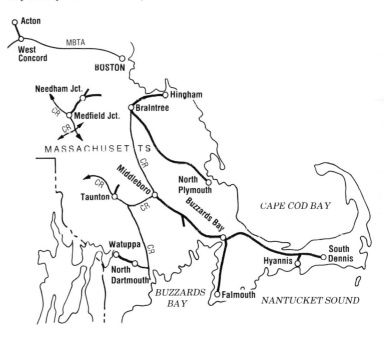

Bay Colony Alco S2 1052, brings freight alongside tidewater at Buzzards Bay, Mass., on June 30, 1984. Photo by Tom Nelligan.

BC RAIL

BC Rail began its existence in 1912 as the Pacific Great Eastern Railway. It constructed a 12-mile line from North Vancouver westward to Horseshoe Bay and took over a bankrupt line that had built a few miles north from Squamish, which was 28 miles west of Horseshoe Bay. In 1918 the government of the province of British Columbia acquired the remaining capital stock of the railway. The PGE reached Quesnel in 1921 and stopped. In 1928 it abandoned its initial line between North Vancouver and Horseshoe Bay.

In 1952 the line was pushed north from Quesnel to a junction with Canadian National's Jasper-Prince Rupert Line at Prince George. It was PGE's first rail connection with another railroad. In 1956 the PGE constructed a line east from Squamish to North Vancouver, replacing the 12 miles of track that it had built in 1912 and abandoned in 1928. It built extensions north from Prince George to Dawson Creek and Fort Nelson in 1958 and 1971, respectively. The name was changed to British Colum-

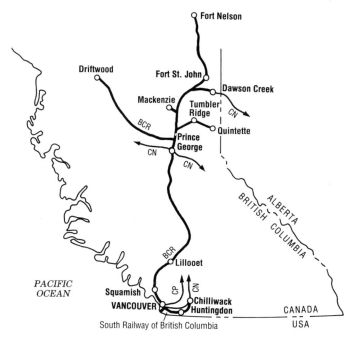

After a tortuous descent into the canyon, two M630s bring a southbound freight across the Fraser River bridge into Lillooet, B. C. The lead unit is painted in the former two-tone green; the second unit wears BC Rail's current red, white, and blue livery. Photo by Alex Mayes.

bia Railway in 1972 and to BC Rail in late 1984. Construction of an extension to Dease Lake in northwestern British Columbia was halted in 1977. The 80-mile Tumbler Ridge Branch, begun in 1981, was completed in 1983. The branch is electrified to preclude the need for extensive ventilation in its tunnels; its principal item of traffic is coal.

BC Rail operates passenger service between North Vancouver and Prince George using RDCs; the Royal Hudson Steam Train, a tourist operation, runs on BC Rail tracks between North Vancouver and Squamish.

Address of general offices: P. O. Box 8770, Vancouver, BC, Canada V6B 4X6
Miles of road operated: 1,387
Reporting marks: BCIT, BCOL, PGE
Number of locomotives: 107

Number of freight cars: 10,090
Number of passenger cars: 12 (self-propelled)
Principal commodities carried: Forest products, coal
Principal shops: North Vancouver, B. C.; Prince George, B. C.; Squamish, B. C.
Junctions with other railroads:
Canadian National: Dawson Creek, North Vancouver, and Prince George, B. C.
CP Rail: North Vancouver, B. C.
Radio frequencies: 159.570, 160.695 (road), 161.370, 161.520 (dispatcher)
Passenger routes: North Vancouver-Squamish-Prince George

BELT RAILWAY OF CHICAGO

The Belt Railway of Chicago was built between 1880 and 1882 as the Belt Division of the Chicago & Western Indiana, a terminal road owned by the predecessors of the Chicago & Eastern Illinois, Monon, Erie, Wabash, and Grand Trunk Western railroads (eventual components, respectively, of Union Pacific, CSX, Conrail, Norfolk Southern, and Canadian National). The railroad was reincorporated in 1882 as the Belt Railway Company of Chicago, and control passed from the C&WI to its owners.

The purpose of the belt line was to provide connections away from the congestion of downtown Chicago between line-haul railroads. The BRC was to have a large yard that could serve as a freight car clearinghouse in Chicago (hence the name Clearing Yard). A circular design for the yard was proposed by A. B. Stickney of the Chicago Great Western. Although only a small portion of that design was built (and of more-or-less conventional layout), when Clearing Yard opened in 1902 it was the largest freight yard in the world and one of the first three hump yards in the U. S. (The other two were the Pennsylvania's East Altoona, Pa., Yard and New York Central's DeWitt Yard at Syracuse, N. Y.)

In 1911 the Lowrey Agreement resulted in flat-rate switching charges for Chicago, and in 1912 the Belt Operating Agreement brought several more railroads into the ownership and operation of the BRC: Atchison, Topeka & Santa Fe; Chesapeake & Ohio; Chicago, Burlington & Quincy; Illinois Central; Pennsylvania; Rock Island; and Soo Line. Pere Marquette became an owner in 1923. Clearing Yard was extensively rebuilt in 1912, and in 1938 retarders were added, eliminating the need for men to ride and brake each car as it rolled down the hump.

BRC is currently owned by Atchison, Topeka & Santa Fe; Burlington Northern; Grand Trunk Western; Illinois Central; Norfolk Southern; Soo

Two MP15s and an SW1500 lead a Belt Railway of Chicago transfer run through Blue Island in April 1983. Photo by R. B. Olson.

Line; and Union Pacific (one twelfth each); CSX (one fourth); and Conrail (one sixth). It connects with all line-haul roads serving Chicago.

Address of general offices: 6900 S. Central Avenue, Chicago, IL 60638

Miles of road operated: 43

Reporting marks: BRC

Number of locomotives: 46

Major yards: Chicago (Clearing Yard)

Shops: Clearing Yard

Connects with:
Atchison, Topeka & Santa Fe
Baltimore & Ohio Chicago Terminal
Burlington Northern
Chicago & North Western
Chicago, Central & Pacific
Chicago Rail Link
Chicago Short Line
Chicago SouthShore & South Bend
Chicago, West Pullman & Southern
Conrail
CSX
Elgin, Joliet & Eastern
Grand Trunk Western
Illinois Central
Indiana Harbor Belt
Manufacturers' Junction
Norfolk Southern
CP Rail System (Soo Line)
Southern Pacific Lines
Union Pacific
Wisconsin & Calumet
Wisconsin Central
all within the Chicago Switching District

Radio frequencies: 160.500, 160.380 (yard)

Recommended reading: "Serving twelve masters," by Jerry A. Pinkepank, in TRAINS Magazine, September 1966, pages 36-46, and October 1966, pages 42-49

BESSEMER & LAKE ERIE RAILROAD

The Bessemer & Lake Erie began life around 1865 as the Bear Creek Railroad, which was built to serve the coalfields southeast of Greenville, Pennsylvania. It was renamed the Shenango & Allegheny Railroad in 1867 and reorganized as the Pittsburgh, Shenango & Lake Erie Railroad in 1888. By then it consisted of a main line from Osgood to Hilliards plus several branches, and its operations included the West Penn & Shenango Connecting Railroad south to Butler. The railroad was extended north, reaching the city of Erie in 1891 and Conneaut, Ohio, in 1892.

In 1896 the railroad joined in a three-way agreement with the Union Railroad and the Carnegie Steel Co. to build a line from Butler to East Pittsburgh. Carnegie already controlled the Mesabi Range iron mines in Minnesota, the railroads from the mines to the docks on Lake Superior, and the Union Railroad, a terminal railroad serving the steel mills in Pittsburgh. By financing the construction of the line from Butler to the connection with the Union Railroad, Carnegie gained control over all the companies involved in transporting ore to his mills.

In 1897 the railroad was renamed the Pittsburg, Bessemer & Lake Erie Railroad, and in 1900 Carnegie Steel chartered the Bessemer & Lake Erie Railroad, which then leased the PB&LE. In 1901 Carnegie Steel became part of the new United States Steel Corporation.

The Bessemer embarked on a series of projects to improve its line, and by the mid-1950s it had relocated or reduced the grade of approximately half the route between Pittsburgh and Conneaut. The topography of the

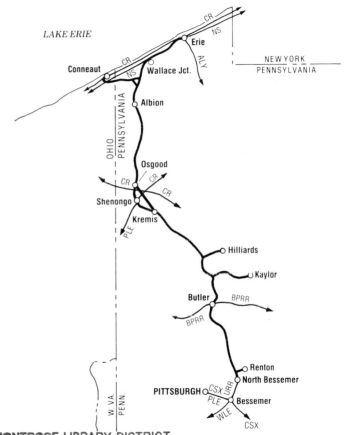

A northbound coal train (right) has just arrived at the transfer facilities at Conneaut, and a southbound train of empty hopper cars awaits departure. Photo by Robert A. Michalka.

area through which the Bessemer runs is hilly and lacks convenient watercourses to follow. The B&LE is noted for its bridges; two of the largest are a 1,724-foot-long viaduct near Osgood, Pa., and the 2,327-foot bridge over the Allegheny River northeast of Pittsburgh, adjacent to the Pennsylvania Turnpike (I-76) bridge.

B&LE purchased the Western Allegheny Railroad from the Pennsylvania Railroad at the end of 1967. B&LE operates over trackage of the Unity Railways Co., a 3.9-mile line between Unity Junction and Renton, Pa.

The railroad was owned by U. S. Steel until 1988, when it was acquired by Transtar, Inc. Blackstone Capital Partners owns a 51 percent interest in Transtar; USX, successor to U. S. Steel owns 49 percent.

Address of general offices: P. O. Box 68, Monroeville, PA 15146
Miles of road operated: 205
Reporting marks: BLE
Number of locomotives: 51

Number of freight cars: 5,127
Principal commodities carried: Iron ore, coal, coke, limestone
Major yards: Albion, Pa.; Conneaut, Ohio
Principal shops: Greenville, Pa.
Junctions with other railroads:
Buffalo & Pittsburgh: Butler, Pa.
Conrail: Conneaut, Ohio, Erie, Pa., Shenango, Pa.
Norfolk Southern: Erie, Pa.; Wallace Junction, Pa.
Pittsburgh & Lake Erie: Shenango, Pa.
Union: North Bessemer, Pa.
Unity Railways: Unity Junction, Pa.
Radio frequencies: 160.830 (road), 161.310 (yard)
Recommended reading: *The Bessemer and Lake Erie Railroad*, by Roy C. Beaver, published in 1969 by Golden West Books, P. O. Box 8136, San Marino, CA 91108 (ISBN 87095-033-9)

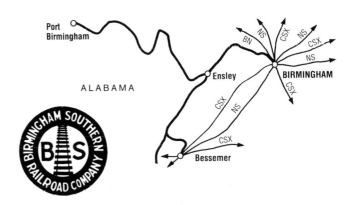

Two Birmingham Southern SW1001s move a string of gondolas at Fairfield, Alabama. Photo by Jim Shaw.

BIRMINGHAM SOUTHERN RAILROAD

The Birmingham Southern was incorporated in 1899. Its original line was built from Birmingham to what is now Pratt City, Alabama, in 1878 and extended to Ensley in 1887. It carried coal from the Pratt Fields to blast furnaces at Ensley and Birmingham and steel products from Ensley to Birmingham for interchange with other railroads. Shortly after its organization the line was purchased by the Louisville & Nashville and the Southern Railway and operated as a joint facility of those companies. It was subsequently acquired by Tennessee Coal, Iron & Railroad Co., which became a part of United States Steel Corporation in 1906.

In 1966 Birmingham Southern acquired Federal Barge Line Railroad, running 18 miles from Birmingham to Port Birmingham on the Black Warrior River. The road performs general terminal service in the Birmingham area. The railroad was owned by U. S. Steel until 1988, when it was acquired by Transtar, Inc. Blackstone Capital Partners owns a 51 percent interest in Transtar; USX, successor to U. S. Steel owns 49 percent.

Address of general offices: P. O. Box 579, Fairfield, AL 35064
Miles of road operated: 84
Reporting marks: BS
Number of locomotives: 35
Number of freight cars: 215
Principal commodities carried: Steel products and raw materials, slag, coal
Junctions with other railroads:
Burlington Northern: Birmingham, Ala.
CSX: Bessemer, Birmingham, Ensley, and Woodward, Ala.
Norfolk Southern: Bessemer, Birmingham, and Ensley, Ala.
Radio frequencies: 160.290, 160.890

BUFFALO & PITTSBURGH RAILROAD

In 1869 the Rochester & State Line Railroad was incorporated to build a railroad south from Rochester, New York. In 1878 the line was open from Rochester through Ashford and Salamanca, New York, and Bradford and DuBois, Pennsylvania, to Punxsutawney. In 1881 it was reorganized as the Rochester & Pittsburgh Railroad.

The Buffalo, Rochester & Pittsburgh Railroad was organized in 1881 to construct a line from Ashford north to Buffalo. In 1887 Adrian Iselin, a New York financier also associated with the Mobile & Ohio Railroad, consolidated the BR&P and the Rochester & Pittsburgh as the Buffalo, Rochester & Pittsburgh Railway.

The BR&P constructed several branch lines, the most important of which ran from Punxsutawney west to Butler and a connection with the Baltimore & Ohio. The road developed into a well-run coal carrier and eventually caught the eye of the Baltimore & Ohio, which wanted to use it as the nucleus of an east-west route across central Pennsylvania. In 1928 the BR&P was acquired by the Van Sweringen brothers (who owned the Nickel Plate and controlled the Chesapeake & Ohio). The B&O still wanted it, though, and traded its interest in the Wheeling & Lake Erie, which the Van Sweringens wanted, for the BR&P, on January 1, 1932. Even though B&O took over operation of the BR&P, the road continued to have a separate corporate existence.

In 1986 Chessie System, successor to the B&O, sold the Rochester-Ashford portion of the BR&P to Genesee & Wyoming Industries. In April 1988 the remainder of the BR&P became the Buffalo & Pittsburgh Railroad, also a Genesee & Wyoming subsidiary.

The Buffalo & Pittsburgh's main line extends from Buffalo, N. Y., to New Castle, Pa. (the last 25 miles are by trackage rights on CSX). Branches extend to Lucerne Junction, Clarksburg, Clearfield, and Bruin, Pa.
Address of general offices: 201 North Penn Street, Punxsutawney, PA 15767
Miles of road operated: 394
Reporting marks: BPRR
Number of locomotives: 27
Number of freight cars: 107

Principal commodities carried: Coal, fuel oil, lumber, pulp, paper
Shops: Butler, Pa.
Junctions with other railroads:
Allegheny: Johnsonburg, Pa.
Bessemer & Lake Erie: Butler, Pa.
Buffalo Southern: Buffalo, N. Y.
Canadian National: Buffalo, N. Y.
Conrail: Buffalo, N. Y., Clearfield, Pa., Salamanca, N. Y.
CSX: Buffalo, N. Y.

CP Rail System (Delaware & Hudson): Buffalo, N. Y.
Mountain Laurel: Falls Creek, Pa.
New York & Lake Erie: Buffalo, N. Y.
Norfolk Southern: Buffalo, N. Y.
Pittsburgh & Lake Erie: New Castle, Pa.
Pittsburg & Shawmut: Dellwood, Pa., West Mosgrove, Pa.
Rochester & Southern: East Salamanca, N. Y.
South Buffalo: Buffalo, N. Y.
Radio frequencies: 160.230, 160.320, 160.530

BURLINGTON NORTHERN RAILROAD

Burlington Northern was created on March 2, 1970, by the merger of four railroads: Northern Pacific Railway; Great Northern Railway; Chicago, Burlington & Quincy Railroad; and Spokane, Portland & Seattle Railway. A decade later BN merged the St. Louis-San Francisco Railway (the Frisco). It is the longest railroad in North America and has a greater extent than any other of the Super Seven: Vancouver, British Columbia, to Pensacola, Florida. If you cross North America from east to west, you have to cross BN rails or get your feet wet in the Gulf of Mexico or find your way around the north side of the city of Winnipeg.

Northern Pacific: The Northern Pacific Railroad was a land-grant railroad chartered in 1864 and completed in 1883 from Carlton, Minnesota, near Duluth, west through Billings, Montana, and Spokane, Washington, to a connection with the Oregon Railway & Navigation Co. at Wallula Junction, Washington. NP already had a line in place from Portland north to Tacoma and soon completed a line over the Cascade Range from Pasco to Tacoma so it could reach tidewater on its own rails.

NP entered receivership in 1893 and was reorganized in 1896. By then its map included lines to St. Paul, to Winnipeg and beyond, and to the Canadian border north of Seattle. In 1901 NP came under the control of James J. Hill, who was intent on eventual merger of NP with his Great Northern Railway.

NP's main line lay across the southern parts of North Dakota and Montana, serving the population centers of those states, but its route across the Rockies was longer and considerably more difficult than those of its northern rival. The portion of the line between Huntley, Montana, east of Billings, and Sandpoint, Idaho, is now a regional railroad, Montana Rail Link.

Great Northern: After an inauspicious start, the St. Paul & Pacific Railroad was acquired by James J. Hill, who reorganized it as the St. Paul, Minneapolis & Manitoba Railway. Hill built northwest from the Twin Cities, then west across the prairie. He acquired an existing charter, renamed it the Great Northern Railway, and pointed it west from Havre, Montana. The road reached Puget Sound at Seattle in 1893; by then Hill had completed a line north to Vancouver, British Columbia.

GN's map eventually included a system of grain-gathering branches north toward and across the Canadian border, lines to the iron-mining area of northeast Minnesota, and a network of branches in southern British Columbia. In 1931 GN completed its Inside Gateway route south from the

Burlington Northern is the top coal hauler in the U. S. because of the development of coalfields in the Powder River Basin of eastern Wyoming. Four BN units, led by SD60M 9289, lug coal uphill at East Coal Creek, Wyo., in 1991. Photo by Wesley Fox.

Columbia River to a junction with the Western Pacific at Bieber, California, using a combination of Spokane, Portland & Seattle's Oregon Trunk Railway, trackage rights on Southern Pacific, and new construction.

Spokane, Portland & Seattle: James J. Hill incorporated the Spokane, Portland & Seattle in 1905 to give Great Northern and Northern Pacific direct access to Portland without having to make a dogleg through Seattle or Tacoma. The road was financed jointly by GN and NP; its route was southwest from Spokane to Pasco, Wash., where it connected with Northern Pacific, then along the north bank of the Columbia River to Van-couver, Wash., across the Columbia River from Portland. It opened in 1909. SP&S subsidiary Oregon Electric Railway connected Portland with Eugene, Ore.; the Oregon Trunk Railway, another subsidiary, followed the Deschutes River south from the Columbia to Bend, Ore.

Chicago, Burlington & Quincy: The Chicago, Burlington & Quincy Railroad, chartered in 1849, was one of the Midwest's first railroads. By 1869 its routes reached from Chicago to Kansas City, Missouri, and Council Bluffs, Iowa. To meet the competitive threat of Jay Gould (who at the time controlled the Union Pacific, Missouri Pacific, and Wabash)

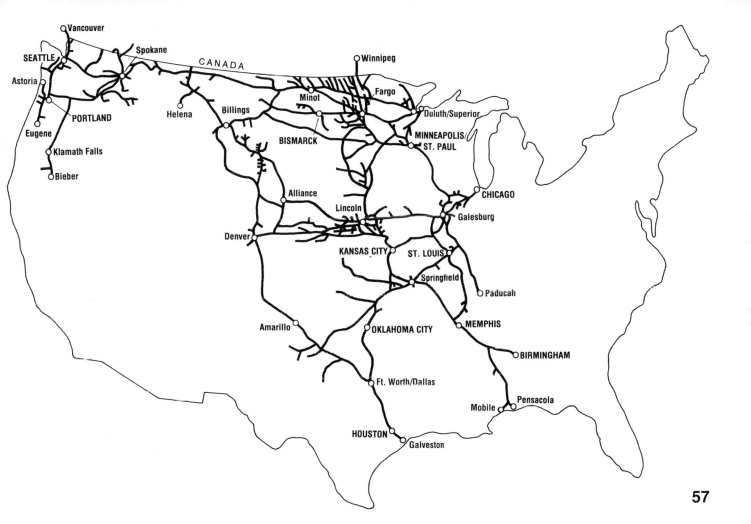

LOUIS W. MENK (1918-   ) was born in Englewood, Colorado. He attended the University of Denver for a year, then hired on with the Union Pacific as a messenger in 1937. In 1940 he moved to the St. Louis-San Francisco. His entry in *Who's Who in Railroading and Rail Transit* for 1971 reads, "telegrapher to chairman and president, St. L-S.F.Ry., 1940-65." While working for the Frisco Menk attended the University of Tulsa, trying to get a college degree one course at a time; there he met  Martha Jane Swan, whom he married in 1942. Later he studied at the Harvard Business School and the Transportation Center at Northwestern University.

Menk successively became a dispatcher, trainmaster, superintendent, and general manager, and in 1962 he became president of the Frisco. Earnings and revenues increased each year of his stewardship. In late 1965 Menk was named president of the Chicago, Burlington & Quincy, and within a year moved to the presidency of the Northern Pacific. He became president of the Burlington Northern when it was formed in 1970, and in 1971 became chairman and chief executive officer. Along the way he was awarded honorary degrees by Drury College, Monmouth College, and the University of Denver, and in 1978 he received the Horatio Alger Award from the American Schools and Colleges Association.

Menk's path to the presidency of the BN gave him a detailed understanding of how the railroad operates. His management techniques included cost control, an integrated approach to marketing, and workable solutions to labor problems. He had little tolerance for money-losing passenger trains. During his tenure as president, the Frisco discontinued most of its passenger trains. A magazine ad during his year on the Burlington blared, "Lou Menk says the Burlington should get out of the railroad business!" adding that Lou Menk was president of the Burlington, and the Burlington was in the distribution business. He chafed against government policies that poured money into competing modes of transportation and at the same time severely restricted the railroads' ability to make an adequate return on investment.

Menk retired from the Burlington Northern in 1983.

the Burlington constructed an extension west to Denver between 1880 and 1882. Construction of the Northern Pacific and the Great Northern prompted the Burlington to build a line north along the east bank of the Mississippi to St. Paul. The line, opened in 1886, was longer than the Milwaukee Road and Chicago & North Western routes but had easier grades. That route, which attracted the attention of James J. Hill, is ultimately responsible for keeping the Burlington out of the difficulties that afflicted the other roads of the Midwest.

The Burlington extended lines northwest to Billings, Montana, and southeast to Paducah, Kentucky, and in 1908 acquired control of the Colorado & Southern and its subsidiaries, which reached from Denver to Galveston, Texas. It surveyed extensions west to the Pacific and considered mergers with practically every other railroad, but the road was managed extremely conservatively. CB&Q seemed content with a network of main lines and branches serving the agricultural area between Chicago and Denver and a single tentacle reaching north to St. Paul for all the traffic its two rich uncles (GN and NP) could provide.

In 1934 the Burlington purchased the nation's first diesel-powered streamlined train, the *Zephyr*. Other *Zephyrs* followed, forming one of the best-known streamliner families. The Burlington constructed the first Vista-Dome car in its shops in 1945.

St. Louis-San Francisco: Frisco's history dates from 1853, when ground was broken for the South-West Branch of the Pacific Railroad of Missouri at Franklin (now Pacific), Missouri. The line was aimed at Springfield, Mo., and eventually the Pacific Ocean. The railroad reached Springfield in 1870 and merged with the Atlantic & Pacific, which was chartered

to build west along the 35th parallel. The western portion of the A&P eventually became the Santa Fe's main line, and the St. Louis-San Francisco, successor to the South-West Branch, altered its destination to Texas.

The Santa Fe purchased the Frisco in 1890 and lost it during receivership a few years later. In 1901 the Frisco acquired a line from Kansas City through Memphis to Birmingham, Alabama.It crossed Frisco's original route at Springfield, Mo., which eventually became the hub of the system. About the same time the Frisco became part of the empire of Benjamin F. Yoakum (along with Rock Island, Chicago & Eastern Illinois, and Gulf Coast Lines). The Frisco regained independence in 1916 and went through receivership in the 1930s and 1940s. Its rails eventually reached the Gulf of Mexico, not in Texas but at Pensacola, Florida, and Mobile, Alabama.

Between 1956 and 1961 the Frisco controlled the Central of Georgia, and in the 1960s it talked merger with Chicago Great Western, Santa Fe, and Southern. The Chicago, Burlington & Quincy purchased a large block of Frisco stock in 1966. BN initiated merger talks in 1977. In 1980 BN merged the Frisco.

Burlington Northern: Great Northern and Northern Pacific covered most of Minnesota north and west of the Twin Cities and the eastern third of North Dakota. West of there, the main lines of the two roads were as much as 200 miles apart, coming together at Spokane but separating again to cross Washington. The two roads were instrumental in settling much of the northern Great Plains, and they pretty much divided the northern tier of the country between the Mississippi and Puget Sound between them (as the Milwaukee Road eventually learned). Burlington Northern existed after a fashion long before the merger formalities of 1970. In 1901 Great Northern and Northern Pacific each acquired almost 49 percent of Burlington's stock, assuring a connection from St. Paul, eastern terminus of GN and NP, to Chicago, and NP came under the control of GN. In 1905 GN

Eastbound train 208, with an SD60 leased from Oakway on the point, crosses Java Bridge a few miles southeast of Essex, Montana, on the former Great Northern main line. The train is headed for a crossing of the Continental Divide at the summit of Marias Pass, in September 1989. Photo by Wesley Fox.

and NP organized and constructed the Spokane, Portland & Seattle Railway. In 1927 the Great Northern Pacific Railway was organized to consolidate GN and NP and lease the Burlington and the SP&S; the Interstate Commerce Commission would approve it only without the Burlington. The companies resumed merger studies in 1956, and in 1960 the directors of GN and NP approved the terms. Government approval and actual merger took another decade.

At the end of 1981 BN absorbed the Colorado & Southern, which had been a CB&Q subsidiary, and transferred C&S's Denver-Texline route to the Fort Worth & Denver, a C&S subsidiary. On January 1, 1983, FW&D was also merged into BN.

BN's former Great Northern line includes the two longest railroad tunnels in North America, the Cascade Tunnel, 7.79 miles, between Scenic and Berne, Wash., and the 7.75-mile-long Flathead Tunnel, east of Libby, Mont. The Crooked River Bridge, north of Redmond, Ore., on the Oregon Trunk line, is second highest (320 feet) in the U. S.

Address of general offices: 777 Main Street, Fort Worth, TX 76102
Miles of road operated: 25,000
Reporting marks: BN, BNFE, CBQ, CS, FWD, GN, NP, SLSF, SPS
Number of locomotives: 2,340
Number of freight cars: 58,769

Principal commodities carried: Coal, grain, forest products, intermodal containers and trailers
Major yards: Chicago (Cicero); Galesburg, Ill.; Kansas City, Mo.; Lincoln, Nebr.; Minneapolis (Northtown); Pasco, Wash.; Seattle; Springfield, Mo.
Principal shops: Alliance, Nebr.; Havelock, Nebr.; Springfield, Mo.; West Burlington, Iowa
Radio frequencies: 161.100, 161.160
Passenger routes:
Amtrak — Chicago-Denver, Galesburg-West Quincy, Mo., St. Paul-Seattle, Spokane-Portland, and Seattle-Portland
Metra — Chicago-Aurora, Ill.
Historical and technical societies:
Burlington Route Historical Society, Box 456, LaGrande, IL 60525
Frisco Railroad Museum, P. O. Box 276, Ash Grove, MO 65604
Great Northern Railway Historical Society, c/o Connie Hoffman, 1781 Griffith, Berkley, MI 48072
Northern Pacific Railway Historical Association, c/o Richard Loop, 550 Amy Lane, Idaho Falls, ID 83406
Spokane, Portland & Seattle Railway Historical Society, c/o Gerald Howard, 6207 North Concord, Portland, OR 97217

BURLINGTON NORTHERN SPINOFFS

Burlington Northern has sold several route segments to become regional railroads or short lines. The principal ones are:
• Arkansas & Missouri Railroad: Ex-Frisco secondary main line from Monett, Mo., to Fort Smith, Ark., 140 miles (September 1, 1986)
• Kiamichi Railroad: Ex-Frisco from Hope, Ark., to Lakeside, Okla., and from Antlers, Okla., to Paris, Texas, 251 miles (July 22, 1987)

• Montana Rail Link: Ex-Northern Pacific main line from Huntley, Mont., to Sandpoint, Idaho, plus branches, 862 miles (November 1, 1987)
• Red River Valley & Western Railroad: Ex-Northern Pacific branches in North Dakota, 656 miles (July 19, 1987)
• Washington Central Railroad: Ex-Northern Pacific main line from Kennewick to Cle Elum, Wash., plus several branches, 344 miles (October 13, 1986)

CALTRAIN (Peninsula Corridor Joint Powers Board)

On July 1, 1980, the California Department of Transportation (Cal-Trans) signed an agreement with Southern Pacific to finance the commute trains SP operated between San Francisco and San Jose, 47 miles. In October 1981 the schedules were revised, with additional trains to accommodate reverse commuting (southbound in the morning and northbound in the evening). In 1985 Electro-Motive delivered 18 F40PH-2 diesels bearing the CalTrain name — two more came in 1987 — and in 1985 and 1986 73 gallery coaches arrived from Nippon Sharyo in Japan.

In 1991 San Francisco, San Mateo, and Santa Clara counties negotiated the purchase of the San Francisco-San Jose line from Southern Pacific. Responsibility for funding and operating the service was shifted from Cal-Trans to the Peninsula Corridor Joint Powers Board, retaining the Cal-Train name for the service.

On July 1, 1992, Amtrak took over operation of the service. Most trains were extended 2 miles south of San Jose to a new station named Tamien, where a connection is made with Santa Clara County's light rail system,

Six trains await duty at San Francisco on July 21, 1989. They will depart for San Jose at 5:20, 5:24, 5:28, and 5:32. The 5:20 runs nonstop to California Avenue, 32 miles; the 5:24, to Hillsdale, 20 miles; and so on. Most commuters reach their home stations a few minutes before or after 6 p.m. Photo by William D. Middleton.

and two weekday trains were extended to Gilroy, 34 miles south of San Jose.

The San Francisco terminal at Fourth and Townsend streets has long been considered temporary, and a 1.5 mile extension to a terminal closer to San Francisco's business district is under study. (The previous station and Third and Townsend was also considered temporary. Not long after 1900 the Southern Pacific formulated plans to extend the line north along the Embarcadero to Market Street opposite the Ferry Building.)

Address of general offices: P. O. Box 3006, San Carlos, CA 94070-1306
Miles of road operated: 81
Number of locomotives: 20
Number of passenger cars: 73
Radio frequencies: 161.550
Passenger routes: San Francisco-San Jose-Gilroy

CANADIAN NATIONAL RAILWAYS

Canadian National Railways was incorporated on June 6, 1919, to operate several railroads that had come under control of the Canadian government because of financial difficulties. Brief histories of CN's principal components follow, in the order they came under government control.

Predecessors

The first component to come under government operation was the Intercolonial Railway. It was built under government auspices to connect Nova Scotia and New Brunswick with Quebec, much as the Canadian Pacific was built as a condition of British Columbia's entering the confederation. It began operation in 1876 between Halifax, N. S., and Riviere du Loup, Que., where it connected with the Grand Trunk. The route through Moncton and Campbellton, N. B., and Truro, N. S., was chosen to be as far as possible from the U. S. border; it is now CN's main route between Halifax and Montreal. Canadian Government Railways took over operation of the Intercolonial in 1913.

The National Transcontinental Railway grew from a Grand Trunk proposal for a line to Winnipeg from Callander, Ontario, near North Bay, at the end of a Grand Trunk line from Toronto. Political forces changed the proposal to a line from Moncton, N. B., in almost a straight line to Winnipeg, far to the north of Montreal and Toronto. Between Quebec City and Winnipeg, 1,372 miles, there was almost no population along the route. The railroad was built by the Canadian government for eventual operation by the Grand Trunk Pacific, but GTP, deep in financial trouble, refused to accept the line upon completion. Canadian Government Railways took it over in 1915.

The Canadian Northern Railway was begun in 1899 by William Mackenzie and Donald Mann as a line from Winnipeg to Vancouver via Saskatoon and Edmonton, well north of the Canadian Pacific's route. The system soon included several lines in Manitoba leased from the Northern Pacific, and an assortment of lines in Ontario, Quebec, and Nova Scotia.

The line to Vancouver was completed in 1915. From Edmonton west to Yellowhead Pass the CNoR paralleled the Grand Trunk Pacific; for many miles in British Columbia Canadian Northern occupied the opposite bank of the Fraser River from the well-established Canadian Pacific. By 1916 the eastern half of the CNoR system stretched from Quebec City to Winnipeg via Ottawa, Toronto, Capreol, and Port Arthur-Fort William (now Thunder Bay), Ont., and Warroad, Minnesota. An Ottawa-Capreol

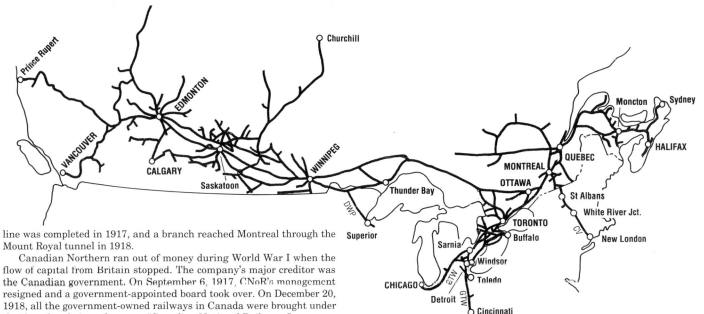

line was completed in 1917, and a branch reached Montreal through the Mount Royal tunnel in 1918.

Canadian Northern ran out of money during World War I when the flow of capital from Britain stopped. The company's major creditor was the Canadian government. On September 6, 1917, CNoR's management resigned and a government-appointed board took over. On December 20, 1918, all the government-owned railways in Canada were brought under that board and given the name "Canadian National Railways."

The Grand Trunk Pacific Railway was incorporated in 1903 to build a railroad from Winnipeg, Manitoba, west to the Pacific at Prince Rupert, British Columbia. Construction costs of the GTP far exceeded the estimates, and revenues were disappointing — Prince Rupert never developed into a major seaport. GTP entered receivership in 1919 and became part of Canadian National Railways in 1920.

The Grand Trunk Railway was the last major addition to Canadian National Railways. It was conceived as a Canadian main line from Montreal through Toronto to Sarnia, Ont., where it would connect with a railroad to Chicago and, via Chicago, the Canadian West. To that was added in 1853 a line from Montreal to the nearest seaport, Portland, Maine. Con-

struction and acquisition at the west end of the line put Grand Trunk across the St. Clair River by ferry and through Michigan and Indiana into Chicago in 1880. Grand Trunk's tunnel under the St. Clair between Sarnia, Ont., and Port Huron, Mich., was completed in 1886. By the early 1900s the Grand Trunk had an extensive network of lines in southern Ontario and reached south to New London, Connecticut, through its control of the Central Vermont Railway.

The Grand Trunk Railway resisted the idea of westward expansion for more than 20 years but finally yielded, backing two railways, the National Transcontinental and the Grand Trunk Pacific Railway. The Grand Trunk bore a huge debt for the construction of the Grand Trunk Pacific but rejected a chance to turn the GTP over to the government. When the GTP sank into financial ruin it dragged Grand Trunk down with it.

The Canadian government took ownership of the Grand Trunk on May 21, 1920, and amalgamated it with Canadian National in 1923. The Grand Trunk name continued in use for the line to Portland, Maine, and the lines in Michigan, Indiana, and Illinois; the latter became the Grand Trunk Western Railway in 1928.

Canadian National

In 1923 Canadian National had two transcontinental routes from Moncton, N. B., to the Pacific (the ex-Canadian Northern route to Vancouver and the ex-Grand Trunk Pacific route to Prince Rupert) plus dense networks of lines in Quebec and Ontario and on the prairies between Winnipeg and the Rockies. In 1923 CN built a 30-mile cutoff in northern Ontario, from Longlac on the former Canadian Northern to Nakina on the former National Transcontinental. The new line shortened CN's Toronto-Winnipeg route by 102 miles. In the 1960s CN pushed lines into the subarctic area north of the prairies to tap mineral deposits. Notable among these is the Great Slave Lake Railway.

In 1961 CN underwent an image change, replacing the maple leaf with a modern logo, and olive green paint on passenger cars and locomotives with black and off-white. Two years later CN kicked off a passenger renaissance with incentive fares, refurbished cars, fast intercity trains, and cars — even domes — purchased secondhand from U. S. railroads. CN's passenger trains carried respectable numbers of passengers and served as the basis for the establishment of VIA Rail Canada in 1977.

The 3 foot 6 inch-gauge Newfoundland Railway became part of CN in 1949 when Newfoundland joined the confederation. In 1979 CN created a subsidiary, Terra Transport, to operate all CN services in Newfoundland. The railway ceased operating on October 1, 1988. Rail service on Prince Edward Island was discontinued at the end of 1989, and in March 1990 CN abandoned its operations on Vancouver Island.

Northern Alberta Railways was incorporated in 1929 to take over several lines owned and operated by the province of Alberta. It was jointly owned by CN and Canadian Pacific until CP sold its half to CN in 1980.

Canadian National also runs hotels, truck and express companies, ferries in the Maritime Provinces, and a communications system. CN divest-

The "comfort cab" or "safety cab" found widespread favor in Canada a decade before it was adopted by railroads south of the border. A CN SD40-2 with such a cab leads an eastbound freight into Winnipeg, Manitoba, in July 1985. Photo by Alex Mayes.

ed itself of its interest in Air Canada in 1978.

Grand Trunk Corporation was incorporated in 1970 to consolidate CN's U. S. subsidiaries: Grand Trunk Western; Central Vermont; and Duluth, Winnipeg & Pacific. The roads are now known collectively as CN North America. The portion of the original Grand Trunk route from Island Pond, Vermont, to Portland, Maine, (which was operated as part of CN proper, not part of Grand Trunk Corporation) was sold in 1989 to become The St. Lawrence & Atlantic Railroad.

Address of general offices: P. O. Box 1800, Montreal, PQ, Canada H3C 3N4

Miles of road operated: 22,518
Reporting marks: BCNE, CN, CNA, CNIS, NAR
Number of locomotives: 1782
Number of freight cars: 56,091
Principal commodities carried: Grain, lumber, coal, potash
Major yards: Edmonton, Moncton, Montreal (Taschereau), Toronto, Winnipeg
Principal shops: Montreal (Pointe St. Charles), Winnipeg (Transcona)
Radio frequencies: 161.415, 161.205, 160.935 (dispatcher to train)
Passenger routes:
VIA Rail Canada — Halifax-Montreal; Moncton-Saint John, N. B.; Gaspé-Matapedia, Que.; Quebec-Montreal; Chicoutimi, Que.-Hervey-Montreal; Hervey, Que.-Cochrane, Ont.; Montreal-Ottawa; Ottawa-Smiths Falls, Ont.; Montreal-Toronto; Toronto-Stratford-London-Sarnia, Ont.; Toronto-Brantford-London-Windsor; Toronto-Hamilton-Niagara Falls; Toronto-Winnipeg-Vancouver; Jasper, Alta.-Prince Rupert, B. C.; Winnipeg-Thompson-Churchill, Man.; The Pas-Lynn Lake, Man.
Ontario Northland — Toronto-North Bay
Montreal Urban Community Transportation Commission — Montreal-Deux Montagnes, Que. (electrified)
GO Transit — Oshawa-Toronto-Hamilton; Toronto-Bradford; Toronto-Stouffville; Toronto-Georgetown
Amtrak — Montreal-East Alburgh, Vt.; Montreal-Rouses Point, N. Y.
Recommended reading: *Canadian National Railways*, by G. R. Stevens, O. B. E., published in 1962 by Clarke, Irwin & Co., Ltd., Toronto and Vancouver

CANEY FORK & WESTERN RAILROAD

The McMinnville & Manchester Railroad was chartered in 1850 to connect McMinnville and Manchester, Tennessee, with the Nashville & Chattanooga Railroad, which at the time hadn't progressed much beyond the city limits of Nashville. Much of the road was dismantled during the Civil War to rebuild the N&C, but the short line was rebuilt after the war and by 1877 was part of the Nashville, Chattanooga & St. Louis. In 1885 the line was extended northeast from McMinnville to Sparta

Ownership and management passed from NC&StL successively to

Caney Fork & Western 531, a GP9, is headed south at Doyle, Tennessee. Photo by Jim Shaw.

Louisville & Nashville, the Seaboard System, and CSX. In 1983 CSX sold the line to the Tri-County Railroad Authority (Coffee, Warren, and White counties), which leased it to the Caney Fork & Western.

Address of general offices: P. O. Box 451, McMinnville, TN 37110
Miles of road operated: 61
Reporting marks: CFWR
Number of locomotives: 3

Number of freight cars: 1,025 (all but 6 are 4750-cubic-foot covered hopper cars)
Principal commodities carried: Grain, fertilizer
Shops: McMinnville, Tenn.
Junctions with other railroads: CSX: Tullahoma, Tenn.
Radio frequencies: 160.545

CARTIER RAILWAY
(La Compagnie de Chemin de Fer Cartier)

The Quebec Cartier Mining Co. (then a subsidiary of U. S. Steel; now owned by Dofasco, Mitsui, and Caemi) was formed in 1957 to mine iron ore in eastern Quebec and transport it south to the St. Lawrence River. Construction of the Cartier Railway began in 1958, and by the end of 1960 the line was completed from Port Cartier, 40 miles west of Sept Iles, 193 miles north to Lac Jeannine, near Gagnon. In the early 1970s the line was extended 85 miles north from a junction at milepost 174 to a mine and concentrator at Mount Wright. Trains are operated year round, because a dryer built into the ore concentrator eliminates the problem of ore freezing in the cars.

Address of general offices: Port Cartier, PQ, Canada G5B 2H3
Miles of road operated: 260
Reporting marks: QCM
Number of locomotives: 31
Number of freight cars: 1,300
Principal commodities carried: Iron ore
Shops: Port Cartier, Que.
Junctions with other railroads: None

Two six-motor 3600-h.p. units built by Montreal bring an ore train south toward Port Cartier, Que., in June 1981. Photo by Greg McDonnell.

Radio frequencies: 161.130, 160.800, 160.980
Map: See Quebec North Shore & Labrador, page 000

66

CENTRAL MICHIGAN RAILWAY

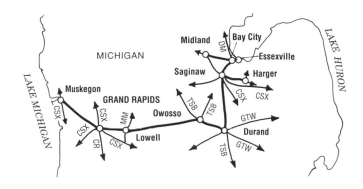

In September 1987 the Central Michigan Railway purchased a cluster of rail lines in Michigan's Lower Peninsula: from Durand through Bay City to Essexville, from Bay City to Midland, from Durand through Grand Rapids to Muskegon (since then partly abandoned), and from Grand Rapids to Coopersville, plus a segment of a former Conrail line from Saginaw to Harger. The routes are generally of Grand Trunk Western heritage, but the Grand Rapids-Muskegon segment was once part of the Pennsylvania Railroad, and the Midland-Bay City and Saginaw-Harger lines are former Conrail (ex-New York Central; previously Michigan Central) routes.

Address of general offices: 120 Oak Street, Tawas City, MI 48763
Miles of road operated: 214
Reporting marks: CMGN
Number of locomotives: 11
Principal commodities carried: Auto parts, chemicals, grain
Shops: Bay City
Junctions with other railroads:
Conrail: Grand Rapids
CSX: Grand Rapids, Midland, Saginaw
Grand Trunk Western: Durand
Huron & Eastern: Harger
Lake State: Bay City
Mid-Michigan: Lowell
Tuscola & Saginaw Bay: Durand, Owosso
Radio frequencies: 161.280, 161.310

General Electric and Electro-Motive team up on a Central Michigan freight at Bay City on July 3, 1990. Photo by Jim Shaw.

67

RAILROAD COMPANY OF INDIANAPOLIS

CENTRAL RAILROAD COMPANY OF INDIANAPOLIS

Central Railroad of Indianapolis began operation August 14, 1989, on two ex-Norfolk & Western (previously Nickel Plate) lines in Indiana, from Marion to Frankfort and from Argos to Tipton. The two routes cross at Kokomo. Since January 1, 1992, it has also operated the former CSX line between Marion and Amboy, Ind., owned by Kokomo Grain Co.

The Marion-Frankfort route was part of the narrow gauge Toledo, Delphos & Burlington, itself part of an ambitious scheme to create a narrow gauge route all the way from Toledo, Ohio, to Mexico City. It eventually became the Toledo, St. Louis & Western — the Clover Leaf — which briefly around 1911 was under common management with the Alton, the Iowa Central, and the Minneapolis & St. Louis. The Clover Leaf was acquired by the Van Sweringen brothers in 1922, and it became part of

Three Central Railroad of Indianapolis units probe through early-morning fog with a freight train in April 1990. CERA photo.

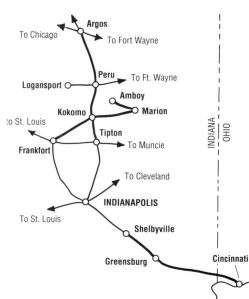

the Nickel Plate (the New York, Chicago & St. Louis Railroad) in 1923.

The Argos-Tipton line was built by the Peru & Indianapolis Railroad in the 1840s and 1850s. By the time it was acquired by the Lake Erie & Western Railway in 1887 it reached from Indianapolis north to Michigan City. The Lake Erie & Western came under control of the Lake Shore & Michigan Southern (New York Central) in 1899 and was purchased by the Van Sweringens in 1922 to become part of the Nickel Plate.

Central Railroad of Indianapolis leases its routes from Norfolk Southern; the Peru-Argos segment is subleased to Indiana Hi-Rail Corporation.

Under the same management is the 84-mile Central Railroad Company of Indiana, which began operating the former Conrail (New York Central; Big Four) line from Cincinnati, Ohio, to Shelbyville, Ind. CIND has trackage rights over Conrail between Shelbyville and Frankfort, where it connects with the Central Railroad of Indianapolis.

Address of general offices: P. O. Box 554, Kokomo, IN 46903-0554
Miles of road operated: 87
Reporting marks: CERA
Number of locomotives: 10
Number of freight cars: 78
Principal commodities carried: Grain, fertilizer, sand, soda ash, pulpboard
Junctions with other railroads:
Conrail: Kokomo, Ind.; Marion, Ind.
Central of Indiana: Frankfort, Ind.
Indiana Hi-Rail: Peru, Ind.
Norfolk Southern: Frankfort, Ind.; Peru, Ind.; Tipton, Ind.
Radio frequencies: 160.455, 161.295

CENTRAL VERMONT RAILWAY

The Vermont Central Railroad was opened in 1849 between the Connecticut River at Windsor, Vermont, and Lake Champlain at Burlington. Like many New England railroads of the time, it aimed to capture traffic moving between Boston and the Great Lakes. By 1850 connections were in place at each end, creating a through route from Boston to Ogdensburg, New York, on the St. Lawrence River.

In the early 1850s the Vermont Central came under the control of one of those connections, the Vermont & Canada Railroad, which ran from Essex Junction, near Burlington, around the north end of Lake Champlain to Rouses Point, N. Y.

By 1871 the Vermont Central controlled a system reaching from New London, Connecticut, north to Montreal and west to Ogdensburg. The system included the Rutland Railroad and steamship lines from New London to New York and from Ogdensburg to Chicago. In 1873 the Vermont Central was reorganized as the Central Vermont Railroad.

After the financial panic of 1893 the Central Vermont surrendered the leases of the Rutland and the Ogdensburg & Lake Champlain. The company was reorganized again in 1898 as the Central Vermont Railway with Canada's Grand Trunk Railway as its majority stockholder.

Control passed from Grand Trunk to Canadian National Railways in 1923. A flood in 1927 wiped out almost all of the original portion of CV's main line between White River Junction and Essex Junction; Canadian National funded the rebuilding of the line. CV was in receivership between 1927 and 1929; during the Depression it trimmed back several branch lines.

After World War II CV discontinued its New London-New York steamship service; in the mid-1950s it abandoned its own line to Montreal in favor of trackage rights on CN. The railroad dieselized relatively late, in 1957.

In 1971 CN placed all its U. S. subsidiaries under the control of the

Three Central Vermont GP9s accelerate out of Palmer, Massachusetts, with a northbound freight, on October 7, 1989. The track in the foreground is Conrail's Boston-Albany main line. Photo by Jim Shaw.

Grand Trunk Corporation, headquartered in Detroit. Later in the 1970s CV regained a measure of independence and local control. However, traffic and revenues diminished, and in 1983 the CV was for sale briefly. CV made several attempts to increase business: a piggyback train, a unit train carrying wood chips to a power plant, a unit train carrying lumber and building materials, and a TankTrain operation (linked tank cars). Some of those trains ran only for a short time; others are still in service. Most of CV's traffic is received from CN and Conrail and terminates on line.

The map of today's CV looks essentially like it has for decades, other than the abandonment of a few branches and one addition. In 1987 Boston & Maine's Connecticut River line was in such bad condition that Amtrak suspended the operation of its Washington-Montreal *Montrealer* and used its condemnation powers to take ownership of the Brattleboro-Windsor portion of the route. Amtrak transferred the line to CV, which rehabilitated the track, and the *Montrealer* resumed operation in 1989 on a new route — the entire length of CV's main line, from New London, Conn., to East Alburgh, Vt., instead of using Amtrak rails from New Haven, Conn.,

to Springfield, Mass., and B&M from Springfield to Brattleboro. The CV is grouped with Canadian National's other United States subsidiaries in a unit named CN North America.

Address of general offices: 2 Federal Street, St. Albans, VT 05478
Miles of road operated: 366
Reporting marks: CV
Number of locomotives: 8
Number of freight cars: 223
Principal commodities carried: Forest products, agricultural products
Major yards: St. Albans, Vt., Palmer, Mass.
Principal shops: St. Albans, Vt.
Junctions with other railroads:
Guilford Transportation Industries (Boston & Maine): Brattleboro, Vt.; White River Junction, Vt.
Canadian National: East Alburgh, Vt.
Claremont Concord: Claremont Junction, N. H.
Conrail: Palmer, Mass.
Delaware & Hudson: Rouses Point, N. Y.
Green Mountain: Bellows Falls, Vt.
Lamoille Valley: St. Albans, Vt.
Providence & Worcester: New London, Conn.
Vermont Railway: Burlington, Vt.
Washington County: Montpelier Junction, Vt.
Radio frequencies: 161.415 (road), 161.205 (yard and maintenance of way), 160.935 (yard)
Passenger routes: Amtrak — New London, Conn.-East Alburgh, Vt.
Recommended reading:
The Central Vermont Railway, by Robert C. Jones, published in 1981 and 1982 by Sundance Publications, Silverton, CO 81433 (ISBN 0-913582-27-1, -28-X, -29-8, -30-1, -31-X, and 32 8)
"Central Vermont ... a survivor," by Scott Hartley, in TRAINS Magazine, February 1991, pages 30-42

CENTRAL WESTERN RAILWAY

Central Western Railway operates 105 miles of the former Stettler Subdivision of Canadian National Railways from Ferlow Junction, south of Camrose, Alberta, south through a grain-growing area to Dinosaur, north of Drumheller. The road also operates a former CP Rail line from Stettler east 121 miles to Compeer, Alta., on the Saskatchewan border. Operating headquarters are at Stettler.

The north-south line was originally Canadian Northern Railway's Battle River Branch. It formed a long-way-around route between Edmonton and Calgary for CNoR (259 miles versus CP Rail's 192-mile route). The line retained passenger service until late 1981 in the form of an Edmonton-Drumheller RDC operated by VIA Rail Canada.

The Stettler-Compeer line was part of CP Rail's Lacombe and Coronation subdivisions. Before it was severed east of Compeer, the line reached southeast to Moose Jaw, Sask. Central Western acquired it in March 1992.

Central Western began operating on November 21, 1986. Its principal business is carrying grain. Alberta Prairie Railway Excursions operates steam-powered excursion trains over most of the north-south route.

Address of general offices: P. O. Box 4690, South Edmonton, AB T6E 5G5
Miles of road operated: 236
Reporting marks: CWR
Number of locomotives: 4
Principal commodities carried: Grain
Shops: Stettler, Alta.
Junctions with other railroads:
Canadian National: Ferlow Junction, Alta.; Dinosaur, Alta.
CP Rail: Stettler, Alta.
Radio frequencies: 160.590, 161.445
Passenger routes: Alberta Prairie Railway Excursions — Edberg-Stettler-Morrin, Alta.

CHATTAHOOCHEE INDUSTRIAL RAILROAD

The Chattahoochee Industrial Railroad was built by the Great Northern Nekoosa Paper Co. to serve a new plant near Cedar Springs, in the southwest corner of Georgia. The railroad began operation in 1963. Other customers of the line are plywood, chemical, and steel tubing plants and several forest-products-related industries.

The railroad was acquired by the Georgia Pacific Corporation in 1991 and placed under the same management as the Ashley, Drew & Northern; Arkansas Louisiana & Mississippi; and Fordyce & Princeton.

Address of general offices: P. O. Box 253, Cedar Springs, GA 31732
Miles of road operated: 15
Reporting marks: CIRR

Number of locomotives: 10
Number of freight cars: 816
Principal commodities carried: Paper products, coal
Shops: Saffold, Ga.
Junctions with other railroads:
CSX: Saffold, Ga.
Georgia Southwestern: Saffold, Ga.
Norfolk Southern: Hilton, Ga.
Radio frequencies: 160.860, 160.620, 161.235 (shops)
Map: see Apalachicola Northern, page 29

For years GP7 1830 was Chattahoochee Industrial's odd man — the rest of the roster was Alco RS1s. Of late modernism has appeared in the form of SW1500s. Photo by R. C. Thomason.

CHICAGO & ILLINOIS MIDLAND RAILWAY

In 1888 the Pawnee Railroad was chartered to build west from Pawnee, Illinois, a few miles south of Springfield, to a connection with the St. Louis & Chicago (now Illinois Central), a distance of 4 miles. In 1892 the road more than doubled its mileage with an extension west to the Chicago & Alton (now Southern Pacific) at Auburn.

The Illinois Midland Coal Co., owned jointly by Peabody Coal Co. and Samuel Insull's Chicago Edison and Commonwealth Electric companies, had mines in the area. In 1905 the coal company purchased the railroad and organized it as the Central Illinois Railway. Later that year the railroad's name was changed to Chicago & Illinois Midland to avoid confusion with the neighboring Illinois Central. During the teens the railroad was extended east to Taylorville to connect with the Baltimore & Ohio and the Wabash and west to a connection with the Chicago & North Western.

In 1926 the railroad purchased the Springfield-Peoria trackage of the defunct Chicago, Peoria & St. Louis and obtained trackage rights from Illinois Central from Pawnee Jct. (now Cimic) to Springfield. As a result the coal traffic pattern changed. Instead of moving to connecting roads for rail haulage north to Chicago, it moved to the Illinois River at Havana, then north by barge.

C&IM's steam power was noteworthy on a couple of counts. Passenger trains were handled by a trio of 4-4-0s built in 1927 and 1928 by Baldwin, the last of their type built for a Class 1 railroad. In the 1940s and early 1950s C&IM purchased a number of Wabash and Atlantic Coast Line 2-10-2s to replace smaller locomotives; the road dieselized relatively late in 1955.

Construction of a mine-mouth generating plant in the 1960s and later the restrictions against burning high-sulfur Illinois coal in generating stations again altered the railroad's traffic pattern. Now much of C&IM's traffic is unit coal trains of low-sulfur coal from Wyoming and Montana received from the Burlington Northern and Chicago & North Western at Peoria for delivery to Edison's generating station at Powerton, near Pekin, and to Havana for shipment by barge to generating stations near Chicago.

Commonwealth Edison, which was formed in 1907 by the merger of Chicago Edison and Commonwealth Electric, owned the Chicago & Illi-

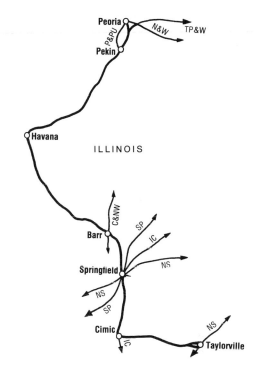

nois Midland until 1987. The railroad is now privately held.

Address of general offices: P. O. Box 139, Springfield, IL 62705
Miles of road operated: 121
Reporting marks: CIM
Number of locomotives: 18
Number of freight cars: 405

Shops: Springfield, Ill.
Principal commodities carried: Coal, wheat, roofing granules, municipal solid waste
Junctions with other railroads:
Burlington Northern: Peoria
Chicago & North Western: Barr, Peoria
Conrail: Peoria
Gateway Western: Springfield
Illinois Central: Cimic, Pekin, Peoria, Springfield
Iowa Interstate: Peoria
Keokuk Junction: Peoria
Norfolk Southern: Peoria; Springfield; Taylorville
Peoria & Pekin Union: Pekin; Peoria
Southern Pacific: Springfield
Toledo, Peoria & Western: East Peoria
Radio frequencies: 160.950, 160.290 (yard)
Recommended reading: *Chicago & Illinois Midland*, by Richard R. Wallin, Paul H. Stringham, and John Szwajkart, published in 1979 by Golden West Books, P. O. Box 8136, San Marino, CA 91108 (ISBN 0-87095-077-0)

Three dark-green SD38-2s bring empty hopper cars through Forest City, Illinois, on August 15, 1983. Photo by J. David Ingles.

CHICAGO & NORTH WESTERN TRANSPORTATION COMPANY

The railroad capital of the United States, Chicago, saw its first locomotive in 1848: the *Pioneer* of the Galena & Chicago Union Rail Road. The G&CU, chartered in 1836, lay dormant for 12 years before construction began. By 1850, though, its rails reached west to Elgin and in 1853 to Freeport, where it connected with the Illinois Central Railroad under construction from Cairo at the southern tip of Illinois to Galena in the northwest corner of the state. The Galena & Chicago Union then built westward from what is now West Chicago, reaching Fulton, Illinois, on the Mississippi River, in 1855.

In 1855 the Chicago, St. Paul & Fond du Lac Rail Road was organized

to extend an existing road northwest from Cary, Ill., through Madison and La Crosse, Wisconsin, to St. Paul, Minnesota, and north through Fond du Lac, Wisconsin, to the iron and copper country south of Lake Superior. It was reorganized in 1859 as the Chicago & North Western Railway. In

1864 it was consolidated with the Galena & Chicago Union. In 1866 the C&NW leased the Chicago & Milwaukee Railroad, which linked the two cities of its name.

The C&NW continued to acquire other railroads, notable among them the Chicago, St. Paul, Minneapolis & Omaha Railway (the "Omaha Road", which retained a separate corporate existence until 1972). By the early part of the twentieth century C&NW rails reached west to Rapid City, South Dakota, and Lander, Wyoming; north to Duluth, Minn.; and south almost to St. Louis. The road became Union Pacific's preferred eastern connection and handled UP's fleet of *City* streamliners between Chicago and Omaha until 1955, when they were transferred to the Milwaukee Road.

In the late 1950s and 1960s C&NW merged several smaller railroads: Litchfield & Madison in 1958, extending C&NW into St. Louis; Minneapolis & St. Louis in 1960; Chicago Great Western in 1968; and Des Moines & Central Iowa (which owned the Fort Dodge, Des Moines & Southern) in

1968. C&NW gradually dismantled the lines of these railroads, keeping only a few strategic segments in service. In 1972 C&NW joined with Missouri Pacific to purchase the Alton & Southern from Alcoa, but a year later sold its half to St. Louis Southwestern.

There was also a change in corporate structure in 1972. The Chicago & North Western Transportation Company was incorporated in 1970 as the North Western Employees Transportation Co., owned by nearly 1,000 C&NW employees. In 1972 it purchased the transportation assets of the Chicago & North Western Railway and changed its name to Chicago & North Western Transportation Co. For some time thereafter the road's herald carried the words "Employee Owned." In 1989 Chicago & North Western Holdings Corp., which owns the transportation company, was formed by Blackstone Capital Partners. It was privately held until 1992.

After the 1980 demise of the Rock Island the C&NW acquired Rock's Minneapolis-Kansas City "spine line," and by the mid-1980s abandoned

A coal train moves south on the joint BN-C&NW line near Walker, Wyoming, behind C&NW and Union Pacific General Electric Dash 8 diesels. Photo by Wesley Fox.

the somewhat longer Chicago Great Western route between those cities.

The North Western's other major expansion has been into the Powder River Basin of northeastern Wyoming. C&NW (through a subsidiary, Western Railroad Properties) and Burlington Northern jointly operate a line north into the coalfields from Orin and Shawnee, Wyoming (the line was constructed by BN between 1976 and 1979). In 1984 C&NW opened a new line along the Wyoming-Nebraska state line to a connection with Union Pacific's line along the North Platte River rather than rebuild more than 500 miles of its line across northern Nebraska.

The North Western has spun off two major groups of lines to form regional railroads:
• Dakota, Minnesota & Eastern Railroad: Winona, Minn., to Rapid City, S. D., plus branches, 965 miles in all (September 1986)
• Fox River Valley Railroad: two lines from Green Bay to Granville and Cleveland, Wis., plus branches, 214 miles (December 9, 1988). Sale of the two main lines south of Green Bay had the effect of isolating C&NW's lines in northern Wisconsin and Michigan's Upper Peninsula from the rest of the system.

Most of Chicago & North Western's traffic today is concentrated on two lines: Chicago to Council Bluffs, Iowa, essentially an eastern extension of Union Pacific's transcontinental main line (UP owns 25 percent of C&NW), and the Wyoming and Nebraska coal lines.

Address of general offices: 1 North Western Center, Chicago, IL 60606
Miles of road operated: 5,800
Reporting marks: CGW, CMO, CNW, FDDM, MSTL
Number of locomotives: 1,040
Number of freight cars: 29,355
Principal commodities carried: Coal, grain, automobiles, double-stack containers
Major yards: Chicago (Proviso)
Principal shops: Chicago, Marshalltown, Iowa (locomotives); Clinton, Iowa (cars)
Radio frequencies: 160.890 (road), 160.455 (maintenance of way and road), 161.040 (road)
Passenger routes: Regional Transportation Authority — Chicago-Kenosha, Wis.; Chicago-Harvard, Ill.; Chicago-McHenry, Ill.; Chicago-Geneva, Ill.
Historical and technical society: Chicago & North Western Historical Society, 17004 Locust Drive, Hazel Crest, IL 60429
Recommended reading:
"Powder River Country," by Fred W. Frailey, in TRAINS Magazine, November 1989, pages 40-63

CHICAGO, CENTRAL & PACIFIC RAILROAD

The original route of the Illinois Central Railroad was from Cairo, at the southern tip of Illinois, north to Galena, in the northwest corner of the state. That line was completed in 1856, but the road's Centralia-Chicago branch proved to be more important than the main line to Galena. Nonetheless, the IC pushed the line west to the Mississippi River and across it into Iowa. In 1867 the Illinois Central leased the Dubuque & Sioux City Railroad; by 1870 that railroad had reached Sioux City. In the 1880s IC began serious expansion westward. It built branches to Cedar Rapids, Iowa, Sioux Falls, South Dakota, and Omaha, Nebraska, and a line from Chicago west to Freeport, Ill., connecting the Iowa lines with Chicago.

In the early 1980s Illinois Central Gulf (the product of the 1972 merger of IC and Gulf, Mobile & Ohio) decided to concentrate on its north-south main line and spin off its east-west routes. The first to be sold was the route to Omaha and Sioux City. In December 1985 Jack Haley's Chicago,

Central & Pacific Railroad purchased ICG's Chicago-Omaha line and its branches to Sioux City and Cedar Rapids, Iowa. Haley had started his railroad empire in 1984 by purchasing ICG's Cedar Falls, Iowa-Albert Lea, Minnesota, branch and operating it as the Cedar Valley Railroad. In 1986 the road later bought Chicago & North Western's line between Wall Lake and Ida Grove, Iowa, 24 miles.

The Chicago Central got off to a good start, but in 1987 General Electric Credit Corporation, which had provided the financing, became anxious when Haley fell behind in loan payments. Haley took the Chicago Central into bankruptcy on September 1, 1987, so he could retain control. The Chicago Central was released from bankruptcy in October under the leadership of Don Wood, formerly executive vice-president, operations, of Burlington Northern. Wood trimmed the road's car fleet, reduced train miles, and lowered speed limits to save fuel and wear on the track. The CC undertook several track repair projects to recover from ICG's policy of deferred maintenance.

The Cedar Valley Railroad ceased operation on May 22, 1991, and the Interstate Commerce Commission let Chicago Central serve customers on the line. At the end of 1991 CC bought the Cedar Valley through a subsidiary, the Cedar River Railroad.

Address of general offices: P. O. Box 1800, Waterloo, IA 50704
Miles of road operated: 708
Reporting marks: CC
Number of locomotives: 88
Number of freight cars: 2165
Principal commodities carried: Corn, soybeans, coal
Major yards: Cicero, Ill. (Hawthorne), Freeport, Ill. (Wallace)
Principal shops: Waterloo, Iowa
Radio frequencies: 160.755, 161.190
Recommended reading: "Seared, burned, but now cooking," by Steve Glischinski, in Trains Magazine, July 1992, pages 34-41

A Chicago Central freight rolls through New Hartford, Iowa, on September 5, 1991. The lead unit, GP10 No. 1705, is a product of Illinois Central's Paducah shops. Photo by Jim Shaw.

CHICAGO SOUTHSHORE & SOUTH BEND RAILROAD
NORTHERN INDIANA COMMUTER TRANSPORTATION DISTRICT

Late in 1901 the Chicago & Indiana Air Line Railway was incorporated. Two years later it opened a 3.4-mile streetcar line between Indiana Harbor and East Chicago, Indiana. In 1904 the name of the company was changed to Chicago, Lake Shore & South Bend. The pace of construction accelerated, and in 1908 the entire line was in service from Hammond to South Bend, 76 miles. The line was electrified at 6600 volts AC, unusual for an interurban, and the grades and curves of the line were more typical of a heavy steam railroad than of a light electric railway. A year later the line was extended west across the state line to a connection with Illinois Central at Kensington, Illinois.

Samuel Insull acquired control of the company in 1925, reorganized it as the Chicago South Shore & South Bend, and undertook a reconstruction that changed it from an interurban to a heavy electric railroad. The modernization included steel cars, change of power to 1500 volts DC, and operation through to Chicago over IC's newly electrified suburban line.

Insull's control ended in 1932 and the company entered bankruptcy. New management continued to improve the road, though, and moved it further into the steam-road category — interurbans were dying off faster than they had been born a few decades before — with interline passenger ticketing, off-line freight solicitation, rebuilt passenger cars, and in 1956 a bypass around the city streets of East Chicago on a right of way shared with the new Indiana Toll Road.

Chesapeake & Ohio acquired control of the South Shore in 1967. Electric freight operation ended in 1981, but passenger service continued under the wires, and the arrival in 1982 of new cars purchased by the Northern Indiana Commuter Transportation District (NICTD) permitted the retirement of the Insull-era cars, which had long since begun to show their age.

In 1984 the Venango River Corporation purchased the South Shore from the C&O. (Venango River is better known for its purchase in April 1987 of the Joliet-St. Louis-Kansas City portion of the Illinois Central Gulf to create the Chicago, Missouri & Western Railway.) In 1988 NICTD did not pay its share of an insurance premium, so the South Shore paid the entire amount, in the process defaulting on other payments that were due. Its financial trouble was even deeper: it had made a large loan to the CM&W, which declared bankruptcy in April 1988. The South Shore petitioned to discontinue passenger service in mid-1989, and won ICC approval, but put off the cessation of service while agreements could be worked out with NICTD. The South Shore declared bankruptcy on April 7, 1990.

The Anacostia & Pacific Corporation acquired the South Shore from Venango River on January 1, 1990, and immediately sold the physical plant and the passenger operations to NICTD. Anacostia & Pacific retained freight rights on the line as the Chicago SouthShore & South Bend Railroad.

NICTD and Metra jointly operate and subsidize the passenger service. North of Kensington, Ill., the trains use Metra's ex-Illinois Central electrified tracks. At Randolph Street in Chicago NICTD trains use their own tracks and platforms. NICTD and Amtrak share the South Bend station.

Chicago SouthShore & South Bend
Address of general offices: 505 North Carroll Avenue, Michigan City, IN 46360-5082
Miles of road operated: 74
Reporting marks: CSS
Number of locomotives: 11

Number of freight cars: 268
Shops: Michigan City
Junctions with other railroads:
Baltimore & Ohio Chicago Terminal: East Chicago, Ind.
Chicago, Central & Pacific: Kensington, Ill.
Chicago Rail Link: Kensington, Ill.
Conrail: South Bend, Ind.
CSX: Gary, Michigan City, Ind.
Elgin, Joliet & Eastern: Gary, Ind.
Grand Trunk Western: Stillwell, Ind.
Illinois Central: Kensington, Ill.
Indiana Harbor Belt: Burnham, Ill.
Norfolk Southern: Kensington, Ill., Michigan City, Ind.
Radio frequencies: 161.355, 161.010
Northern Indiana Commuter Transportation District
Address of general offices: 33 East U.S. Highway 12, Chesterton, IN 46304
Miles of road operated: 73 (plus 15 miles on Metra)
Number of passenger cars: 44
Shops: Michigan City
Radio frequencies: 161.355, 161.010, 161.025 (on Metra)
Passenger routes: Chicago (Randolph Street)-South Bend (Randolph Street to Kensington on Metra)
Recommended reading:
South Shore — The Last Interurban, by William D. Middleton, published in 1970 by Golden West Books, P. O. Box 8136, San Marino, CA 91108
Duneland Electric, by Donald R. Kaplan, published in 1984 by PTJ Publishing, a division of Interurban Press, P. O. Box 6444, Glendale, CA 91225 (ISBN 0-9-37658-11-1)

A South Bend-Chicago train made up of three Japanese-built coaches meets South Shore's line car (rebuilt from an Indiana Railroad car) at Miller, Indiana, on June 28, 1986. Photo by William D. Middleton.

COE RAIL

Coe Rail operates freight and excursion service between West Bloomfield and Wixom, Michigan. The line was acquired from Grand Trunk Western in 1984. It was part of a route from Port Huron through Pontiac to Jackson, Mich. The railroad is notable for its large fleet of box, flat, and covered hopper cars. In addition to its excursion trains, Coe Rail operates the Star Clipper dinner train.

Address of general offices: 840 North Pontiac Trail, Walled Lake, MI 48390

Miles of road operated: 9

Reporting marks: CRLE
Number of locomotives: 3
Number of freight cars: 709
Number of passenger cars: 6
Principal commodities carried: Plastic, lumber
Junctions with other railroads: CSX: Wixom, Mich.
Radio frequencies: 161.025
Passenger routes: West Bloomfield-Wixom, Mich.

COLUMBIA & COWLITZ RAILWAY

The Columbia & Cowlitz connects the Longview, Washington, plant of its owner, Weyerhaeuser Company, with the Burlington Northern and the Union Pacific at Rocky Point, north of Kelso, which is across the Cowlitz River from Longview. Weyerhaeuser also operates a logging railroad in conjunction with the Columbia & Cowlitz.

The Columbia & Cowlitz merits inclusion in this guide because of its large fleet of freight cars in interchange service — chances are pretty good you'll see a box car with CLC reporting marks, most likely carrying Weyerhaeuser products.

Address of general offices: P. O. Box 209, Longview, WA 98632
Miles of road operated: 8
Reporting marks: CLC
Number of locomotives: 2
Number of freight cars: 743
Principal commodities carried: Lumber, forest products
Junctions with other railroads:
Burlington Northern: Rocky Point, Wash.
Union Pacific: Rocky Point, Wash.

Columbia & Cowlitz's two GP9s tiptoe across the trestle at Rocky Point, Washington, on September 18, 1991. Photo by Jim Shaw.

Shops: Longview, Wash.
Radio frequencies: 160.425, 161.385, 161.115

COLUMBUS & GREENVILLE RAILWAY

The narrow gauge Greenville, Columbus & Birmingham Railroad was chartered in 1878 to build a railroad across Mississippi. (According to Poor's *Manual* for 1880, the president of the road was C. P. Huntington — Charles Perrit Huntington. Collis Potter Huntington of Central Pacific fame was pushing his Louisville, New Orleans & Texas through Mississippi about the same time, unintentionally setting snares for unwary researchers a century later.) The Greenville, Columbus & Birmingham was soon allied with the Georgia Pacific Railway (no relation to the present-day wood products company) and was standard-gauged in 1889. The Georgia Pacific eventually became part of the Southern Railway System, but the line in Mississippi remained a separate entity because of a state law requiring that railroads operating in the state be incorporated there.

In 1920 Southern cast off its Mississippi stepchild as the Columbus & Greenville Railroad. It quickly went bankrupt, was purchased by A. T. Stovall, reorganized as the Columbus & Greenville Railway, and operated at a profit into the 1960s. The road asked to be included in the merger of Illinois Central and Gulf, Mobile & Ohio — it intersected IC at six points and GM&O at three — and in September 1972 the road became part of Illinois Central Gulf.

Floods in 1973 closed part of the line. Shippers petitioned and the state public service commission ordered Illinois Central Gulf to restore service. The ICG suggested that local interests buy the railroad and return it to independent status.

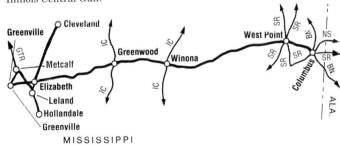

A westbound Columbus & Greenville freight rolls through the North 7th Street crossing in Columbus, Mississippi, in March 1982 with GP7 614 in the lead. Photo by David Hurt.

Local management took over on October 30, 1975. Its first task was to rebuild the track. In 1985 the road acquired a group of Illinois Central Gulf lines in western Mississippi: from Greenville through Metcalf to Leland and from Cleveland through Leland to Hollandale.

Address of general offices: P. O. Box 6000, Columbus, MS 39701

Miles of road operated: 232

Reporting marks: CAGY

Number of locomotives: 20

Number of freight cars: 1,147

Principal commodities carried: Steel, agricultural products, pulpwood, food products, mineral wool

Shops: Columbus, Miss.

Junctions with other railroads:

Burlington Northern: Columbus, Miss.

CSX: Brookwood, Ala.

Golden Triangle: Columbus, Miss.

Great River: Great River Junction, Miss.

Illinois Central: Greenwood, Miss.; Winona, Miss.

Norfolk Southern: Columbus, Miss.

SouthRail: Columbus, Miss.; West Point, Miss.; Artesia, Miss.

Radio frequencies: 160.230 (switching), 160.245 (road)

Recommended reading: *Delta Route*, by Louis R. Saillard, published in 1981 by the Columbus & Greenville Railway, P. O. Box 6000, Columbus, MS 39701

CONNECTICUT DEPARTMENT OF TRANSPORTATION

In May 1990 Shore Line East commuter service began between Old Saybrook and New Haven, Connecticut, 36 miles. Amtrak, which owns the Northeast Corridor line the trains run on, operates the service for the Connecticut Department of Transportation. The cars and locomotives used at first came from the Port Authority of Allegheny County's discontinued service between Pittsburgh and Versailles, Pennsylvania. However, ridership quickly exceeded expectations, so Connecticut Department of Transportation ordered additional cars from Bombardier and leased locomotives from Guilford Transportation industries.

Connecticut Department of Transportation F7s 6691 and 6690 and GP38 257 wait on the ready track at New Haven, Connecticut, on June 18, 1990. The units are painted and lettered for the New York, New Haven & Hartford Railroad, owner until 1968 of the line on which they run. Photo by J. W. Swanberg.

OLD PAINT SCHEMES RIDE AGAIN

The locomotives used on Shore Line East commuter trains are painted and lettered for the New Haven — in the color scheme introduced when Patrick B. McGinnis was president of the road between 1954 and 1956. This practice started when four FL9 diesels owned by Connecticut DOT and assigned to Metro-North trains serving Connecticut were repainted in their original colors.

The choice of the New Haven livery is curious: The black, white, and red-orange livery is distinctive and visible, but in its day it symbolized a railroad that was the butt of criticism and humor among Connecticut commuters (it was, nonetheless, the only way to get to New York) and a management they despised. However, when the fresh paint was applied it had been 30 years since McGinnis ran the New Haven into the ground. Time truly does heal all wounds.

It was logical to use the FL9 paint scheme on the Shore Line East F7s, but New Haven never had GP38s or any second-generation EMD hood units. NH's second-generation hood units were mostly black, but the use of the tri-color scheme on an EMD hood unit wasn't entirely new — one brand of HO scale models had included a New Haven SDP40 for years.

Other old paint schemes have reappeared. It all began in 1977 when Amtrak repainted GG1 4935 in its original 1943 Pennsylvania Railroad colors. Maine Central repainted a GP7 in maroon and gold, and Massachusetts Bay Transportation Authority used the same colors on a GP9 as a nod to the Boston & Maine. Escanaba & Lake Superior resurrected Great Northern's Omaha orange and Pullman green, and New Jersey Transit painted a pair of E8s in Erie two-tone green. Santa Fe's newest diesels wear the best-known diesel livery of all, the red, yellow, and silver "warbonnet" paint scheme introduced in 1937.

All of this is evidence of a wider movement in railroad preservation. Instead of being content to recreate the liveries of years gone by on museum equipment, enthusiasts now seek to apply these paint schemes to equipment in daily use.

At present ConnDOT operates six westbound morning trains and eight eastbound afternoon and evening trains. ConnDOT also subsidizes Metro-North services from New Haven, Waterbury, Danbury, and New Canaan to New York City.

Address of general offices: Office of Rail Operations, Union Station, Third Floor West, New Haven, CT 06511
Miles of road operated: 36
Number of locomotives: 5
Number of passenger cars: 10
Radio frequencies: 160.920 (Amtrak)
Passenger routes: Old Saybrook-New Haven, Conn

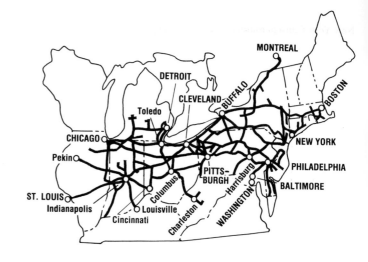

CONRAIL (Consolidated Rail Corporation)

Shortly after Penn Central went bankrupt in 1970, Congress created the United States Railway Association to plan a reorganization of the railroad and act as its banker. The result was Consolidated Rail Corporation (it was soon abbreviated to ConRail, then to Conrail), which began operation on April 1, 1976. It took over the railroad properties and operations of six bankrupt eastern railroads — Central Railroad of New Jersey, Erie Lackawanna, Lehigh & Hudson River, Lehigh Valley, Penn Central, and Reading — plus one railroad that was not bankrupt but neither was it financially robust, Pennsylvania-Reading Seashore Lines.

Penn Central was the product of the merger in 1968 of the two rival giants of eastern railroading, Pennsylvania and New York Central, with the later addition of the New Haven. Its collapse, hastened by the depressed steel and automobile industries which provided much of its traffic, was the precipitating factor in the formation of Conrail. The other railroads included the "anthracite railroads," those traditionally associated with mining and carrying hard coal. Their financial problems had been aggravated by damage from hurricanes that had hit Pennsylvania and New York in 1972. Conrail's predecessors are described in detail in *The Historical Guide to North American Railroads*, but brief summaries follow.

Central Railroad of New Jersey was opened in 1852 between Elizabeth and Phillipsburg, New Jersey. In 1864 the line was extended a few miles east to Jersey City, and in 1871 the railroad expanded into Pennsylvania by leasing the Lehigh & Susquehanna Railroad. In 1946 CNJ's

lines in Pennsylvania were reorganized as the Central Railroad of Pennsylvania in an attempt to avoid taxation by New Jersey. Separate operation of the CRP ended in 1952. In 1961 CNJ purchased about 40 miles of the defunct Lehigh & New England.

CNJ came under the control of the Reading Company in 1901, about the same time the Reading came under the control of the Baltimore & Ohio Railroad. The three railroads formed a Jersey City-Philadelphia-Washington passenger route to compete with the Pennsylvania Railroad.

Erie Lackawanna Railroad was created in 1960 by the merger of the Erie Railroad and the Delaware, Lackawanna & Western Railroad. The Erie, built with a track gauge of 6 feet, was completed from Piermont, N. Y., on the Hudson, to Dunkirk, on Lake Erie, in 1851. It was later extended to Jersey City, Buffalo, and Chicago. It was converted to standard gauge in 1880. The Erie always seemed to be the subject of one financial manipulation or another; eventually it achieved some stability as a New York-Chicago route, primarily for freight.

The Delaware, Lackawanna & Western — also 6-foot gauge — was built from Scranton, Pa., to the Delaware River in 1856 and made a connection with the Central of New Jersey in 1857 for a route to New York. In 1868 it leased the Morris & Essex Railroad to gain its own route to the Hudson. In 1882 the Lackawanna reached Buffalo, which became its western terminus.

In the early part of the twentieth century the Lackawanna embarked on a number of engineering projects: line relocations, massive concrete viaducts, and a general upgrading of the property. In 1930 DL&W electrified the suburban lines that radiated from its terminal at Hoboken, N. J. The hardware of that electrification was finally replaced in 1986.

The Lackawanna advertised that it used clean-burning anthracite for fuel. The road's symbol was Phoebe Snow, a young woman whose gown, to quote one of the many verses, "stayed white from morn 'til night upon the Road of Anthracite."

Lehigh & Hudson River Railway was incorporated in 1882. Its line from Easton, Pa., to Maybrook, N. Y., was a bridge route, connecting the Central of New Jersey and the Lehigh Valley at Easton and the Pennsylvania at Phillipsburg, N. J., with the New Haven's route from Maybrook to New Haven, Conn. Inclusion of the New Haven in Penn Central in 1968 altered traffic patterns, drying up much of L&HR's business; and destruction of New Haven's bridge over the Hudson at Poughkeepsie by fire in 1974 rendered L&HR even more redundant. L&HR was owned by Central of New Jersey, Erie Lackawanna, Lehigh Valley, Pennsylvania, and Reading.

Lehigh Valley Railroad's earliest ancestor was the Delaware, Lehigh, Schuylkill, & Susquehanna Railroad. It was incorporated in 1846 to haul anthracite from Mauch Chunk, Pa., to Easton. In 1853 it changed its name to Lehigh Valley Railroad, and it opened its rail line in 1855. By construction and by acquisition of other railroads LV made a connection with the Erie at Waverly, Pa., in 1869. In 1876 the road reached Buffalo by financing the addition to Erie's broad gauge track of a third rail for standard gauge trains, and in 1892 extended its own line to Buffalo. The eastern end of the railroad was pushed east to Perth Amboy, N. J., in 1875 and to

Two brand-new General Electric C23-8s and a C30-7A wheel Conrail piggyback train TV-9 west through Weston, Massachusetts, in 1984. Photo by Tom Nelligan.

Newark and a terminal on New York Harbor in 1891.

LV discontinued the last of its passenger trains in 1961, one of the first major roads to do so. In 1962 the ICC authorized the Pennsylvania Railroad, which through subsidiaries had held a substantial interest in LV since the late 1920s, to acquire control of Lehigh Valley. By 1965 PRR had acquired 97 percent of LV's stock.

The Reading Company began as the Philadelphia & Reading Railroad, chartered in 1833 and opened from Philadelphia through Reading to Pottsville, Pa., in 1842. An affiliated company, the Philadelphia & Reading Coal & Iron Co., began to buy much of the anthracite land in the area. In a reorganization in 1896 the Reading Company, a holding company, acquired the railroad and the coal and iron company, and in 1901 got control of the Central Railroad of New Jersey. In 1923 the Reading Company merged a large number of wholly owned subsidiaries and became an operating company.

Reading's passenger business was almost all suburban, and its freight business was also largely short-haul. Reading had considerable anthracite

L. STANLEY CRANE (1915-   ) was born in Cincinnati, Ohio. He graduated from George Washington University in 1938 with an engineering degree; by then he was already working for the Southern Railway as a laboratory assistant. Over the next 25 years he rose to become Southern's chief mechanical officer.

In 1963 he went to the Pennsylvania Railroad as director of industrial engineering. In 1965 he returned to the Southern as vice president, engineering and research. He became president and chief executive officer in 1977 and chairman in 1979. He reached Southern's mandatory retirement age in 1980.

In January 1981 he went back to work as chairman and chief executive of Conrail. He arrived when the government was considering selling the road off, either whole or, more likely, in parts. When asked why he would take on Conrail after years at the Southern, generally considered the best-run railroad in the U. S., he replied that he recognized that Conrail, which served 35 percent of the nation's industry, had a chance of success. He told the *Philadelphia Inquirer* "I hope to be able to say to you that we can run this railroad so efficiently that it ain't up for sale!"

He did just that. With the cooperation and support of Conrail's employees he changed Conrail from a company that lost a million dollars a day to one that earned a million dollars a day. In 1983 Modern Railroads magazine selected him as the 1983 railroad industry man of the year. Crane retired from Conrail at the end of 1988.

---

traffic, and its route west from Allentown through Reading and Harrisburg carried much freight that bypassed Philadelphia, Baltimore, and Washington.

Pennsylvania-Reading Seashore Lines was formed in 1933 to consolidate the operations of Pennsylvania's West Jersey & Seashore Railroad and Reading's Atlantic City Railroad between Camden, New Jersey, across the Delaware River from Philadelphia, and the seashore resort cities.

Penn Central Company was formed in 1968 by the merger of the Pennsylvania Railroad and the New York Central Railroad. At the end of 1968 PC purchased the properties of the New York, New Haven & Hartford. PC declared bankruptcy in June 1970. As for PC's antecedents:

New York Central started with the Mohawk & Hudson Rail Road, opened between Albany and Schenectady in 1831. In 1853 it merged with nine other railroads to form the New York Central Railroad, extending from Albany to Buffalo. The Hudson River Railroad was opened in 1851 from New York to Albany; in 1869 it was merged with NYC to form the New York Central & Hudson River Railroad. The New York Central name returned in 1914 to designate the product of the merger of the NYC&HR and the Lake Shore & Michigan Southern Railway.

Cornelius Vanderbilt purchased control of the New York & Harlem Railroad in 1857 and the Hudson River Railroad in 1863, and he bought a block of New York Central stock in 1864. He and his son, William K. Vanderbilt, continued to add to their railroad holdings so that by the turn of the century their New York Central System extended from New York and Boston through Albany and Buffalo to Chicago via both Cleveland and Detroit, with lines reaching out to St. Louis, Cincinnati, Montreal, and Ottawa. Among NYC's subsidiaries were Boston & Albany; Michigan Central; Big Four (Cleveland, Cincinnati, Chicago & St. Louis); West Shore; Peoria & Eastern; and Toledo & Ohio Central. In addition NYC owned large interests in Pittsburgh & Lake Erie; Indiana Harbor Belt; and Toronto, Hamilton & Buffalo.

NYC's main line followed the Hudson and Mohawk rivers and avoided the mountains that other eastern lines had to battle — hence the road's slogan, "The Water Level Route." NYC's New York-Chicago *20th Century Limited* was generally acknowledged to be the country's finest passenger train. The road's Grand Central Terminal in New York was — and is — a notable feat of railroad engineering.

New York, New Haven & Hartford Railroad was incorporated in 1872 as a consolidation of the New York & New Haven and Hartford & New Haven railroads. It leased and purchased other lines and soon expanded to cover all of southeastern Massachusetts, Rhode Island, and Connecticut. The New Haven was an early experimenter with electrification — it owned a number of street railways and interurbans — and between 1905 and 1914 it electrified its four-track main line between New York and New Haven.

The New Haven entered bankruptcy in 1935 and emerged from reorganization in 1947 only to go bankrupt again in 1961. There were several causes of its financial problems: flamboyant and shady management, construction of parallel superhighways that allowed trucks to siphon off much of the freight traffic, revenues that were derived almost as much from passenger service as from freight traffic, and flood damage from hurricanes.

The Pennsylvania Railroad was incorporated in 1846. It was opened from Harrisburg west to Altoona in 1850 and all the way to Pittsburgh in 1852. It extended itself east of Harrisburg and west of Pittsburgh by acquiring other railroads. Its principal eastern lines were New York-Philadelphia-Washington, Philadelphia-Harrisburg-Pittsburgh, and Baltimore-Harrisburg-Buffalo, with branches, secondary lines, and freight bypasses blanketing the region. West of Buffalo and Pittsburgh it reached Chicago, St. Louis, Cincinnati, Louisville, Cleveland, Detroit, and Mackinaw City — most of the same places that the New York Central System served.

Pennsy was for many years the largest U. S. railroad in terms of tonnage and revenue, and its slogan was "The Standard Railroad of the World." In spite of the slogan, a number of traits were distinctive to PRR rather than industry standard: steam locomotives with Belpaire boilers (simply put, a flat-topped firebox), a random numbering scheme for steam locomotives, and position-light signals, whose aspects were made up of vertical, horizontal, and diagonal rows of amber lights.

Recognizing the advantage that a terminal in Manhattan gave the New York Central, Pennsy responded with Pennsylvania Station, opened in 1910. Included in the project were tunnels under the Hudson and East rivers, massive yards on Long Island, and, a few years later, construction

of the Hell Gate Bridge to afford a connection with the New Haven. Another piece of engineering that was became a Pennsy trademark was Horse Shoe Curve west of Altoona, Pa. Although one of the four tracks has been removed and traffic is far less than it once was, it remains an impressive sight. PRR electrified most of its mainline trackage east of Harrisburg in the late 1920s and 1930s.

Either directly or through subsidiaries Pennsy controlled a number of other railroads: Norfolk & Western; Wabash; Detroit, Toledo & Ironton; Long Island; Toledo, Peoria & Western; and Lehigh Valley.

Conrail started out with $2.1 billion from the U. S. government, which purchased Conrail debentures and preferred stock, and perhaps $2.10 worth of confidence in its success — after all, six times bankrupt equals bankrupt, and the road was a department of the federal government (or so it was perceived). Conrail began operation in 1976 with 17,000 route miles, 5,000 locomotives, and 162,000 freight cars. It had 95,000 employees and 278 different labor agreements. It had excess plant; it had labor-protection agreements; and it had extensive commuter train operations serving Boston, New York, and Philadelphia.

When Conrail came into existence the Northeast Corridor lines (Boston-Washington, Springfield-New Haven, and Philadelphia-Harrisburg) were conveyed to Amtrak. Conrail abandoned, sold to short lines, or agreed to operate with state subsidy another 6,000 route miles, and embarked on an intense program of rebuilding roadbed and track, repairing old locomotives and cars, and purchasing new ones. In the second quarter of 1979 Conrail posted a modest net income, but an economic recession wiped any chance of that recurring.

L. Stanley Crane assumed the presidency of Conrail at the beginning of 1981, about the time the Reagan administration proposed selling the railroad. Crane continued to trim Conrail's physical plant and payroll and managed to shed its commuter operations. He took advantage of deregulation; he improved the quality of Conrail's service; he sharpened Conrail's image. Conrail posted a profit for 1981, and kept doing better, even as almost everyone in sight was (a) bidding to purchase it at a bargain price and (b) protesting anyone else's doing so. In February 1986 the U. S. Senate voted to sell Conrail to Norfolk Southern, but in October 1986 President Reagan signed a bill authorizing the sale of Conrail stock to the public. It

87

went on sale March 25, 1987, at $28 a share, the largest single initial public stock offering in the history of the New York Stock Exchange. It netted the government $1.6 billion, plus $300 million of Conrail cash and a return of $2 billion worth of tax credits.

Crane retired as chairman at the end of 1988 and was succeeded by Richard D. Sanborn, who had become president of Conrail in March 1988. Sanborn died suddenly of a heart attack after only 6 weeks as chairman; James Hagen was brought from CSX to succeed Sanborn.

During the recession of 1990 and 1991 Conrail reacted quickly to the anticipated drop in revenue by cutting expenses, storing locomotives and cars, and restructuring its services, with the result that it was still able to declare a stock dividend. In 1990 Conrail bought back about one third of its common stock as part of a restructuring to thwart possible takeover bids. By the end of 1991 the price of Conrail stock had risen to $84.50 a share — just one indicator of the company's robust health.

Address of general offices: 6 Penn Center Plaza, Philadelphia, PA 19104
Miles of road operated: 12,700
Number of locomotives: 2,100

Number of freight cars: 74,277
Reporting marks: CNJ, CR, EL, ERIE, LV, NYC, PAE, PC, PCA, PRR, RDG
Principal commodities carried: Coal, grain, intermodal traffic
Major yards: Albany, N. Y. (Selkirk); Columbus, Ohio (Buckeye); Elkhart, Ind.; Harrisburg, Pa. (Enola); Indianapolis (Avon); Pittsburgh (Conway); Syracuse, N. Y. (DeWitt)
Principal shops: Altoona, Pa.; Meadville, Pa.; Hollidaysburg, Pa.; Reading, Pa.
Radio frequencies: 160.800, 161.070
Passenger routes:
Amtrak — Poughkeepsie, N. Y.-Albany-Buffalo-Cleveland-Chicago; Buffalo-Niagara Falls; Harrisburg, Pa.-Pittsburgh-Cleveland, Framingham, Mass.-Albany, Toledo-Detroit-Kalamazoo; Indianapolis-Crawfordsville, Ind., Maynard, Ind.-Chicago
Metro-North — Suffern-Port Jervis, N. Y.
Historical and technical society: Conrail Technical Society, c/o Matt McGill, Route 1, 5111 Grant, Riverdale, MI 48877-9705

COPPER BASIN RAILWAY

The Phoenix & Eastern Railroad was chartered in 1901 and opened in 1904 from Phoenix east to Winkelman, Arizona. In 1910 it was purchased by the Arizona Eastern Railroad, a subsidiary of the Southern Pacific.

The line begins at Magma Junction, where it connects with SP's Picacho-Phoenix route. It heads southeast to Florence, then east and southeast again along the Gila River through Hayden to Winkelman. From Ray Junction a branch runs 7 miles north to a Kennecott Minerals copper mine at Ray. (The branch was built by the Ray & Gila Valley Railroad, a Kennecott subsidiary, and was a common carrier until 1943.) At Hayden the Copper Basin Railway connects with the San Manuel Arizona Railway, which is owned by the Magma Copper Co.

The principal item of traffic on the railroad is copper ore moving from the mine at Ray to a smelter at Hayden.

Address of general offices: P. O. Drawer I, Hayden, AZ 85235
Miles of road operated: 61
Reporting marks: CBRY
Number of locomotives: 14
Number of freight cars: 1,087
Principal commodities carried: Copper, copper ore
Shops: Hayden, Ariz.
Junctions with other railroads:
Southern Pacific: Magma, Ariz.
San Manuel Arizona: Hayden, Ariz.
Radio frequencies: 160.545, 161.505

Recommended reading:
Railroads of Arizona, Volume II, by David F. Myrick, published in 1980 by Howell-North Books, 850 North Hollywood Way, Burbank, CA 91505 (ISBN 0-8310-7118-3)
"Espee's sandy satellites," by James W. Terrell, in TRAINS Magazine, July 1986, pages 18-19
Map: See Arizona & California, page 30

Three Copper Basin diesels, two SD39s and a GP9, lead empty ore cars at Kearny, Arizona, on May 30, 1990. Photo by Jim Shaw.

CP Rail

CP RAIL SYSTEM

The history of CP Rail is intimately tied to Canadian politics. British Columbia joined the Canadian confederation in 1871 on the condition that a railroad would link the province to the rest of the country within 10 years. The geographic barriers to such a railroad were formidable: the wilderness of northern Ontario, the vast emptiness of the prairies, the Rocky Mountains.

The financial barrier was also formidable. The principal railroad in Canada, the Grand Trunk Railway, was not interested in the project, so in 1881 the Canadian Pacific Railway was incorporated to build a railroad to the Pacific at what is now Vancouver. The starting point of the new railway was Callander, Ontario, near North Bay, at the end of a Grand Trunk

line from Toronto. Construction started at several points, and the line across the prairie was completed before the more difficult sections east and west.

In 1881 CP absorbed the Canada Central Railway, which was building northwest toward Callander from Brockville and Ottawa. In 1882 CP purchased the Western Division of the Quebec, Montreal, Ottawa & Occidental Railway, a line from Montreal to Ottawa along the north bank of the Ottawa River. The acquisitions ensured that CP would have a route to Ottawa and Montreal, even if at the time there was still a gap of several hundred miles between those lines and the new railroad CP was building.

Construction along the north shore of Lake Superior was extremely difficult, but nationalistic feelings precluded an easier route south of Lake Superior through the United States. The crossing of the Rockies at Kicking Horse Pass was accomplished only by resorting to 4.5 percent grades as an interim solution and later a pair of spiral tunnels. The last spike was driven at Craigellachie, B. C., on November 7, 1885.

In 1884 CP leased the Ontario & Quebec Railway, gaining a line from Toronto to Perth, Ont. In 1887 that line was extended east to Montreal and west to Windsor Ont., on the Detroit River. By 1890 the CP had built east from Montreal across Maine to Saint John, New Brunswick, creat-

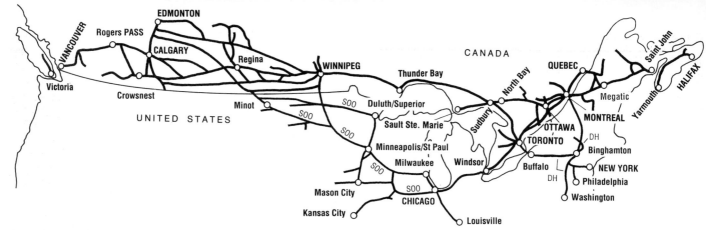

ing a true transcontinental railroad from the Atlantic to the Pacific.

Southeastern British Columbia was geographically and economically much closer to the U. S. (and to James J. Hill's Great Northern Railway) than to Canada. The discovery there of silver in 1887 sparked an outbreak of railroad fever. CP built a line from Medicine Hat, Alberta, west across Crows Nest Pass into the Kootenay region. The Canadian government provided a cash grant for its construction in exchange for a permanent reduction in grain rates — the Crows Nest Pass Agreement of 1897. In 1916 the Kettle Valley Railway, a CP subsidiary, extended that route west to a connection with CP's main line at Hope, B. C., creating a secondary main line across the southern tier of British Columbia and part of Alberta. The line ran across the mountains rather than along the valleys and was expensive to build and operate. Much of the western portion of the Kettle Valley line has been abandoned in recent years.

Rogers Pass in the Selkirk Mountains of British Columbia had long been a bottleneck on CP's main line, not only because of 2.2-percent grades against westbound traffic but also because of snow in the winter. Much of the traffic moving over Rogers Pass was export grain moving to Vancouver. Because the Crows Nest Pass Agreement kept rates artificially low, CP

calculated that it lost $200 million a year on grain traffic. It couldn't reconcile such losses against the $600 million needed to improve the Rogers Pass line. In 1983 the Canadian parliament passed the Western Grain Transportation Act, which established subsidies to the railways from grain producers and the federal government, giving CP the encouragement it needed to undertake the Rogers Pass project.

On May, 1989, CP completed a new line for westbound traffic through Rogers Pass. The keystone of the project is the 9.1-mile Mount Macdonald Tunnel, longest railroad tunnel in the western hemisphere. The new line reduced the westbound grade from 2.2 percent to 1 percent. Eastbound traffic continues to use the 5-mile Connaught Tunnel, opened in 1916.

Through the years the Canadian Pacific Railway grew to become, in its own words, the world's greatest travel system. Its properties included ships, hotels, and an airline. In 1968 Canadian Pacific revised its image, much as Canadian National had done in 1961. Wine-red and gray gave way to bright red; the shield, sometimes surmounted by a beaver, was replaced by the "multimark," a black triangle on a white semicircle, and "Canadian Pacific Railway" became CP Rail, a unit of Canadian Pacific Limited.

Canadian subsidiaries

In 1912 CP Rail leased three railroads: the Dominion Atlantic Railway (Halifax-Yarmouth, Nova Scotia); the Quebec Central Railway (Quebec City-Newport, Vermont); and the Esquimault & Nanaimo Railway (Victoria-Courtenay, B. C., on Vancouver Island). They continue to maintain their corporate identities, as do two former electric lines in Ontario, the Lake Erie & Northern Railway and the Grand River Railway. All are operated as part of CP Rail.

On January 1, 1987, CP Rail absorbed the Toronto, Hamilton & Buffalo Railway, a wholly owned subsidiary. Its main line connected Hamilton and Welland, Ont., and was the middle third of a Buffalo-Toronto route operated in conjunction with CP and New York Central. In 1895 TH&B was purchased by four railroads: 27 percent by CP and 73 percent by New York Central and two subsidiaries. NYC's majority interest passed to Penn Central; CP purchased PC's interest in 1977.

On September 1, 1988, CP created the Canadian Atlantic Railway, a wholly owned subsidiary consisting of CP's lines east of Megantic, Que.: light-traffic branches in New Brunswick, the Dominion Atlantic Railway, and the main line across Maine to Saint John, N. B. (Halifax and Montreal are Canada's major Atlantic seaports). CP hopes to take advantage of railroad deregulation in Canada and to cut labor costs on those routes. As of mid-1992, though, there was no mention of Canadian Atlantic in *The Official Guide*, *The Official Railway Equipment Register*, and the *Pocket List of Railroad Officials*.

U. S. subsidiaries

In the late 1880s CP gained control of the Soo Line — the Minneapolis, St. Paul, and Sault Ste. Marie Railway — (Sault Ste. Marie to the Twin Cities) partly for the wheat traffic and partly to block the Grand Trunk Railway from doing so. The latter was also the primary reason for acquiring the Duluth, South Shore & Atlantic Railway (Sault Ste. Marie to Duluth) in 1888. The Soo Line leased the Wisconsin Central Railway in 1909, gaining access to Chicago, and by 1930 the Soo and the DSS&A had the same officers.

DSS&A declared bankruptcy in 1937 and was reorganized in 1949. In 1961 the DSS&A, Wisconsin Central, and the Soo Line merged to form the Soo Line Railroad (official name, not nickname). Soo Line purchased the

An SD60M, with safety cab and full width body, leads a coal train on a new track alignment through a new rock cut near Albert Canyon in 1989 — note the old single-track tunnel to the left. Photo by T. O. Repp.

bankrupt Milwaukee Road in 1985 and merged it at the beginning of 1986. Soo briefly tried operating its light-density lines in Michigan and Wisconsin as Lake States Transportation Division (don't confuse it with Michigan's Lake State Railway, which is the former Detroit & Mackinac). Then Soo Line consolidated its Chicago-Twin Cities operations on the former Milwaukee Road route and sold what had been its own lines to Wisconsin Central Limited in 1987 (in many ways re-creating the pre-1909 Wisconsin Central). CP went through a brief spell of trying sell off Soo Line, then decided to try for full ownership. By early 1990 CP Rail had acquired full ownership of Soo Line's stock.

Guilford Transportation Industries placed the Delaware & Hudson Railway in bankruptcy in June 1988 and put the railroad up for sale. CP Rail purchased in January 1991, eyeing D&H's trackage rights (acquired when Conrail was formed) to Washington, Philadelphia, and Newark, New Jersey, in the light of the U. S.-Canada free trade pact of 1990. CP Rail undertook a rehabilitation of the D&H, purchased Conrail's Buffalo-Binghamton, N. Y., line, over which D&H had trackage rights, and began regular freight service to Philadelphia and Newark. The operations of CP Rail, the Delaware & Hudson, and the Soo Line have been integrated under a new name, CP Rail System.

Address of general offices: P. O. Box 6042, Station A, Montreal, PQ, Canada H3C 3E4
Miles of road operated: 19,506 (system total)
Reporting marks: CP, CPAA, CPI, CPT, DA, THB
Number of locomotives: 1,669 (system total)
Number of freight cars: 53,270 (system total)
Principal commodities carried: Coal, grain, potash, petrochemicals, autos and auto parts, intermodal trailers and containers
Major yards: Calgary, Montreal, Toronto, Vancouver, Winnipeg
Principal shops: Calgary (Ogden), Winnipeg (Weston)
Radio frequencies: (CP proper) 161.475, 161.115 (yard)
Passenger routes:
Montreal Urban Community Transportation Commission — Montreal-Rigaud, Que.
GO Transit — Toronto-Milton, Ont.
VIA Rail Canada — Smiths Falls-Brockville, Ont.; Victoria-Courtenay, B. C.

CSX TRANSPORTATION

The history of CSX, one of the Super Seven, includes the oldest common carrier railroad in the United States, the Baltimore & Ohio, and one of the shortest-lived, Seaboard System. It is the product of a series of mergers, many of them recent. The lineage is complicated enough that genealogy computer software might create a more understandable explanation than a word processor — but even that might have trouble with the shirttail cousins that make up the West Point Route, the *ménage à trois* of the Chessie System, and the Clinchfield, an unincorporated offspring of Atlantic Coast Line and Louisville & Nashville. For histories of the components, particularly the pre-1950 railroads that are rapidly becoming ancient history, see *The Historical Guide to North American Railroads*.

On November 1, 1980, Chessie System, the holding company that was the parent of the Chesapeake & Ohio, Baltimore & Ohio, and Western Maryland, merged with Seaboard Coast Line Industries, the parent of the Seaboard Coast Line Railroad, to form CSX Corporation ("C" for Chessie, "S" for Seaboard, and "X" for a multiplication symbol). The intention then was for the subsidiary railroads to maintain their identities. However, on July 1, 1986, the name of the Seaboard System Railroad was changed to CSX Transportation, and on August 31, 1987, CSX Transportation merged the Chesapeake & Ohio Railway.

Chessie System was incorporated on February 26, 1973. On June 15, 1973, the Baltimore & Ohio Railroad, the Chesapeake & Ohio Railway, and the Western Maryland Railway were made subsidiaries of the Chessie System. The C&O had controlled the B&O since the early 1960s. B&O had held almost half of WM's stock since 1927, and by 1973 C&O and B&O between them held more than 90 percent. The individual railroads continued in existence, and rolling stock continued to carry their initials along with the Chessie herald.

On May 1, 1983, B&O took over operation of WM and merged it later that year, reducing Chessie System to two railroads. Four years later, on April 30, 1987, C&O merged B&O, becoming the sole Chessie System Railroad, and on August 31, 1987, C&O was in turn merged by CSX Transportation.

Seaboard System Railroad was the product of the merger of the Seaboard Coast Line Railroad and the Louisville & Nashville Railroad on December 29, 1982. The Seaboard Coast Line was formed in 1967 by the merger of the Seaboard Air Line Railway and the Atlantic Coast Line Railroad; ACL had controlled the L&N since 1902.

On January 1, 1983, three days after the creation of the Seaboard System, the Clinchfield Railroad became the Clinchfield Division of the Seaboard System. The Clinchfield was an unincorporated entity that operated the Carolina, Clinchfield & Ohio Railway for the ACL and the L&N, which had leased the CC&O in 1924.

Also in 1983 Seaboard System purchased the Georgia Railroad, another member of the ACL-L&N family, and merged it, and took over operations of the Atlanta & West Point Rail Road and the Western Railway of Alabama (taken together, the West Point Route), both of which had long been affiliated with the Georgia Railroad.

The locomotives on this CSX train of empty coal hoppers moving north at Kittrell, North Carolina, in March 1991 include a GP40, a U18B, and a GP40-2 still in Chessie colors. Photo by Curt Tillotson Jr.

CSX Transportation absorbed the Richmond, Fredericksburg & Potomac Railroad by the end of 1991. The RF&P linked Richmond and Washington, connecting Seaboard System (earlier ACL and SAL) with Chessie System and Conrail (earlier, Baltimore & Ohio and Pennsylvania Railroad). Simplifying somewhat, it was owned partly by the commonwealth of Virginia and partly by six railroads (historically, ACL, B&O, C&O, SAL, Pennsylvania, and Southern; Penn Central relinquished the PRR share in 1978, giving CSX 80 percent of the pie).

With one exception CSX has not spun off great stretches of secondary lines to become regional railroads but rather nibbled away at redundant

HAYS T. WATKINS JR. (1926-   ) was born in Fern Creek, Kentucky. He graduated from Bowling Green University in 1947 (his college career was interrupted by two years in the U. S. Army) and went on to Northwestern University, where he received an MBA degree in 1948. He joined the Chesapeake & Ohio as a staff analyst in 1949. Not long afterward he was discharged because a coal strike had cut traffic and revenues; three weeks later, just as abruptly, he was rehired. He married Betty Wright in 1950. He rose through C&O's accounting department to become vice president, administrative group, of the C&O and Baltimore & Ohio in 1964. He was named president in 1971, and became chairman and chief executive officer of Chessie System in 1973.

Watkins' management style is that of an accountant (he is, in his own words, "a bean counter") tempered with a quest for balance both in the demands of different factions and in the allocation of resources. He is approachable and enjoys first-name relationships with many of the employees. He also cheerfully admits to being a rail enthusiast and, as chairman of its board, is largely responsible for survival of the B&O Railroad Museum in Baltimore, one of the oldest and most respected railroad museums in the United States.

He became chairman and chief executive officer of CSX Corporation in 1980 and served in that post until February 1991, when he reached the company's mandatory retirement age. He heads the Board of Visitors of the College of William and Mary and is chairman of Richmond Tomorrow.

lines, a few miles here, a few there. The two former main lines that have been decommissioned are the Baltimore & Ohio route between Clarksburg, W. Va., and Cincinnati, and the Seaboard Air Line main line from Petersburg, Va., to Norlina, North Carolina. The exception cited is the B&O route from Eidenau, Pa., north of Pittsburgh, to Buffalo and Rochester (the one-time Buffalo, Rochester & Pittsburgh Railway), and even that was sold in two pieces.

Address of general offices: 500 Water Street, Jacksonville, FL 32202
Miles of road operated: 19,356
Reporting marks: ACL, AWP, BO, CO, CRR, CSXT, GA, LN, MON, NC, SAL, SBD, SCL, WA, WM
Number of locomotives: 3,097
Number of freight cars: 115,510
Principal commodities carried: Coal, phosphate rock, wood and paper products
Major yards: Chicago (Barr); Cincinnati (Queensgate); Russell, Ky.; Toledo (Walbridge); Atlanta (Tilford); Birmingham (Boyles); DeCoursey, Ky.; Hamlet, N. C.; Nashville (Radnor); South Louisville, Ky. (Osborn);

Waycross, Ga. (Rice); Jacksonville (Moncrief)
Principal shops: Cumberland, Md.; Huntington, W. Va.; Raceland, Ky.; Jacksonville, Fla.; Tampa Fla.; Waycross, Ga.
Radio frequencies: 160.230 (road, ex-Chessie), 160.590 (road, ex-SCL), 161.100 (road, ex-SCL), 161.370 (road, ex-L&N)
Passenger routes:
Amtrak
Washington-Cumberland-Pittsburgh-Willard-Garrett-Chicago
Washington-Charlottesville-Huntington-Cincinnati-Indianapolis
Washington-Selma-Charleston-Jacksonville-Orlando-Tampa
Richmond-Newport News
Raleigh-Columbia-Savannah
Jacksonville-Ocala-Miami
Birmingham-Mobile
Crawfordsville-Dyer, Ind.
Grand Rapids-New Buffalo, Mich.
MARC — Washington-Baltimore, Washington-Martinsburg, W. Va.
Virginia Railway Express — Washington-Fredericksburg, Va.

D&I RAILROAD

D&I Railroad, owned by the L. G. Everist Co., runs from Dell Rapids, South Dakota, south through Sioux Falls to Sioux City, Iowa, over former Milwaukee Road track. The line between Dell Rapids and Sioux Falls is owned by Everist; the remainder is owned by the state of South Dakota and the Sioux Valley Regional Railroad Authority. D&I began operation in 1982. For its name it uses just the initials — for "Dakota & Iowa."
Address of general offices: P. O. Box 829, Sioux Falls, SD 57117
Miles of road operated: 138

Reporting marks: DAIR
Number of locomotives: 14
Principal commodities carried: Sand, gravel, grain, fertilizer
Shops: Dell Rapids, S.D.
Junctions with other railroads:
Burlington Northern: Sioux City, Iowa; Sioux Falls, S. D.
Chicago & North Western: Sioux City, Iowa
Chicago, Central & Pacific: Sioux City, Iowa
Radio frequency: 161.190
Map: See Dakota, Minnesota & Eastern, page 98

Six D&I Geeps bring freight through Hawarden, Iowa, on September 6, 1991. Photo by Jim Shaw.

DAKOTA, MINNESOTA & EASTERN RAILROAD

Chicago & North Western's line from the Mississippi River at Winona, Minnesota, west to Pierre, South Dakota, was built between 1864 and 1880. In 1906 and 1907 it was extended west to Rapid City, S. D. The line was instrumental in settling the South Dakota prairie, and it settled down to a long existence as a grain gatherer and carrier. The line achieved minor notoriety among rail enthusiasts in the 1970s as the home territory for C&NW's Alco diesels.

In late 1985 the Chicago & North Western applied to abandon its light-density line between Pierre and Rapid City, South Dakota. It was the only rail route connecting the eastern and western parts of the state (the Milwaukee Road's line to Rapid City was already gone). The state protested, even while agreeing that C&NW would not have to operate the line at a loss — the solution was to sell it.

C&NW worked with the Railroad Management Services Venture Team, a division of L. B. Foster, a railroad supply firm in Pittsburgh, Pennsylvania, to put together a package that might attract a buyer. No one leaped up to buy the Pierre-Rapid City segment, so the property offered was extended east to Huron, S. D., then to Mankato, Minn., and finally all the way to Winona, Minn. The Foster group liked the final package well enough to purchase it and several branch lines on September 4, 1986, for operation as the Dakota, Minnesota & Eastern Railroad.

The DM&E's primary commodity is wheat, usually moving to midwestern flour mills or to a rail-barge transfer facility at Winona. Corn and soybenas move in unit trains destined for the Northwest, but agricultural products make up less than half the road's traffic. The road has undertaken a major track improvement project allowing a maximum speed of 25 mph over the entire length of the main line.

Address of general offices: P. O. Box 178, Brookings, SD 57006

SD40-2 No. 6384, named *City of New Ulm*, and five other units lead a freight west at Arlington, South Dakota. Photo by Jim Shaw.

Miles of road operated: 965
Reporting marks: DME
Number of locomotives: 46
Principal commodities carried: Grain, clay, cement, minerals
Shops: Huron, S.D.
Junctions with other railroads:
Burlington Northern: Aberdeen, Huron, Redfield, Watertown, and
Wolsey, S. D.
Chicago & North Western: Mankato, Minn.; Mason City, Iowa; Rapid
City, S. D.; Winona, Minn.
CP Rail System (Soo Line): Owatonna, Minn.
Radio frequencies: 160.395, 160.965
Recommended reading: "DM&E: the hardworking regional," by Jim
Zierke, in TRAINS Magazine, December 1991, pages 68-79

DAKOTA SOUTHERN RAILWAY

Dakota Southern Railway operates former Milwaukee Road trackage
from Mitchell, South Dakota, west to Chamberlain and Kadoka. The state-
owned line is part of the former Milwaukee Road route from Madison,
Wisconsin, west through Marquette and Mason City, Iowa, to Rapid City,
S. D. It was built between 1880 and 1907.
Address of general offices: P. O. Box 436, Chamberlain, SD 57325
Miles of road operated: 187
Reporting marks: DSRC
Number of locomotives: 5
Number of freight cars: 177 (mostly 4650- and 4750-cubic-foot cov-
ered hopper cars)
Principal commodities carried: Grain, agricultural products, aggre-
gates
Shops: Chamberlain, S. D.
Junctions with other railroads: Burlington Northern: Mitchell, S.D.
Radio frequency: 161.535
Map: See Dakota, Minnesota & Eastern, above

Dakota Southern 522, an SD9, brings a trainload of grain through rolling
hills at Oacoma, South Dakota, on September 8, 1991. Photo by Jim
Shaw.

98

DELAWARE & HUDSON RAILROAD

The Delaware & Hudson rated five pages in the 1991 edition of *The Historical Guide to North American Railroads* because it appeared likely that the railroad would qualify for inclusion in that book by disappearing, if not by abandonment, at absorption into CP Rail. It appears likely that D&H will remain an entity just barely long enough to be included here.

The D&H dates from 1823, when the Delaware & Hudson Canal Co. was chartered to build a canal from Honesdale, Pennsylvania, to Rondout, New York, on the Hudson River. The purpose of the canal was to carry anthracite coal from the mines of Pennsylvania to New York City. Access to the mines near Carbondale, Pa., was by a gravity railroad.

The demand for coal increased, and the D&H increased its coal holdings and began building railroads: north from Carbondale to Nineveh, N. Y., to connect with the Albany & Susquehanna, which it leased; and south from Carbondale to Scranton. In 1871 D&H leased the Rensselaer & Saratoga Railroad, which reached from Albany and Schenectady north to Lake Champlain at Whitehall, N. Y. By the end of 1875 D&H had assembled a rail route all the way north to the Canadian border.

D&H had two Canadian subsidiaries. In 1906 it acquired the Quebec, Montreal & Southern Railway, which extended 62 miles from St. Lambert northeast through Sorel to Pierreville, Quebec, and from Sorel south to Noyan Junction just north of the U. S. border. More important was the 28-mile Napierville Junction Railway, opened in 1907 between Rouses Point, N. Y., and Delson, Quebec, where it connected with Canadian Pacific and Canadian National.

Leonor F. Loree became president of the D&H in 1907. He undertook an upgrading of the D&H, but he had definite ideas about locomotives. He shunned most advances in steam locomotive technology — the initial demonstration of Lima's Super Power concept took place practically under his nose — and pushed the Consolidation type to its limit. The road's traffic was primarily coal — not a time-sensitive commodity — and speed was secondary to tractive effort.

When Loree retired in 1938, coal traffic had fallen off as oil replaced coal for heating, so D&H turned its attention to developing bridge traffic (traffic received from one railroad and passed on to another) between the

Midwest and New England and Canada. In 1957 D&H studied merger with Erie and Delaware, Lackawanna & Western, but was deterred by the long-term debt of those roads. A condition of the 1964 Norfolk & Western merger was that Delaware & Hudson be allowed in because the impending merger of the Pennsylvania and the New York Central would surround it. In 1968 Dereco, a subsidiary of N&W, acquired control of D&H and Erie Lackawanna, but neither road was ever considered part of the N&W system. D&H entered a period of joint management with Erie Lackawanna, which lasted until EL's bankruptcy in 1972.

In the thrashing around that preceded the formation of Conrail, D&H acquired trackage rights to Buffalo, N. Y., Newark, New Jersey, and Alexandria, Virginia. It sought loans from the United States Railway Association to enable it to compete with Conrail, yet the USRA was charged with seeing that Conrail succeeded; parent Norfolk & Western provided no help.

On January 4, 1984, Guilford Transportation Industries purchased the D&H and began to consolidate its operations with those of the Boston & Maine and the Maine Central. D&H entered bankruptcy in June 1988, and the New York, Susquehanna & Western was designated to operate it while Guilford put it up for sale. CP Rail purchased the road in January 1991, eyeing D&H's trackage rights to Washington, Philadelphia, and Newark, New Jersey, in the light of the U. S.-Canada free trade pact of 1990. CP undertook a rehabilitation of the D&H and began regular freight service to Philadelphia and Newark.

The office functions of the D&H have been combined with those of parent CP Rail in Montreal; the first D&H locomotive to be rehabilitated under the new ownerships was painted in D&H's traditional blue and gray — but by CP's Calgary, Alberta, shops rather than D&H's Colonie Shops near Albany. D&H's identity, like that of CP's other U. S. subsidiary, Soo Line, is rapidly giving way to that of CP Rail System.

Address of general offices: CP Rail, P. O. Box 6042, Station A, Montreal, PQ, Canada H3C 3E4
Miles of road operated: 1,699
Reporting marks: DH, DHNY
Number of locomotives: 17 (plus leased units and CP Rail units)
Number of freight cars: 1,562
Principal commodities carried: Chemicals, wood products, paper products, piggyback and container traffic
Radio frequencies: 160.590, 160.530, 161.100
Passenger routes: Amtrak — Schenectady-Rouses Point, N. Y.
Historical and technical society: Bridge Line Historical Society, Box 7242, Capitol Station, Albany, N. Y. 12224
Recommended reading: "Delaware & Hudson thrives under CP Rail," by Bill Stephens, in TRAINS Magazine, July 1992, pages 24-26

DENVER & RIO GRANDE WESTERN RAILROAD

The Denver & Rio Grande Western is now part of Southern Pacific Line (see page 202), but its absorption by SP is recent enought that it merits its own entry here. The Denver & Rio Grande Railway was incorporated by William Jackson Palmer in 1870 to build a railroad from Denver south along the eastern edge of the Rockies to El Paso, Texas. Palmer, who had risen to the rank of brigadier general during the Civil War, chose a track gauge of 3 feet for reasons of economy. The line was completed to the

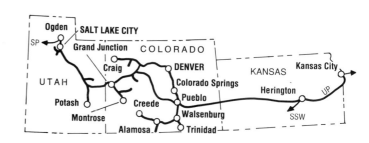

new town of Colorado Springs in 1871. In 1872 it was extended south to Pueblo, then west to tap coal deposits near Canon City, Colorado. There the railroad remained for a few years.

In 1878 the Rio Grande engaged in two railroad wars with the Santa Fe — perhaps "skirmishes" is more accurate than "wars." Palmer's forces narrowly lost Raton Pass in southern Colorado, but won occupancy of the Royal Gorge of the Arkansas River west of Canon City. Shortly afterward the D&RG was leased to the Santa Fe for a year.

In 1879 the Rio Grande was on its own again under the management of Palmer and Jay Gould. It made an agreement with the Santa Fe a year later to head in different directions: the Santa Fe south into New Mexico and the D&RG west into the Rockies. In 1881 the Rio Grande reached Gunnison and Durango, and foreshadowing changes to come, it added a third rail for standard gauge trains to its tracks between Denver and Pueblo.

In 1882 D&RG leased the affiliated Denver & Rio Grande Western Railway, which was building and consolidating lines southeastward from Salt Lake City. In 1883 the two railroads met near Green River, Utah, forming a narrow gauge route from Denver to Salt Lake City via Pueblo and Marshall Pass. In the early 1880s the D&RG built a new route from Leadville north over Tennessee Pass (10,239 feet, the highest point reached by a standard gauge main line in North America), then along the Eagle and Grand rivers, reaching Glenwood Springs in 1887. Two years later it was extended west to Rifle. The line from there to Grand Junction was built by the Rio Grande Junction Railway, which was jointly owned with the standard gauge Colorado Midland Railway — which in 1890 came under the control of the Santa Fe. Meanwhile, D&RG had been adding a third rail to its line east of Leadville. The lines west of Grand Junction were converted to standard gauge, and by 1890 D&RG had standard gauge track all the way from Denver to Ogden, Utah.

At the same time D&RG's narrow gauge network continued to expand south and west of the Pueblo-Grand Junction main line. In 1880 a line was extended south from Antonito, Colo., to Española, N. M. Rails reached Silverton from Durango in 1882, and in 1890 a line was built north from Alamosa to connect with existing lines southwest of Salida. In 1886 the Texas, Santa Fe & Northern Railroad constructed a line north from Santa

A Rio Grande coal train winds beside the Eagle River at Belden, Colorado, between Minturn and Red Cliff on the Tennessee Pass route. Photo by Wesley Fox.

Fe to Española. The company was reorganized as the Santa Fe Southern in 1888, and the Rio Grande acquired it in 1895.

The Rio Grande was deeply involved in financing the construction of the Western Pacific Railway between Salt Lake City and San Francisco,s completed in 1910. When WP entered bankruptcy in 1915, it pulled the Rio Grande in after it. The Rio Grande was sold in 1920 to interests affiliated with the WP. The new company was the Denver & Rio Grande Western Railroad. It entered receivership in 1921 and emerged in 1924 under the joint ownership of Western Pacific and Missouri Pacific — and encumbered with debt that put it back in trusteeship again in 1935. There was a difference this time. The trustees were not East Coast bankers but local men: Wilson McCarthy of Salt Lake City and Henry Swan of Denver.

The Moffat Tunnel and Dotsero Cutoff

David Moffat's Denver, Northwestern & Pacific Railway had built westward from Denver over Rollins Pass. In 1912 it was reorganized as the Denver & Salt Lake Railroad, but it got no closer to the goal in its name than Craig, in northwestern Colorado. The city of Denver, which for decades had wanted a direct rail route to the west, constructed the 6-mile Moffat Tunnel under James Peak for the D&SL (and also to bring Western Slope water to Denver). The tunnel, opened in 1928, let D&SL avoid the steep and often snowy climb over Rollins Pass, but D&SL had little traffic to send through the tunnel.

At Bond, the D&SL was about 40 miles up the Colorado River from D&RGW's main line at Dotsero. Both railroads wanted to build a cutoff connecting the routes; the Interstate Commerce Commission gave the nod to the Rio Grande. The Dotsero Cutoff was opened in 1934 and the Rio Grande acquired trackage rights on the D&SL between Denver and Bond. Denver finally was on a transcontinental main line, and D&RGW's route between Denver and Salt Lake City was 175 miles shorter. The D&RGW came out of trusteeship and merged the D&SL on April 11, 1947.

The California Zephyr

In 1939 the D&RGW, Western Pacific, and Chicago, Burlington & Quincy teamed up to operate a through passenger train, the *Exposition Flyer*, between Chicago and San Francisco via Denver and the Moffat Tunnel. The *Flyer* did not set the world on fire with its speed, but westbound it offered magnificent views of the Rockies west of Denver and California's

Feather River Canyon. In 1949 the train became the *California Zephyr*. The *CZ* was slower than its competition, but it was scheduled and equipped — five Vista-Domes per train — to take advantage of the scenery it traversed. The *CZ* was more than a train — it was a long-distance land cruise. It was an immediate success, and it continued to carry good loads even in the late 1960s. In 1970 the Western Pacific managed to disencumber itself of the passenger business, and the *CZ* degenerated into a triweekly Chicago-Salt Lake City-Ogden operation designated "California service."

When Amtrak took over the nation's passenger trains in 1971, the Rio Grande elected to continue operating its sole passenger train, the Denver-Salt Lake City *Rio Grande Zephyr*, a remnant of the *CZ*. D&RGW joined Amtrak in 1983, and the triweekly *RGZ* was replaced by the daily operation of Amtrak's three-pronged service from Chicago to San Francisco, Los Angeles, and Seattle. Rio Grande still operates a seasonal ski train between Denver and Winter Park.

Narrow gauge lines

By the 1920s Rio Grande had worked its narrow gauge lines down to two routes: from Salida west to Montrose via Marshall Pass, the original main line, then south to Ridgway and a connection with the Rio Grande Southern Railroad, which D&RG had controlled since 1893; and from Alamosa west to Durango. From Antonito the "Chili Line" ran south to Santa Fe, N. M.; at Durango there were branches to Farmington, N. M., and Silverton, and another connection with the Rio Grande Southern. A narrow gauge line between Salida and Alamosa connected the two routes. It was possible to ride a complete circle on narrow gauge lines, until a bus replaced the passenger trains on the Salida-Alamosa branch in the mid-1920s.

The Chili Line was abandoned in 1942 for lack of traffic, and the narrow gauge circle was broken at Cerro Summit on the Marshall Pass route in 1949. The pace of narrow gauge abandonments accelerated (a few short segments were standard gauged), so that by the mid-1950s only the Alamosa-Durango-Farmington-Silverton line was left — and it remained operational until 1967. Two segments of that route, from Antonito to Chama and from Durango to Silverton, survive as tourist carriers.

Merger with Southern Pacific

Even though coal from mines in northwestern Colorado became increasingly important to the D&RGW, the road's principal role was that of a fast-freight bridge route between Denver and Pueblo on the east and Salt Lake City and Ogden on the west. Mergers and abandonments changed the railroad map in the 1980s. The Rock Island, a good source of interchange traffic at Denver, ceased operation. The Union Pacific acquired Rio Grande's principal eastern connection, the Missouri Pacific, and principal western connection, Western Pacific. D&RGW acquired trackage rights east over the former MP route to Kansas City as a condition of the UP-MP merger. Then Rio Grande's other western connection, Southern Pacific, began talking merger with Santa Fe. Had the SP-SF merger occurred, D&RGW would have gotten an exclusive lease of SP's line from Ogden west to Roseville, Calif., and Klamath Falls, Oregon, plus trackage rights to Bakersfield, Oakland, and Ogden.

Philip Anschutz, a Denver businessman, acquired control of D&RGW in 1984. When the Interstate Commerce Commission rejected the SP-Santa Fe merger, Anschutz submitted an offer to purchase SP, and the ICC approved it on August 9, 1988.

Address of general offices: P. O. Box 5482, Denver, CO 80217
Miles of road operated: 2,248
Reporting marks: DRGW
Number of locomotives: 282
Number of freight cars: 9,779
Number of passenger cars: 19
Major yards: Denver (North Yard), Salt Lake City (Roper)
Principal shops: Denver (Burnham)
Radio frequencies: 160.455 and 160.920 (road frequencies in different zones), 161.490 (yard), 160.395 and 161.565 (Moffat Tunnel)
Passenger routes: Amtrak — Denver to Salt Lake City
Recommended reading:
Rebel of the Rockies, by Robert G. Athearn, published in 1962 by Yale University Press, New Haven, CT 06520 (LCC: 62-16560)
Rio Grande to the Pacific, by Robert A. Le Massena, published in 1974 by Sundance Ltd., 100 Kalamath St., Denver, CO 80223 (ISBN 0-913582-10-7)

DULUTH, MISSABE & IRON RANGE RAILWAY

The Duluth & Iron Range Rail Road was chartered in 1874 to bring iron ore from the Vermilion Range of northeastern Minnesota down to the Lake Superior ore docks at Two Harbors. The Duluth, Missabe & Northern Railway was incorporated in 1891 to link the open-pit iron mines of the Mesabi Range with docks at Duluth. Both railroads came under the ownership of U. S. Steel in 1901.

The Duluth, Missabe & Iron Range Railway was incorporated in 1937 to consolidate the DM&N and the Spirit Lake Transfer Railway. In 1938 the company acquired the D&IR, which DM&N had leased since 1930, and the Interstate Transfer Railway.

In recent years as veins of high-grade ore have been depleted, mining companies have turned to lower-grade taconite. The taconite is processed into round pellets, which have a lower density than iron ore.

The DM&IR, the largest carrier of iron ore in the U. S., was owned by

U. S. Steel until 1988, when it was acquired by Transtar, Inc. Blackstone Capital Partners owns a 51 percent interest in Transtar; USX, successor to U. S. Steel, owns 49 percent.

Address of general offices: 500 Missabe Building, Duluth, MN 55802
Miles of road operated: 272
Reporting marks: DMIR
Number of locomotives: 61
Number of freight cars: 4,343
Principal commodities carried: Iron ore

Major yards: Proctor, Minn.
Principal shops: Proctor, Minn.
Radio frequencies: 160.800, 160.350
Historical and technical society: Missabe Historical Society, 719 Northland Avenue, Stillwater, MN 55082
Recommended reading: *The Missabe Road*, by Frank A. King, published in 1972 by Golden West Books, P. O. Box 8136, San Marino, CA 91108 (ISBN 87095-040-1)

A Duluth, Missabe & Iron Range ore train enters Proctor Yard on June 29, 1986. Ahead is a steep descent to the ore docks in Duluth. Photo by Jim Shaw.

DELIVERED WITH PRIDE

DULUTH, WINNIPEG & PACIFIC RAILWAY

The first portion of the Duluth, Winnipeg & Pacific was the middle — a logging railroad, the Duluth, Virginia & Rainy Lake Railway, opened in 1901 from Virginia, Minnesota, to nearby Silver Lake. The road was soon purchased by Canadian Northern Railway interests and its name changed to Duluth, Rainy Lake & Winnipeg Railway. In 1908 the line was extended north to a connection with Canadian Northern (a predecessor of Canadian National Railways) at Fort Frances, Ontario. In 1909 the road acquired its present name and built southward to Duluth, reaching there in 1912. In 1918 control of Canadian Northern passed to the Canadian government and the DW&P became part of Canadian National Railways.

In November 1984 the road abandoned its long, twisting descent into Duluth and opened a new facility, Pokegama Yard in Superior, Wisconsin. It reaches the yard by trackage rights on Duluth, Missabe & Iron Range's Spirit Lake branch. The reason for the move was highway construction in downtown Duluth.

The "Peg" is grouped with Canadian National's other United States subsidiaries in a unit named CN North America.

Address of general offices: R. R. 4, Box 3008, Superior, WI 54880
Miles of road operated: 167
Reporting marks: DWC, DWP
Number of locomotives: 13
Number of freight cars: 2,338
Principal commodities carried: Potash, lumber, paper

Junctions with other railroads:
Burlington Northern: Pokegama, Wis.; Superior, Wis.
Canadian National: Fort Frances, Ont.; Ranier, Minn.
Chicago & North Western: Pokegama, Wis.; Superior, Wis.
Duluth, Missabe & Iron Range: Pokegama, Wis.; Virginia, Minn.
Lake Superior Terminal & Transfer: Superior, Wis.
Minnesota, Dakota & Western: Ranier, Minn.
Soo Line: Pokegama, Wis.; Superior, Wis.
Wisconsin Central: Superior, Wis.
Radio frequencies: 161.415, 161.205, 160.935
Recommended reading: "No more Duluth for DW&P," by Steven Glischinski, in Trains Magazine, March 1985, pages 16-17
Map: See Duluth, Missabe & Iron Range, page 103

Most rail enthusiasts know the Duluth, Winnipeg & Pacific only through its fleet of freight cars, such as this box car seen at Butler, Wisconsin, in 1973. Photo by Stanley H. Mailer.

ELGIN, JOLIET & EASTERN RAILWAY

In 1884 a group of Joliet, Illinois, businessmen incorporated a railroad that would run from the Indiana-Illinois state line west through Joliet and Aurora to the Mississippi River opposite Dubuque, Iowa. It would afford Joliet's steel mills and stone quarries connections to railroads that didn't serve Joliet directly. In 1886 the Joliet, Aurora & Northern Railway began operation between Joliet and Aurora. The anticipated traffic was slow to develop, and JA&N's builders got the idea of making the road into a belt line around Chicago.

The proposal attracted the attention of financier J. P. Morgan. A syndicate purchased the JA&N and chartered the Elgin, Joliet & Eastern Railway to extend the JA&N north to Elgin and east into Indiana. Even while the road was under construction it backed two other railroads: the Gardner, Coal City & Northern, which built a line south from Plainfield into a coal-mining area, and the Waukegan & Southwestern, which extended the EJ&E northeast to Waukegan, Ill., on the shore of Lake Michigan just south of the Wisconsin state line (the EJ&E absorbed both roads in 1891).

In 1893 the EJ&E pushed its line east to Porter, Ind., a few miles east of the south end of Lake Michigan. The completed main line formed an arc 30 to 40 miles from the center of Chicago, intersecting with every railroad entering Chicago — giving the "J" its other nickname, Chicago Outer Belt.

In 1898 the EJ&E, Illinois Steel, and Minnesota Iron were all brought under the ownership of a new company, Federal Steel, presided over by Elbert H. Gary. In 1901 Federal Steel and Carnegie Steel merged to form U. S. Steel. The new company chose as the site for a huge new steel mill a tract of sand dunes at the south end of Lake Michigan; it also laid out and incorporated a city nearby and named it for Gary.

From one of its predecessors the EJ&E inherited trackage rights on the Chicago & Eastern Illinois Railroad south to coalfields near Danville, Ill. — but only for trains carrying coal and limestone northbound. The EJ&E continued to exercise those trackage rights until 1947. For two months in 1980 the "J" found itself in a similar situation, as designated operator of the former Rock Island between Joliet and Peoria. The "J" abandoned part of its Aurora branch in 1976 and the rest in 1985; also in

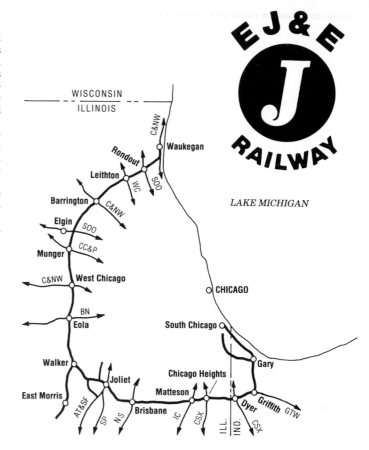

1985 it abandoned the easternmost 20 miles of its line, between Griffith and Porter.

The "J" was the first railroad to install welded rail on its main line, and its Kirk Yard at Gary had the world's first electrically operated automatic car retarders. The road dieselized in 1949.

The railroad was owned by U. S. Steel until 1988, when it was acquired by Transtar Corporation. Blackstone Capital Partners owns a 51 percent interest in Transtar; USX, successor to U. S. Steel owns 44 percent.

Address of general offices: P. O. Box 880, Joliet, IL 60434
Miles of road operated: 231
Reporting marks: EJE
Number of locomotives: 58
Number of freight cars: 5,009
Principal commodities carried: Coal, iron, steel
Major yards: Gary, Ind.; Joliet, Ill.
Principal shops: Joliet, Ill.
Connects with:

Atchison, Topeka & Santa Fe	Conrail
Baltimore & Ohio Chicago Terminal	CSX
Belt Railway of Chicago	Grand Trunk Western
Burlington Northern	Illinois Central
Chicago & North Western	Indiana Harbor Belt
Chicago, Central & Pacific	Iowa Interstate
Chicago Heights Terminal Transfer	Norfolk Southern
Chicago Rail Link	Soo Line
Chicago Short Line	Southern Pacific
Chicago SouthShore & South Bend	Union Pacific
Chicago, West Pullman & Southern	Wisconsin Central

Radio frequencies: 160.350 (road and dispatcher), 160.260 (yard)
Recommended reading: "The J: A Centennial History," by Michael W. Blaszak, in TRAINS Magazine, August 1989, pages 26-35, and September 1989, pages 28-41.

Through industrial-looking landscape an SD38 and an SD38-2 take an Elgin, Joliet & Eastern freight train north out of Eola, Illinois, in March 1983. Photo by William S. Christopher.

ESCANABA & LAKE SUPERIOR RAILROAD

The Escanaba & Lake Superior was incorporated in 1898. It constructed a line from Escanaba, Michigan, on the shore of Lake Michigan, 63 miles northwest to Channing, Mich., where it connected with the Milwaukee Road. For a time (before the Milwaukee Road-Chicago & North Western ore pooling agreement of the 1930s) Milwaukee Road ore trains moved over the E&LS to ore docks at Escanaba.

On March 10, 1980, E&LS took over operation of Milwaukee Road lines from Channing to Green Bay, Wisconsin, Republic, Mich., and Ontonagon, Mich., and purchased them in 1984.

Address of general offices: One Larkin Plaza, Wells, MI 49894
Miles of road operated: 342
Reporting marks: ELS
Number of locomotives: 23
Number of freight cars: 645
Principal commodities carried: Paper, pulpwood
Shops: Wells, Mich.; Menominee, Mich.
Radio frequencies: 160.320
Junctions with other railroads:
Chicago & North Western: Escanaba, Mich.; Iron Mountain, Mich.; Marinette, Wis.
Fox River Valley: Green Bay, Wis.
Green Bay & Western: Green Bay, Wis.
Wisconsin Central: Green Bay, Wis.; North Escanaba, Mich.; Pembine, Wis.
Recommended reading: "The elongated Escanaba & Lake Superior," by Steven Glischinski, in TRAINS Magazine, July 1984, pages 31-41

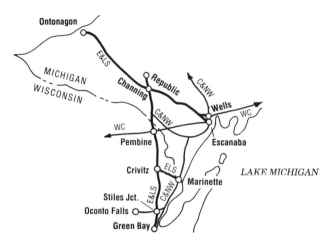

Escanaba & Lake Superior 300, a Baldwin RS12 built for the Seaboard Air Line Railroad in 1953, pulls an inspection train for state legislators between Channing and Wells, Michigan, in November 1982. Photo by William S. Christopher.

FLORIDA CENTRAL RAILROAD
FLORIDA MIDLAND RAILROAD
FLORIDA NORTHERN RAILROAD

During the Florida land boom of the 1920s the Atlantic Coast Line and the Seaboard Air Line both constructed spider webs of branch lines in central Florida. A few of those lines were abandoned before the two railroads merged in 1967 to create the Seaboard Coast Line. Post-merger rationalization took care of many of the redundant lines — ACL and SAL had 38 points in common in Florida — but in the 1980s when conditions favored selling off routes to new shortline railroads, SCL still had plenty of likely properties. The Pinsly Railroad Company formed three railroads to operate former SCL branches in central Florida.

Florida Central Railroad operates several former ACL and SAL branches northwest of Orlando: Orlando through Toronto to Tavares (ex-SAL), Tavares to Umatilla (ex-ACL), Tavares to Sorrento (ex-ACL), and Winter Garden-Toronto-Forest City (ex-ACL). The Florida Central began operation in November 1986.

Florida Midland operates three lines: Wildwood to Leesburg, a portion of a former SAL branch to Tavares; West Lake Wales to Frostproof, part former SAL and part former ACL track; and Winter Haven to Gordonsville, ex-ACL. The Florida Midland purchased the lines and began operation in November 1987.

Florida Northern purchased and began operating a portion of a former ACL route from Lowell through Ocala to Candler in November 1988.

Address of general offices: P. O. Box 967, Plymouth, FL 32768
Miles of road operated: 68 (FCEN), 34 (FMID), 27 (FNOR)
Reporting marks: FCEN, FMID, FNOR
Number of locomotives: 5 (FCEN), 4 (FMID), 1 (FNOR)
Principal commodities carried: Limestone, fertilizer, citrus products
Junctions with other railroads: CSX: Ocala, Orlando, West Lake Wales, Wildwood, Winter Haven
Radio frequencies: 160.545, 161.475

Florida Northern's CF7 rolls into Ocala, Florida, on May 10, 1989, with three CSX covered hopper cars on its drawbar. Photo by Jim Shaw.

FLORIDA EAST COAST RAILWAY

In 1885 Henry M. Flagler took over the Jacksonville, St. Augustine & Halifax, a 36-mile, narrow gauge railroad extending south from Jacksonville, Florida. He converted the line to standard gauge, built a bridge across the St. Johns River to connect with other railroads at Jacksonville, and pushed the line southward, reaching Miami in 1896.

Then, to tap the Cuban trade and also because Key West was the closest port to the Panama Canal, then under construction, he decided to build a line south across the Florida Keys to Key West. Construction was set back by hurricanes in 1906, 1909, and 1910, but the line reached Key West early in 1912, only months before Flagler's death.

The Florida land boom came in 1924, and FEC went whole hog: new cutoffs, branches, double track, signals, and 90 new locomotives of the 4-8-2 type. The boom peaked and receded in 1926, the Seaboard Air Line Railway reached Miami in 1927 — and then the Great Depression hit. FEC entered receivership in 1931.

A hurricane in 1935 wiped out most of the Key West Extension. What remained was used as the right of way for U. S. Highway 1 to Key West. Twenty of the Mountain types were sold off to such roads as Cotton Belt and Western Pacific; eventually 30 more went to National Railways of Mexico.

In 1944 Atlantic Coast Line, whose streamliners FEC operated between Jacksonville and Miami, offered to purchase the FEC; later Seaboard Air Line and Southern Railway came up with a joint counterproposal. There was, however, considerable pressure to keep control of the railroad within the state of Florida.

The railroad was reorganized in 1960. Control was assumed by the St. Joe Paper Co. (which also owns Apalachicola Northern, page 29), owned by the Alfred I. duPont estate. In 1963 the nonoperating unions struck the railroad, which had refused to go along with an industry-wide pay increase. Within two weeks management personnel was operating freight service. The strike became increasingly bitter, with bombings and destruction. In spite of the strike, FEC was required to restore passenger service in 1965 to comply with provisions of its charter. The two-car Jacksonville-Miami train was discontinued in 1968. It was an odd end to the passenger service that in some years had contributed nearly half of FEC's revenues.

The initial strike lasted until 1971; the strike by the operating unions was not settled until 1976. By then the railroad had instituted sweeping changes: two-man freight crews running trains the length of the railroad, where formerly three five-man crews had been required; extensive rebuilding of the railroad, including many miles of concrete ties; single track and CTC; several branches abandoned; and — a harbinger of an industry-wide development — no cabooses. Revenues and earnings began to climb, and in

1980 FEC broke its dividend record — none ever — by declaring a dividend on its common stock.

In 1984 FEC's corporate structure was revised to make the railroad a subsidiary of FEC Industries, a holding company that had been a subsidiary of the railroad.

Address of general offices: 1 Malaga Street, St. Augustine, FL 32084

Miles of road operated: 554

Reporting marks: FEC

Number of locomotives: 73

Number of freight cars: 2,600

Principal commodities carried: Agricultural products, piggyback traffic

Major yards: Jacksonville (Bowden), Miami (Hialeah)

Principal shops: Jacksonville (cars), New Smyrna Beach (locomotives)

Junctions with other railroads:

CSX: Jacksonville, Fla.; Lake Harbor, Fla.; Marcy, Fla.; Miami, Fla.; West Palm Beach, Fla.

Norfolk Southern: Jacksonville, Fla.

Port of Palm Beach District: Port of Palm Beach Jct., Fla.

St. Johns River Terminal: Jacksonville, Fla.

Radio frequencies: 160.530 (road and dispatcher to train), 160.770 (train to dispatcher)

Recommended reading: *Speedway to Sunshine*, by Seth H. Bramson, published in 1984 by Boston Mills Press, 98 Main Street, Erin, ON, Canada N0B 1T0 (ISBN 0-919783-12-0)

A GP40-2 and a GP38-2 bring a southbound Florida East Coast freight, heavy with auto racks, through Korona, Florida, on May 7, 1989. Photo by Jim Shaw.

FOX RIVER VALLEY RAILROAD

Between 1854 and 1862 the Chicago & North Western Railway pushed a line north from Janesville, Wisconsin, to the Fox River Valley towns of Fond du Lac, Oshkosh, Appleton, and Fort Howard (now Green Bay). In 1873 it opened a line from Milwaukee to Oshkosh and through a subsidiary began building a line north from Milwaukee along the shore of Lake Michigan. The latter route reached Manitowoc in 1873 and was extended northwest to Green Bay in 1906.

The Fox River Valley Railroad began operating former Chicago & North Western lines in eastern Wisconsin on December 9, 1988. Its routes extend from Granville, in the northwest corner of Milwaukee, north through Fond du Lac and Appleton to Green Bay; from Cleveland, north of Sheboygan, to Duck Creek (Green Bay); and to New London from Kaukauna South. Fox River Valley has trackage rights on C&NW from Granville to Butler Yard, just west of Milwaukee. The road is owned by Itel Corporation, which also owns Green Bay & Western. In late 1991 Itel placed the two roads under the same management.

As this book goes to press negotiations are under way for purchase of the Fox River Valley and Green Bay & Western by Wisconsin Central.

Address of general offices: P. O. Box 2527, Green Bay, WI 54306
Miles of road operated: 214
Reporting marks: FRVR
Number of locomotives: 28
Number of freight cars: 60
Principal commodities carried: Paper, agricultural products
Shops: Green Bay, Wis.
Junctions with other railroads:
Chicago & North Western: Butler, Wis.; Green Bay, Wis.
Escanaba & Lake Superior: Green Bay, Wis.
Green Bay & Western: Green Bay, Wis.
Soo Line: Milwaukee, Wis.
Wisconsin Central: Appleton, Fond du Lac, Green Bay, Manitowoc, Neenah, and Oshkosh, Wis.
Wisconsin & Southern: Granville, Wis.
Radio frequencies: 160.845, 160.335

A southbound Fox River Valley train leaves Neenah, Wisconsin, on June 29, 1989. Both GP9s are ex-Chicago & North Western; the lead unit has yet to be repainted in Fox River's red and yellow livery. The distant track belongs to the Wisconsin Central. Photo by Eric Hirsimaki.

GALVESTON RAILROAD

The Galveston Railway is a switching line owned by the city of Galveston, Texas. It began operation in 1900 as the Galveston Wharves Railway. It is leased to Rail Management & Consulting Corporation, which operates it as the Galveston Railroad. It is included here because of its large and conspicuous fleet of interchange freight cars.

Address of general offices: P. O. Box 5985, Dothan, AL 36302
Track miles: 43
Reporting marks: GVSR
Number of locomotives: 5
Number of freight cars: 1,052
Principal commodities carried: Grain, sugar
Connects with:
Atchison, Topeka & Santa Fe
Burlington Northern
Southern Pacific
Union Pacific
Radio frequency: 161.355

Galveston Railroad does its work with five SW1001s like orange-and-white No. 303, photographed in 1982. Photo by Tom Eisenhour.

GATEWAY WESTERN RAILWAY

In 1878 the Chicago & Alton Railroad created a Chicago-Kansas City route by leasing the Kansas City, St. Louis & Chicago Railroad, a line between Kansas City and Mexico, Missouri. The new route was shorter than the existing Chicago-Kansas City routes (Burlington, Rock Island, and Milwaukee Road), and the C&A developed a respectable Chicago-Kansas City business. An even shorter route was opened by the Santa Fe in 1888, and C&A's line began a long, slow descent into branchline status. It began losing money in 1912 and entered receivership in 1922. The Baltimore & Ohio purchased it in 1929 and reorganized it as the Alton Railroad. It operated as part of the B&O from 1931 to 1943.

The Gulf, Mobile & Ohio Railroad merged the Alton in 1947, becoming a Great-Lakes-to-Gulf railroad. GM&O, Burlington, and Santa Fe got

Gateway Western GP38s 2044 and 2055 await assignment at East St. Louis, Illinois, on February 11, 1991. Photo by Michael W. Blaszak.

tric car repowered with a diesel engine — to keep from stumbling over Western Pacific's *Zephyrette*, a Budd Rail Diesel Car, which lasted a few months longer and covered almost three times the mileage.)

Illinois Central merged the GM&O in 1972, creating Illinois Central Gulf. In the 1980s ICG underwent a major restructuring, spinning off its east-west routes to form new regional railroads. Most of the old Alton was set loose and became the Chicago, Missouri & Western Railway in 1987. The CM&W entered bankruptcy less than a year after its creation. Southern Pacific purchased the St. Louis-Joliet, Ill., main line to create SPCSL (Southern Pacific Chicago St. Louis). The Kansas City line was purchased by Wertheim Schroeder & Co. and became the Gateway Western Railway.

Gateway Western's main line runs from East St. Louis, Ill., to Kansas City. Short branches reach Fulton, Mo., Jacksonville, Ill., and Springfield, Ill. The line between East St. Louis and Godfrey, Ill., is owned jointly with SPCSL.

Address of general offices: 15 Executive Drive, Fairview Heights, IL 62208
Miles of road operated: 408
Reporting marks: CMNW, GWWR
Number of locomotives: 22
Number of freight cars: 75
Principal commodities carried: Farm products, chemicals
Radio frequencies: 161.280
Historical and technical society: Gulf, Mobile & Ohio Historical Society, P. O. Box 463, Fairfield, IL 62837
Recommended reading: "Road of misfortune," by Michael W. Blaszak and Randy Wood, in TRAINS Magazine, September 1992, pages 54-63; October 1992, pages 36-43; and November 1992, pages 48-53

together and proposed selling GM&O's Kansas City line to the Burlington, which would grant Kansas City-St. Louis trackage rights to the Santa Fe, which would in turn let Burlington use part of its Kansas City-Chicago line. Other railroads protested, and GM&O's Kansas City line remained an east-west route for an otherwise north-south carrier.

The Kansas City line gained some measure of fame among rail enthusiasts in the late 1950s when its Bloomington, Ill.-Kansas City trains qualified as the longest (and among the last) motor car runs in the country. (Careful definition is necessary here — "motor car" means an old gas-elec-

GENESEE & WYOMING RAILROAD

The Genesee & Wyoming Valley Railway was opened in 1894 to carry salt from mines at Retsof, New York (a man named Foster financed the development of the salt mines; Retsof is his name in reverse), to a point

just west of Caledonia known as Pittsburgh & Lehigh Junction (at times just P&L Junction). There the road connected with the Buffalo, Rochester & Pittsburgh and the Lehigh Valley. In 1899 it emerged from receivership and sale as the Genesee & Wyoming Railroad. The Genesee & Wyoming spent three-quarters of the twentieth century as a short line, hauling salt on 12 miles or so of track. After Conrail was formed in 1976, G&W acquired trackage rights over Baltimore & Ohio (successor to the BR&P) north to Rochester and south to Silver Springs. Then Genesee & Wyoming extended its lines south from Retsof by purchasing part of the old Lackawanna main line and the Dansville & Mount Morris.

Genesee & Wyoming is controlled by Genesee & Wyoming Industries, which also controls the Buffalo & Pittsburgh, Rochester & Southern, Dansville & Mt. Morris, and Louisiana & Delta railroads.

Address of general offices: 3546 Retsof Road, Retsof, NY 14539
Miles of road operated: 47
Reporting marks: GNWR

Number of locomotives: 8
Number of freight cars: 455
Principal commodities carried: Salt, coal, fertilizer, grain
Shops: Retsof, N. Y.
Junctions with other railroads:
Conrail: Rochester, N. Y.
Dansville & Mt. Morris: Groveland, N. Y.
Delaware & Hudson: Caledonia, N. Y.
Rochester & Southern: Pittsburgh & Lehigh Junction
Radio frequency: 160.500
Map: See Buffalo & Pittsburgh, page 54

Three cars of salt trail Genesee & Wyoming 46, an MP15DC, at Genesee & Wyoming Junction, New York, in 1982. Photo by Jim Shaw.

GEORGETOWN RAILROAD

Soon after Edwin Snead's Texas Crushed Stone Company opened a new rock quarry near Georgetown, Texas, in 1957, the Missouri Pacific filed a petition to abandon its branch from Round Rock to Georgetown. A group of Georgetown businessmen purchased the line to operate it as the Georgetown Railroad — the same name under which it had been built in the 1880s.

In the 1960s and 1970s the road acquired its own large fleet of cars for carrying crushed rock. Snead, an engineer, experimented extensively to develop a car that could dump its load quickly and completely. The experiments, which continued after Snead's death in 1982, resulted in the Dump Train, a train of hopper cars connected by a conveyor to a boom-mounted dumping belt at one end.

Address of general offices: P. O. Box 529, Georgetown, TX 78627
Miles of road operated: 8
Reporting marks: GRR
Number of locomotives: 20
Number of freight cars: 1,192
Principal commodities carried: Crushed rock
Shops: Feld, Texas
Junctions with other railroads:
Southern Pacific: Kerr, Texas
Union Pacific: Georgetown, Texas; Kerr, Texas
Recommended reading: "Rock-hauler extraordinaire," by J. Parker Lamb, in TRAINS Magazine, August 1988, pages 24-32
Map: See Austin & Northwestern, page 44

Georgetown Railroad's Dump Train rolls along Missouri-Kansas-Texas track near Georgetown on April 12, 1986. Photo by J. Parker Lamb.

GEORGIA & ALABAMA DIVISION — SOUTH CAROLINA CENTRAL RAILROAD

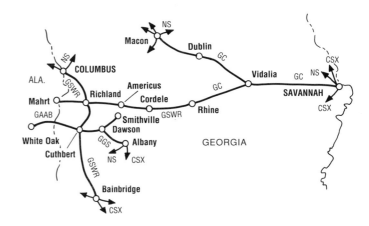

Three divisions of the South Carolina Central Railroad, part of the RailTex group, operate a cluster of former CSX and Central of Georgia lines in southwest Georgia.

The Georgia & Alabama Division operates a former Central of Georgia line from Smithville, Ga., west through Eufaula, Alabama, to White Oak. The line was part of the South Western Railroad, which was leased by the Central of Georgia in 1869. At one time it formed part of CofG's line to Montgomery, Ala. The Georgia & Alabama leased the line from Norfolk Southern in June 1989.

Address of general offices: P. O. Box 62, Dawson, GA 31742
Miles of road operated: 74
Reporting marks: GAAB
Number of locomotives: 2
Principal commodities carried: Agricultural products
Shops: Dawson, Ga.
Junctions with other railroads:
Georgia Great Southern Division: Dawson, Ga.
Georgia Southwestern Division: Cuthbert, Ga.
Norfolk Southern: Smithville, Ga.
Radio frequency: 161.085

GEORGIA SOUTHWESTERN DIVISION — SOUTH CAROLINA CENTRAL RAILROAD

The Georgia Southwestern Division operates former CSX (ex-Seaboard Air Line) routes from Rhine, Ga., west through Cordele and Americus to Mahrt, Alabama, and from Columbus south to Bainbridge, Ga. The two routes cross at Richland, Ga.

The east-west route was built in the 1880s by the Savannah, Americus & Montgomery Railroad, which was absorbed by the Georgia & Alabama Railroad in 1895; that in turn came under control of the Seaboard Air Line in 1901. The north-south route was part of the Georgia, Florida & Alabama Railway, which extended south from Richland, Ga., through Tallahassee to the Gulf of Mexico at St. Marks, Fla. Seaboard Air Line acquired it in 1928. CSX sold the lines to South Carolina Central in June 1989.

Address of general offices: 908 Elm Avenue, Americus, GA 31709
Miles of road operated: 243
Reporting marks: GSWR
Number of locomotives: 8
Number of freight cars: 147
Principal commodities carried: Forest products, paper, chemicals, fertilizer, aggregate
Shops: Americus, Ga.; Damascus, Ga.
Junctions with other railroads:
Chattahoochee Industrial: Saffold, Ga.
CSX: Bainbridge, Ga.; East Cordele, Ga.
Georgia & Alabama Division: Cuthbert, Ga.
Norfolk Southern: Americus, Ga.; Columbus, Ga.; Arlington, Ga.
Radio frequencies: 160.335, 161.325

GEORGIA GREAT SOUTHERN DIVISION — SOUTH CAROLINA CENTRAL RAILROAD

The Georgia Great Southern Division of the South Carolina Central Railroad extends from Dawson, Ga., southeast 22 miles to Albany. It was opened by the Columbus Southern Railroad in 1890 and soon became part of the Georgia & Alabama. South Carolina Central purchased the line from CSX in December 1990.

Address of general offices: P. O. Box 62, Dawson, GA 31742
Miles of road operated: 22 miles
Reporting marks: GGS

Number of locomotives: 1
Principal commodities carried: Agricultural products
Shops: Dawson, Ga.
Junctions with other railroads:
Atlantic & Gulf: East Albany, Ga.
Georgia & Alabama Division: Dawson, Ga.
Norfolk Southern: Albany, Ga.
Radio frequency: 161.085

GEORGIA CENTRAL RAILWAY

The Georgia Central extends west from Savannah, Georgia to Rhine, 132 miles, and from Vidalia northwest to Macon, 92 miles.

The Savannah-Vidalia-Rhine route is part of a line that was opened in 1891 by the Savannah, Albany & Montgomery Railway. It became the Georgia & Alabama Railroad in 1895, and by 1900 it was the Savannah-Montgomery, Ala., route of the Seaboard Air Line.

The Vidalia-Macon branch is the former Macon, Dublin & Savannah Railroad. It was incorporated in 1885 and built during the decade or so that followed. In 1904 the Atlantic Coast Line purchased an interest in the road, but sold it to Seaboard Air Line in 1906. SAL gradually acquired the rest of its stock and absorbed it in 1958.

CSX spun off the lines in 1990 to the Georgia Central. It has received authority to abandon the Helena-Rhine segment of its line, about 19 miles.

Address of general offices: P. O. Box 28300, Panama City Beach, FL 32411
Miles of road operated: 224
Reporting marks: GC
Number of locomotives: 20
Number of freight cars: 67
Principal commodities carried: Paper, clay, chemicals, pulpwood
Shops: Lyons, Ga.
Junctions with other railroads:
CSX: Savannah, Ga.
Norfolk Southern: Dublin, Ga.; Helena, Ga.; Macon, Ga.
Radio frequencies: 160.800, 160.680
Map: See previous page

GOVERNMENT OF ONTARIO TRANSIT

Toronto, like most large cities in the 1950s, faced the related problems of commuter traffic and strangulation by highways. In 1959 Canadian National Railways announced a plan to build a large freight classification yard northwest of Toronto. Freight trains would be rerouted on a belt line, freeing CN's route along the shore of Lake Ontario for commuter trains — but CN added that any commuter service would have to be financed by someone else.

In 1965 the government of Ontario approved a plan to operate a 60-mile commuter service between Pickering on the east, Toronto, and Hamilton on the west. Government of Ontario Transit — GO Transit for short — began operation in 1967 and was an immediate success.

GO Transit added service to Georgetown on CN's secondary main line to London in 1974 (it has since been extended west to Guelph), north to Richmond Hill on CN's Bala Subdivision in 1978, and west to Milton on CP Rail in 1981. In 1982 GO took over VIA Rail Canada's Toronto-Stouffville and Toronto-Bradford trains. In recent years service has been extended east from Pickering to Whitby and Oshawa and north from Bradford to Barrie.

Address of general offices: 1120 Finch Avenue West, Downsview, ON, Canada M3H 5Y6
Miles of road operated: 212
Number of locomotives: 32, plus 14 auxiliary power units, some with cabs
Number of passenger cars: 272
Number of self-propelled passenger cars: 9
Major yards: Mimico (Willowbrook Maintenance Depot), Toronto (Bathurst North)
Shops: Mimico (Willowbrook Maintenance Depot)
Radio frequency: 161.295
Passenger routes:
Hamilton-Oakville-Toronto-Pickering (CN)
Toronto-Bradford (CN)
Toronto-Georgetown (CN)
Toronto-Milton (CP)
Toronto-Richmond Hill (CN)
Toronto-Stouffville (CN)

GO Transit's green-and-white bilevel cars are North America's most distinctive commuter rolling stock. Ten appear here rolling east behind two F59PHs on May 6, 1990. Photo by William D. Middleton.

GRAND TRUNK WESTERN RAILROAD

The Grand Trunk Western's ancestor was Canada's Grand Trunk Railway, conceived in 1852 to connect Montreal and Toronto. To that was added a line from Montreal to the nearest seaport, Portland, Maine. Construction and acquisition at the west end of the line in 1858 put Grand Trunk across the St. Clair River between Sarnia, Ontario, and Port Huron, Michigan, first by ferries and later by a tunnel. The line was extended through Michigan and Indiana, reaching Chicago in 1880.

Grand Trunk stockholders guaranteed the bonds for construction of the Grand Trunk Pacific Railway from Winnipeg, Manitoba, to Prince Rupert, British Columbia. The GTP proved expensive, and GT's financial problems brought it under Canadian government ownership and absorption into the nationalized Canadian National Railways in 1923.

The Grand Trunk Western Railway was incorporated in 1928 by CN to consolidate the Grand Trunk properties in Michigan, Indiana, and Illinois.

In 1980 the Grand Trunk Western purchased the 580-mile Detroit, Toledo & Ironton, whose main line ran from Detroit south to the Ohio River at Ironton, Ohio. DT&I's checkered history includes control by Henry Ford, an experiment in electrification, ownership by subsidiaries of the Pennsylvania Railroad and its successor, Penn Central, and ownership of the now-defunct Ann Arbor Railroad.

In 1981 GTW purchased the Norfolk & Western's half interest in the jointly owned Detroit & Toledo Shore Line (Detroit to Toledo, 50 miles). N&W had acquired its share of the D&TSL when it merged the Nickel Plate.

Grand Trunk Western's main line extends from Port Huron, Mich., to Chicago. A branch extends from Durand southeast through Pontiac to Detroit. The former DT&I line extends south from Detroit to Springfield, Ohio, then to Cincinnati by trackage rights on Conrail. In 1987 GTW sold most of its branch lines in Michigan north of the Port Huron-Chicago main line to the Central Michigan Railway.

Since 1991 Canadian National and its United States subsidiaries have been marketed and publicized as CN North America. In 1991 the company began construction of a new tunnel between Sarnia and Port Huron that

will have sufficient clearance for double-stack containers.

Address of general offices: 1333 Brewery Park Boulevard, Detroit, MI 48207

Miles of road operated: 925

Reporting marks: DTI, DTS, GTW

Number of locomotives: 286

Number of freight cars: 7,441

Principal shops: Battle Creek (locomotives), Port Huron (cars)

Principal commodities carried: Motor vehicles and parts, fuel, chemicals

Major yards: Battle Creek, Flat Rock, Flint, Pontiac, and Port Huron, Mich.; Toledo, Ohio

Radio frequencies: 160.590, 160.530, 160.845

Passenger routes: Amtrak — Battle Creek-Port Huron, Mich.

Historical and technical society: Grand Trunk Western Historical Society, 912 West Broomfield, Mount Pleasant, MI 48858

A GP9 and a GP38-2 bring a Grand Trunk Western freight west through Lansing, Illinois, just west of the Indiana state line. Like its parent Canadian National, GTW specified the long hood as the front of its early hood units. Photo by R. B. Olson.

GREEN BAY & WESTERN RAILROAD

The Green Bay & Lake Pepin Railway was chartered in 1866 to build west from Green Bay, Wisconsin, to the Mississippi River. The road was to provide a Lake Michigan port for Minnesota's wheat and serve the growing lumber industry of northern Wisconsin. The first spike was driven in 1871, and the road reached the Mississippi at East Winona, Wis., in 1873. After several name changes and a period of control by the Lackawanna Iron & Coal Co., an affiliate of the Delaware, Lackawanna & Western, the road was reorganized as the Green Bay & Western Railway in 1896.

The railroad's eastern extension to Lake Michigan was incorporated in 1890 as the Kewaunee, Green Bay & Western Railroad. It opened in 1891, connecting with the ferries that plied Lake Michigan between Frankfort and Ludington, Mich., and Kewaunee, Wis. The KGB&W came under GB&W control in 1897; its corporate existence lasted long enough that one of GB&W's Alco FA1s was lettered for the subsidiary.

The importance of GB&W's bridge traffic diminished in the late 1970s — Ann Arbor's ferries ceased running in 1982, and Chesapeake & Ohio was down to a single Ludington-Kewaunee run — and the importance of Wisconsin's paper industry increased to the point that Burlington Northern expressed interest in acquiring the GB&W. The road was acquired by the Itel Corporation in 1979. In late 1991 Itel placed the GB&W and the Fox River Valley Railroad under the same management. As this book goes

to press Wisconsin Central is negotiating to purchase both roads.

Address of general offices: P. O. Box 2507, Green Bay, WI 54306
Miles of road operated: 255
Reporting marks: GBW
Number of locomotives: 16
Number of freight cars: 1,125
Principal commodities carried: Paper products
Shops: Green Bay, Wis.
Junctions with other railroads:
Ahnapee & Western: Casco Junction, Wis.
Burlington Northern: East Winona, Wis.
Chicago & North Western: Merrilan, Wis.; Wisconsin Rapids, Wis.
Fox River Valley: Green Bay, Wis.
Wisconsin Central: Black Creek, Wis.; Green Bay, Wis.; Plover, Wis.; Stevens Point, Wis.; Wisconsin Rapids, Wis.
Radio frequencies: 161.250, 161.070
Recommended reading: *Green Bay & Western*, by Stan Mailer, published in 1989 by Hundman Publishing Inc., 5115 Monticello Drive, Edmonds, WA 98020 (ISBN 0-945434-01-4)
Map: See Fox River Valley, page 112

Green Bay & Western has been an all-Alco railroad since its dieselization. Here a pair of bright-red C424s roll east through Blair, Wisconsin, with train 2 on September 23, 1989. No. 312 is named for a past GB&W president. Photo by Eric Hirsimaki.

GUILFORD TRANSPORTATION INDUSTRIES

During much of the twentieth century the trend has been for heavy manufacturing industry to move out of New England, making the region primarily a receiver of freight traffic rather than an originator. The ways to make money in the railroad business are to originate freight or carry it a long distance. New England's railroads have long been been handicapped by a traffic flow that makes them delivery agents for other railroads and by short distances. Practically the longest one-railroad haul in New England was Boston & Maine's route from the Hudson River to Portland, Maine, 267 miles — less than one-eighth of the distance from Seattle to Chicago on Burlington Northern.

Merger of Boston & Maine, Maine Central, and Delaware & Hudson along with one or more other New England railroads was proposed as long ago as 1929 by the Interstate Commerce Commission as part of its nationwide merger proposal. In more recent times Frederick C. Dumaine Jr., president at various times of New Haven, Bangor & Aroostook, and Delaware & Hudson, proffered much the same idea. The benefits of such a merger would include economies of scale and longer hauls.

In 1977 Timothy Mellon of Guilford, Connecticut, teamed up with David Fink to form Perma Treat, a railroad tie treatment company. Mellon wanted to acquire a railroad and considered several: Illinois Central Gulf, Pittsburgh & Lake Erie, and Detroit, Toledo & Ironton. None of those ventures worked out, but Mellon's interest in railroads continued. In June 1981 he purchased the Maine Central Railroad and its wholly owned subsidiary Portland Terminal Company through his holding company, Guilford Transportation Industries.

In June 1983 the Boston & Maine Railroad became the second piece of the Guilford system, bringing with it a subsidiary, the 6.5-mile Springfield Terminal Railway, a former electric line connecting Charlestown, New Hampshire with Springfield, Vermont. (During their ownership by Guilford, both Maine Central and Boston & Maine have had a now-you-see-them-now-you-don't existence. For that reason they are described fully in *The Historical Guide to North American Railroads*.)

The formation of Penn Central in 1968 and its takeover of the New Haven at the end of that year had left New England with only one non-Penn Central connection to the rest of the country: B&M's interchange with Delaware & Hudson at Mechanicville, N. Y. The D&H made a logical extension to the Guilford system — and a necessary one if Guilford was to be something more than a terminal company for Conrail traffic moving into New England. D&H was surrounded by Conrail and not doing well. The state of New York, which had financed much of D&H's rehabilitation program, approached Guilford about acquiring the road. In October 1981

Norfolk & Western, which owned D&H through a subsidiary holding company, agreed to sell it to Guilford. The purchase was completed at the beginning of 1984.

By the time the Guilford system was formed, the one-time multiplicity of connecting railroads had become a single, healthy, well-managed railroad: Conrail. Any New England-bound traffic Conrail originated would move as far as possible on Conrail before being handed over to Guilford — to Springfield, Mass., rather than Buffalo, N. Y., for example — and it would move faster. Guilford remained a short-haul, terminating railroad.

Another way make money, at least for a while, is to cut costs. Maine Central's route from Portland to St. Johnsbury, Vt., carried almost no local traffic and served only to give MEC a connection with a railroad other than Boston & Maine. With the formation of the Guilford system it was deemed redundant: B&M was now part of the family, and interchanging traffic with CP Rail at Mattawamkeag, Maine, was easier than battling the grades of Crawford Notch in New Hampshire. Similarly, the only business on MEC's branch from Bangor to Calais, Maine, was at the extreme eastern end, which could be reached by CP Rail. Service on most of the branch was discontinued, and the line was sold to the state. MEC's Rockland Branch was also abandoned (it is now the Maine Coast Railroad) as was part of the Lower Road, the Portland-Waterville route via Augusta.

Guilford also had two north-south routes to Canada, the D&H line north from Albany and B&M's Connecticut River Line. The D&H line was in better shape, so Guilford downgraded the B&M route, reducing maintenance. Complications arose, however. B&M and Central Vermont each owned part of the route. South of Brattleboro and north of Windsor, Vt., CV maintained its track so that good speeds were possible, but between those two points was a 50-mile stretch of B&M track, much of it limited to 10 mph. Amtrak, whose *Montrealer* used the route, found the slow running intolerable. The train was suspended in 1987, and the ICC ordered B&M to sell the Windsor-Brattleboro segment to Amtrak, which immediately resold it to CV. Central Vermont rehabilitated the track. The *Montrealer* was restored in 1989 on a new route: CV all the way from New London, Conn., to Cantic, Que., bypassing B&M entirely.

Guilford announced layoffs, shop closings, and pay cuts. MEC's maintenance workers went on strike in March 1986, and the strike spread to

A westbound Boston & Maine freight works upgrade alongside the Deerfield River at Rices, Massachusetts, on February 1, 1986, with a Delaware & Hudson U33C in Guilford colors on the point. Photo by Scott Hartley.

B&M and D&H. To take advantage of a lower wage scale and the more flexible work rules that apply to short lines, Guilford began leasing portions of the Maine Central and the Boston & Maine to B&M subsidiary Springfield Terminal for operation. Another strike ensued in 1987. In 1988 an arbitrator ruled that Guilford could not lease D&H to Springfield Terminal and had to abide by pre-Springfield Terminal labor agreements. The ruling precipitated D&H into bankruptcy. Guilford withdrew from D&H, and the New York, Susquehanna & Western was designated to operate the road. In 1991 the D&H was sold to CP Rail (see page 89).

Address of general offices: Iron Horse Park, North Billerica, MA 01862

Miles of road operated: 1,218

Reporting marks: BM, MEC
Number of locomotives: 91
Number of freight cars: 1,210 (BM); 2,844 (MEC)
Principal commodities carried: Paper, foodstuffs, fuels
Major yards: East Deerfield, Mass.; South Portland, Maine (Rigby)
Principal shops: North Billerica, Mass.; Waterville, Maine

Radio frequencies: 161.160, 161.520, 161.400 (BM); 160.620, 160.380 (MEC)
Recommended reading: *Guilford — Five Years of Change*, by Scott Hartley, published in 1989 by Railpace Company, P. O. Box 927, Piscataway, NJ 08855-0927 (ISBN 0-9621541-1-3)

HARTFORD & SLOCOMB RAILROAD

The Chattahoochee & Gulf Railroad was chartered in 1899. A little more than a year it later began service between Dothan and Sellersville, Alabama, 47 miles. The road was eventually extended to Lockhart and Columbia, Ala., and was leased by the Central of Georgia in 1900.

The line was abandoned west of Hartford, Ala., in 1940, and about 1950 the CofG decided to abandon the Dothan-Hartford portion. The Hartford & Slocomb Railroad was incorporated in 1953 to purchase and operate the line. The company was acquired by Itel Corporation in 1975. It serves as a home road for a large fleet of freight cars, including many that formerly belonged to the Ferdinand Railroad and Louisville, New Albany & Corydon.

Address of general offices: P. O. Box 2243, Dothan, AL 36302
Miles of road operated: 22
Reporting marks: FRDN, HS, LNAC
Number of locomotives: 2
Number of freight cars: 7,630
Principal commodities carried: Agricultural products
Shops: Hartford, Ala.
Junctions with other railroads:
Atlanta & St. Andrews Bay: Dothan, Ala.
CSX: Dothan, Ala.
Norfolk Southern: Dothan, Ala.
Radio frequencies: 161.250
Map: See Apalachicola Northern, page 29

A Hartford & Slocomb freight rolls into Dothan, Alabama, behind No. 1051, an NW2. The train includes trailers on flat cars, uncommon for a short line. Photo by Jim Shaw.

HOUSTON BELT & TERMINAL RAILWAY

The Houston Belt & Terminal was incorporated in 1905. It is owned by Union Pacific (formerly Missouri Pacific, 50 percent), Santa Fe (25 percent), and Burlington Northern (25 percent). HB&T built and maintained the passenger station used by its owners — indeed, Amtrak's Chicago-Houston *Texas Chief* and *Lone Star* used the station until 1974. HB&T is now out of the passenger business but is nonetheless a busy railroad serving both the fourth largest city in the U. S. and its deepwater port on Buffalo Bayou.

Address of general offices: 501 Crawford Street, Room 100, Houston, TX 77002

Miles of road operated: 57
Reporting marks: HBT
Number of locomotives: 14
Connects with:
Atchison, Topeka & Santa Fe
Burlington Northern
Port Terminal Railroad Association
Southern Pacific
Union Pacific
Radio frequencies: 160.530 (road), 160.380 (yard)

Houston Belt & Terminal 62, an MP15, poses on a highway overpass with Houston's impressive skyline as a backdrop. HB&T photo.

HURON & EASTERN RAILWAY

On March 27, 1986, the Huron & Eastern Railway purchased several former Chesapeake & Ohio branches (previously Pere Marquette) in the thumb of Michigan's lower peninsula: Bad Axe to Croswell; Poland to Sandusky, Palms to Harbor Beach, and Bad Axe to Kinde. The company subsequently took over the former PM line from Bad Axe to Saginaw.

In January 1991 Huron & Eastern took over the lease and operation of several former New York Central branches (previously Michigan Central) radiating out of Vassar, Mich., to Colling, Munger, Millington, and Harger. They had previously been operated by the Tuscola & Saginaw Bay.

The Saginaw-Bad Axe-Croswell line was built in 1882 as the narrow-gauge Port Huron & Northwestern Railroad. It was acquired in 1889 by the Flint & Pere Marquette Railroad and standard-gauged. In 1900 the Flint & Pere Marquette became part of the Pere Marquette Railroad. The Pere Marquette came under the control of the Van Sweringen brothers of Cleveland in 1924; it was merged by the Chesapeake & Ohio Railway in 1947.

The lines out of Vassar were part of Michigan Central's route from Detroit through Bay City to Mackinaw City.

Address of general offices: 538 East Huron Avenue, Vassar, MI 48768

Miles of road operated: 196

Reporting marks: HESR

Number of locomotives: 6

Number of freight cars: 200

Principal commodities carried: Sugar-beet pulp, grain, fertilizer, auto parts, chemicals

Shops: Bad Axe and Vassar

Junctions with other railroads:
Central Michigan: Harger, Mich.
CSX: Saginaw, Mich.

Radio frequencies: 160.440

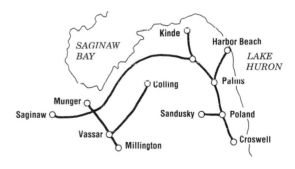

Huron & Eastern GP9 No. 100, wearing a blue-and-yellow paint scheme reminiscent of the Pere Marquette streamliners of 1946, switches covered hopper cars at the grain elevators in Kinde, Michigan, on August 4, 1986. Photo by Ronald Cady.

ILLINOIS CENTRAL RAILROAD

Illinois Central and Illinois Central Gulf are both described in *The Historical Guide to North American Railroads*, a book about railroad companies that have disappeared, and here is Illinois Central again, in a book about active railroads. To summarize what happened between 1972 and 1988 in 23 words: Illinois Central got married, put on weight, had a bunch of kids, got divorced, slimmed way down, and took its old name back.

The Illinois Central Railroad was chartered in 1851 to build a line from Cairo, at the southern tip of Illinois — the confluence of the Ohio and Mississippi rivers — to Galena, in the extreme northwestern corner of the state, with a branch to Chicago. A previous undertaking had resulted in a few miles of grading north of Cairo but nothing else; the IC was aided, however, by a land-grant act signed by President Millard Fillmore in 1850. Finished in 1856, the line was a Y-shaped railroad with its junction just north of Centralia (named for the railroad). The IC gave Chicago an outlet to the Mississippi for north-south traffic, and the railroad operated a steamboat line between Cairo and New Orleans.

South of the Ohio River

On the southern front, IC entered into a traffic agreement with the New Orleans, Jackson & Great Northern Railroad and the Mississippi Central Railway. The former had been opened in 1858 from New Orleans north through Jackson, Mississippi, to Canton, Miss.; the latter was completed in 1860 from Canton north to Jackson, Tennessee. IC completed its own line between Jackson, Tenn., and Cairo in 1873. (Traffic had previously used the Mobile & Ohio Rail Road between Jackson and Colum-

bus, Kentucky, and a riverboat between Columbus and Cairo.) In 1874 IC, the principal bondholder of the NOJ&GN and the Mississippi Central, took them over. The lines south of Cairo were built to the 5-foot track gauge that was standard in the South. The Cairo-New Orleans route was converted to standard gauge in one day on July 29, 1881.

In the 1870s railroads began to penetrate the fertile Yazoo Delta along the western edge of the state of Mississippi. IC's entry was the Yazoo & Mississippi Valley Railroad, incorporated in 1882 to build a railroad westward from Jackson, Miss. Meanwhile, a rival, the Louisville, New Orleans & Texas Railway, was under construction between Memphis and New Orleans via Vicksburg and Baton Rouge, west of IC's main line. That company obtained the backing of C. P. Huntington, who saw the route as a connection between his Southern Pacific at New Orleans and his Chesapeake, Ohio & Southwestern at Memphis. Huntington's forces completed the LNO&T in 1884, then purchased the Mississippi & Tennessee Railroad, whose line from Memphis to Grenada, Miss., funneled traffic to IC. Saber-rattling ensued — in the form of canceled traffic agreements — but Huntington's empire was in financial trouble. IC purchased the LNO&T and the Mississippi & Tennessee and consolidated them with the Yazoo & Mississippi Valley. The acquisition increased IC's mileage by 28 percent and greatly expanded IC's presence in the South.

IC's southern lines were connected by rail to the northern part of the system in 1889 with the completion of the Ohio River bridge at Cairo. In 1893 IC purchased the Chesapeake, Ohio & Southwestern (Louisville to Memphis) and in 1895 built a line into St. Louis from the southeast.

Later expansion

IC's line had been extended west of Galena to the Mississippi River, then across Iowa by leasing the Dubuque & Sioux City Railroad, which reached Sioux City in 1870. In the late 1880s under the leadership of E. H. Harriman the road undertook a westward expansion program. The Chicago, Madison & Northern was incorporated in 1886 to build from Chicago to a connection with the Centralia-Galena line at Freeport, Ill., then north to Madison and Dodgeville, Wisconsin. IC also constructed branches to Cedar Rapids, Iowa; Sioux Falls, South Dakota; and Omaha, Nebraska.

In 1906 the IC completed a line from Effingham, Ill., to Indianapolis, partly through new construction and partly through acquisition of narrow gauge lines. In 1908 it assembled a route from Fulton, Kentucky, to Birmingham, Alabama, largely on trackage rights, and in 1909 it acquired control of the Central of Georgia. In 1926 IC electrified its suburban line along the Chicago lakefront, and in 1928 it constructed a cutoff line between Edgewood, Ill., and Fulton, Ky., to bypass congestion at Cairo.

After World War II IC began to simplify its corporate structure, absorbing the Yazoo & Mississippi Valley and the Gulf & Ship Island, purchasing the Chicago, St. Louis & New Orleans, and acquiring control of the Alabama & Vicksburg and Vicksburg, Shreveport & Pacific, which had been leased by the Y&MV. In the 1950s it purchased several short lines: Waterloo, Cedar Falls & Northern (jointly with the Rock Island through a subsidiary, the Waterloo Railroad); Tremont & Gulf; Peabody Short Line; Louisiana Midland; and the west end of the Tennessee Central.

Illinois Central Gulf

In 1972 IC merged the parallel Gulf, Mobile & Ohio to create the Illinois Central Gulf Railroad. GM&O was itself the product of several mergers; its predecessors include the Gulf, Mobile & Northern; Mobile & Ohio; New Orleans Great Northern; and Alton railroads. (They are described in *The Historical Guide to North American Railroads*.) GM&O was a likely merger partner for the Illinois Central. It was a north-south railroad through much the same area as Illinois Central. In the 1960s the young management team that had put together the GM&O was no longer young, and there were no replacements in sight. At the same time ICG acquired three short lines, the Columbus & Greenville, the Bonhomie & Hattiesburg Southern, and the Fernwood, Columbia & Gulf.

The north-south lines of the resulting ICG map resembled an hourglass. Driving across Mississippi or Illinois from east to west you could encounter as many as eight ICG lines. The former IC routes converged at Fulton, Kentucky, just north of the Tennessee line, and the former GM&O line was less than 10 miles west of Fulton at Cayce. In addition to the north-south lines, ICG had eight routes that ran generally east and west:
• Chicago to Omaha and Sioux City (ex-IC)
• Springfield, Ill., to Kansas City (ex-GM&O)
• Indianapolis to Effingham, Ill. (ex-IC)
• Louisville to Paducah, Ky. (ex-IC)
• Birmingham, Alabama, through Corinth, Miss., to Memphis, Tenn. (a

mix of ex-IC track and ex-IC and ex-GM&O trackage rights)
• Montgomery, Ala., to Greenville, Miss. (ex-GM&O east of Columbus, Miss., and ex-Columbus & Greenville west of there)
• Meridian, Miss., to Shreveport, Louisiana (ex-IC; previously Alabama & Vicksburg and Vicksburg, Shreveport & Pacific)
• Mobile, Ala., to Natchez, Miss. (a combination of former GM&O, Bonhomie & Hattiesburg Southern, and Mississippi Central lines)

Shrinkage

ICG soon decided that the east-west lines didn't fit with a north-south railroad. Its 515-mile Chicago-Council Bluffs route was the longest of the six railroads connecting those cities. GM&O had tried to sell the Kansas City line to the Burlington in 1947, but it remained a long rural branch of the GM&O. The Louisville line, once the Chesapeake, Ohio & Southwestern, ultimately proved more valuable for its route to Memphis from the north than for the line east to Louisville. The Mobile-Natchez route had a ferry, not a bridge, at its west end, and the connecting railroads west of the Mississippi River led mostly to junctions with the Meridian-Shreveport line. In most cases, use of one of ICG's east-west routes as a bridge route required one of the connecting railroads to shorthaul itself (get less than the maximum possible haul and revenue from a carload of freight).

ICG decided to divest itself of the east-west routes. During the 1980s it shed more than two-thirds of its mileage, going from a peak of 9,634 route miles in 1973 to 2,872 miles at the end of 1989. In addition, on February 29, 1988, the railroad changed its name back to Illinois Central, having divested itself of nearly all the former Gulf, Mobile & Ohio routes it acquired in 1972, when it added "Gulf" to its name.

At the end of 1988 the Whitman Corporation (formerly IC Industries) spun off the IC, and in August 1989 control of the railroad was gained by the Prospect Group, which formerly controlled MidSouth Rail Corporation, another ICG spinoff. In late 1990 Illinois Central made an offer to purchase MidSouth. MidSouth rejected the offer; then as stock prices changed, IC withdrew the offer.

IC's slimming down has included not only routes but track and rolling stock. More than half its Chicago-New Orleans main line was double track; most of it is now single track with a computerized CTC system. IC scrapped its surplus cabooses and box cars and sold its excess locomotives. The result of all this is that IC is now a railroad that concentrates on long-haul business between Chicago and the Gulf of Mexico and works hard to capture traffic now moving by truck or barge.

Address of general offices: 233 N. Michigan Ave., Chicago, IL 60601
Miles of road operated: 2,900
Reporting marks: CIW, GMO, IC, ICG
Number of locomotives: 491

ILLINOIS CENTRAL SPINOFFS

The regional railroads created from IC's divestitures were:
• Gulf & Mississippi Railroad: Most former GM&O routes south of Tennessee (July 10, 1985). It is now part of MidSouth
• Chicago, Central & Pacific Railroad: Chicago-Omaha line and its branches to Cedar Rapids and Sioux City, Iowa (December 24, 1985).
• Paducah & Louisville Railway: Louisville-Paducah plus branches west and south of Paducah, and Paducah shops (August 27, 1986).
• MidSouth Rail Corporation: Meridian, Miss.-Shreveport, La., the former Alabama & Vicksburg and Vicksburg, Shreveport & Pacific; and Hattiesburg-Gulfport, Miss., the southern half of the former Gulf & Ship Island (March 31, 1986).
• Chicago, Missouri & Western Railway: Joliet, Ill.-St. Louis and Springfield, Ill.-Kansas City, Mo. (April 28, 1987). Chicago, Missouri & Western, which went bankrupt, was sold, the Chicago line to Southern Pacific and the Kansas City line to an independent group which operates it as the Gateway Western.
In addition, Norfolk Southern purchased the Fulton, Ky.-Birmingham, Ala. route in 1988.

Number of freight cars: 19,813
Principal commodities carried: Chemicals, coal, grain, paper products, piggyback and container traffic
Major yards: Champaign, Ill.; Chicago; Jackson, Miss.; Memphis
Principal shops: Centralia, Ill.; Jackson, Tenn. (Iselin); McComb, Miss.; Woodcrest, Ill.
Radio frequencies: 161.190 (road), 160.920 (road), 161.460 (yard), 161.025 (commuter)

Passenger routes:
Amtrak — Chicago-New Orleans, Chicago-Joliet
Metra — Chicago-Joliet
Historical and technical society: Illinois Central Historical Society, 556 South Elizabeth Drive, Lombard, IL 60148
Recommended reading: "Illinois Central: A railroad for the Nineties," by Michael W. Blaszak, in TRAINS Magazine, August 1992, pages 32-40

INDIANA & OHIO RAIL CORPORATION

The Indiana & Ohio Rail Corporation operates four railroads in southern Ohio; one of them reaches into southeast Indiana. The four roads all use some variant of the Indiana & Ohio name, and motive power is pooled.

Indiana & Ohio Railroad operates the former New York Central Whitewater District from Valley Junction, Ohio, northwest to Brookville, Ind. The line was built by the Whitewater Valley Railroad, which was incorporated in 1865 to build a railroad along the towpath of the Whitewater Valley Canal from Harrison, Ohio, to Hagerstown, Ind. Indiana & Ohio purchased the line and began service in 1979.

Indiana & Ohio Railway operates a former Pennsylvania Railroad line from Monroe, Ohio, to Lebanon and Mason and from Blue Ash, Ohio, to McCullough. Excursion service is operated between Lebanon and Mason by the Indiana & Ohio Scenic Railway. The Lebanon-Mason and Blue Ash-McCullough segments are both part of the former Pennsylvania Railroad route between Dayton and Cincinnati (the former Cincinnati, Lebanon & Northern). The line from Hageman Junction, between Mason and Lebanon, to Monroe is also former Pennsy track. The Indiana & Ohio Railway began operation in 1985.

Indiana & Ohio Central Railroad has three routes on which it operates freight service. It began service in July 1987 on a former Chesapeake & Ohio route (previously Hocking Valley) from Columbus southeast to Logan, Ohio. In October 1988 it began operation between Midland City and Greenfield, Ohio, on what was once part of Baltimore & Ohio's Wash-

ington-St. Louis main line. Service began in October 1990 on the third segment, from Fayne (Washington Court House) northwest to Springfield, Ohio, on a former Grand Trunk Western line (previously Detroit, Toledo & Ironton).

Indiana & Ohio Eastern Railroad operates a former Baltimore & Ohio line from Vauces, near Chilicothe, Ohio, east to Red Diamond, and from

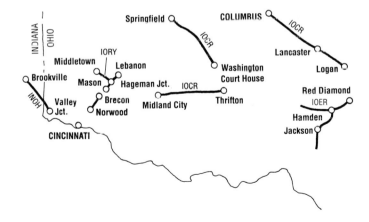

Hamden south through Wellston and Jackson to Firebrick. The Vauces-Red Diamond line was once also part of B&O's Washington-St. Louis line.

Address of general offices: 2856 Cypress Way, Cincinnati, OH 45212
Miles of road operated: 220
Reporting marks: INOH, IOCR, IOER, IORY
Number of locomotives: 5
Number of freight cars: 100
Shops: Logan, Ohio; Mason, Ohio
Passenger routes: Lebanon-Mason (Indiana & Ohio Scenic Railway)

Junctions with other railroads:
Conrail: Columbus, Ohio; Valley Junction, Ohio; Monroe, Ohio; Cincinnati, Ohio; Springfield, Ohio
CSX: Cincinnati, Ohio; Columbus, Ohio; Fayne, Ohio; Middletown, Ohio; Midland City, Ohio; Vauces, Ohio
Grand Trunk Western: Cincinnati, Ohio; Springfield, Ohio
Norfolk Southern: Cincinnati, Ohio; Columbus, Ohio
Radio frequencies: 161.385, 160.575 (INOH); 161.295, 160.695 (IOCR and IOER)

INDIANA HARBOR BELT RAILROAD

The Indiana Harbor Belt was incorporated in 1896 as the East Chicago Belt Railroad. It received its present name in 1907, when it took over the Michigan Central's rights in the Chicago Junction Railway, which had a route from Whiting, Indiana, to Franklin Park, Illinois. Until 1911 the IHB was jointly owned by Michigan Central and Lake Shore & Michigan Southern, both part of the New York Central System. At that time 20 percent interests were sold to Chicago & North Western and the Milwaukee Road. Penn Central and later Conrail inherited NYC's interest. Present ownership is divided between Conrail and CP Rail System (Soo Line).

IHB's main line extends from the industrial area at the southern end of Lake Michigan west and north through Blue Island and La Grange, Ill., to Franklin Park, forming a belt line much of the way around Chicago. The

Two representatives of Indiana Harbor Belt's all-switcher locomotive roster move a cut of cars in Blue Island Yard in September 1985. Photo by R. B. Olson.

route bypasses the rail congestion of Chicago and reduces transit time through the Chicago gateway.

Address of general offices: 2721 161st St., Hammond, IN 46323-1099
Miles of road operated: 114
Reporting marks: IHB
Number of locomotives: 90
Number of freight cars: 1,177
Major yards: Hammond, Ind. (Gibson); Riverdale, Ill. (Blue Island)
Shops: Hammond, Ind. (locomotives); Riverdale, Ill. (cars)
Connects with:
Atchison, Topeka & Santa Fe
Baltimore & Ohio Chicago Terminal
Belt Railway of Chicago
Burlington Northern
Chicago & North Western
Chicago, Central & Pacific
Chicago Short Line
Chicago SouthShore & South Bend
Chicago, West Pullman & Southern
Conrail
CSX
Elgin, Joliet & Eastern
Grand Trunk Western
Illinois Central
Iowa Interstate
Norfolk Southern
CP Rail System (Soo Line)
Southern Pacific
Union Pacific
Wisconsin Central
Radio frequencies: 160.980, 161.070, 160.665 (Gibson hump), 161.565 (Blue Island hump)
Recommended reading: "Change on the Harbor," by Michael W. Blaszak, in TRAINS Magazine, March 1986, pages 22-37

INDIANA HI-RAIL CORPORATION

Indiana Hi-Rail operates on numerous separate segments of track in Illinois, Indiana, Kentucky, and Ohio. They are grouped below by ancestry. In addition, Indiana Hi-Rail operates two short lines, the Poseyville & Owensville Railroad and the Spencerville & Elgin Railroad, under contract.

Ex-Conrail (New York Central)

Connersville to Beesons, Ind., purchased in December 1981. This is Indiana Hi-Rail's original line.

Ex-Conrail (Pennsylvania Railroad)

Woodville to Tiffin, Ohio. Indiana Hi-Rail acquired the line in 1990. It was once part of the Pennsylvania Railroad route between Mansfield and Toledo, Ohio.

Ex-Illinois Central

Newton, Illinois, through Olney and Browns, Ill., and Evansville, Ind., to Henderson, Kentucky. Indiana Hi-Rail purchased the southern part of the line in May 1986 and the rest in August 1990.

Cisco, Ill., through Decatur and Elwin to Assumption, on a segment of Illinois Central's original north-south line through Illinois. Indiana Hi-Rail began operation on the line in November 1986.

Ex-Norfolk & Western (Nickel Plate)

New Castle, Ind., to Connersville on a former Nickel Plate branch (long ago, Lake Erie & Western). Operation of the line began in December 1981.

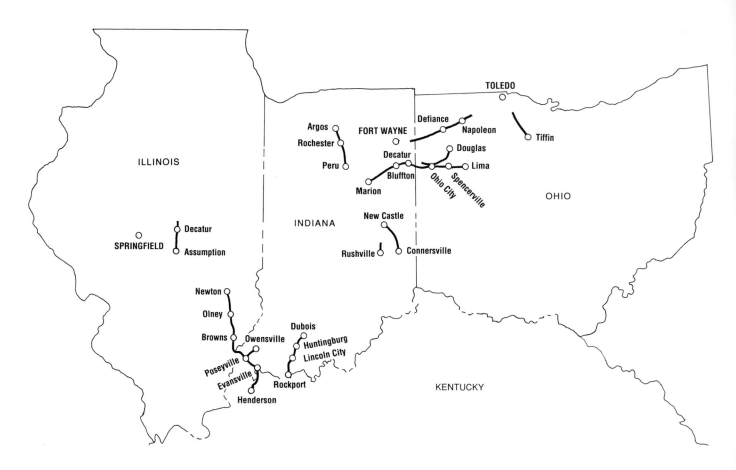

ILLINOIS

TOLEDO

Argos
Rochester
Peru

FORT WAYNE

Defiance
Napoleon

Tiffin

Decatur
Bluffton

Douglas
Lima

Marion

Ohio City

Spencerville

OHIO

INDIANA

New Castle

Rushville

Connersville

SPRINGFIELD

Decatur
Assumption

Newton

Olney

Browns
Owensville
Poseyville
Evansville
Henderson

Dubois
Huntingburg
Lincoln City
Rockport

KENTUCKY

Rushville, Ind., to a point about 5 miles north on a line that used to go to New Castle (also ex-LE&W). Operation began in February 1983.

Peru north to Argos, Ind., a short segment of the former Nickel Plate line from Indianapolis to Michigan City, Ind. (ex-LE&W). The Peru-Rochester segment is slated for abandonment.

Marion, Ind., east through Warren to Douglas, Ohio, part of the Toledo to St. Louis route (ex-Toledo, St. Louis & Western).

Ex-Norfolk & Western (Wabash)

Woodburn, Ind., near Fort Wayne, through Defiance, Ohio, to Liberty Center, Ohio, on what was once Wabash's Fort Wayne-Toledo route.

Ex-Southern Railway

Huntingburg, Ind., north to Dubois, southeast to Tell City, and south to Rockport. The three lines are former Southern Railway branches. The line to Dubois used to continue to the resort of French Lick; the main route south of Huntingburg was part of a line to Evansville; and the Tell City and Rockport routes were branches that reached south to the Ohio River. Indiana Hi-Rail leased the lines from Norfolk Southern in 1989. The Santa Claus-Tell City segment was abandoned in 1991.

Poseyville & Owensville Railroad

The 11-mile Poseyville & Owensville extends from Poseyville, Ind., northeast to Owensville on a short piece of the former Louisville & Nashville (ex-Chicago & Eastern Illinois) branch to Mount Vernon, Indiana. Poseyville & Owensville acquired the line in 1987.

Spencerville & Elgin Railroad

The Spencerville & Elgin Railroad runs from Glenmore, Ohio, east to Lima. The line is ex-Conrail, part of the former Erie-Lackawanna main line to Chicago. It is owned by the Van Wert County-Allen County Port Authority. It began operation of the line in 1978; Indiana Hi-Rail took over the operation in 1991.

Address of general offices: R. R. 1, Box 242, Connersville, IN 47331
Miles of road operated: 470
Reporting marks: GSOR, IHRC
Number of locomotives: 26
Number of freight cars: 520
Junctions with other railroads:
Central Railroad of Indianapolis: Marion, Ind.
Conrail: Delphos, Ohio; Lima, Ohio; New Castle, Ind.; Woodville, Ohio
CSX: Connersville, Ind.; Defiance, Ohio; Evansville, Ind.; Henderson, Ky.; Olney, Ill., Rushville, Ind., Tiffin, Ohio
Grand Trunk Western: Lima, Ohio
Illinois Central: Decatur, Ill.; Newton, Ill.
Indiana Rail Road: Newton, Ill.
Indiana Southern: Evansville, Ind.
Norfolk Southern: Argos, Ind.; Bluffton, Ind.; Browns, Ill.; Evansville, Ind.; Huntingburg, Ind.; Maple Grove, Ohio; Peru, Ind.; Woodburn, Ind.
Radio frequencies: 160.590, 160.845, 160.695, 161.505

INDIANA RAIL ROAD

In 1906 the Indianapolis Southern Railroad, a subsidiary of the Illinois Central, completed a line from Effingham, Illinois, on IC's main line, east and north to Indianapolis, Indiana. Part was new construction; the segment between Sullivan and Switz City, Ind., was the former narrow gauge Illinois & Indiana Railroad — incorporated in 1880 and reorganized and renamed several times before it came under IC control in 1900.

In 1977 Illinois Central Gulf petitioned to abandon 89 miles of the line from Switz City to Indianapolis. Much of it had a 10-mph speed limit because of track conditions. A year later the Federal Railroad Adminis-tration embargoed 56 miles of that segment, from Bloomington to Indianapolis, because of track conditions.

In the late 1970s Thomas Hoback wanted to buy a railroad and began negotiations with ICG to purchase the Indianapolis line. Negotiations ended when ICG obtained state and federal funds to repair the track sufficiently to raise the speed limit to 25 mph. In 1983 ICG changed its course and decided to sell the line. Hoback resumed negotiations, and in December 1985 he purchased the Sullivan-Indianapolis segment through a holding company, Indianapolis Terminal Corporation.

Indiana Rail Road began operations March 18, 1986. Its principal jobs are to carry coal to an Indianapolis Power & Light power plant at Indianapolis and a Central Illinois Public Service plant at Lis, Ill., and to serve Marathon Oil's refinery at Robinson, Ill.

In August 1989 Indiana Rail Road acquired a 40-mile line from Indianapolis north to Tipton, the south end of the former Norfolk & Western (ex-Nickel Plate) line between Indianapolis and Michigan City. It abandoned the line in November 1991. Indiana Transportation Museum operates excursion service on it by agreement with Norfolk Southern. In 1990 the Indiana Rail Road purchased the Sullivan-Newton, Ill., segment of the line and also IC's Newton-Browns, Ill., line, but sold the latter to Indiana Hi-Rail in May 1992. In addition to freight trains, the road operates a dinner train, the *Hoosierland Limited*, out of Indianapolis.

Address of general offices: Senate Avenue Terminal, Box 2464, Indianapolis, IN 46206-2464

Miles of road operated: 160

Reporting marks: INRD

Number of locomotives: 12

Number of freight cars: 71

Principal commodities carried: Coal, lumber, petroleum products

Shops: Indianapolis

Junctions with other railroads:

Conrail: Indianapolis, Ind.

CSX: Bloomington, Ind.; Indianapolis, Ind.; Sullivan Ind.

Illinois Central: Newton, Ill.

Indiana Hi-Rail: Newton, Ill.

Indianapolis Union: Indianapolis, Ind.

Indiana Southern: Switz City, Ind.

CP Rail System (Soo Line): Linton, Ind.

Radio frequencies: 161.100

Passenger routes: Indianapolis-Morgantown, Ind. (*Hoosierland Limited* dinner train)

Recommended reading: "High times on the Hi-Dry," by Gary W. Dolzall and Stephen F. Dolzall, in TRAINS Magazine, June 1988, pages 24-29

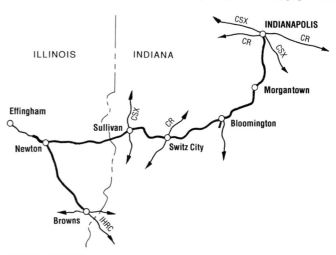

INTERSTATE COMMERCE COMMISSION

The Constitution of the United States, Article I, Section 8, gave Congress the power to regulate commerce among the several states. In 1886 the Supreme Court of the U. S. ruled that the Illinois Railroad Act of 1871 (which established a commission to fix maximum rates) was in violation of the Fourteenth Amendment to the Constitution (no state may deprive a person of property without due process) and that therefore the states could not regulate interstate commerce.

The Interstate Commerce Act was passed in February 1887. The Act applied to all railroads engaged in interstate commerce, even if their lines were located entirely within one state, and it also applied to riverboats, barges, ferries, and the like owned or controlled by railroads. The Act required railroads to publish their rates and give advance notice of change, and stated that rates charged by the railroads had to be "just and reasonable," but set no standards for reasonableness. Railroads were forbidden to give preference, advantage, special rates, or rebates to any person, company, location, or type of traffic. They were not allowed to charge more for a short haul than for a long haul under the same circumstances when the short haul was a segment of a longer haul — it could not cost more to ship an item from New York to Baltimore than to ship it from New York to Washington. The act prohibited pooling, the sharing of revenue.

Finally, the Act created the Interstate Commerce Commission. Its members were to be appointed by the President, and the commission was authorized to investigate violations of the Act and order the cessation of wrongdoing. However, ICC orders required an order by a federal court to become effective. The Interstate Commerce Act was the first important federal regulation of big business, and the ICC was the first independent regulatory body.

Initially the ICC had little power. In 1897 the Supreme Court ruled that the ICC had no power to fix rates and took most of the bite out of the clause stating that the short haul should cost no more than the long haul. The situation began to change around the turn of the century. The Elkins Act (1903) increased the penalties for rate discrimination and made those who sought rebates as guilty as the railroads that granted them. The Hepburn Act (1906) gave the commission power to determine maximum rates and declared that any order of the ICC had the force of a court order. It also introduced new accounting methods and raised the number of commissioners to seven. The Mann-Elkins Act of 1910 set up a special court to hear ICC cases and gave the ICC authority to begin judicial proceedings against railroads without the need for the Attorney General to initiate the action. It gave the ICC power to suspend rate increases pending hearings and laid on the railroads the burden of proof that the rate — not just the increase — was just and reasonable. The 1910 Act also extended the ICC's jurisdiction to telephone and telegraph companies (that authority was transferred to the Federal Communications Commission in 1934).

The ICC soon grew to have authority over almost every aspect of railroading: locomotive boilers, passenger accounting, diameter of grab irons, and speed limits, to cite a few items at random. The railroads reached their peak in extent and influence about 1915, about the time the ICC was

The Interstate Commerce Commission building stands on the northwest corner of 12th Street and Constitution Avenue in Washington. Photo by Don Phillips.

hitting its stride. Ironically, just as the railroads began to suffer from the competition of highways and waterways, the ICC set out to protect the public from the railroads.

The Transportation Act of 1920 contained a clause granting the railroads a fair return. The Act (which was repealed in 1933) also allowed the ICC to set minimum rates and instructed the ICC to prepare a plan to consolidate the railroads of the U. S. into a few large systems. By 1952 the ICC had jurisdiction over railroads, ferries, pipelines, bridges, internal and coastal shipping, trucks, and buses — but the majority of internal waterway and truck traffic was, by virtue of one law or another, exempt from ICC control. The ICC's authority over the railroads extended to the setting of maximum and minimum rates, approving or disapproving consolidations and mergers, authorizing construction and abandonment of lines, and issuance of securities — indeed, every aspect of the railroad business but labor relations.

The Transportation Act of 1958 gave the ICC jurisdiction over passenger train discontinuances, previously under the authority of the state commissions, and the ICC earned a reputation for capriciousness in such matters. In the matter of mergers the ICC functioned at a glacial pace. Proceedings in connection with the proposed merger of Rock Island and Union Pacific stretched out for ten years. (Some blame can be placed on the protestations of other roads, which usually adopt not the attitude "We're still better than they'll ever be," but "They'll take away all our business.")

Regulation of railroads reached the point that the ICC could and did require railroads to continue operations that lost money — it was depriving the railroads of property without due process. In 1962 President John F. Kennedy criticized the regulatory structure in a message to Congress, but it fell to his successor, Lyndon B. Johnson, to establish the Department of Transportation in 1966. The DOT was to develop and coordinate policies that would encourage a national transportation system (some rate-making and regulatory functions remained with the ICC). The Federal Railroad Administration is the DOT agency that deals with railroads.

Deregulation came on October 14, 1980, when President Jimmy Carter signed into law the Staggers Rail Act, named for Rep. Harley O. Staggers of West Virginia. It constituted massive deregulation of the railroads, including provisions to raise any rate that fell below 160 percent of out-of-pocket costs (later 180 percent) and to enter into contracts with shippers to set price and service, both without ICC approval.

Recommended reading:

Enterprise Denied, by Albro Martin, published in 1971 by Columbia University Press, 440 West 110th Street, New York, NY 10025 (ISBN: 0-231-03508-X)

Transportation: The Domestic System, by Robert C. Lieb, published in 1978 by Reston Publishing Co., Reston, VA 22090 (ISBN: 0-87909-843-0)

IOWA INTERSTATE RAILROAD

The Rock Island & La Salle Rail Road was chartered in 1847 to build a railroad between the Mississippi River at Rock Island, Illinois, and the Illinois & Michigan Canal at La Salle. The charter was soon amended to extend the railroad all the way to Chicago and rename the company the Chicago & Rock Island Rail Road. Construction began in 1851, and the railroad was opened between Chicago and Rock Island in 1854. The railroad built the first bridge across the Mississippi in 1856 to join its rails with those of the Mississippi & Missouri Railroad. Through sale and consolidation the two railroad companies became the Chicago, Rock Island & Pacific Railroad. The rails reached the Missouri River at Council Bluffs, Iowa, opposite Omaha, on May 11, 1869, just one day after the golden spike was driven linking the Union Pacific and Central Pacific at Promontory, Utah.

When the bankrupt Rock Island ceased operation on March 31, 1980, several agencies took over operation on portions of the line. Chicago's Regional Transportation Authority purchased the Chicago-Joliet line so Rock Island's commuter service could continue. Freight service on that segment was operated by Chicago Rail Link (later purchased by Chicago West Pullman Transportation). The Joliet-Bureau-Peoria portion was operated briefly by the Elgin, Joliet & Eastern, then equally briefly in part by Burlington Northern and in part by Winchester & Western. In August 1980 Baltimore & Ohio began operating the Joliet-Bureau portion of the main line and part of the Peoria branch, with trackage rights from Joliet east to Blue Island. Farther west, short segments of the main line were operated by Davenport, Rock Island & Northwestern; Milwaukee Road; and Chicago & North Western

In November 1981 the Iowa Railroad began operating the west end of the route from Council Bluffs to Dexter, Iowa, 97 miles, plus branches to Audubon and Oakland. In June 1982 the Iowa Railroad extended its operation east to Bureau, Illinois, in hopes of capturing traffic moving between

Union Pacific at Council Bluffs and B&O at Bureau. An interesting quirk in Iowa's operations was a shared-track arrangement with the Milwaukee Road between Iowa City and West Davenport — Iowa Railroad used the track from 8 p.m. to 8 a.m., and Milwaukee Road used it from 8 a.m. to 8 p.m. The Iowa Railroad was able only to lease the track, not purchase it, and it was unable to obtain trackage rights east of Bureau. Iowa Railroad's operation was not particularly successful.

Several industries along the route and the Cedar Rapids & Iowa City Railway formed Heartland Corporation, which purchased the railroad between Council Bluffs and Bureau (except for a short piece at Des Moines that Chicago & North Western had bought) in October 1984. Included in the deal were branches to Oakland, Audubon, and Pella, Iowa, and Milan, Illinois, and trackage rights from Bureau to Blue Island. Heartland established an operating subsidiary, the Iowa Interstate Railroad, but startup was delayed while the new company asked the ICC for help in evicting the tenants, Iowa Railroad and Milwaukee Road.

Iowa Interstate Railroad began operations on November 2, 1984. The road's freight traffic is primarily local, moving to and from customers along the line. (It carries little bridge traffic moving between connecting railroads at Blue Island and Council Bluffs.) Iowa Interstate operates the Lincoln & Southern Railroad, a B. F. Goodrich subsidiary that owns the former Rock Island track from the Goodrich plant in Henry, Ill., south to Peoria.

Address of general offices: 800 Webster St., Iowa City, Iowa 52240
Miles of road operated: 598

Reporting marks: IAIS
Number of locomotives: 37
Number of freight cars: 398
Principal commodities carried: Steel, home appliances, grain, coal
Shops: Iowa City, Iowa, Council Bluffs, Iowa
Junctions with other railroads:
Atchison, Topeka & Santa Fe: Joliet, Ill.
Burlington Northern: Rock Island, Ill.; Council Bluffs, Iowa
Cedar Rapids & Iowa City: Iowa City
Chicago & North Western: Des Moines, Iowa; Grinnell, Iowa; Council Bluffs, Iowa
Chicago Central & Pacific: Council Bluffs, Iowa
Davenport, Rock Island & North Western: Davenport, Iowa
Elgin, Joliet & Eastern: Joliet, Ill., Minooka, Ill.
Grand Trunk Western: Blue Island, Ill.
Indiana Harbor Belt: Blue Island, Ill.
Kansas City Southern: Council Bluffs, Iowa
Norfolk Southern: Des Moines, Iowa
CP Rail System (Soo Line): Davenport, Iowa
Union Pacific: Council Bluffs, Iowa
Radio frequencies: 161.220, 160.305
Recommended reading: "Iowa Interstate: Humility, and profits, in the heartland," by Gary W. Dolzall, in TRAINS Magazine, June 1989, pages 44-55.

KANSAS CITY SOUTHERN RAILWAY

In 1890 Arthur Stilwell began construction of the Kansas City, Pittsburg & Gulf Railroad, a line intended to carry agricultural products to the Gulf of Mexico. The line was built directly south from Kansas City, creating the shortest Kansas City-to-Gulf route. In 1897 its rails reached the Gulf at the new city of Port Arthur, Texas — also built by Stilwell. Within two years the railroad entered receivership. Stilwell was squeezed out (he turned his hand to building the Kansas City, Mexico & Orient Railway)

and the KCP&G was reorganized as the Kansas City Southern Railway.

Discovery of oil in eastern Texas changed KCS's fortunes. Northbound petroleum and chemicals complemented southbound grain. To build up the railroad for increased traffic, Leonor F. Loree was brought in. He served from 1906 to 1936 as chairman of the executive committee. (For most of that period he was also president of Delaware & Hudson, explaining, perhaps, the similarity of the steam locomotive rosters of the two railroads.)

Between 1896 and 1907 William Edenborn built a railroad between New Orleans and Shreveport, Louisiana — the Louisiana Railway & Navigation Co. In 1923 he extended the line west to McKinney, Texas, within hailing distance of Dallas, by purchasing a Missouri-Kansas-Texas branch. William Buchanan started a logging railroad in southwestern Arkansas in 1896; by 1906 it was the Louisiana & Arkansas Railway, with a main line from Hope, Arkansas, south to Alexandria, La., and a short branch from Minden, La., to Shreveport.

L&A and LR&N merged in 1928 as the Louisiana & Arkansas Railway. Its New Orleans-Shreveport route and its line to Dallas were natural extensions of the Kansas City Southern, which in 1939 purchased almost all the capital stock of the L&A. The two roads unified their operations, but L&A continued to have some measure of separate existence.

The 1940s and 1950s saw KCS rebuilt with heavy rail, new ties, CTC, and diesels under the leadership of William N. Deramus, who was succeeded in 1961 by his son, William N. Deramus III. In the late 1960s, though, the road began to fall apart — the new rail, new ties, and new diesels of the previous decade all wore out at the same time, and the attention of management was taken up by an effort to diversify through the formation of a holding company, KCS Industries.

In late 1972 KCS experienced a rash of derailments and a traffic surge at the same time. The road recognized it had two problems: undermaintained track and midtrain helper locomotives positioned so they were pushing rather than pulling. The helper problem was easy to solve; the track required (and got) a massive rebuilding program. While the rebuilding was in process, the road landed a contract to move coal to power plants in Arkansas, Louisiana, and Texas — further justifying reconstruction.

The KCS has been surrounded by a storm of mergers, but an attempt to purchase the Gulf, Mobile & Ohio's Kansas City line in 1972 has been its only move toward expansion, and the road has remained independent.

Address of general offices: 114 W. 11th Street, Kansas City, MO 64105

Miles of road operated: 1,663

Reporting marks: KCS

Number of locomotives: 284

Number of freight cars: 7,025

Principal commodities carried: Coal, chemicals, paper products

Major yards: Shreveport, La. (Deramus)

140

Principal shops: Shreveport, La.
Radio frequencies: 160.260 (road and dispatcher to train), 160.350 (train to dispatcher)
Historical and technical society: Kansas City Southern Historical Society, 9825 Bellaire, Kansas City, MO 61571
Recommended reading: "The Kansas City Southern Story," by Fred W. Frailey, in TRAINS Magazine, August 1979, pages 22-29, and September 1979, pages 22-32

Five Kansas City Southern SD40-2s bring a unit coal train south through Pittsburg, Kansas, on August 31, 1985. Photo by G. E. Lloyd.

KANSAS CITY TERMINAL RAILWAY

The Kansas City Terminal was incorporated in 1906. In 1910 it absorbed the Kansas City Belt Railway and the Union Depot Co. of Kansas City. The company built Kansas City Union Station, which opened in 1914 (Amtrak now uses a new station just east of the old building). KCT is owned equally by Santa Fe, Burlington Northern, Chicago & North Western, Gateway Western, Kansas City Southern, Norfolk Southern, St. Louis Southwestern, Soo Line, and Union Pacific, one-twelfth each except for Burlington Northern, which owns one-sixth (because it inherited shares from Chicago, Burlington & Quincy and St. Louis-San Francisco), and Union Pacific, one-fourth (its own share plus those of Missouri Pacific and Missouri-Kansas-Texas).

Address of general offices: P. O. Box 412737, Kansas City, MO 64141-2737
Miles of road operated: 27
Reporting marks: KCT
Number of locomotives: 8
Number of freight cars: 60
Connects with:
Atchison, Topeka & Santa Fe
Burlington Northern
Chicago & North Western
Gateway Western
Kansas & Missouri Railway & Terminal Co.
Kansas City Southern
Norfolk Southern
St. Louis Southwestern (Cotton Belt)
CP Rail System (Soo Line)
Union Pacific
all at Kansas City, Mo., or Kansas City, Kans.
Radio frequencies: 161.310 (road and yard), 161.010 (dispatcher)

The visors over the rear windows of SW1200s 73 and 78 are a feature unique to KCT. Photo by Louis A. Marre.

KIAMICHI RAILROAD

In 1886 the Fort Smith & Southern Railway, which was financed by the St. Louis & San Francisco, was incorporated to construct a line from Fort Smith, Arkansas, southwest through Indian Territory (now Oklahoma) to the Red River; another company, also backed by the Frisco, built a line from the Red River to Paris, Texas. The line got the Frisco into Texas, but a little over a decade later an easier route lying well west of the Ozarks was completed, and the Monett, Missouri-Fort Smith-Paris route was reduced to secondary status. The route was severed north of Antlers, Okla., about 1980.

In 1902 the Frisco bought a short line running west from Ashdown, Ark., and extended it east to Hope, Ark., and west to Ardmore, Indian Territory. Burlington Northern, which acquired the Frisco in 1980, abandoned the west end of the line, from Madill, Okla., to Ardmore, Okla., in 1982.

Both routes were light-traffic lines, good candidates for spinning off to a short line.

The purchase of the two lines by Jack Hadley in 1987 aroused curiosity. The area was characterized by high unemployment, shippers were forsaking the railroad, and there was opposition from BN employees. Already reduced to approximately one-third the number that had been employed by the Frisco, they feared the loss of their jobs. The Kiamichi Railroad began operation July 22, 1987.

The Antlers-Paris line and the eastern half of the Hope-Madill line were at best 90-pound jointed rail on ties that had long since earned retirement, so the road undertook a track rehabilitation project. It offered improved service and attracted new customers, and within a two years it was employing more persons than BN had.

Kiamichi's offices are divided between a building in downtown Hugo and a building near the Hugo yard. The former Frisco depot in Hugo is now a museum run by the Choctaw County Historical Society; it is also the base for Hugo Historical Railroad's excursion trains, which are operated by the Kiamichi Railroad.

Address of general offices: P. O. Box 786, Hugo, OK 74743
Miles of road operated: 227
Reporting marks: KRR
Number of locomotives: 14
Number of freight cars: 120
Principal commodities carried: Coal, forest products, cement, grain

Kiamichi Railroad 3803 is a GP35 that Missouri Pacific, its previous owner, deturbocharged and downrated to 2000 h.p. Photo by Louis A. Marre.

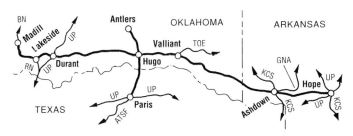

Shops: Hugo, Okla.
Junctions with other railroads:
Burlington Northern: Madill, Okla.
Chaparral: Paris, Texas
Graysonia, Nashville & Ashdown: Ashdown, Ark.
Kansas City Southern: Ashdown, Ark.; Hope, Ark.

Texas Northeastern: Paris, Texas
Texas, Oklahoma & Eastern: Valliant, Okla.
Union Pacific: Durant, Okla.; Hope, Ark.
Radio frequencies:
Recommended reading: "The Kiamichi Railroad Story," by Bob Thompson, in TRAINS Magazine, September 1989, pages 54-59

KYLE RAILROAD

In 1883 the Rock Island, the Milwaukee Road, and the Union Pacific made a tripartite agreement covering interchange of traffic at Omaha. The Chicago & North Western and a predecessor of the Wabash soon joined the pact; the Burlington, left out, protested, then Union Pacific fell into financial troubles. In 1889 the Rock Island completed its own line across northern Kansas to Colorado Springs, Colorado, with trackage rights to reach Denver, at first over the Rio Grande from Colorado Springs, later over the Union Pacific from Limon, Colo.

Rock Island shut down on March 31, 1980. The Union Pacific, Burlington Northern, Wabash Valley, Brandon, and Cadillac & Lake City railroads operated portions of RI's Colorado main line in 1980 and 1981, but none of the operations had any permanence. Fourteen counties along the route formed the Mid States Port Authority to acquire the line.

The Authority contracted with Kyle Railways, a shortline operator, to provide service. Kyle began operating between Limon, Colo., and Courtland, Kan., on February 16, 1982, and soon extended its operations east to Clay Center and Mahaska. In 1976 Kyle purchased a former Missouri Pacific line between Scandia and Yuma Junction, Kan.

On June 2, 1991, Kyle began operation on its Solomon division: 347 miles of leased Union Pacific track in Kansas: Frankfort to Lenora, Downs to Stockton, Jamestown to Burr Oak, and Beloit to Solomon, plus trackage rights from Solomon to Salina. The first three segments are former Missouri Pacific lines; Beloit-Solomon-Salina is Union Pacific proper.

The principal reason for the line's existence is wheat. The railroad serves a wheat-growing area remote from other railroads and is at its busiest during the summer wheat harvest.

Address of general offices: Third and Railroad Avenue, Phillipsburg, KS 67661
Miles of road operated: 778
Reporting marks: KYLE
Number of locomotives: 21
Number of freight cars: 696 (all covered hoppers)
Principal commodities carried: Grain
Shops: Phillipsburg, Kan.
Junctions with other railroads:
Atchison, Topeka & Santa Fe: Concordia,Courtland, and Osborne, Kan.
Burlington Northern: Norton, Kan.
Union Pacific: Colby, Kan.; Limon, Colo.; Salina, Kan.
Radio frequencies: 160.440, 160.275
Recommended reading: "Not a Rocket, but it moves," by Frank W. Bryan, in TRAINS Magazine, October 1988, pages 48-53

RAILROAD LABOR RELATIONS

The industrialization of America required that workers migrate to the new factories from farms and small shops. Working conditions were often bad, and there was little incentive for the factory owners to improve them because there was a ready supply of cheap labor; an employee who was dissatisfied could be replaced quickly.

Like other industries, railroading was labor-intensive and working conditions were difficult — much of the work was done out in the weather — but it differed in some aspects. Train crews regularly had to travel long distances and remain away from home; they worked not until the whistle blew at the end of a shift but until they reached their destination; and they worked in small groups without direct management supervision.

Railroad unions began as fraternal and protective organizations. Operating trains was a dangerous occupation — dismemberment and death were frequent, and there were widows and orphans to care for. The Brotherhood of Locomotive Engineers was formed in 1863. Other brotherhoods followed: conductors in 1868, firemen in 1873, trainmen in 1883. The brotherhoods were conservative — the engineers even had a no-strike policy. Railroaders felt some distrust of the unions that were forming in other industries because of their strong association with socialism.

The first major railroad strike occurred in 1877. During the economic depression that followed the Panic of 1873, the Baltimore & Ohio cut wages. A spontaneous strike against the B&O spread to other railroads. The strike turned into riots, and public sympathy for the railroad workers disappeared. President Rutherford Hayes used federal troops to quell the riots and restore railroad operation. The strike increased management's distrust of the unions and spurred the unions to better organization.

Eugene Debs attempted to organize railroad workers in 1892 as the American Railway Union. His activities culminated in the disastrous Pullman strike of 1894. He was jailed, and without his leadership his union collapsed. Several rail craft unions were formed soon afterward and eventually came under the American Federation of Labor.

The federal government initially sided with managment as it grappled with the problem of the labor unions. In 1894 federal judge William Howard Taft (later president) said that railroads should be off limits to organized labor, because railroads were necessary to the life, health, and comfort of the people. The Sherman Antitrust Act of 1890, which was supposed to protect the public from monopoly and conspiracy, was used far more often against labor than against big business. The Erdman Act of 1898 cleared up the railroad labor situation to a degree by providing for mediation and arbitration and for the continuance of work while they were in progress. There were no major strikes for 25 years thereafter.

In 1915, the brotherhoods asked for overtime to start after 8 hours rather than 10. At that time freight rates had been frozen for 20 years and the railroads were losing money. The threat of a national strike loomed just as the United States was about to become involved in World War I. On September 2, 1916, President Woodrow Wilson signed into law the Adamson Act, which provided that 8 hours or a trip of 100 miles, whichever was completed first, constituted a day's work. That standard remained in force until 1985.

The U. S. entered World War I on April 6, 1917. In December President Wilson placed the railroads under the direction of the United States Railroad Administration. The Railroad Wage Commission was established, and wages were standardized nationwide, even though railroad management complained that working and living conditions differed across the country. By the end of the war railroad wages had doubled and new work rules had established the amount of work that could be done and by whom. For example, a road engine crew couldn't perform a switching maneuver if a switching crew was available (or the crew would have to be paid an extra day's wages for it); an electrician couldn't be asked to connect an air hose. There was considerable pressure from labor to nationalize the railroads, and about that time the Interstate Commerce Commission put forth its plan to consolidate the railroads of the U. S. into 19 systems. Government's attitude toward labor was changing rapidly, because organized labor had been recognized as a voting force.

About this same time the regulatory processes of the ICC were coming up to speed, and the federal government began programs of highway and waterway construction, in effect subsidizing the railroads' competitors. The Transportation Act of 1920 increased government's role in settling labor disputes and established the U. S. Railroad Labor Board. The Board immediately supported a 22 percent wage increase, just before the economy took a turn downward, then recommended a 12 percent cut. A strike ensued.

The Railway Labor Act became law in 1926. It guaranteed workers the right to organize and bargain collectively, and it ordered the railroads to make and maintain agreements and to settle disputes peaceably. Both unions and management were happy with it.

Through much of the 20th century, railroad workers have been paid well. Between 1926 and 1987 railroad wages rose at an average annual rate of 5.27 percent. Manufacturing wages rose at 4.84 percent per year over the same period (in 1926 they had been considerably lower than railroad wages), and the Consumer Price Index rose at 3.07 percent. Railroad unions have gained from Congress some unique arrangements, including income protection when jobs are affected by mergers, employer-funded unemployment benefits for striking workers, and the right to engage in secondary picketing — a union can extend the strike to other railroads to get them to apply pressure to the primary railroad, so a local strike can quickly become national. Further complicating matters, railroad management must deal with a dozen unions, each a little different and each wanting just a bit more than another union got in their last round of talks. In other industries a single union represents most workers.

Management has traditionally tried to avoid strikes, because railroading has high fixed costs and what it produces — transportation — can't be stored up. Rail strikes no longer shut down the country as thoroughly as when railroads were the sole mode of transportation, but the effects of auto parts not reaching assembly lines or commuters not reaching work are quickly felt. Congress often intervenes in railroad labor matters and imposes its own settlement under the authority of the commerce clause of the Constitution.

Progress in the revision of work rules has been spotty. A 1963 measure abolishing full-crew laws and eliminating firemen from diesel locomotives was effectively nullified by subsequent agreements aimed at getting labor to withdraw its objection to the Penn Central merger. Demands for income protection when jobs are changed or abolished because of merger or abandonment have come up against the practical matter of how to get money from an insolvent railroad. The issue currently being grappled with is whether sale of a railroad or part of a railroad should impose existing labor agreements on the purchaser, who has not been a party to those agreements and where such an agreement is likely to result in the abandonment of the line rather than continued operation.

As railroads and the brotherhoods prepare to enter the 21st century, railroad labor laws and labor agreements remain an uneven patchwork. Recent deregulation of rail rates and the growth of nonunion trucking companies have not been paralleled by reform of railroad work rules, and restrictive labor agreements in force on the large railroads have in large part been responsible for the emergence of short lines and regional railroads. The situation remains complex and defies a simple solution.

Recommended reading:
The Railway Labor Act & the Dilemma of Labor Relations, by Frank N. Wilner, published in 1991 by Simmons-Boardman Books, Inc., 1809 Capitol Avenue, Omaha, NE 68102 (ISBN 0-911382-12-7)
"Income protection sets carriers, unions apart," by Frank N. Wilner, in TRAINS Magazine, March 1991, pages 23-24

LAKE STATE RAILWAY

The earliest ancestor of Lake State Railway began operation in 1878 as the Lake Huron & Southwestern Railroad, a 38-inch-gauge logging railroad at Tawas City, Michigan. In 1883 the railroad made a connection with the Michigan Central Railroad (later New York Central) at Alger. In 1886 the road was standard-gauged and extended north along the west shore of Lake Huron to Alpena. It was renamed the Detroit & Mackinac Railway in 1895. A year later the railroad was extended south to Bay City. In 1904 it reached Cheboygan, near the northern tip of Michigan's lower peninsula.

In 1976 D&M acquired portions of the former New York Central line from Bay City north through Cheboygan and on to Mackinaw City, essentially doubling its mileage and creating a second line the length of the peninsula. The state of Michigan owned the middle of the ex-NYC line from near Linwood to Gaylord; D&M owned the rest and used both that line and the "old" D&M line along the shore of Lake Huron as needed.

In 1984 the state ended its subsidy to the carferry that plied the Mackinac Strait, linking Michigan's two peninsulas. Industries along the line closed. D&M embargoed its line north of Gaylord and began dismantling it. In early 1992 the road was purchased by two of its vice presidents and became the Lake State Railway.

Address of general offices: P. O. Box 250, Tawas City, MI 48763
Miles of road operated: 275
Reporting marks: DM, LSRC
Number of locomotives: 16

Number of freight cars: 688
Principal commodities carried: Gravel, gypsum, shale, wood products, paper products
Shops: Tawas City, Mich.
Junctions with other railroads:
Central Michigan: Bay City, Mich.
CSX: Bay City, Mich.
Radio frequencies: 161.310
Recommended reading: "Detroit & Mackinac adieu," by Ron Cady, in TRAINS Magazine, July 1992, page 28

As this book went to press in the fall of 1992 Lake State had not yet adopted a new paint scheme. Its locomotives still carry the Detroit & Mackinac name, as exemplified by C425 No. 381, switching at Cheboygan, Michigan, in September 1983. TRAINS Magazine photo by J. David Ingles.

147

LAKE SUPERIOR & ISHPEMING RAILROAD

In 1896 the Cleveland Cliffs Iron Mining Co. opened the Lake Superior & Ishpeming Railway. The purpose of the railroad was to transport iron ore from Cleveland Cliffs' mines in Michigan's Upper Peninsula to the docks on Lake Superior at Marquette, Mich. Previously the ore had been handled by the Duluth, South Shore & Atlantic; the mining company saw economies in having its own railroad. In 1927 the LS&I was merged with the Munising, Marquette & Southeastern Railway, also a Cleveland Cliffs operation and a product of a merger of two small roads between Marquette and Munising, Mich. The new road became the Lake Superior & Ishpeming Railroad. Between 1952 and 1974 the LS&I built branch lines to serve mines and pellet plants near Ishpeming, and in 1963 it sold the Big Bay branch, which ran northwest from Marquette, to the Marquette & Huron Mountain Railroad. In 1979 LS&I abandoned its trackage east of Marquette, except for a 5-mile segment between Munising and the Soo Line at Munising Junction. That branch was sold to Wisconsin Central in 1989. LS&I continues to haul iron, both as ore and as magnetite and hematite pellets for its owner, Cleveland Cliffs Iron Co.

Address of general offices: 105 East Washington Street, Marquette, MI 49855
Miles of road operated: 49
Reporting marks: LSI
Number of locomotives: 21
Number of freight cars: 1,233
Principal commodities carried: Iron ore
Shops: Eagle Mills, Mich.
Junctions with other railroads:
Chicago & North Western: Eagle Mills, Mich.
Wisconsin Central: Eagle Mills, Mich.
Radio frequencies: 160.230

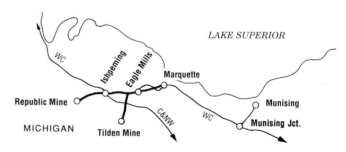

A pair of U30Cs purchased from the Burlington Northern brings a train of empty ore cars past Lake Superior & Ishpeming's last Alco diesel on July 3, 1989. Photo by Eric Hirsimaki.

LITTLE ROCK & WESTERN RAILWAY

The Little Rock & Western is one of several short lines created from the remains of the Rock Island. The LR&W bought the Perry-Pulaski, Arkansas, portion of RI's Choctaw Route (Little Rock-Oklahoma City-Amarillo, Texas-Tucumcari, New Mexico) to provide a rail outlet for the Arkansas Kraft Paper Mill located 3 miles east of Perry. Operation began in June 1980. In June 1986 the road leased another 35 miles of track from Perry west to Danville to serve a chicken farm operated by Continental Grain. The railroad is owned by Green Bay Packaging. It has a large fleet of interchange freight cars, primarily box cars and covered hoppers.

Address of general offices: P. O. Box 146, Perry, AR 72125
Miles of road operated: 79
Reporting marks: LRWN
Number of locomotives: 3
Number of freight cars: 797
Principal commodities carried: Paper products, corn
Shops: Perry, Ark.
Junctions with other railroads:
Union Pacific: North Little Rock, Ark.
St. Louis Southwestern: North Little Rock, Ark.

Little Rock & Western 102 is an Alco C420 formerly listed on Louisville & Nashville's roster as No. 1307. It was rebuilt by the Green Bay & Western. Photo by Jim Shaw.

Radio frequency: 160.965
Map: See Arkansas Midland, page 33

The Long Island Rail Road Company

LONG ISLAND RAIL ROAD

The Long Island Rail Road was chartered in 1834. It was intended to be one link in a complex New York-Boston route: ferry from Manhattan to Brooklyn; rail to Greenport, New York, at the northeastern tip of Long Island; steamer across Long Island Sound to Stonington, Connecticut; and rail to Boston. The line was completed to Greenport in 1844, but by 1850 the engineers who had assured LIRR backers that a railroad could never be built along the Connecticut shore had been proven wrong — an all-rail route between New York and Boston was capturing most of the business. The Long Island entered receivership and turned its attention away from Boston and toward local matters for several decades.

In 1880 Austin Corbin gained control of the railroad. He planned to make Montauk, N. Y., at the eastern tip of Long Island, a port for transatlantic shipping. His plans came to naught, but the capital he provided was useful to the railroad. The LIRR absorbed its competitors, including the New York & Flushing and the South Side Railway, and became the only railroad on the island. In 1885 LIRR began operating trains of flatcars to carry farmers' wagons into New York City — the first piggyback service.

Passenger service in Long Island's electrified zone is provided by Budd-built *Metropolitan* M-1 and M-3 M. U. cars. Two such trains are shown on July 5, 1984, meeting at Nassau tower in Mineola, New York, where the Oyster Bay branch, left, diverges from the main line. Photo by Tom Nelligan.

Under Alexander J. Cassatt the Pennsylvania Railroad acquired control of the Long Island in 1900 and included it in plans for Pennsylvania Station in New York City. Because of its involvement in the Penn Station project, LIRR was able to boast of mainline electrification with 600-volt DC third rail (1905), the first steel passenger car (1905), and the first all-steel passenger fleet (1927). The suburban boom on Long Island began in

the early 1920s, and LIRR's access to a terminal in Manhattan was a decided asset in building its commuter business.

The Long Island Rail Road found it was difficult to make money in the commuter business. Commuter service requires large amounts of rolling stock and correspondingly large numbers of employees to run it for two short periods each day, plus, of course, the track and stations to handle

Penn Station (Manhattan) LONG ISLAND SOUND
Flatbush Avenue (Brooklyn)
Port Washington
Oyster Bay
Port Jefferson
Greenport
Montauk
AMTK
Jamaica
Bay Ridge
Far Rockaway
Long Beach
Babylon
ATLANTIC OCEAN

In 1965 the Metropolitan Commuter Transportation Authority was created; it purchased the railroad from the Pennsylvania in 1966. In 1968 the Metropolitan Transportation Authority was formed; it now owns the LIRR.

The Long Island is the busiest passenger railroad in the U. S., carrying approximately 250,000 passengers on an average weekday. Its trains run from three western terminals —Penn Station in Manhattan, Flatbush Avenue in Brooklyn, and Hunterspoint Avenue in Queens — to destinations on ten routes. Most of the trains run through Jamaica station, the busiest through station in the U. S. New York-Port Washington trains branch off the main line west of Jamaica. Freight accounts for only one-tenth of LIRR's revenue.

Address of general offices: Jamaica Station, Jamaica, NY 11435
Miles of road operated: 320
Reporting marks: LI
Number of locomotives: 62, plus 14 push-pull control units
Number of locomotive-hauled passenger cars: 213
Number of self-propelled passenger cars: 935
Principal commodities carried: Foodstuffs, copper, rock salt
Shops: Queens, N. Y.
Junctions with other railroads:
Conrail: Fresh Pond Junction, N. Y.
New York Cross Harbor: Brooklyn, N. Y.
Radio frequencies: 160.380 (road and towers), 161.445 (dispatcher), 161.265 (yard)
Passenger routes: New York (Penn Station), Brooklyn (Flatbush Avenue), and Hunterspoint Avenue via Jamaica to Far Rockaway, Long Beach, Babylon, West Hempstead, Hempstead, Oyster Bay, Port Jefferson, Ronkonkoma, Greenport, and Montauk; New York (Penn Station) to Port Washington
Recommended reading: *Steel Rails to the Sunrise*, by Ron Ziel and George Foster, published in 1987 by Amereon House, P. O. Box 1200, Mattituck, NY 11952 (ISBN 0-8488-0368-X)

large crowds. Nor was the railroad helped by a New York Public Service Commission freeze on commuter fares from 1918 to 1947. LIRR went into the red in 1935. Taxes, the cost of grade-crossing elimination projects, and the maintenance required by heavy World War II traffic drove the railroad into bankruptcy.

New York State and LIRR's owner, the Pennsylvania Railroad, both proposed plans for bringing the road out of bankruptcy, and the two reached agreement in 1954. The plan adopted called for a 12-year rehabilitation period during which Pennsy would receive no dividends (indeed, Pennsy had received a return on its investment for perhaps 10 of the 50 years it had owned the Long Island) and fares could be increased to cover expenses. The plan also included relief from property taxes. Rehabilitation included modernization of cars and purchase of new ones, dieselization of the nonelectrified portion of the line, plant improvements, and increased service. LIRR's passengers were happy even if the accountants soon found themselves looking at balance sheets similar to those they had seen before.

MARYLAND & PENNSYLVANIA RAILROAD

The Maryland & Pennsylvania — the Ma & Pa, for short — used to be the quintessential, archetypal short line. It had to go 77 miles to get from Baltimore, Maryland, to York, Pennsylvania, which are less than 50 miles apart. Its steam locomotives were small and old, and its passenger cars were innocent of such modernities as steel construction, cast trucks, and vestibules.

The Maryland Central Railroad was chartered in 1867. It started construction in Baltimore, and entered receivership in 1884, about the time its three-foot-gauge track entered the town of Delta, Md., 44 miles northeast of Baltimore. It was reorganized in 1888 as the Maryland Central Railway.

The Peach Bottom Railway was opened in 1874 from York, Pennsylvania, to Peach Bottom, about 35 miles away on the Susquehanna River. By 1881 the narrow gauge railroad was in receivership; it was reorganized in 1882 as the York & Peach Bottom. In 1891 the York & Peach Bottom and the Maryland Central were merged as the Baltimore & Lehigh Railroad.

The new company went bankrupt in 1892. In 1894 the Pennsylvania portion of the road was reorganized as the York Southern, and the Maryland portion as the Baltimore & Lehigh Railway. They were standard-gauged in 1895 and 1900, respectively, and merged in 1901 to form the Maryland & Pennsylvania.

The Ma & Pa eked out an existence for more than half a century on local traffic, most of it on the northern part of the route. In 1958 the railroad abandoned the Maryland portion of its line, from Baltimore to Delta. In 1969 the road restored its Peach Bottom branch, which had been pulled up in 1903. Philadelphia Electric Co. was constructing a nuclear power plant at Peach Bottom, and inbound construction materials furnished revenue for the road for several years.

Emons Industries purchased the railroad in 1971, primarily as a means for entering the freight car leasing field. The railroad built a new shop at York in 1977 and began building new freight cars. When Conrail was formed, Ma & Pa picked up the former Pennsylvania Railroad line from York southwest to Walkersville, Md., plus a three-mile segment of the old Northern Central, Pennsy's direct route from Harrisburg through York to Baltimore. The Walkersville line was cut back to Hanover, Pa., in 1978, and the original Ma & Pa line was abandoned south of Red Lion, Pa., that same year. In 1983 Ma & Pa abandoned the rest of its original line between York and Red Lion.

Affiliated with the Maryland & Pennsylvania is Yorkrail, which operates 16 miles of a former CSX branch (earlier, Western Maryland) from

Maryland & Pennsylvania 84, an SW9, takes a short local freight out of York, Pennsylvania, in 1986. Photo by Jim Shaw.

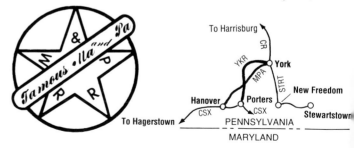

York southwest to Porters, where it connects with CSX.
Address of general offices: 96 South George Street, York, PA 17401
Miles of road operated: 26
Reporting marks: MPA
Number of locomotives: 10
Number of freight cars: 1,967
Principal commodities carried: Paper products, foodstuffs, furniture
Shops: York, Pa.
Radio frequencies: 160.335, 160.695

Junctions with other railroads:
Conrail: York, Pa.
CSX: Hanover, Pa.
Stewartstown: York, Pa.
Yorkrail: York, Pa.
Historical and technical society: Maryland & Pennsylvania Railroad Preservation and Historical Society, P. O. Box 224, Spring Grove, PA 17362

MARC (Maryland Rail Commuter)

When Amtrak took over long-distance trains in 1971, Baltimore & Ohio still operated a modest commuter service to Washington from Baltimore and Brunswick, Maryland (38 and 49 miles, respectively) plus one Baltimore-Washington train scheduled for persons working in Baltimore. Penn Central operated two local trains from Baltimore to Washington each morning and two back in the evening.

The Maryland Department of Transportation began subsidizing the B&O trains in 1975, and it acquired rebuilt locomotives and cars for those train in 1981. Increased service brought increased ridership, a new name, and increased service on the electrified Pennsylvania-Penn Central-Amtrak route, for which MARC bought 4 electric locomotives built by EMD under license from ASEA and acquired 11 coaches through Sumitomo Corporation of America.

At present MARC operates local trains throughout the day on Amtrak's electrified line between Washington and Baltimore; peak-hour trains operate another 36 miles northeast to Perryville, Md. Service on the two CSX (ex-Baltimore & Ohio) routes from Washington to Baltimore and from Washington to Martinsburg, West Virginia, is limited to peak hours because of freight traffic, but MARC is installing centralized traffic control on those routes. The CSX Baltimore-Washington route is the oldest rail passenger route in the U. S.; between West Baltimore and Relay, Md., passenger service has been operated continuously since May 1830. The ex-B&O Balti-

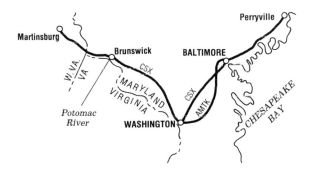

more-Washington route was also the location of the first telegraph line in the U. S.

MARC is planning extensions of the Brunswick route to Frederick and Hagerstown, a branch from the Amtrak route at Bowie south to La Plata, and extension of the Amtrak route northeast to Newark, Delaware. MARC coordinates its commuter rail services with connecting bus, light rail, and subway services in Maryland, and the routes to Washington offer direct connections at several stations with the Washington Metro.
Address of general offices: P. O. Box 8755, Baltimore-Washington

153

International Airport, MD 21240
Miles of road operated: 186
Number of locomotives: 11 diesel, 4 electric
Number of passenger cars: 88
Radio frequencies: CSX: 160.230, 160.320; Amtrak: 160.920
Passenger routes:
Amtrak: Washington-Baltimore-Perryville, Md.
CSX: Washington-Baltimore, Washington-Martinsburg, W. Va.

A Washington-Baltimore MARC train approaches Bowie, Maryland, on Amtrak's Northeast Corridor route. The body of the AEM7 was built in Austria; EMD built the running gear under license from ASEA. The coaches were built in Japan. Photo by William D. Middleton.

MASSACHUSETTS BAY TRANSPORTATION AUTHORITY

In 1947 the Metropolitan Transit Authority of Massachusetts took over the Boston Elevated Railway, a transit system serving Boston and 13 surrounding cities and towns with subway and elevated trains, streetcars, trackless trolleys, and buses. The MTA was succeeded in 1964 by the Massachusetts Bay Transportation Authority, whose scope encompassed 79 municipalities in eastern Massachusetts.

In 1964 three railroads operated commuter service to Boston: Boston & Maine to North Station and New Haven and New York Central (Boston & Albany) to South Station. None of the three was financially healthy, and in 1965 MBTA made its first assistance payment to Boston & Maine for operating commuter trains. Soon MBTA was underwriting all rail commuter service into Boston. In 1973 MBTA purchased former New Haven commuter lines to Attleboro, Stoughton, and Franklin, Mass., and a segment of the former New York Central line between Riverside and Framingham, Mass. In 1975 MBTA purchased Boston & Maine's rolling stock

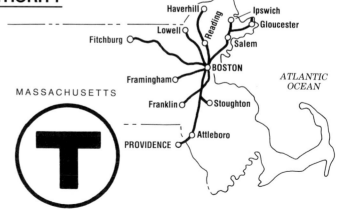

Boston's South Station, which also serves Amtrak, received high-level platforms in 1987 (the entire rebuilding of the station took 6 years, from 1984 to 1990). Three Massachusetts Bay Transportation Authority commuter trains stand at the platforms awaiting homeward-bound commuters. Photo by William D. Middleton.

and physical plant used for commuter service; B&M continued to operate the service for MBTA as before.

Penn Central operated the service out of South Station for MBTA; PC was succeeded by Conrail on April 1, 1976. In 1977 Conrail asked for a large subsidy increase for the ex-New Haven and ex-New York Central commuter service it had inherited from Penn Central. MBTA sought another operator and chose Boston & Maine, which took over the former New Haven and New York Central operations. In 1987 Amtrak was awarded the contract to operate the services.

In recent years MBTA's commuter equipment has undergone extensive modernization. New coaches built by Bombardier and new diesels from EMD and Morrison-Knudsen have replaced the fleet of ex-B&M Budd RDCs (the world's largest), long-distance coaches from the New Haven, an assortment of ex-NH diesels and RDCs, and rebuilt ex-Gulf, Mobile & Ohio F3s and F7s.

MBTA also operates Boston's transit system, which extends well into the suburbs, and an extensive suburban bus service.

Address of general offices: 10 Park Plaza, Boston, MA 02116
Miles of road operated: 244 (excluding transit)
Number of locomotives: 52
Number of passenger cars: 385
Radio frequencies: 160.320, 160.920, 160.800
Passenger routes:
Boston (North Station) to Fitchburg, Lowell, Haverhill, Reading, Ipswich, and Rockport, Mass.; Boston (South Station) to Stoughton, Forge Park, Needham Heights, Framingham, and Attleboro, Mass., and Providence, R. I.

Recommended reading:
Route of the Minute Man, by Tom Nelligan and Scott Hartley, published in 1980 by Quadrant Press, New York, NY (ISBN 0-915276-26-7)
Boston's Commuter Rail, by Thomas J. Humphrey and Norton D. Clark, published in 1985 and 1986 by Boston Street Railway Association, P. O. Box 102, Cambridge, MA 02238-0102
Change at Park Street Under, by Brian J. Cudahy, published in 1972 by Stephen Greene Press, P. O. Box 1000, Brattleboro, VT 05301 (ISBN 0-8289-0173-2)

McCLOUD RAILWAY

The McCloud River Railroad was incorporated in 1897 to provide access to the forests east of Mt. Shasta in northern California. It connects with Southern Pacific at Mt. Shasta and with Burlington Northern (formerly Great Northern) at Hambone (BN owns the line from Hambone east to Lookout, but McCloud River maintains and operates it). The line from Mt. Shasta over Signal Butte to McCloud has a single switchback east of the summit about 5 miles west of McCloud and 1000 feet higher — trains departing from Mt. Shasta in normal fashion arrive McCloud in reverse.

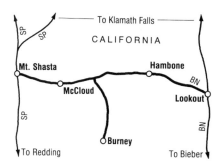

The McCloud River was owned for many years by the McCloud Lumber Company and later U. S. Plywood. In 1977 it was purchased by Itel Corporation. The line was completely rehabilitated in 1982 with the help of a grant from the Federal Railroad Administration. In May 1992 the road was purchased by its president, Jeff Forbis, and given its present name.
Address of general offices: P. O. Box 1500, McCloud, CA 96057
Miles of road operated: 132
Reporting marks: MR
Number of locomotives: 2
Number of freight cars: 20
Principal commodities carried: Forest products
Shops: McCloud, Calif.
Junctions with other railroads:

SD38-2 No. 39 and SD38 No. 38 are in charge of a McCloud River train at Bartle, California, in July 1983. Photo by Jim Shaw.

Burlington Northern: Hambone, Calif.
Southern Pacific: Mt. Shasta, Calif.
Radio frequencies: 160.695 (road), 161.025 (switching), 161.860 (switching)
Recommended reading: *Pine Across the Mountain*, by Robert M. Hanft, published in 1970 by Golden West Books, P. O. Box 8136, San Marino, CA 91108 (ISBN 0-87095-038-X)

METRA

Metra is the rail commuter service operator for northeast Illinois. The Regional Transportation Authority, under whose name the service was operated for several years, is a financial oversight agency which funnels state and federal funds to Metra; Chicago Transit Authority; and Pace, the suburban bus system.

Metra operates service with its own crews on its Milwaukee District to Fox Lake and Big Timber, Illinois, west of Elgin; on its Rock Island District to Joliet; and on Metra/Electric (ex-Illinois Central electrified lines) to University Park, South Chicago, and Blue Island. Metra subsidizes and equips service operated under contract by Burlington Northern to Aurora, by Chicago & North Western to Geneva, Harvard, and McHenry, Ill., and Kenosha, Wisconsin, and by Norfolk Southern (ex-Wabash) to Orland Park,

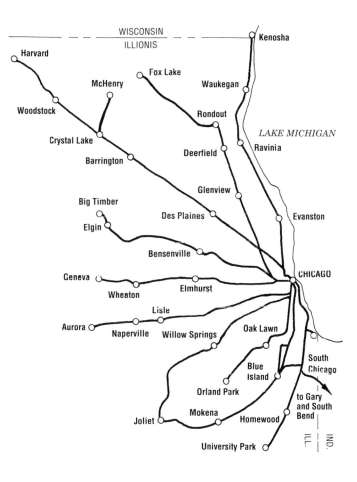

Ill.. Metra subsidizes the Illinois portion of Northern Indiana Commuter Transportation District's Chicago-South Bend service. Metra operates Heritage Corridor service on IC (ex-Gulf, Mobile & Ohio) to Joliet by trackage rights.

Local transit districts own some of the rolling stock: Chicago South Suburban Mass Transit District owns the Metra/Electric cars; West Suburban Mass Transit District owns the cars used on the BN; and Northwest Suburban Mass Transit District owns some of the cars and locomotives used on the routes to Fox Lake and Big Timber.

Several companies operate freight service on Metra's tracks. Chicago Rail Link, a subsidiary of the Broe Corporation, provides freight service on the Rock Island District lines north of Blue Island. Iowa Interstate operates freight service on the ex-RI lines southwest of Blue Island. CSX and Southern Pacific have overhead rights from Blue Island to Joliet. CP Rail System (Soo Line) provides the freight service on the Milwaukee District. The Wisconsin & Calumet Railroad, another Broe subsidiary, has overhead trackage rights from Chicago to Fox Lake.

Metra carries approximately 270,000 passengers on an average weekday. Two expansions of Metra service are planned: from Chicago to Antioch, Ill., on Wisconsin Central and a circumferential route from Aurora to Barrington, Ill., on the Elgin, Joliet & Eastern.

Address of general offices: 547 West Jackson Boulevard, Chicago, IL 60661.

Miles of road operated: 495

Reporting marks: RTA

Number of locomotives: 159

Number of passenger cars: 691

Number of electric M. U. cars: 173 (including 8 for South Shore service)

Shops:

Locomotive: 47th Street, Chicago (Rock Island District); 40th Street, Chicago (Chicago & North Western); Western Avenue, Chicago (Milwaukee District); 14th Street, Chicago (Burlington Northern)

Car: 49th Street, Chicago (Rock Island District); California Avenue, Chicago (Chicago & North Western); Western Avenue, Chicago (Milwaukee District); 14th Street, Chicago (Burlington Northern)

Four Metra/Electric "Highliners" slip out of subterranean Randolph Street Station in Chicago. Photo by William D. Middleton.

Radio frequencies:

BN: 161.100
C&NW: 161.040
IC (ex-GM&O): 160.920
Metra/Electric: 161.025

Milwaukee District: 161.520 (Big Timber)
Milwaukee District: 160.770 (Fox Lake)
NS: 160.440
Rock Island District: 161.610

Passenger routes:
Chicago (ex-C&NW station) to Geneva, Harvard, and McHenry, Ill., and Kenosha, Wis. (Chicago & North Western)
Chicago (Union Station) to Big Timber and Fox Lake (Metra)
Chicago (Union Station) to Orland Park (Norfolk Southern, ex-Wabash)
Chicago (Union Station) to Aurora (Burlington Northern)
Chicago (Union Station) to Joliet (Illinois Central, ex-Gulf, Mobile & Ohio)
Chicago (LaSalle Street Station) to Joliet (Metra)
Chicago (Randolph Street Station) to University Park, South Chicago, and Blue Island, Ill. (Metra/Electric), and South Bend, Ind. (jointly with Northern Indiana Commuter Transportation District — electrified)

COMMUTER EQUIPMENT

Nowadays commuter service is subsidized by city, regional, and state authorities as a cheaper, more efficient alternative to building more highways and parking lots. It is not viewed as a money-making operation — but, come to think it, neither is a freeway.

Before 1960, when railroads ran commuter service for their own accounts, it was traditionally the refuge of old coaches and locomotives that had been replaced in mainline service. Most railroads were reluctant to spend money on equipment that was used 4 hours a day, 5 days a week, for business that was marginally profitable — if it was profitable at all.

Chicago, Burlington & Quincy 700 was the first gallery car. Note how much higher it is than the conventional coach behind it. CB&Q photo

Driven by the idea that purpose-built equipment might bring efficiency, in the 1920s and 1930s a few roads purchased high-capacity coaches of lightweight construction. Others electrified their commuter operations. Double-deck cars had been around since the early days of

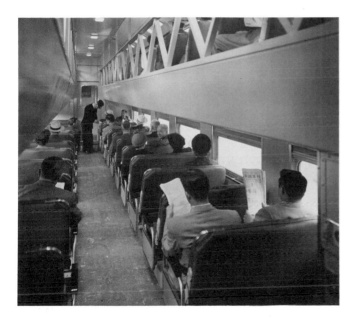

The interior of the gallery car has double seats on the main floor and single seats upstairs. The conductor can collect tickets from both levels while standing in the aisle. CB&Q photo.

railroading — you've seen etchings depicting people sitting on the roofs of the stagecoach-like cars. In 1932 the Pennsylvania Railroad designed and built for the Long Island a semi-double-deck coach in which seats were arranged two steps up or down from the aisle; after World War II Long Island used the design for self-propelled electric cars.

In 1950 the Chicago, Burlington & Quincy Railroad undertook modernization of its commuter service between Chicago and Aurora. The centerpiece of the modernization was a group of Budd-built coaches, "gallery" cars, which had a wide vestibule at the center of the car, low-back 2-and-2 seating on the main floor, balconies or galleries with single seats above the lower-level seats, and clear space above the lower-level aisle for headroom and to allow the conductor to collect tickets by reaching up for them. The cars seated 144 persons; almost half again as many as the single-level cars they replaced. They were comfortable and quiet, and they were air-conditioned — still a novelty in 1950.

Gallery cars appeared on Southern Pacific and Chicago & North Western in 1955, but the next major development occurred in 1959, when C&NW purchased gallery cars with an engineer's cab at one end and wiring that enabled the diesel locomotive to be controlled from that cab, enabling push-pull operation. The C&NW cars also had lighting, air conditioning, and heating powered by an auxiliary generator in the locomotive. Head-end-powered lighting wasn't a new concept, and head-end-powered heating was the norm — but with steam, not electricity. The third major development was in 1971 when Illinois Central received self-propelled electric gallery cars from St. Louis Car Co.

The gallery car is 28 inches taller than a standard coach (and 4 inches lower than an Amtrak Superliner), too tall for clearances in the East. Commuter fleets on the East Coast include the single-level coach previously built by Pullman and now by Bombardier (it's also the basis of Amtrak's Horizon Fleet coaches) and a variety of single-level electric cars.

A compromise car was developed by Hawker Siddeley for GO Transit in 1977. If it were a house it would be called split level. The center

GO Transit's coaches have full width upper and lower decks between the trucks and short sections at normal floor level at each end of the car. Photo by N. S. Helm.

portion of the car, between the trucks, is of true double-deck design. At the ends of the car is a floor at conventional height. Short stairways connect the ends with the upper and lower decks in the middle. The roof slopes down at each end over the vestibule. Tri-Rail has cars identical to GO Transit's; Massachusetts Bay Transportation Authority has split-level cars with a straight roofline.

The cab end of Chicago & North Western's first cab coach, No. 151 (now Metra 8700), sports headlights, horns, bell, ladders to permit cleaning the windows, and a pilot below the coupler. The cab occupies the full width of the car on the upper level. Trane Company photo.

METRO-NORTH COMMUTER RAILROAD CO.

The Northeast Rail Service Act of July 1981 instructed Conrail to divest itself of the commuter operations it had inherited from Penn Central by the end of 1982. The Metropolitan Transportation Authority of the state of New York established Metro-North Commuter Railroad as a subsidiary to operate the services. These ex-New York Central and New Haven trains serve New York and Connecticut from Grand Central Terminal in New York City. Metro-North began operation on January 1, 1983.

MTA provides operating subsidies for Metro-North service on the Hudson (New York-Poughkeepsie) and Harlem (New York-Brewster-Dover Plains) lines; MTA and the Connecticut Department of Transportation

Drawing power from the third rail, blue and silver Metro-North M. U. cars roll south along the Harlem Division on a run from Brewster to Grand Central Terminal in New York on May 6, 1904. Photo by Howard Pincus.

Metro-North Commuter Railroad

jointly subsidize service on the New Haven line. Approximately 90,000 passengers ride Metro-North trains each weekday.

MTA also subsidizes service operated by NJ Transit on former Erie-Lackawanna lines from Hoboken, New Jersey, to Spring Valley and Port Jervis, N. Y.; some Metro-North rolling stock is assigned to that service.

Other Metropolitan Transportation Authority subsidiaries are the Long Island Rail Road, the New York City Transit Authority, and the Staten Island Rapid Transit Operating Authority.

Address of general offices: 347 Madison Avenue, New York, NY 10017

Miles of road operated: 262

Reporting marks: MNCW
Number of locomotives: 48 (45 diesel, 3 electric)
Number of passenger cars: 156
Number of self-propelled passenger cars: 579 (566 electric, 13 diesel)
Radio frequencies: 160.950 (Hudson Division), 161.280 (Harlem Division), 160.545 (New Haven Division)
Passenger routes: New York (Grand Central Terminal) to Poughkeepsie and Dover Plains, N. Y., and New Haven, Waterbury, Danbury, and New Canaan, Conn.

161

MIDSOUTH RAIL CORPORATION

The Clinton & Vicksburg Railroad was incorporated in 1833. By 1840 it had been renamed the Vicksburg & Jackson and was operating between the Mississippi cities of its name. Across the Mississippi River from Vicksburg, the Vicksburg, Shreveport & Texas had a line as far west as Monroe, Louisiana. The Civil War destroyed both roads, but they were rebuilt. By 1890 both had new corporate structures and new names (Alabama & Vicksburg Railway and Vicksburg, Shreveport & Pacific Railway) and were part of the Queen & Crescent System, a group of affiliated railroads reaching from Cincinnati to New Orleans and from Meridian, Miss., west to Shreveport, La.

The Cincinnati-New Orleans portion of the Queen & Crescent eventually became part of the Southern Railway system, and Illinois Central acquired the Vicksburg Route in 1926. The Mississippi River was bridged at Vicksburg in 1930, eliminating the need for a ferry.

A MidSouth local freight returns to Vicksburg from a trip to a paper mill at Redwood, Mississippi. Photo by Louis R. Saillard.

On March 31, 1986, MidSouth Rail Corporation purchased Illinois Central Gulf's line from Meridian, Mississippi, to Shreveport, Louisiana, plus short branches north and south from Vicksburg, remnants of ICG's Memphis-Baton Rouge line, and a line not connected with the others extending from Hattiesburg to Gulfport, Miss., once part of the Gulf & Ship Island Railroad.

Illinois Central Gulf had operated a single daily train each way; MidSouth increased that to two trains a day over much of its main line, and scheduled those to minimize delay to cars delivered to the railroad. MidSouth's biggest customer is a paper mill at Redwood, just north of Vicksburg. Pulpwood, paper, and chemicals constitute more than 60 percent of the road's traffic. About one-third of MidSouth's traffic originates on line; another third is received from another road and terminates on line; and the remainder is bridge or overhead traffic, cars received from one railroad to be delivered to another.

Address of general offices: P. O. Box 1232, Jackson, MS 39215
Miles of road operated: 420
Reporting marks: MSRC
Number of locomotives: 111
Number of freight cars: 509
Principal commodities carried: Pulpwood, wood products, paper, chemicals
Shops: Hodge, La
Radio frequencies: 160.545 (road), 161.010 (yard), 160.215 (joint with MidLouisiana)
Recommended reading: "Rebirth of the Vicksburg Route," by Louis R. Saillard, in TRAINS Magazine, April 1989, pages 30-41

MIDLOUISIANA RAIL CORPORATION

On September 8, 1987, MidSouth purchased the 40-mile North Louisiana & Gulf Railroad, with which it connected at Gibsland, La. The NL&G was incorporated in 1906 and was owned by Continental Can Co., which has a large paper mill at Hodge, La. Along with the NL&G came a subsidiary, the Central Louisiana & Gulf Railroad, which in 1980 acquired a short segment of former Rock Island track between Hodge and Winnfield, La. MidSouth renamed its acquisition MidLouisiana Rail Corporation.

Miles of road operated: 113
Reporting marks: MDR, NLG
Number of freight cars: 2,064
Radio frequencies: 160.755 (road), 160.230 (yard), 160.215 (joint with MidSouth)

SOUTHRAIL CORPORATION

Even before MidSouth was created, ICG spun off most of its ex-Gulf, Mobile & Ohio lines in Mississippi and Alabama to the Gulf & Mississippi Railroad on July 10, 1985. The new road was handicapped by poor track conditions and competition from ICG and Burlington Northern lines. It was facing bankruptcy when a MidSouth subsidiary, SouthRail Corporation, acquired it on April 14, 1988.

Miles of road operated: 732
Reporting marks: GMSR, SR
Number of freight cars: 1,258
Radio frequencies: 161.085

MINNESOTA, DAKOTA & WESTERN RAILWAY

In 1912 the International Bridge & Terminal Company of International Falls, Minnesota, which had been incorporated in 1902, acquired a nearby railroad with the intention of pushing it west across Minnesota and North Dakota and into Montana. The company took a new name to reflect those intentions, Minnesota, Dakota & Western Railway. By the late 1920s, after getting as far as Loman, Minn., about 20 miles out of town, it had given up its aspirations and settled down to the job of carrying raw materials and finished products for its owner, Minnesota & Ontario Paper Co. The road was acquired by Boise Cascade Corporation in 1965. It is best known for its large fleet of bright-green-and-white box cars.

Address of general offices: P. O. Box 7747, Boise, ID 83707
Miles of road operated: 5
Reporting marks: MDW
Number of locomotives: 5
Number of freight cars: 1,406
Principal commodities carried: Paper, wood pulp, pulpwood, chemicals
Shops: International Falls, Minn.
Junctions with other railroads:
Burlington Northern: International Falls, Minn.
Duluth, Winnipeg & Pacific: Ranier, Minn.
Radio frequencies: 160.530, 160.410, 160.680

Minnesota, Dakota & Western 19, shown at International Falls in June 1985, is one of five Alco S2s on the road's roster. Photo by Jim Shaw.

MISSISSIPPI DELTA RAILROAD

Mississippi Delta operates a former Illinois Central line from Swan Lake, Mississippi, north through Clarksdale to Lula, Mississippi. The Clarksdale-Lula segment was part of a Memphis-Baton Rouge line built by the Louisville, New Orleans & Texas Railroad, part of C. P. Huntington's empire. It came under the control of the Yazoo & Mississippi Valley Railroad, an Illinois Central subsidiary, in 1885.

In the 1980s Illinois Central Gulf abandoned most of its lines in the Mississippi Valley south of Memphis, severing the former Louisville, New Orleans & Texas route in several places. Clarksdale, one of the few large towns in the area, lost its north-south main line and maintained its rail service only through a branch south to the main line at Swan Lake.

Mississippi Delta purchased the Clarksdale-Lula line and leased the Swan Lake-Clarksdale line in 1986. The road also operates Delta Oil Mills' private railroad from Lula southeast to Jonestown, Miss. The road has a large fleet of freight cars.

Address of general offices: P. O. Box 1446, Clarksdale, MS 38614

Mississippi Delta 8068, a GP10, has northbound freight in tow at Mattson, Mississippi, on June 3, 1987. Photo by Jim Shaw.

Miles of road operated: 49
Reporting marks: MSDR
Number of locomotives: 2
Number of freight cars: 2,827
Radio frequencies: 160.500

Principal commodities carried: Soybeans, cotton seed, carbon black, rubber
Shops: Clarksdale, Miss.
Junctions with other railroads: Illinois Central: Swan Lake, Miss.

MONTANA RAIL LINK

The last spike of the Northern Pacific Railroad was driven near Garrison, Montana, on September 8, 1883, completing a line from Carlton, Minnesota, near Duluth, to Wallula Junction, Washington. Within a few years extensions were in place to St. Paul, Minn., and Seattle and Tacoma, Wash. In 1901 the NP came under the control of James J. Hill, who had built the parallel Great Northern Railway, and NP and GN jointly purchased the Chicago, Burlington & Quincy. All that was needed to bring what would become Burlington Northern into existence was a nod from the Interstate Commerce Commission — and that took almost 70 years.

BN began operation March 2, 1970. It had two main lines all the way from St. Paul to Seattle, and alternate routes and cutoffs made it three or more for much of the distance. In the mid-1980s BN began to prune its route structure. The ex-GN line across Montana was 10 years newer than the ex-NP line and had easier grades; BN thought it could easily concentrate its traffic on the GN line.

In 1987 Montana Rail Link acquired the ex-NP line from Huntley, Mont., east of Billings, through Helena to Sandpoint, Idaho, plus trackage rights from Sandpoint to Spokane, Wash. It leased the main line and purchased branches to Harrison, Alder, Phillipsburg, Darby, St. Regis, and Polson, Mont. BN retained ownership of the line from Helena to Phosphate for access to the Montana Western Railway, a short line created from the Garrison-Butte segment of the former NP line via Butte (the steep line over Homestake Pass east of Butte has been abandoned). BN also has trackage rights from Huntley through Billings to Laurel, Mont.

The start of operations on October 31, 1987, was marked by picketing by the United Transportation Union (MRL's operating employees are all

A Montana Rail Link freight rolls across Skyline Trestle on Mullan Pass, west of Helena, Montana. There is a four-unit helper about halfway back in the 98-car train. Photo by Wesley Fox.

members of the Brotherhood of Locomotive Engineers) and vandalism at Livingston, Mont., the location of a major NP shop that had been closed by BN.

In 1988 the Washington Corporation, MRL's parent, reopened the Livingston shops as a contract repair shop, not only for its own locomotives but for those of other roads. In 1991 MRL petitioned for and was granted exemption from the Interstate Commerce Commission's Class 1 status, citing the cost of the extra paperwork involved in being a Class 1 railroad. In August 1992 MRL leased the Helena-Phosphate line, known as "The Gap." In mid-1992 the Phillipsburg and Alder lines were out of service.

Montana Rail Link's principal items of traffic are paper, lumber and other forest products, grain, and BN trains moving between Spokane and Billings — the MRL route is 125 miles shorter, and BN's own route is operating at capacity.

Address of general offices: P. O. Box 8779, Missoula, MT 59807

Miles of road operated: 944

Reporting marks: MRL

Number of locomotives: 98

Number of freight cars: 1,184

Principal commodities carried: Paper, forest products, grain, cement, talc, petroleum products

Shops: Livingston, Mont. (locomotives); Laurel, Mont. (cars)

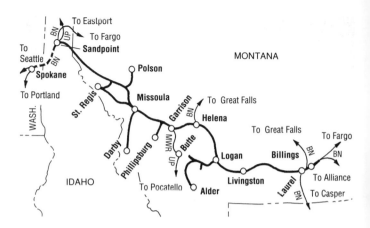

Radio frequencies: 161.100, 161.160

Junctions with other railroads:

Burlington Northern: Helena, Mont.; Laurel, Mont.; Spokane, Wash.

Union Pacific: Sandpoint, Idaho

MONTREAL URBAN COMMUNITY TRANSPORTATION COMMISSION
(Société de Transport de la Communaute Urbaine de Montréal)

At one time Montreal, Quebec, was served by commuter trains converging on the city from all points of the compass. They were operated by Canadian National, Canadian Pacific, and New York Central. By the 1970s, though, trains ran on only two routes, Canadian National's line through the Mount Royal tunnel to Deux Montagnes, and Canadian Pacific's "Lakeshore" route west to Vaudreuil and Rigaud.

Both routes had a long history of commuter service. When the Canadian

Northern Railway was planning its line into Montreal about 1910 it found the easy routes to the center of the city already taken by Canadian Pacific and Grand Trunk. Canadian Northern used a temporary station in the eastern part of the city and started planning a downtown terminal. Part of the project was a 3.2-mile tunnel under Mount Royal; another aspect was laying out a model community, the Town of Mount Royal, at the west portal of the tunnel. The length of the tunnel and the ascending westbound

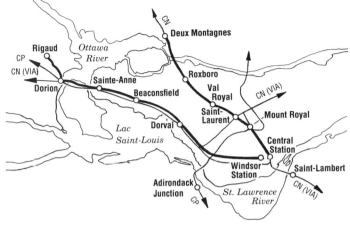

Montreal-Dorion train 19 glides into the Vendome station to pick up homeward-bound commuters on August 4, 1986. The station also serves line 2 of the Montreal Metro and several bus routes. In the distance can be seen the old Westmount station. Photo by William D. Middleton.

grade required electrification of the line, Canada's first (and only) mainline electrification.

Work began in 1912, but World War I delayed the opening of the tunnel and the terminal until 1918. A year later Canadian Northern was absorbed by Canadian National Railways. In 1943 Canadian National consolidated its Montreal passenger facilities in a new station, Central Station, at the site of Canadian Northern's terminal. For the expanded terminal electrification (all trains were hauled in and out of the new station with electric power) CN augmented the six boxcab electrics built by General Electric in 1914 and 1916 with nine English Electric locomotives acquired

from the National Harbours Board. Three General Electric steeplecabs were added in 1950, and in 1952 CN bought 6 motor cars and 12 trailers from Canadian Car & Foundry. With the dieselization of CN passenger service some of the electrification was pruned, leaving only one route under wires.

Commuters were part of the passenger business on Canadian Pacific's route west of Montreal as early as 1889. The area along the line made a gradual transition from rural to suburban, and the commuter business did well enough that CP purchased 40 new coaches for the Montreal-Rigaud trains in 1953 and 9 gallery cars in 1969. (Canadian National discontinued its parallel commuter service in 1957.)

As the 1980s began, the usual progression of increased fares and decreased service affected patronage on both routes, and it was clear that some kind of government subsidy was necessary. On July 1, 1982, MUCTC

167

Canadian National boxcab electric 6713 (General Electric, class of 1914) and an equally ancient classmate roll commuters toward Montreal near Roxboro, Quebec, on August 6, 1986. Photo by William D. Middleton.

took over management and funding of the CN service between Montreal and Deux Montagnes, 17 miles. Frequency of service was increased and fares were reduced to equal competing bus fares. On November 1, 1982, MUCTC acquired Canadian Pacific's 40-mile commuter service to Rigaud and the equipment necessary to operate it, making the same initial fare reductions and service increases that it did on the CNR route. New rolling stock arrived for the former CP route in 1989 in the form of 24 Bombardier coaches, 8 of them with cabs for push-pull service.

The railroads continue to operate the service for MUCTC. The commission also operates subways and bus systems in Montreal.

Address of general offices: 159 St. Antoine Street West, Montreal, PQ H2Z 1H3

Miles of road operated: 57

Number of locomotives: 11 diesel, 13 electric

Number of passenger cars: 122

Number of self-propelled electric passenger cars: 5 motors, 11 trailers

Radio frequencies: 161.415 (CN), 161.475, 161.115 (CP)

Passenger routes: Montreal (Central Station)-Deux Montagnes, Que.; Montreal (Windsor Station)-Rigaud, Que.

NATIONAL RAILWAYS OF MEXICO
(Ferrocarriles Nacionales de México)

The National Railways of Mexico is an amalgamation of several railroads built separately and at different times — and the most recent of those amalgamations occurred in the 1980s, when NdeM absorbed four regional railroads: Pacific Railroad, Chihuahua Pacific Railway, Sonora-Baja California Railway, and United South Eastern Railways.

Both lines from the U. S. border to Mexico City were built by companies that received concessions from the Mexican government. The line from Ciudad Juárez south to Mexico City through Chihuahua, Torreón, Aguascalientes, and Querétaro was built by Atchison, Topeka & Santa Fe inter-

ests as the Mexican Central Railway. It was completed in 1884.

The route south from Laredo was built as the 3-foot-gauge Mexican National Railroad. It was begun in 1881 by Gen. William Jackson Palmer (of Denver & Rio Grande fame). It was completed to Mexico City via Monterrey, Saltillo, San Luis Potosí, Acámbaro, and Toluca, with branches from Monterrey east to Matamoros and from Acámbaro southwest to Uruapan. The main line was standard-gauged as far south as Escobedo in 1903, and a new line was built from there to Mexico City paralleling the Mexican Central.

National Railways of Mexico was organized on March 28, 1908. It took over operations of the Mexican National at the beginning of 1909 and that same year purchased the Mexican Central. In the 1930s, a period of political upheaval, control of the railroad was tossed from government to a syn-

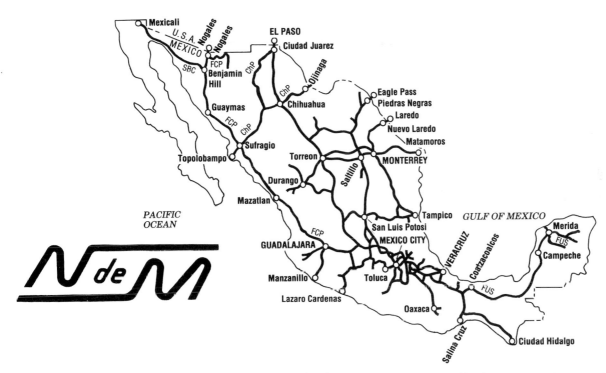

dicate of railroad workers to the railroad's own management and back to the government.

The line from Mexico City to Veracruz via Jalapa is the former 3-foot-gauge Interoceanic Railway, converted to standard gauge in 1948. A branch of this line running from Oriental to Teziutlán is still 3-foot gauge. The Mexico City-Veracruz line through Orizaba is the former Mexican Railway (Ferrocarril Mexicano), built with British capital between 1864 and 1873. It was acquired by the government in 1946 and absorbed by NdeM in 1959. The Maltrata Incline between Esperanza and Paso del Macho, with grades in excess of 4 percent, was electrified in the 1920s; electric operation ceased in the 1970s.

In recent years NdeM has undertaken several line relocations and built a number of new lines. Among them are a cutoff northeast of Queretaro for traffic moving between Monterrey and Mexico City; extensive reconstruction of the line between the north end of that cutoff and Saltillo; a new line from a point south of Uruapan to the Pacific port city of Lázaro Cardenas; a new double-track electrified line from Mexico City to Queretaro; and a line that bypasses the Maltrata Incline.

The four regional railroads absorbed by National Railways of Mexico still maintain some identity; brief descriptions follow.

Pacific Railroad (Ferrocarril del Pacífico)

In 1881 and 1882 the Santa Fe built the Sonora Railway north from the Gulf of California port of Guaymas to the U. S. border at what is now Nogales, Arizona. In 1898 Santa Fe traded the line to Southern Pacific for a strategic stretch of track between Needles and Mojave, California. Southern Pacific incorporated a subsidiary, the Southern Pacific of Mexico, to extend the line south along the coast from Guaymas to Guadalajara, 1,095 miles from Nogales. The line was completed in 1927, and SP sold it to the Mexican government in 1951. It was renamed the Pacific Railroad (Ferrocarril del Pacífico). The railroad outgrew its stepchild beginnings and developed a good business in moving fruit and vegetables northward. On June 22, 1987, the 1,435-mile Ferrocarril del Pacífico became the Pacific Region of the National Railways of Mexico.

Chihuahua Pacific Railroad
(Ferrocarril de Chihuaha al Pacífico)

In 1899 Arthur Stilwell, who had built the Kansas City Southern, proposed a railroad to run southwest from Kansas City to the nearest Pacific port, Topolobampo, on the Gulf of Mexico in the state of Sinaloa. By 1912 three separate sections of the Kansas City, Mexico & Orient Railway were in operation: from Wichita, Kansas, southwest to the Pecos River in west Texas; from a point 34 miles east of the city of Chihuahua west to Miñaca, mostly on trackage rights; and from El Fuerte across the coastal plain to Topolobampo. Mexico was in revolution, and the KCM&O entered receivership. A new company scraped along for a while. The discovery of oil in west Texas made the U. S. portion of the property attractive enough that the Santa Fe bought it in 1928, then sold the Mexican portion to the United Sugar Co. In 1930 the Texas and Mexico portions of the line were joined. (In 1992 the Santa Fe spun off the 394-mile San Angelo Junction-Presidio, Texas, segment to become the South Orient Railroad; and the 351-mile Cherokee, Oklahoma-Maryneal, Texas portion as the Texas & Oklahoma Railroad.)

Freight and passenger trains stand in the station at San Luis Potosí, on February 26, 1982. The city is the location of National of Mexico's principal diesel shop. Photo by George H. Drury.

The Mexican government purchased the Mexican part of the KCM&O in 1940 and announced it would join the two disconnected segments. The KCM&O was merged with the Mexico North-Western Railway, with which it had been associated off and on, in 1955 to form the Chihuahua Pacific Railway. Construction resumed in earnest through some of the most rugged topography in North America, and the line was completed in 1961. Topolobampo never developed into a major port, but the Chihuahua Pacific opened the Copper Canyon area of northwest Mexico to tourism. The 942-mile ChP became the Northern Region of National Railways of Mexico in 1987.

Sonora-Baja California Railway
(Ferrocarril Sonora-Baja California)

The Sonora-Baja California had its beginning in 1923 when the Ministry of Communications and Public Works began construction of a railroad southeast from Mexicali, Baja California. It remained a 43-mile stub to nowhere until 1936, when work resumed and the line was extended to Puerto Peñasco on the Gulf of California. There it remained until 1946, when construction resumed. In 1948 the road was completed to a connection with the Southern Pacific of Mexico (now NdeM's Pacific Region) at Benjamin Hill, Sonora, 332 miles from Mexicali. On April 2, 1987, the S-BC became the Baja California Division of the National Railways of Mexico.

United South Eastern Railways
(Ferrocarriles Unidos del Sureste)

By the beginning of the 20th century the United Railways of Yucatan comprised several lines, some standard gauge, some narrow, radiating from Yucatán's capital city, Mérida, into the state of Yucatán and southwest into the neighboring state of Campeche. It had no rail connections with other railroads until 1950, when the Mexican government completed the Southeastern Railway from Allende, in the state of Veracruz, to a connection with the United of Yucatán at the city of Campeche. In 1969 the two railroads were merged to form United South Eastern Railways. In 1987 it became part of National Railways of Mexico.

Address of general offices: Avenida Central No. 140, México, D. F. 06358

Miles of road operated: 12,396 standard gauge, 263 narrow gauge
Reporting marks: CHP, FCM, FCP, FUS, NDM, SBC
Number of locomotives: 1,887 standard gauge, 14 narrow gauge
Number of freight cars: 43,706 standard gauge

Major yards: Mexico City (Valle de México)
Principal shops: Aguascalientes, Mexico City, Monterrey, San Luis Potosí
Junctions with other railroads:
Atchison, Topeka & Santa Fe: Ciudad Juárez, Chihuahua
Southern Pacific:
    Agua Prieta, Sonora
    Ciudad Juárez, Chih.
    Matamoros, Tampaulipas
    Mexicali, Baja California
    Nogales, Son.
    Piedras Negras, Coahuila
South Orient: Ojinaga, Chih.
Texas Mexican: Nuevo Laredo, Tamps.
Union Pacific:
    Ciudad Juárez, Chih.
    Matamoros, Tamps.
    Nuevo Laredo, Tamps.
Radio frequencies: 173.225, 173.600, 172.450 (former NdeM proper and ChP); 167.100, 167.150 (former FCP and SBC)
Passenger routes:
The principal long-distance passenger routes are Mexico City-Nuevo Laredo, Mexico City-Ciudad Juárez, Mexico City-Guadalajara-Nogales, Benjamin Hill-Mexicali, Mexico City-Toluca-Uruapan, Mexico City-Oaxaca, Mexico City-Ciudad Hidalgo, Mexico City-Coatzacoalcos-Mérida, Mexico City-Veracruz, Saltillo-Piedras Negras, Monterrey-Torreón-Durango, Monterrey-Matamoros, Monterrey-Tampico, San Luis Potosí-Tampico, and Chihuahua-Los Mochis. Most lines have local or mixed-train service.

NEW ORLEANS PUBLIC BELT RAILROAD

The New Orleans Public Belt is a switching railroad owned and operated by the city of New Orleans. It was formed by a city ordinance in 1900 to provide rail service to the port area. Operation of the line, which extends along the Mississippi River waterfront and the Industrial Canal, began in 1908. Like most such railroads it goes about its business without fanfare, but two items are worth noting. First, NOPB once owned a trio of 900-h.p. Baldwin diesel switchers built in 1937, the only ones of their type. They were among the earliest Baldwin diesels, and they have long since been scrapped. Second, NOPB owns the Huey P. Long Bridge across the Mississippi. It was opened in December 1935. Including approach trestles it is nearly 4 miles long; the eight main spans total 3524 feet. There are highway lanes on each side of the tracks.

Address of general offices: P. O. Box 51658, New Orleans, LA 70151
Miles of road operated: 45
Reporting marks: NOPB
Number of locomotives: 6
Number of freight cars: 204
Connects with:
CSX
Illinois Central
Louisiana & Arkansas (Kansas City Southern)
Louisiana Southern
New Orleans Terminal Co.
Norfolk Southern
Southern Pacific
Union Pacific
all in the New Orleans switching district
Radio frequencies: 160.320, 160.530

The Huey P. Long bridge was still under construction when this view was taken from the west bank of the Mississippi River. Southern Pacific photo.

Red-and-white SW1000s and SW1500s congregate at New Orleans Public Belt's engine terminal. TRAINS Magazine photo by J. David Ingles.

NEW YORK, SUSQUEHANNA & WESTERN RAILWAY

In 1966 the New York Central abandoned the western end of its Ulster & Delaware branch. The Delaware Otsego Corporation purchased 2.6 miles of the line at Oneonta, New York, and operated it as a steam-powered tourist carrier. DO also offered freight service, but there was little market for it.

Five years later DO's Oneonta operation was in the path of highway construction, and Delaware & Hudson wanted to abandon its Cooperstown branch. DO bought the D&H branch and operated it as the Cooperstown & Charlotte Valley Railway. Although the passenger operation was not a success, freight was and DO management saw potential in acquiring low-traffic branches that larger roads couldn't operate profitably.

Between 1973 and 1986 Delaware Otsego acquired several other branches and short lines: the Richfield Springs branch of the Erie Lackawanna, EL's line between Lackawaxen and Honesdale, Pennsylvania, the Fonda, Johnstown & Gloversville Railroad, the Staten Island Railway, and the Rahway Valley Railroad.

Delaware Otsego's major success, though, was the New York, Susquehanna & Western. The Susquehanna's original purpose was to be part of a route from New York to the Great Lakes. Its partner in this endeavor was the New York, Ontario & Western. (During the first half of the 20th century, railroads that were down on their luck took comfort from knowing the NYO&W was worse off.) The Susquehanna reached west to the Delaware River and leased the Wilkes-Barre & Eastern for access to the coalfields of northeastern Pennsylvania. It was the weakest of the Pennsylvania-to-Hudson River coal roads, and it came under the control of the Erie Railroad in 1898.

The Susquehanna entered bankruptcy in 1937 (the Erie was right behind it) and took charge of its own affairs in 1940. It modernized its commuter service with ACF Motorailers and connecting bus service to New York, and dieselized its other operations by the end of World War II; then it upgraded its commuter service again in the early 1950s with RDCs and new coaches from Budd. The Susquehanna fell on hard times during

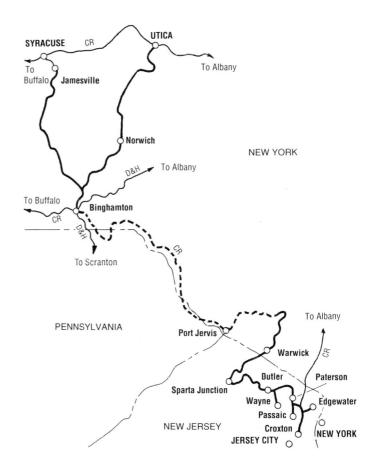

173

In 1981 Conrail proposed abandonment of the former Erie Lackawanna line between Binghamton, N. Y., and Jamesville, just south of Syracuse, and the Utica branch of that line. Delaware Otsego purchased the lines and organized them as the Northern Division of the NYS&W. To connect the two divisions, DO also purchased a portion of the former Lehigh & Hudson River Railway between Warwick, N. Y., and Franklin, N. J., from Conrail and secured trackage rights on Conrail from Binghamton to Warwick and from Franklin to Sparta Junction.

DO's management early recognized the potential in coast-to-coast container traffic. Sea-Land leased property adjacent to NYS&W's yard at Little Ferry, N. J., and contracted with the railroad to operate container trains. Almost all their mileage west to Binghamton was on Conrail track by virtue of the trackage and haulage rights agreements. After a few years Conrail, which operated container trains of its own, wanted to raise the rates it charged NYS&W for moving the trains. The process required renegotiating trackage rights and haulage agreements; as a result, NYS&W reopened its line west of Butler and got more favorable operating arrangements on Conrail track.

The Susquehanna has been quite successful with its container trains and has become a regional railroad. It offers the only non-Conrail access to northern New Jersey. Delaware Otsego's short lines all operated with some degree of success through most of the 1980s but ceased operation around 1990.

Address of general offices: 1 Railroad Ave., Cooperstown, NY 13326
Miles of road operated: 403
Reporting marks: NYSW
Number of locomotives: 20
Principal commodities carried: Intermodal containers, grain, chemicals, paper products, lumber
Shops: Little Ferry, N. J.
Junctions with other railroads:
Conrail: Binghamton, N. Y.; Passaic Junction, N. J.; Utica, N. Y.
CP Rail System (Delaware & Hudson): Binghamton, N. Y.
Stourbridge Railroad: Lackawaxen, Pa.
Radio frequencies: 161.295 (New York Division), 160.485 (New Jersey Division)

A Susquehanna double-stack train rolls through Deposit, New York, on January 16, 1988, behind a pair of SD45s. Photo by Alex Mayes.

the economic recession of 1957. It sold its modern passenger cars and replaced them with third-hand coaches (and later offered its commuters $1,000 each to stop using the trains); two of its connecting railroads, the NYO&W and the Lehigh & New England, ceased operation; and washouts cut off its other western connections.

The Susquehanna declared bankruptcy in 1976 but stayed out of Conrail, which had surrounded it. The bankruptcy court ordered that the road be abandoned and its assets sold. By then the road was down to a 43-mile line from Croxton and Edgewater through Paterson to Butler. The state of New Jersey, aware of Delaware Otsego's reputation at rehabilitating short lines, asked DO to take over the railroad. A new DO subsidiary, the New York, Susquehanna & Western Railway, began operation in September 1980 under a lease agreement. In 1982 DO purchased the NYS&W.

Recommended reading:
"The Delaware Otsego Story," by Scott Hartley, in TRAINS Magazine, January 1988, pages 28-41

Susquehanna From Shortlines to Stackpacks, by Ken Karlewicz and Scott Hartley, published in 1987 by Railpace Company, P. O. Box 927, Piscataway, NJ 08855-0927 (LCC 87-20698)

NJ TRANSIT RAIL OPERATIONS

As early as 1968 the Department of Transportation of the state of New Jersey was subsidizing rail commuter service by furnishing equipment for the railroads that ran the trains. That year NJDOT purchased 13 GP40Ps for use on the Central Railroad of New Jersey. In the early 1970s the state DOT bought more locomotives, this time 32 U34CHs for service on Erie Lackawanna's non-electrified routes, and cars to go with them. More equipment was purchased — secondhand passenger diesels and long-distance coaches — largely for use on the New York & Long Branch Railroad, which was jointly owned and operated by the Pennsylvania and the Central of New Jersey. Later purchases have included F40PHs, Jersey Arrow M. U. cars for service on former Pennsylvania Railroad and Lackawanna lines, and nonpowered Comet II coaches for ex-CNJ lines. Gradually the services began to look more like an operation of the state than of the railroads.

The railroads operating the commuter service — Penn Central, Erie Lackawanna, and Central of New Jersey — became part of Conrail on April 1, 1976, and the Northeast Rail Service Act of July 1981 instructed Conrail to divest itself of its commuter operations by the end of 1982. The NJ Transit Rail Division of NJ Transit Corporation was formed in April 1982 to take them over, and it began operation on January 1, 1983. (NJ

During conversion of the former Lackawanna electrification, diesel-hauled trains worked the line. F40PH-2 No. 4116 has a train of Pullman-built coaches in tow at Summit, New Jersey, in January 1982. Photo by Scott Snell.

Transit Corporation is the operating arm of the New Jersey Department of Transportation; it also operates the Newark subway, and there is an NJ Transit Bus division.)

NJ Transit owns most of the lines on which it provides commuter service. The two exceptions are the ex-Pennsylvania Northeast Corridor line between New York and Trenton and the Atlantic City line, which are owned by Amtrak. NJ Transit operates the New York portion of the former Erie Lackawanna Hoboken-Port Jervis, N. Y., line for New York's Metropolitan Transportation Authority; Metro-North provides cars and locomotives for that route.

Conrail inherited Camden-Atlantic City passenger trains from Pennsylvania-Reading Seashore Lines. They ceased operation on July 1, 1982, because federal officials had imposed a 15 mph limit on the track. On September 17, 1989, NJ Transit began operating local service between Atlantic City and Lindenwold, where it connects with the PATCO rapid transit line to Camden and Philadelphia.

In 1986 NJ Transit completed the conversion of the former Lackawanna electrification from 3,000 volt DC to 25,000 volt, 60-cycle AC. The New York & Long Branch was electrified from South Amboy to Matawan in 1982; the electrification was extended 16 miles to Long Branch in 1988. In September 1991 NJ Transit opened a connecting line that permits Northeast Corridor, North Jersey Coast, and Raritan Valley trains to reach the former EL terminal at Hoboken. A similar connector, scheduled to open in 1995, will permit trains on former Erie Lackawanna routes to travel to and from Penn Station in New York.

Address of general offices: One Penn Plaza East, Newark, NJ 07105-2246

Miles of road operated: 490

Number of locomotives: 83 diesel, 23 electric

Number of passenger cars: 715

Number of self-propelled passenger cars: 300 electric

Shops: Kearny, Hoboken

Radio frequencies: 161.400, 161.235 (North Jersey Coast and Raritan Valley routes), 161.355 (Atlantic City route)

Passenger routes: (NJ Transit's route name and historical operator in parentheses)

Newark-High Bridge (Raritan Valley — Central Railroad of New Jersey)

New York-Trenton, Princeton Jct. Princeton (Northeast Corridor — Pennsylvania)

New York and Hoboken-Bay Head (North Jersey Coast — Pennsylvania and Central Railroad of New Jersey)

Hoboken-Dover, Hoboken-Gladstone, Hoboken-Montclair (Morris & Essex — Lackawanna)

Hoboken-Dover-Netcong (Boonton Line — Lackawanna)

Hoboken-Port Jervis (Main Line, Bergen County Line — Erie)

Hoboken-Spring Valley, N. Y. (Pascack Valley — Erie)

Lindenwold-Atlantic City (Atlantic City — Pennsylvania-Reading Seashore Lines)

NORFOLK SOUTHERN RAILWAY

In describing today's Norfolk Southern Railway it is necessary first to say what it is not — or at least not anymore. Until 1974 the Norfolk Southern Railway was a 600-mile regional railroad running south from Norfolk, Virginia, then west through Raleigh, North Carolina, to Charlotte. Its history was peppered with receiverships and a period of management by Patrick B. McGinnis; the skeletons in its rolling stock closet included electric interurban cars, ACF Motorailers, five lightweight 2-8-4s, and a fleet of Baldwin diesel hood units.

In 1974 the Southern Railway purchased the Norfolk Southern and merged into it the Carolina & Northwestern, another Southern subsidiary. In 1982 the name of the Norfolk Southern Railway was changed to Carolina & Northwestern. The Southern tucked the Norfolk Southern name in its briefcase, stopped in Roanoke to pick up a friend, and went to Washington.

On March 25, 1982, the Interstate Commerce Commission approved acquisition of the Southern Railway and the Norfolk & Western by Norfolk Southern Corporation, a newly organized holding company. The transaction took place on June 1, 1982. At first the two railroads maintained separate identities, but gradually a new Norfolk Southern image took over. At the end of 1990 the Norfolk & Western became a subsidiary of the Southern Railway (it had been a subsidiary of Norfolk Southern Corporation), and the Southern Railway changed its name to Norfolk Southern Railway.

Norfolk Southern's map consists of a skein of lines from Buffalo, New York, southwest across the Midwest to Kansas City, and a complex network of lines from Washington and Norfolk southwest to New Orleans. Just three lines connect these webs: the former N&W main line from Roanoke to Columbus and Cincinnati, the Cincinnati, New Orleans & Texas Pacific subsidiary from Chattanooga north to Cincinnati, and a route linking Birmingham with St. Louis: the former Illinois Central line from Haleyville, Alabama, to Fulton, Kentucky, acquired in 1988, plus trackage rights on IC from Fulton north to Centralia, Illinois.

Southern Railway

The Southern Railway of recent decades was a well-run, well-maintained, profitable railroad extending from Washington through Atlanta and Birmingham to New Orleans and from Cincinnati south through Chattanooga to Birmingham, with lines extending to Atlantic tidewater at various points from Norfolk, Virginia, south to Jacksonville, Florida, and west to the Mississippi at St. Louis and Memphis. Southern's subsidiaries retained their identity far longer than those of most other roads. Two, the Alabama Great Southern Railway and the Cincinnati, New Orleans & Texas Pacific Railway, were Class 1 railroads in their own right.

Between 1847 and 1892 the Richmond & Danville Railroad and the East Tennessee, Virginia & Georgia Railroad each assembled a string of railroads extending from Virginia to Georgia and the Mississippi River. The central point of the systems was Atlanta. Both railroads failed financially and were consolidated in 1894 as the Southern Railway. The Southern soon acquired control of the AGS and the CNO&TP, and in 1916 purchased the New Orleans & Northeastern Railroad, putting the entire Cincinnati-New Orleans route under Southern control. In 1895 Southern

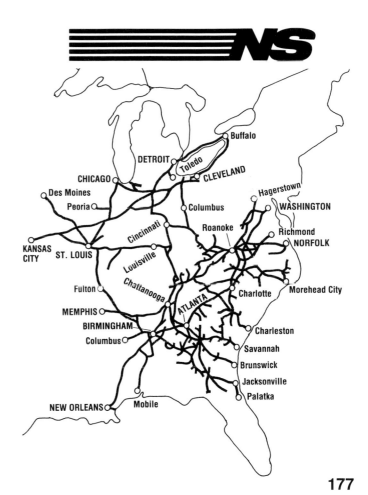

Norfolk Southern has wholeheartedly adopted the RoadRailer, a highway trailer with a set of railroad wheels and trailer-to-trailer couplers. Train 248, the Atlanta-Washington RoadRailer, speeds through Pelham, North Carolina, on June 14, 1991. Photo by Curt Tillotson Jr.

incorporated the Georgia Southern & Florida Railway to reorganize a line from Macon, Ga., to Palatka, Florida; it soon acquired a branch to Jacksonville. Latter-day acquisitions include the Central of Georgia, Georgia & Florida, and Savannah & Atlanta railroads, acquired in 1963, the Interstate Railroad (1960), and the previously noted Norfolk Southern (1974).

Norfolk & Western

By 1858 the predecessors of the N&W were in place from Norfolk through Petersburg and Lynchburg to Bristol, Va. They were consolidated in 1867 and became the Atlantic, Mississippi & Ohio Railroad in 1870. In 1881 the AM&O was purchased by the owners of the Shenandoah Valley Railroad and renamed the Norfolk & Western. The N&W was extended west through the West Virginia coalfields to the Ohio River. It reached Columbus in 1892 and Cincinnati in 1901. The Pennsylvania Railroad began purchasing N&W stock in 1900, and by 1964 it held approximately a one-third interest.

The N&W was the consummate coal-hauler, and it stayed with coal-burning steam locomotives, most of which it built in its Roanoke shops, until the late 1950s. Most of the coal it carried moved toward the Midwest until the mid-1950s, when a demand for high-quality coal developed in Europe. N&W's route east from Roanoke crossed several summits; the parallel Virginian Railway had a gentle descent all the way to tidewater. In 1925 N&W had made arrangements to lease the Virginian, but the Interstate Commerce Commission had said "No." The regulatory climate changed over three decades — N&W merged the Virginian in 1959.

The merger plans of the Pennsylvania and the New York Central and Chesapeake & Ohio's acquisition of control of the Baltimore & Ohio spurred N&W to look for merger partners. In 1964 N&W merged the Nickel Plate, leased the Wabash and the Pittsburgh & West Virginia, and purchased the Akron, Canton & Youngstown to create a system reaching to the Great Lakes and as far west as the Missouri River. An often-forgotten part of the merger was the purchase of Pennsylvania Railroad's line from Columbus north to Sandusky, Ohio, which connected the N&W to its acquisitions. (Much later, N&W also purchased the former PRR line from Cincinnati to New Castle, Ind.)

In 1965 N&W and Chesapeake & Ohio announced merger plans that would have encompassed practically everything east of the Mississippi and north of the Ohio and the Potomac that wasn't part of the Pennsylvania-New York Central proposal. The merger was killed by the bankruptcy of Penn Central and several other railroads in the early 1970s. A residue of the plans was the ownership through a subsidiary holding company of the Delaware & Hudson and the Erie Lackawanna. In 1981 N&W purchased the Illinois Terminal Railroad, a former interurban line between Peoria and St. Louis.

Virginian Railway

The Virginian Railway was built between 1904 and 1909 to carry coal from West Virginia to tidewater. It was notable for a 134-mile stretch of electrified main line west of Roanoke. VGN purchased new electric locomotives in 1948 and 1956; N&W found the electrification unnecessary with the one-way traffic pattern it established on the lines west of Roanoke and dismantled it in 1962.

Nickel Plate Road

The Nickel Plate was formally the New York, Chicago & St. Louis Railroad. It was begun in 1881 as a Buffalo-Cleveland-Chicago line to spite the New York Central, which promptly bought it to keep it out of the hands of Jay Gould. It remained a neglected part of the NYC system until 1916, when NYC sold it to Cleveland real estate developers Oris and Mantis Van Sweringen to keep it out of the hands of the Pennsylvania Railroad.

The Van Sweringens extended the NYC&StL to Peoria and St. Louis by acquiring the Lake Erie & Western, another NYC ward, and the Toledo, St. Louis & Western, a former narrow gauge road; then made alliances with Chesapeake & Ohio, Pere Marquette, Hocking Valley, and Erie. Nickel Plate and C&O both attempted to merge each other, but in each case groups of stockholders objected. In 1946 and 1947 Nickel Plate bought a majority interest in the Wheeling & Lake Erie, and in 1949 leased it.

Like the Norfolk & Western, the Nickel Plate dieselized late; its modern high-drivered 2-8-4s outperformed visiting diesel demonstrators. In the early 1960s Nickel Plate's principal Buffalo connections, Lehigh Valley and Lackawanna, suddenly found themselves affiliated with other railroads (Pennsylvania and Erie, respectively), and there was a general shift in alliances in the East. Norfolk & Western merged Nickel Plate on October 16, 1964.

Wheeling & Lake Erie

The Wheeling & Lake Erie was incorporated in 1871 to build from the Lake Erie ports of Sandusky and Toledo, Ohio, southeast through the coalfields of Ohio to Wheeling, West Virginia. The road got off to a slow, narrow gauge start; it took the backing of Jay Gould to convert it to standard gauge and get it to Wheeling in 1891. It gathered in a Cleveland-Zanesville railroad and continued to limp along, gathering strength only when the automobile industry in Detroit burgeoned — plants and factories along W&LE's line produced many automobile components.

In 1927 Nickel Plate, New York Central, and Baltimore & Ohio bought W&LE stock. The ICC ordered them to sell it. The Van Sweringens bought

it and added it to what they already had. The Nickel Plate purchased control in 1947 and leased the road in 1949. The lease passed to Norfolk & Western in 1964, and N&W merged the Wheeling & Lake Erie in 1988.

On May 17, 1990, a new Wheeling & Lake Erie Railway began operating most of the old W&LE plus the Pittsburgh &West Virginia (leased from the N&W) and what remains of the Akron, Canton & Youngstown (see page 236).

Pittsburgh & West Virginia

George Gould, son of Jay Gould, built the Wabash Pittsburgh Terminal Railway as an eastern extension of the Wheeling & Lake Erie. It reached Pittsburgh in 1904 with the intention of continuing southeast to meet a planned extension of the Western Maryland, also under Gould's control. The Panic of 1907 put the WPT, the Wheeling, and the Western Maryland into receivership. Western Maryland completed its extension to Connellsville, Pa., in 1912.

In 1916 the Wabash Pittsburgh Terminal was reorganized as the Pittsburgh & West Virginia. The ICC denied its request to acquire control of WM and W&LE, and not until 1931 did the road complete its line southeast to Connellsville. By then it had been acquired by a holding company subsidiary of the Pennsylvania Railroad.

In the 1930s the P&WV became a vital component of a multi-road fast freight route between the Midwest and the East made up of the Nickel Plate, Wheeling & Lake Erie, P&WV, Western Maryland, and Reading — collectively known as the Alphabet Route.

Akron, Canton & Youngstown

The AC&Y extended from Mogadore, Ohio, 8 miles east of Akron, west (in the opposite direction from Canton and Youngstown) across northern Ohio to Delphos. Much of its traffic consisted of tires (and inner tubes, in the old days) moving from Akron to Henry Ford's Detroit, Toledo & Ironton at Columbus Grove, Ohio. Both the AC&Y and the P&WV requested inclusion in the enlarged Norfolk & Western. N&W agreed to take them in, fearing their protests would delay N&W's merger with the Nickel Plate.

Wabash

The Wabash was assembled by Jay Gould in 1879 from the St. Louis, Kansas City & Northern Railroad, which had lines from St. Louis to Kansas City and Omaha, and the Toledo & Wabash Railway, which ran from Tole-

ROBERT B. CLAYTOR

(1922-) was born in Roanoke, Virginia. He graduated cum laude from Princeton University in 1943, and that same year married Frances Tice (Mrs. Claytor died in 1989). He served in the Army for three years, then attended Harvard Law School, from which he received the Juris Doctor degree in 1948. He worked for American Telephone & Telegraph as an attorney from 1948 to 1951, then joined the Norfolk & Western as a solicitor. He became vice-president, law, in 1964, president of the railroad in 1980, and chairman of the board of Norfolk Southern Corporation in 1982. In 1986 he reached the company's mandatory retirement age. He is still a director of Norfolk Southern.

Claytor engineered the merger of Norfolk & Western and Southern. A difficult aspect of that project was that both railroads were well and profitably run. He was quoted in *Focus*, the NS magazine: ". . . a consolidation of equals is tough and demanding. People from both companies are asked to accept a new way of life. We had to take the best of predecessors' ways and develop new ways; we wanted to make it work; we had to do what the New York Central and Pennsylvania failed utterly to do."

Claytor is an active rail enthusiast. He was instrumental in the return to active service of two Norfolk & Western steam locomotives, 4-8-4 No. 611 and 2-6-6-4 No. 1218, and he could often be found at their throttles. He is also active in civic and cultural affairs — in particular, he has served on the boards of the Virginia Opera Association and the Roanoke Symphony Society.

do, Ohio, to the Mississippi River at Keokuk, Iowa, and Quincy, Illinois. Gould constructed lines to Detroit and Chicago and acquired other railroads, and by 1884 the Wabash reached from Detroit to Kansas City and from the southern tip of Illinois to the northwest corner of Iowa. That year it collapsed into receivership, fell apart, then was reassembled in 1889 as the Wabash Railroad.

In 1904 George Gould pushed the Wabash into Pittsburgh as the Wabash Pittsburgh Terminal Railway. The Pittsburgh venture fell apart, as did Gould's plan for a coast-to-coast system. The Wabash was reorganized in 1915 as the Wabash Railway. Its main line ran from Buffalo through southwest Ontario and Detroit to Kansas City; there were branches to Toledo, Chicago, Des Moines, Omaha, and St. Louis. The Wabash was one of the few railroads that crossed an imaginary north-south line from Chicago through Peoria to St. Louis, then down the Mississippi.

In 1928 the Pennsylvania gained control of the Wabash, and by 1963 owned 87 percent of its stock. Divestiture was necessary before the ICC would approve the Pennsylvania-New York Central merger. Acquiring the Wabash gave the N&W access to the automobile industry in Detroit and a line all the way to the Missouri River.

Address of general offices: Three Commercial Place, Norfolk, VA 23510-2191

Miles of road operated: 14,700

Reporting marks: ACY, CG, CHW, ITC, NKP, NS, NW, SOU, VGN, WAB

Number of locomotives: 2,043

Number of freight cars: 110,121

Principal commodities carried: Coal, automobiles and parts, wood and paper, chemicals, intermodal containers and trailers

Major yards: Atlanta, Ga. (Inman); Bellevue, Ohio; Birmingham, Ala. (Norris); Chattanooga, Tenn. (DeButts); Decatur, Ill.; Fort Wayne, Ind.; Knoxville, Tenn. (Sevier); Linwood, N. C. (Spencer); Macon, Ga. (Brosnan); Roanoke, Va.; Muscle Shoals, Ala. (Sheffield)

Principal shops: Chattanooga, Tenn.; Roanoke, Va. (locomotives); Roanoke, Va.; Knoxville, Tenn.; Spartanburg, S. C. (cars)

Radio frequencies: 161.190 (original N&W), 161.250 (former Nickel Plate), 160.440 (former Wabash), 160.245, 160.830 (former Southern)

Passenger routes: Amtrak — Washington-New Orleans; Selma-Raleigh-Greensboro, N. C.; Centralia, Ill.-St. Louis, Mo.
Recommended reading:
The Norfolk & Western: A History, by E. F. Pat Striplin, published in

1981 by the Norfolk & Western Railway
The Southern Railway: Road of the Innovators, by Burke Davis, published in 1985 by the University of North Carolina Press, P. O. Box 2288, Chapel Hill, NC 27514 (ISBN 0-8078-1636-1)

STEAM ON THE MAIN LINE

By 1960 steam power had all but disappeared from North American railroads. A few steam locomotives could be found operating scheduled service on museum railroads, and you might encounter operating steam on short lines and industrial railroads, but it was largely a matter of luck — those roads were dieselizing, too.

In 1963 Paul Merriam, a railroad enthusiast and a member of the Tennessee Valley Railroad Museum, bought a steam locomotive, Kentucky & Tennessee Railway 12 (formerly Southern Railway 4501, the road's first 2-8-2), and asked the Southern to move it under its own power 145 miles from Stearns, Kentucky, to Chattanooga, Tennessee. The Southern, which had completed dieselization in 1953, pondered the matter and agreed to it. The locomotive got to Chattanooga without tying up the railroad, and 4501 underwent a two-year restoration project.

Meanwhile, the Atlanta Chapter of the National Railway Historical Society began operating excursions powered by Savannah & Atlanta 4-6-2 No. 750 on Southern rails. W. Graham Claytor, vice-president, law, of the Southern Railway (later its president) recognized that the steam locomotives were excellent advertisements for the Southern. Under his direction the Southern developed a steam locomotive program that over the years operated nine steam locomotives on excur-

The locomotive that started Norfolk Southern's steam program, No. 4501, leads a Danville, Kentucky-Chattanooga excursion train out of a tunnel and across a bridge south of Lancing, Tennessee, on June 30, 1970. Photo by Don Phillips.

sion trains nearly every weekend from March through November. Claytor assigned a former diesel shop in Birmingham, Alabama, to the steam program and, more important, staffed the effort.

Graham Claytor's retirement from the Southern in 1977 had no effect on the steam program; Southern's merger with Norfolk & Western accelerated it. In 1980 Robert Claytor, president of the Norfolk & Western and like his brother Graham a railroad enthusiast, made arrangements to have Norfolk & Western 611, a J-class streamlined 4-8-4, removed from the Roanoke Tranportation Museum in Wasena Park and sent to Birmingham to be restored to operating condition. In 1985 another N&W engine, A-class 2-6-6-4 No. 1218, was moved from the museum to Birmingham — it began excursion service in 1987.

Norfolk Southern has not been alone in operating steam. Union Pacific dieselized its operations but never removed 4-8-4 No. 844 from its locomotive roster. In 1979 UP began restoration of 4-6-6-4 No. 3985, which had been displayed next to the station in Cheyenne, and in March 1981 the articulated moved under its own power — and quickly took its place in UP's steam excursion program. There has been some good-natured banter between NS and UP about which has the larger locomotive: UP 3985 is heavier; N&W 1218 is more powerful. All the Super Seven railroads and most of the other Class 1 railroads have hosted steam power within the last two decades.

When they dieselized, many railroads wrote off the scrap value of a few steam locomotives and donated them to cities and towns along their lines. A few went to museums — but there weren't many railroad museums in the 1950s. Most of the donated locomotives ended up on display in parks, prey to weather, neglect, and vandalism.

There is something unsatisfying about static display of a dynamic machine. For every locomotive that was placed on a short piece of track with a fence around it at least one person wondered, "Could it run again?" Some of those people did more than wonder: they painted, they lubricated, they got together and asked, "How can we make it run again?"

The process of restoration begins with moving a chunk of machinery that has sat in one place for a long time and may weigh upwards of 200 tons. Next, every piece of the locomotive has to be made able to slide or turn or hold water or withstand air or steam pressure. Parts have to be made from scratch; most of the companies that built the locomotives and supplied the components are long gone. Much of the restoration work has been done by volunteers, though the railroad companies have often proved cooperative once projects are under way.

There are several significant differences between the mainline steam operations and the tourist railroads. The locomotives have generally been larger — 2-8-4s and 4-8-4s predominate. They run greater distances, and they share the tracks with freight, piggyback, and passenger trains which have schedules to meet. It is to a railroad's credit that it can deal with the vagaries of steam-powered excursion trains.

In 1991 Norfolk Southern celebrated 25 years of operating steam-powered excursion trains on its main lines and gave every indication that steam locomotives would continue to burnish NS rails beyond the turn of the century.

Recommended reading:

Weekend Steam, edited by Bill Schafer, published in 1991 by Southern Railway Historical Association, P. O. Box 33, Spencer, NC 28159
"Steam-powered public relations," by Jim Wrinn, in TRAINS Magazine, August 1991, pages 30-44

NORTHWESTERN OKLAHOMA RAILROAD

The Northwestern Oklahoma has operated a short stretch of former Missouri-Kansas Texas track between Woodward and Fisk, Oklahoma, since 1973. Long ago the line was part of the Wichita Falls & Northwestern Railway, which extended from Wichita Falls, Texas, north through western Oklahoma, then turned west through the panhandle of the state. The road operates a commercial freight car repair shop and has a large fleet of interchange freight cars.

Address of general offices: Box 1131, Woodward, OK 73801
Miles of road operated: 9
Reporting marks: NOKL
Number of locomotives: 1
Number of freight cars: 2,020
Principal commodities carried: Cement, oil drilling mud, grain
Shops: Woodward, Okla.
Junctions with other railroads: Atchison, Topeka & Santa Fe: Woodward, Okla.

Northwestern Oklahoma No. 1 is a GE 44-tonner built in 1946 for the Sacramento Northern. Photo by Jim Shaw.

ONTARIO NORTHLAND RAILWAY

Shortly after the boundary between the Canadian provinces of Ontario and Quebec was defined in 1884, the settlers living just west of that boundary near Lake Temiskaming began to demand a railway, both for colonization and to link the area to Toronto. In 1902 the legislative assembly of Ontario passed an act creating a commission to construct and operate the Temiskaming & Northern Ontario Railway. The commission chose to create a government railway rather than finance construction by a private

Ontario Northland SD40-2s lead a northbound freight across the Driftwood River bridge at Monteith, Ontario on February 17, 1977. Photo by Len Thompson.

corporation or build a railway for eventual operation by one of the existing carriers.

Construction began at North Bay, Ont., on the Canadian Pacific line between Montreal and Sudbury, Ont., and at the end of a Grand Trunk line from Toronto. The T&NO reached Englehart in 1906 and a junction with the National Transcontinental Railway, still under construction, at Cochrane, 252 miles from North Bay, in 1909. In its early days T&NO carried supplies for construction of the National Transcontinental, and for a period T&NO formed part of a through route to the West in conjunction with Grand Trunk from Toronto to North Bay and NTR west of Cochrane.

T&NO's fortunes changed with the discovery of silver at Cobalt, Ont., in 1903 and the discovery of gold in the Porcupine area, near what is now Timmins, in 1909. The road was instrumental in the development of the Clay Belt agricultural area and the forest lands through which it lay. In 1928 the Nipissing Central Railway, a T&NO subsidiary, constructed a branch east from Swastika to the gold-mining area at Noranda and Rouyn, Que. In 1931 T&NO completed a line from Cochrane north to the shore of James Bay at Moosonee.

The name of the railway was changed in 1946 to Ontario Northland to be more descriptive of the area it served and also to avoid confusion with the Texas & New Orleans Railroad, Southern Pacific's Texas and Louisiana subsidiary.

Ontario Northland's principal business is still carrying the products of Ontario's forests and mines. It operates its own passenger trains (rather than turn them over to VIA Rail Canada), the daytime Toronto-Cochrane *Northlander*, which runs on Canadian National rails between Toronto and North Bay, and the *Polar Bear*, a mixed train between Cochrane and Moosonee.

Ontario Northland Transportation Commission, parent company of the railway, also operates buses, trucks, boats, airplanes, and communications services in northern Ontario.

Address of general offices: 555 Oak Street East, North Bay, ON, Canada P1B 8L3
Miles of road operated: 574
Reporting marks: ONT, ONTA
Number of locomotives: 38

Number of freight cars: 690
Number of passenger cars: 64
Principal commodities carried: Newsprint, pulpwood, lumber, ores and concentrates
Shops: Cochrane, Ont.; Englehart, Ont.; North Bay, Ont.; Rouyn, Que.; Timmins, Ont.
Radio frequencies: 160.545, 161.265, 160.995

Junctions with other railroads:
Canadian National: Cochrane, Ont.; Noranda, Que.; North Bay, Ont.
CP Rail: North Bay, Ont.
Passenger routes: Toronto-North Bay-Cochrane-Moosonee, Ont.
Recommended reading: *Steam Into Wilderness*, by Albert Tucker, published in 1978 by Fitzhenry & Whiteside, 150 Lesmill Road, Don Mills, ON, Canada M3B 2T5 (ISBN 0-88902-444-8)

PADUCAH & LOUISVILLE RAILWAY

A railroad was opened between Elizabethtown and Paducah, Kentucky, by the Elizabethtown & Paducah Railroad in 1872. The railroad company went through several reorganizations and name changes; in 1877 the route became part of the Chesapeake, Ohio & Southwestern Railroad, extending from Elizabethtown and Louisville through Paducah to Memphis, Tennessee. It was to be a link in a transcontinental system that C. P.

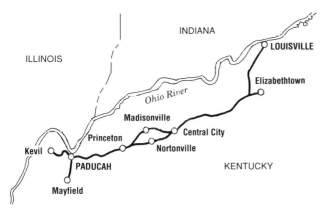

Huntington was trying to create, with the Southern Pacific and the Chesapeake & Ohio as the two ends.

In 1888 the Illinois Central Railroad, by then under the control of E. H. Harriman, purchased the Chesapeake, Ohio & Southwestern, gaining access to Louisville, the coalfields east of Paducah and, more important to IC in the long run, Memphis.

Illinois Central grew and prospered. In 1972 IC merged the Gulf, Mobile & Ohio Railroad to create Illinois Central Gulf. Not long after ICG reached its maximum extent (with lines reaching to Sioux Falls, South Dakota, Shreveport, Louisiana, and Montgomery, Alabama), its owner, IC Industries, began to look for a buyer so it could get out of the railroad business. No one wanted the whole railroad. In 1981 IC Industries decided to sell pieces to trim ICG to a Chicago-New Orleans trunk line. It soon found buyers for ICG's east-west routes, and within a few years ICG's route mileage shrank by 70 percent.

In 1985 ICG approached two western Kentucky businessmen, Jim Smith and David Reed, who singly or jointly owned coal mines, a highway construction firm, a quarry, and a rail-to-barge transfer operation. ICG suggested that with the impending downsizing of the railroad, the best way for the men to preserve rail service would be to operate their own. On August 27, 1986, the Paducah & Louisville took ownership of the Paducah-Louisville main line (there are two routes between Central City and Dawson Springs), branches to Elizabethtown, Kevil, and Clayburn, and ICG's shop complex at Paducah, which was spun off to a subsidiary, VMV Enterprises.

A Paducah & Louisville GP35 — an ex-Gulf, Mobile & Ohio unit riding on Alco trucks — leads a train across Barkley Dam at Lake City, Kentucky. Photo by Gary Dolzall.

Most of P&L's traffic either originates or terminates on line, and more than 60 percent of it is coal.

Address of general offices: 1500 Kentucky Avenue, Paducah, KY 42001
Miles of road operated: 309
Reporting marks: PAL
Number of locomotives: 71
Number of freight cars: 1,183
Principal commodities carried: Coal, chemicals, stone
Major yards: Paducah, Ky.
Principal shops: Paducah, Ky.
Junctions with other railroads:
Burlington Northern: Paducah, Ky.
Conrail: Louisville, Ky.
CP Rail System (Soo Line): Louisville, Ky.
CSX: Louisville, Ky.; Madisonville, Ky.
Illinois Central: Paducah, Ky.
Norfolk Southern: Louisville, Ky.
Tradewater: Princeton, Ky.
Radio frequencies: 160.740 (road), 160.695 (yard), 161.325 (yard)
Recommended reading: "The Paducah & Louisville story," by Gary W. Dolzall and Jerry Mart, in TRAINS Magazine, March 1988, pages 24-33

PITTSBURGH & LAKE ERIE RAILROAD

The Pittsburgh & Lake Erie was chartered in 1875 and opened from Pittsburgh, Pennsylvania, to Youngstown, Ohio, in 1879. Cornelius Vanderbilt of the New York Central subscribed to 15 percent of the railroad's stock, because he saw the P&LE as the route by which his New York Central system could enter Pittsburgh to compete with the Pennsylvania Railroad to serve the steel industry. NYC gained control of P&LE in 1889, and from then on it was for all practical purposes a division of the NYC and a highly profitable one.

The portion of the P&LE south of Pittsburgh was incorporated in 1881 as the Pittsburgh, McKeesport & Youghiogheny. It was jointly owned by

P&LE and NYC and was operated as part of P&LE. In 1965 P&LE bought NYC's half interest in the road.

When Penn Central, successor to New York Central, went bankrupt in 1970 it owed P&LE $15 million and it owned 92.6 percent of P&LE's stock. Officials who held positions with both PC and P&LE were replaced with new management, and P&LE began to chart an independent course. Local congressmen were persuaded by P&LE management, labor, and shippers to amend the Regional Rail Reorganization Act of 1973 to allow solvent subsidiaries of Penn Central to stay out of Conrail. Later negotiations gave P&LE access to Norfolk & Western's ex-Nickel Plate line at Ashtabula, Ohio, via trackage rights on Conrail north from Youngstown. On February 27, 1979, Penn Central sold the Pittsburgh & Lake Erie Rail-

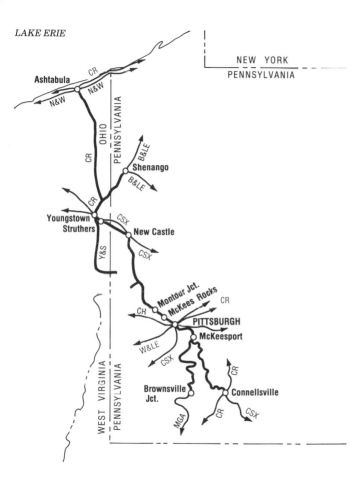

Five Pittsburgh & Lake Erie diesels wait in the rain at Lowellville, Ohio, on May 1, 1992. Photo by Michael W. Blaszak.

road to the new Pittsburgh & Lake Erie Company, which subsequently became a private corporation.

As the steel industry along its Pittsburgh-Youngstown route declined, so did the P&LE. In the late 1980s the road was up for sale. Several prospective buyers came and went while the labor unions fought for income protection. In June 1989 the United States Supreme Court reversed the decision of a lower court and upheld a company's right to sell its business without having to bargain with the unions. In May 1990 P&LE reached agreement with its 14 unions on severance benefits and sold the railroad to Railroad Development Corporation on June 6, 1990.

In July 1991 P&LE sold 61 miles of its main line from McKeesport, Pa., through Pittsburgh to New Castle to CSX. Baltimore & Ohio had obtained trackage rights on the route in 1934 to bypass the steep grades and sharp curves of its own line west of Pittsburgh. The sale reversed the owner-tenant relationship and generated some much-needed cash for P&LE. Negotiations are in process for government agencies to buy 265 miles of Conrail's former Erie Lackawanna main line between Hornell, New York, and Pymatuning, Pa., southwest of Shenango. P&LE has been selected to operate the line.

P&LE operated few branch lines but had several subsidiary railroads. The Montour Railroad was a short line serving the area west of Pittsburgh. It was owned jointly with Penn Central; P&LE bought PC's half interest in 1975. The Montour ceased operation in 1983; abandonment was approved in 1986. The Montour owned the Youngstown & Southern Railway, a 35-mile road running south and east from Youngstown, Ohio. It remains in operation.

The Monongahela Railway, a 162-mile coal carrier running southwest from Brownsville, Pa., was owned jointly with Chessie System (ex-Baltimore & Ohio) and Conrail (ex-Pennsylvania Railroad interest). Conrail has acquired full ownership and has applied to merge the Monongahela.

The Pittsburgh, Chartiers & Youghiogheny Railway, a 12-mile switching line between Pittsburgh, McKees Rocks, and Carnegie, is owned jointly by P&LE and Conrail.

Address of general offices: 4 Station Square, Pittsburgh, PA 15219
Miles of road operated: 404
Reporting marks: MTR, PLE
Number of locomotives: 39
Number of freight cars: 3,174
Principal commodities carried: Coal, iron ore, coke, limestone, steel
Major yards: Youngstown, Ohio (Gateway); McKees Rocks, Pa. (Riverton)
Principal shops: McKees Rocks, Pa.
Radio frequencies: 160.995 (road), 160.890 (yard)
Historical and technical society: New York Central System Historical Society, P. O. Box 10027, Cleveland, OH 44110
Recommended reading:
Pittsburgh and Lake Erie R. R., by Harold H. McLean, published in 1980 by Golden West Books, P. O. Box 8136, San Marino, CA 91108 (ISBN 0-87095-080-0)
"The Little Giant, free again," by Lee A. Gregory, in TRAINS Magazine, July 1981, pages 36-47

PRIVATE CARS, LUXURY TRAINS, AND DINNER TRAINS

Once upon a time, long before first class consisted of two-and-two seating at the front of the plane, luxury travel was your own private railroad car. To go to Saratoga Springs or French Lick or Bar Harbor, you asked your personal secretary to make the arrangements. At the proper time your chauffeur brought the limousine around to the porte cochere (this was before "limousine" got shortened to "limo" and became a van). Your chauffeur took you to the station, where you found your car at the rear of the train, offering an unobstructed view from the observation platform. Your car's staff (who may have been your household staff, too) welcomed you aboard; by then your luggage, which had come earlier, was unpacked and its contents were in drawers and closets, so you could dress for dinner. You didn't have to adjust the routine of your life at all — if you were one of the privileged few who had that sort of routine.

Most private cars were alike in configuration if not in decor. The kitchen was typically at the front end of the car; off the pantry was a small bedroom for the chef and the waiter. Next was a dining room seating 8 to 12 at a large central table, then several staterooms. The master stateroom had its own bathroom; occupants of other staterooms might have to share a bathroom or the stateroom might contain a folding washstand and a toilet disguised as a hassock. At the rear of the car was an observation room with windows looking out to the rear across the brass-railed platform.

Everything about a private car was expensive — the purchase price, maintenance, staff, and the cost of moving it (traditionally 18 first-class fares). As J. P. Morgan is reputed to have said of a yacht, if you had to ask

Private car 353, owned by Richard Horstmann of Syracuse, N. Y., once served the officials of the Lehigh Valley Railroad, and keeps its historic livery and lettering. Photo by Don Jilson.

what it cost, you couldn't afford it. Those who didn't own a private car could charter one from the Pullman Company, which maintained a fleet of about two dozen cars for the purpose.

After 1930 the private car began to drop out of favor, partly because of the cost and partly because train travel was becoming passé. In 1959 Lucius Beebe wrote in *Mansions on Rails* that only two private cars remained, one of them his. He blamed their demise on the railroads' "urge toward suicide and bankruptcy" that manifested itself in "such monumental follies as Dieselization." (He also predicted that the supply of old-time steam locomotive photos would soon be exhausted, bringing an end to railroad books and magazines.)

There was a subtle difference between the private car and the railroad or corporation business or office car. Exterior appearance and configuration were much the same, but the interior of the business car was less ornate. The purpose of the car was not luxury travel but simply conveyance for company officials to where they were needed. The business car furnished meals, lodging, and office space, and, just as important, let the officials see the railroad.

Railroads trimmed back their business car fleets for the same reasons that private cars disappeared. Did it make sense to hang 80 tons of business car on the rear of a passenger train, when a roomette in the sleeping car and a voucher for breakfast in the dining car would suffice? (As passenger trains were discontinued it became a moot question. An official could fly somewhere and be back the same evening, sometimes on the railroad's own plane.)

Some business cars that were trimmed from railroad fleets found their way into the hands of individuals. By the 1970s a private-car renaissance was at hand. There was a difference, though. The man in the dining room wearing black tie was still the owner, but he might be serving the dinner he prepared to the people who had chartered the car — and an hour or so later he might be found, no longer in black tie, prodding a balky air conditioner back to life or unplugging a toilet.

Private cars have continued to increase in number. Many of those in service today have been converted from other types of cars (sleepers and diners, for example) and the accommodations and facilities are more varied than anything found in the 1920s. Excursion trains of private cars are no longer uncommon, and cars available for charter to move on Amtrak trains are plentiful.

Luxury trains

Most railroads had a flagship passenger train. Usually it had the fastest schedule between the most important cities on the railroad, the newest cars, and the best crews. Often it provided a level of service better than the other trains on the road; often it was all-Pullman (first-class sleeping cars); and occasionally an extra fare was charged. Examples that spring to mind immediately are New York Central's *20th Century Limited* between New York and Chicago, Santa Fe's *Super Chief* between Chicago and Los Angeles, and Illinois Central's *Panama Limited* between Chicago and New Orleans.

One by one these premier trains were democratized: the extra fare was abolished, coaches were added, the observation car was removed, special items on the menu were deleted — and other inferior trains were discontinued. By the time Amtrak took over passenger railroading in 1971, deluxe

189

passenger travel seemed to have been taken over by the airlines. There were no first-class-only trains left in the United States. (Some will make a case for the *Panama*, but between the locomotive and the first sleeper were the coaches of the *Magnolia Star*, which operated on the same schedule. The *Super Chief*? Up front were the hi-level coaches of *El Capitan* — another example of schedule-sharing — and there was no observation car on the rear end.)

The next development was in Europe. In 1976 the *Nostalgie Istanbul Orient Express* began operating a train of restored sleeping and dining cars on several routes. The trips were not frequent enough to be considered regularly scheduled service, but they were more luxurious in both equipment and service than anything else in Europe. In 1982 the *Venice Simplon-Orient-Express* began regular service two or three times a week between London and Venice with restored cars, elaborate food service, and attentive staff. VSOE aims the service at the upscale tourist market and top-level business people and has been quite successful.

Intraflug, owner of the *Nostalgie Istanbul Orient Express*, brought the concept to the United States in November 1989 with the inauguration of the *American European Express* between Washington and Chicago: luxurious sleeping, dining, and lounge cars coupled to the rear of Amtrak's *Capitol Limited*. Passenger counts were disappointing; among the possible reasons for low ridership were a schedule just barely long enough for dinner, a few hours of sleep, and an early breakfast; and fares two to three times what Amtrak was charging in the first-class sleepers just ahead. In May 1980 AEE reduced its Washington-Chicago service and added New York-Philadelphia-Chicago service. Service was discontinued in November 1990 and restored in March 1991 on a new route: New York-Chicago via Washington, White Sulphur Springs, Cincinnati, and Indianapolis — the route of Amtrak's *Cardinal* but operating as a separate train west of Washington. In October 1991 AEE suspended operations because of financial problems.

Dinner trains

Another product of the private-car renaissance and the public's renewed fascination with trains has been the dinner train, typically a 3- to 4-hour out-and-back train ride for the sole purpose of having a nice dinner. Some dinner trains have been successful; others have flourished for a year or two before exhausting their market. The price, which must include what you'd pay for the dinner in a restaurant plus the cost of making the restaurant move, tends to make them special-occasion rather the spur-of-the-moment dining; they do best near major metropolitan areas. The best-known dinner train is the Napa Valley Wine Train, which is well known for the controversy about its startup: Some opponents said the train would bring more tourists to an area where the highways were already glutted with tourists. Others simply objected to the trains as trains (the tracks had been in place since 1868). The California Public Utilities Commission also got into the wrangle, requiring an environmental impact study. Nonetheless, it has elegantly decorated cars and handsome locomotives, serves a superb dinner, and offers in the course of an evening a chance to experience luxury rail travel.

Address: American Association of Private Railroad Car Owners, Inc.,

The Napa Valley Wine Train combines Montreal-built FPA4s and former Southern and Rio Grande coaches rebuilt to kitchen, dining, and lounge observation cars. The colors are, appropriately, champagne and burgundy. Photo by Victor D. Ryerson.

c/o Lawrence C. Haines, 224 Orr Drive, Somerville, NJ 08876
Recommended reading:
Mansions on Rails, by Lucius Beebe, published in 1959 by Howell-North, Berkeley, California

Vanishing Varnish, by Patrick O. McLaughlin, published in 1990 by POM Publishing Company, P. O. Box 3714, Danville, VA 24543
"Going out (and back) for dinner," by Steve Glischinski, in TRAINS Magazine, June 1990, pages 26-35

PROVIDENCE & WORCESTER RAILROAD

The Providence & Worcester was chartered in 1844 and began operation between its namesake cities, Providence, Rhode Island, and Worcester, Massachusetts, in 1847. In 1889 it was leased to the New York, Providence & Boston Railroad, which was in turn leased to the New Haven in 1892. The road was operated thereafter as part of the New Haven.

A Providence & Worcester freight brushes fresh snow off the rails alongside the Thames River at Preston, Connecticut, on March 9, 1984. Photo by Alan M. Crossley.

In 1968, just before the New Haven became part of Penn Central, the Providence & Worcester reincorporated and in 1970 requested independence. On February 3, 1973, P&W resumed independent operation. In 1974 P&W purchased a line from Worcester to Gardner, Massachusetts, from the Boston & Maine.

Rhode Island has become a one-freight-railroad state as a result of P&W's acquisitions. In 1979 P&W bought the Warwick Railway, a railroad only nine-tenths of a mile long at Cranston. In 1981 P&W purchased the Moshassuck Valley Railroad — twice as long as the Warwick, stretching from Woodlawn (Pawtucket) to Saylesville. In 1982 P&W acquired all of Conrail's former New Haven branches in Rhode Island and freight rights on Amtrak's Northeast Corridor line (the former New Haven main line) from Attleboro, Mass., through Providence to Westbrook, Connecticut (later all the way to New Haven).

P&W also acquired the former New Haven line from Worcester south to Groton, Connecticut, plus two branches from that route to Southbridge, Mass., and Willimantic, Conn.

Address of general offices: P. O. Box 1188, Worcester, MA 01601
Miles of road operated: 370
Reporting marks: PW
Number of locomotives: 16
Number of freight cars: 38
Principal commodities carried: Chemicals, newsprint, foodstuffs, sand and gravel, pulp board
Shops: Worcester, Mass.
Junctions with other railroads:
Guilford Transportation Industries (Boston & Maine): Gardner, Mass.
Central Vermont: New London, Conn.
Conrail: Worcester, Mass.
Radio frequencies: 160.650 (road), 161.100 (yard)

QUEBEC NORTH SHORE & LABRADOR RAILWAY

The area north of the St. Lawrence River along the Quebec-Newfoundland border — the Ungava tract in the Labrador Peninsula — was known as early as the 1890s to contain iron ore, but not until the 1930s and 1940s did exploration reveal a large enough deposit — one of the world's largest — to make mining and transportation of the ore economically feasible. In 1949 the Iron Ore Company of Canada (IOC) was formed with the backing of a number of U. S. steelmakers. One of its first projects was the construction of a railroad north from Sept-Îles, Quebec, about 356 miles into the wilderness. Much of the surveying for the line was done from helicopters, and the construction machinery and supplies were brought in by air. Construction began in 1951 and the road was completed in 1954. The southern half of the line is in Quebec; the northern half is in Newfoundland, except for the last few miles into Schefferville, Que.

In 1960 a 36-mile branch was completed west from Ross Bay Junction, Newfoundland (224 miles from Sept-Îles), to the Carol Lake mining area near Labrador City and Wabush Lake. The branch is jointly owned by IOC and Wabush Lake Railway Co. An automated electrically operated railroad serves the mines near Carol Lake. Ore trains from that area move south on the QNS&L to Arnaud Junction, 8 miles north of Sept-Îles. From there the Arnaud Railway takes them to ore docks at Pointe-Noire, Que., 21 miles west of Sept-Îles. Like the Cartier Railway, QNS&L and Arnaud have no rail connection to the rest of the North American rail system.

QNS&L is a heavy-duty single-track railroad characterized by such modern technology as welded rail, long sidings, centralized traffic control, roller bearings, and radio control of mid-train helper locomotives. QNS&L's trains are among the longest and heaviest in the world — usually 230 cars, or about 1.6 miles and 28,000 tons.

Because ore freezes, the railroad carries raw ore only during summer and autumn, but trains run year round to carry beneficiated (processed) ore in the form of concentrate or pellets.

QNS&L is a common carrier, and it operates biweekly passenger trains; there are no highways north of Sept-Îles.

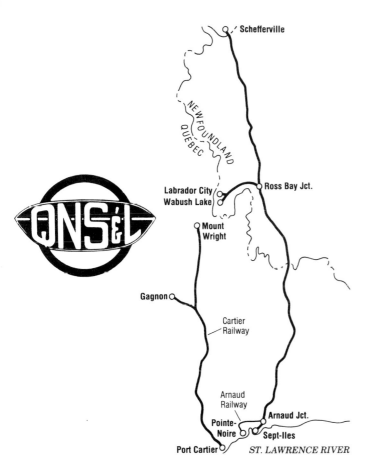

A short train leaves the bank of the St. Lawrence River at Sept-Iles, Que., on June 7, 1981, with tank and covered hopper cars of chemicals bound for the iron mines to the north. Photo by Greg McDonnell.

Address of general offices: P. O. Box 1000, Sept-Îles, PQ, Canada G4R 4L5
Miles of road operated: 394
Reporting marks: QNSL, IOCC
Number of locomotives: 58
Number of freight cars: 4,238
Number of passenger cars: 24
Principal commodities carried: Iron ore
Major yards: Sept-Îles, Que.; Labrador City, Newfoundland
Shops: Sept-Îles, Que.
Junctions with other railroads: Arnaud Railway: Arnaud Junction, Que.
Radio frequencies: 160.215, 160.290
Passenger routes: Sept-Îles to Schefferville, Ross Bay Jct.-Labrador City

RED RIVER VALLEY & WESTERN RAILROAD

In 1986 three Minneapolis investors were looking for a railroad to buy, and Burlington Northern wanted to prune its route map. The investors formed the Red River Valley & Western Railroad and purchased a cluster of BN lines in North Dakota:

- Breckenridge, Minnesota-Wahpeton, N. D.-Oakes-Independence
- Wahpeton-Casselton
- Chaffee Junction-Chaffee
- Horace-Davenport-Sheldon-Edgley
- Casselton-Lucca-Marion
- LaMoure-Pingree-Carrington-New Rockford-Esmond
- Pingree-Regan
- Carrington-Turtle Lake
- Oberon-Minnewaukan

In addition, RRV&W obtained trackage rights on Soo Line from Sheldon to Lucca to connect the Horace-Edgley and Casselton-Marion lines.

All the lines RRV&W purchased are former Northern Pacific branches except for the Wahpeton-Casselton line and its branch to Chaffee, which are ex-Great Northern. The lines were built between 1870 and 1912 to serve the wheat-growing area of eastern North Dakota. Many were built by separate companies, not by NP, whose charter did not allow branch line construction.

The lines were profitable, but BN wanted to concentrate on long-haul traffic. The lines are also profitable for Red River Valley, and the smaller road can pay close attention to shippers' needs. The road has tariff and car-hire arrangements with BN (it owns no freight cars) and in a sense functions as a switching and terminal road for BN. Red River Valley & Western runs unit trains during the harvest season.

Address of general offices: P. O. Box 608, Wahpeton, ND 58074
Miles of road operated: 667
Reporting marks: RRVW

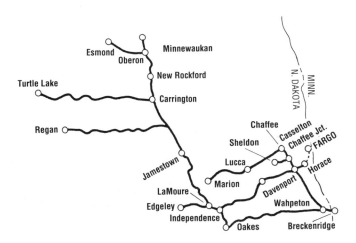

Two Red River Valley & Western CF7s take a long grain train across Highway 13 at Gwinner, North Dakota, on July 19, 1987. Photo by Robert W. Johnston.

Number of locomotives: 10
Shops: Breckenridge, Minn.
Junctions with other railroads:
Burlington Northern: Breckenridge, Minn.; Casselton, N. D.;
Jamestown, N. D.; New Rockford, N. D.
CP Rail System (Soo Line): Carrington, N. D.; Lucca, N. D.; Oakes, N. D.

Principal commodities carried: Wheat, corn, sugar
Radio frequencies: 160.230, 161.445
Recommended reading: "The most mellifluous name in railroading," by Ken C. Brovald and William E. Thoms, in TRAINS Magazine, February 1990, pages 52-61

REGIONAL RAILROADS OF AMERICA

In the mid-1980s several Class 2 and regional railroads formed an association named Regional Railroads of America. Its purpose is to lobby Congress on issues affecting medium-size and small railroads — such issues as the federal railroad retirement and unemployment program, the Federal Employers Liability Act, and labor protection responsibilities during the sale and abandonment of railroads. The group works to educate legislators and the public on the emerging role of regional and feeder railroads. The association's membership numbers about 125 railroads. Associate memberships are available for industry suppliers and others interested in the activities of the association.

Address of general offices: 122 C Street, N. W., Suite 850, Washington, DC 20001

ROCHESTER & SOUTHERN RAILROAD

In 1869 the Rochester & State Line Railroad was incorporated to build a railroad south from Rochester, New York. In 1878 the line was open from Rochester through Ashford and Salamanca, New York, and Bradford and DuBois, Pennsylvania, to Punxsutawney. In 1881 it was reorganized as the Rochester & Pittsburgh Railroad, and in 1887 it became part of the Buffalo, Rochester & Pittsburgh Railway.

The BR&P developed into a well-run coal carrier, and eventually it caught the eye of the Baltimore & Ohio, which wanted to use it as the nucleus of an east-west route across central Pennsylvania. In 1928 it was acquired by the Van Sweringen brothers (who owned the Nickel Plate and controlled the Chesapeake & Ohio). The B&O still wanted it, though, and

Rochester & Southern 104, a GP40, stands in the yard at East Salamanca, New York, on June 3, 1988. Coupled to it is Buffalo & Pittsburgh 886, a GP9 still wearing the solid black of its previous owner, Norfolk & Western. Photo by Jim Shaw.

traded its interest in the Wheeling & Lake Erie, which the Van Sweringens wanted, for the BR&P on January 1, 1932. Even though B&O took over operation of the BR&P, the BR&P continued to have a corporate existence. In 1986 Chessie System, successor to the B&O, sold the Rochester-Ashford portion of the BR&P to Genesee & Wyoming Industries. In April 1988 the remainder of the BR&P became the Buffalo & Pittsburgh Railroad, also a Genesee & Wyoming subsidiary.

Address of general offices: 1372 Brooks Avenue, Rochester, NY 14624
Miles of road operated: 67
Reporting marks: RSR

Number of locomotives: 6
Number of freight cars: 121
Principal commodities carried: Coal, salt, chemicals
Shops: Rochester, N. Y.
Junctions with other railroads:
Buffalo & Pittsburgh: East Salamanca, N. Y.
Conrail: Rochester, N. Y.; Silver Springs, N. Y.
CP Rail System (Delaware & Hudson): Silver Springs, N. Y.
Genesee & Wyoming: Caledonia (P&L Junction), N. Y.
Radio frequencies: 160.770 (road), 161.100 (yard)

SAN JOAQUIN VALLEY RAILROAD

The San Joaquin Valley began operating a cluster of former Southern Pacific branches on January 1, 1992. The lines extend west from Exeter, California, through Visalia and Hanford to Stratford and Huron, from Exeter north through Sanger to Fresno, and from Exeter south to Terra Bella. The road is a division of Kyle Railways.

Address of general offices: P. O. Box 937, Exeter, CA 93221
Miles of road operated: 144
Reporting marks: SJVR
Number of locomotives: 7
Principal commodities carried: Grain, foodstuffs, paper products
Shops: Exeter, Calif.
Junctions with other railroads: Southern Pacific: Fresno, Calif.; Goshen Junction, Calif.

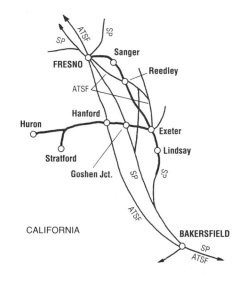

San Joaquin Valley 1754, a GP9 fresh out of the road's shop, crosses the Kings River at Reedley, California, on its way to Fresno on April 23, 1992. The two mechanical refrigerator cars behind the diesel belong to the Ventura County Railway. Photo by Ted Benson

SEMINOLE GULF RAILWAY

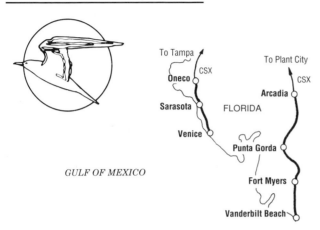

Miles of road operated: 118
Reporting marks: SGLR
Number of locomotives: 8
Number of freight cars: 90
Number of passenger cars: 6
Principal commodities carried: Limestone, building materials, forest products, newsprint
Shops: Fort Myers, Fla.; Oneco, Fla.
Junctions with other railroads: CSX: Arcadia, Fla.; Oneco, Fla.
Radio frequencies:
Passenger routes: Punta Gorda-Fort Myers-Bonita Springs, Fla.

Seminole Gulf Railway operates a former Seaboard Air Line route from Oneco, Florida, through Sarasota to Venice and a former Atlantic Coast Line branch from Arcadia, Fla., through Fort Myers to the north outskirts of Naples. The Venice route was opened to Sarasota in 1903 and extended south to Venice in 1912. The Fort Myers route was built as a narrow gauge line by the Florida Southern Railway. It reached Punta Gorda in 1886 and was converted to standard gauge in 1892. The line was later extended to Fort Myers as part of the Plant System, then farther south through Naples to Marco Island — under Atlantic Coast Line auspices. By the 1950s it had been trimmed back to Naples, and in the 1980s Seaboard Coast Line trimmed it further to a point about 10 miles north of downtown Naples. CSX sold the lines to Seminole Gulf in 1987. The company is affiliated with Bay Colony Railroad in southeastern Massachusetts.
Address of general offices: 4110 Centerpointe Drive, Fort Myers, FL 33916

Seminole Gulf GP9 575 switches tank cars alongside Evans Avenue in Fort Myers, Florida, on July 24, 1992. Photo by George H. Drury.

SOO LINE RAILROAD

In the 1870s the flour millers of Minneapolis sought a new outlet for their products to avoid the exorbitant freight rates charged by existing railroads through Chicago. James J. Hill, who later built the Great Northern, tried to persuade the Canadian Pacific to construct its line to the west through Sault Ste. Marie and Minneapolis, but nationalistic feeling in Canada dictated CP's all-Canada route north of Lake Superior.

In 1883 a group of Minneapolis men incorporated the Minneapolis,

Sault Ste. Marie & Atlantic Railway to construct a line from the Twin Cities east to a connection with the Canadian Pacific at Sault Ste. Marie. (Sault is pronounced "Soo." The area that includes the St. Marys River, its rapids, and cities named Sault Ste. Marie in Michigan and Ontario is called "the Soo.") A year later the Minneapolis & Pacific Railway was incorporated by many of the same men to build northwestward into the wheat-growing areas of Minnesota and North Dakota. In 1888 these two roads and two others were consolidated to form the Minneapolis, St. Paul & Sault Ste. Marie Railway. Canadian Pacific acquired control of the railroad largely to block any attempt by CP's rival Grand Trunk Railway to build toward western Canada via the U. S. In 1893 the Soo Line, as it was nicknamed, built northwest to connect with CP at Portal, N. D., and in 1904 completed a line north from Glenwood, Minn., to a connection with CP at Noyes, Minn.

In 1909 Soo Line leased the properties of the Wisconsin Central Railroad, a 1,000-mile road extending from Chicago to St. Paul, Duluth, and Ashland, Wis. In addition to gaining access to Chicago, Soo Line also obtained routes to the industrial Fox River Valley of Wisconsin and the iron ore deposits in the northern part of the state.

The Duluth, South Shore & Atlantic Railway was formed by the merger of several lines along the south shore of Lake Superior. Its traffic consisted largely of iron ore and forest products. Its line ran east from Duluth along the south shore of Lake Superior to Sault Ste. Marie and to St. Ignace, where it connected via carferry to Mackinaw City at the northern tip of Michigan's lower peninsula. Canadian Pacific obtained control of the DSS&A in 1888 for the same reason it had bought into the Soo Line to block possible construction by Grand Trunk. By 1930 the DSS&A shared officers with the Soo Line.

In 1961 the Minneapolis, St. Paul & Sault Ste. Marie; the Duluth, South Shore & Atlantic; and the Wisconsin Central merged to form the Soo Line Railroad (the corporate structure is that of the 1949 reorganization of the DSS&A). In 1982 Soo Line acquired the Minneapolis, Northfield & Southern Railway, a 74-mile line between Northfield, Minn., and the suburbs of Minneapolis.

Soo Line purchased the bankrupt Chicago, Milwaukee, St. Paul & Pacific Railroad in 1985 and merged it at the beginning of 1986. By then the

Soo Line SD40-2 No. 779 and SD40 No. 740 roll freight east through Wauwatosa, Wisconsin, on the former Milwaukee Road main line on December 23, 1989. Photo by J. David Ingles.

Milwaukee, which had once reached west to Puget Sound, had shrunk to three principal routes: Chicago-Milwaukee-St. Paul-Minneapolis; Chicago-Kansas City; and Chicago-Louisville, Kentucky, the last almost entire-

ly by trackage rights. Soo Line also acquired trackage rights on Chessie System (now CSX) from Chicago to Detroit, where it made a connection with parent CP Rail.

Soo briefly tried operating its light-density lines in Michigan and Wisconsin as Lake States Transportation Division (don't confuse it with Michigan's Lake State Railway, which is the former Detroit & Mackinac Railway). Then Soo Line consolidated its Chicago-Twin Cities operations on the former Milwaukee Road main line and sold what had been its own lines to Wisconsin Central Ltd. in 1987, in many ways re-creating the pre-1909 Wisconsin Central.

In 1990 Soo Line leased two routes in wheat-growing country totaling 293 miles to the Dakota, Missouri Valley & Western Railroad: Flaxton, N. D., west to Whitetail, Montana, and Oakes, N. D., through Wishek and Bismarck to Washburn, N. D., plus a branch from Wishek to Ashley.

For a long time Canadian Pacific owned a little more than half of Soo's outstanding stock. In the late 1980s CP tried briefly to sell off Soo Line, then decided to try for full ownership; by early 1990 CP Rail had acquired full ownership. As this book went to press in fall 1992 CP Rail was reorganizing its U. S. subsidiaries, Soo Line and Delaware & Hudson, as a division of CP Rail Systems.

Address of general offices: CP Rail, P. O. Box 6042, Station A, Montreal, PQ, Canada H3C 3E4

Miles of road operated: 5,807

Reporting marks: MILW, MNS, SOO

Number of locomotives: 370

Number of freight cars: 14,185

Principal commodities carried: Grain, paper, lumber, potash, sulfur, intermodal traffic, automobiles

Major yards: Bensenville, Ill.; Minneapolis, Minn. (Shoreham); Thief River Falls, Minn.

Principal shops: Minneapolis, Minn.

Radio frequencies: 161.370, 161.520, 161.085, 160.770 (road channels 1-4)

Passenger routes: Amtrak — Chicago-St. Paul

Historical and technical society: Soo Line Historical & Technical Society, 3410 Kasten Court, Middleton, WI 53562

SOUTHEASTERN PENNSYLVANIA TRANSPORTATION AUTHORITY

Southeastern Pennsylvania Transportation Authority was created by the Pennsylvania legislature in 1963 to plan, develop, and coordinate a regional transportation system for Philadelphia, Bucks, Chester, Delaware, and Montgomery counties. In 1968 SEPTA acquired Philadelphia Transportation Company, which operated streetcar, subway, elevated, and bus services in Philadelphia. In 1970 it purchased Philadelphia Suburban Transportation Company (Red Arrow Lines), which operated 5'2¼" gauge trolley lines to Sharon Hill and Media, a standard gauge third-rail line (the former Philadelphia & Western Railway) to Norristown, and numer-ous bus routes from a terminal shared with PTC's Market Street elevated at 69th Street in Upper Darby.

Cooperation between governmental authorities and the railroads that operated Philadelphia-area commuter service had begun in 1958. The program, named Operation Northwest, was an experiment with increased service and reduced fares on the Pennsylvania and Reading branches to Chestnut Hill in the northwest corner of Philadelphia. Government's role in commuter service increased. By 1974, SEPTA was purchasing rolling stock for Penn Central and Reading commuter trains.

A Paoli-Doylestown (route R5) train pauses at Wayne, Pennsylvania, to receive Philadelphia-bound passengers on October 18, 1988. Photo by William D. Middleton.

Penn Central and Reading became part of Conrail on April 1, 1976. The Northeast Rail Service Act of July 1981 instructed Conrail to divest itself of its commuter operations by the end of 1982. The transition from Conrail to SEPTA operation did not go smoothly; a strike shut down the system from March 15 to July 1, 1983.

The commuter rail system is now called the SEPTA Regional High Speed Lines. SEPTA owns the ex-Pennsylvania lines to Chestnut Hill, Manayunk, and West Chester, and the ex-Reading lines to Chestnut Hill, Doylestown, Newtown, Norristown, Warminster, and West Trenton, New Jersey. The ex-Pennsy lines to Paoli, Trenton, N. J., and Wilmington, Del., are owned by Amtrak.

SEPTA completed two major construction projects soon after it took over operation of the the commuter trains. In November 1984 it opened a tunnel in downtown Philadelphia connecting the former Reading and Pennsylvania systems, bypassing Reading Terminal and turning Suburban Station into a through station. In April 1985 it opened a line linking 30th Street Station with Philadelphia International Airport, the first railroad connection to an airport in the United States.

Address of General Offices: 1515 Market Street, 6th Floor, Philadelphia, PA 19102
Miles of road operated: 284
Number of locomotives: 7 electric
Number of self-propelled passenger cars: 305 electric
Number of passenger cars: 35
Shops: Paoli, Pa., Wayne Junction, Pa.
Radio frequencies: 160.920 (Amtrak routes), 160.350 (ex-Pennsylvania lines), 161.460 (ex-Reading lines)
Passenger routes:
All routes operate via North Broad Street, Market East, Suburban Station, and 30th Street Station in Philadelphia. There is no R4 route.
R1: Philadelphia to Philadelphia International Airport
R2: Warminster (ex-Reading) to Wilmington, Del. (ex-Pennsylvania)
R3: West Trenton (ex-Reading) to Elwyn (ex-Pennsylvania)
R5: Doylestown (ex-Reading) to Paoli and Parkesburg (ex-Pennsylvania)
R6: Norristown (ex-Reading) to Cynwyd (ex-Pennsylvania)
R7: Trenton (ex-Pennsylvania) to Chestnut Hill East (ex-Reading)
R8: Fox Chase (ex-Reading) to Chestnut Hill West (ex-Pennsylvania)

SOUTHERN PACIFIC LINES

Until the supermergers of recent decades, Southern Pacific was one of the largest railroads in the U. S., ranking third behind Pennsylvania and New York Central in operating revenue and second behind Santa Fe in route mileage. SP's lines stretched over a greater distance than any other railroad — from New Orleans west to Los Angeles, then north to Portland, Oregon, and before 1951 down the west coast of Mexico to Guadalajara. It dominated transportation in California and was (and is) the only large railroad headquartered on the West Coast. Explaining Southern Pacific's history route by route, much as its passenger timetables were arranged years ago, makes it easier to understand.

Overland Route

In 1850 the state of California was admitted to the union. It would need a railroad to connect it to the rest of the country. The route that railroad should take posed a question: south toward the slave states or north toward the free states? The question was answered a decade later by the outbreak of the Civil War.

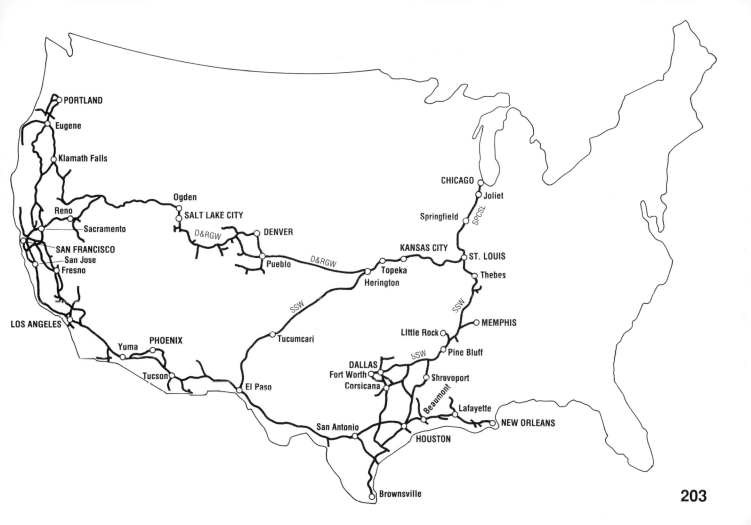

PORTLAND
Eugene
Klamath Falls
Ogden
SALT LAKE CITY
Reno
Sacramento
SAN FRANCISCO
San Jose
Fresno
DENVER
D&RGW
D&RGW
Pueblo
CHICAGO
Joliet
Springfield
SPCSL
KANSAS CITY
ST. LOUIS
Topeka
Herington
Thebes
SSW
SSW
LOS ANGELES
Yuma
PHOENIX
Tucson
El Paso
Tucumcari
MEMPHIS
Little Rock
Pine Bluff
SSW
DALLAS
Fort Worth
Corsicana
Shreveport
Beaumont
Lafayette
NEW ORLEANS
San Antonio
HOUSTON
Brownsville

203

In 1852 the Sacramento Valley Rail Road engaged Theodore D. Judah to lay out its line from Sacramento east a few miles to Folsom and Placerville. The line was opened in 1856, but Judah had higher goals — a railroad over the Sierra Nevada to Virginia City, Nevada. He scouted the mountains for a route and sought financial backing in San Francisco. That city considered itself a seaport, not the terminal of a railroad. In Sacramento he obtained the backing of four merchants: Collis P. Huntington, Mark Hopkins, Charles Crocker, and Leland Stanford. They incorporated the Central Pacific Railroad in June 1861.

In 1862 Congress passed the Pacific Railroad Act. It provided for the incorporation of the Union Pacific Railroad, to build west (the eastern terminal, Omaha, was decided later); empowered the Central Pacific to build east; and provided loans and land for both efforts.

Construction of the Central Pacific began at Sacramento in January 1863. Its first train operated 18 miles east to what is now Roseville in November of that year. By 1867 Central Pacific had crossed the state line into Nevada, and on May 10, 1869, the Central Pacific and the Union Pacific met at Promontory, Utah, creating the first transcontinental railroad.

In 1900 Collis P. Huntington, the last survivor of the four founders of the Central Pacific, died. Edward H. Harriman mortgaged his Union Pacific and bought Huntington's interest in the Southern Pacific. Under Harriman SP built the Lucin Cutoff across the Great Salt Lake, shortening the route by 44 miles (and bypassing Promontory, site of the Golden Spike ceremony in 1869), and double-tracked the line over the Sierra, in many places building a new line with easier grades.

California Lines

After meeting the UP at Promontory, Central Pacific was extended west from Sacramento to San Francisco Bay, first by construction of the Western Pacific Railroad to Oakland over Altamont Pass (don't confuse this Western Pacific with the modern railroad of the same name over the same pass, now part of Union Pacific), then by acquisition in 1876 of the California Pacific Railroad from Sacramento to Vallejo. In 1879 Central Pacific completed a line from Port Costa, across the Carquinez Strait from Vallejo, along the shore of San Francisco Bay to Oakland. Train ferries made the connection between Port Costa and Benicia (just east of Vallejo) until the construction of the bridge across Carquinez Strait in 1929.

The San Francisco & San Jose Railroad was opened along the San Francisco peninsula in 1864. It was merged by the Southern Pacific Railroad, which was intent on building south along the Pacific coast to San Diego, then east to connect with a railroad building west from the Mississippi River. The Central Pacific acquired the Southern Pacific by 1868.

One of Harriman's improvements in California was the Bayshore Cutoff south of San Francisco, which replaced a steeply graded inland route with a water-level route along the shore of San Francisco Bay. The Coast Line between San Francisco and Los Angeles was opened in 1901.

Sunset and Golden State Routes

In 1870 Central Pacific acquired the San Joaquin Valley Rail Road, which had started building a line south from a point near Stockton. Central Pacific pushed the line down the San Joaquin Valley, reaching Bakersfield in 1874. The railroad continued to build south from Bakersfield, now working under Southern Pacific's charter. The line ascended the Tehachapi Mountains and then turned south, reaching Los Angeles in September 1876. From Los Angeles it built east and reached the Colorado River at Yuma, Arizona, in 1877. Further construction, this time as the Galveston, Harrisburg & San Antonio Railway, put the line into El Paso, Texas, in 1881. It met the line that was being constructed west from San Antonio on the bank of the Pecos River in 1883. The line at that point has since been relocated, crossing the Pecos on the highest bridge on a U. S. common carrier (320 feet).

SP constructed a line east from Mojave, Calif., to the Colorado River at Needles, Calif., arriving there on July 1, 1883, little more than a month before the Santa Fe arrived from the east. SP later traded this line to Santa Fe for the Sonora Railway that Santa Fe had constructed between Nogales and Guaymas, Sonora, Mexico. The Sonora Railway became the Southern Pacific of Mexico and later the Ferrocarril del Pacifico.

In 1924 SP acquired the El Paso & Southwestern system, which had a line from Tucson, Ariz., through Douglas, Ariz., and El Paso, Texas, to Tucumcari, New Mexico, where it connected with the Rock Island. The El Paso-Tucumcari line was opened in 1902. The ex-RI line from Tucumcari to Kansas City is now the property of SP subsidiary Cotton Belt.

Texas and Louisiana Lines

The SP lines east of El Paso grew from the Buffalo Bayou, Brazos &

A lumber train bound from Eugene, Oregon, to West Colton, California, rolls through the Sacramento River canyon under the Castle Crags near Dunsmuir, Calif. Photo by Wesley Fox.

Colorado Railroad and the New Orleans, Opelousas & Great Western Railroad, both chartered in 1850. The BBB&C was reorganized as the Galveston, Harrisburg & San Antonio Railway in 1870. It reached San Antonio in 1877, engaged in some machinations with and against Jay Gould's Missouri Pacific system, and continued building west. The Opelousas, sold in 1869 to steamship magnate Charles Morgan and later resold and reorganized as Morgan's Louisiana & Texas Railroad, built across the bayou country west of New Orleans to form a New Orleans-Houston route in conjunction with the Louisiana Western and the Texas & New Orleans.

In 1934 all these railroads were consolidated as the Texas & New Orleans Railroad. Even after the repeal in 1967 of the article in the Texas constitution requiring railroads operating in Texas to be headquartered there, the T&NO lines were operated as a separate entity.

Shasta and Cascade Routes

In 1870 Central Pacific acquired the California & Oregon Railroad, which had built north from Marysville. It pushed north through Redding, Calif., up the Sacramento River canyon, and over the Siskiyou Range to connect with the Oregon & California Railroad at Ashland, Ore., in 1887. SP acquired the O&C at that time, extending its system north to Portland. In 1909 the road opened a line from Black Butte, Calif., at the foot of Mount Shasta, northeast across the state line to Klamath Falls, Ore.

In 1926 SP opened the Natron Cutoff between Klamath Falls and Eugene, Ore. It had been conceived as a line southeast from Eugene to meet a proposed Union Pacific line west from the Idaho-Oregon border. That linkup never happened, but SP saw that extending this line south through the Klamath Basin might head off the Great Northern, which was constructing a line south from the Columbia River to connect with a Western Pacific line being pushed north from Keddie, Calif. As it turned out, GN wound up on SP rails between Chemult, Ore., and Klamath Falls. The new route had much easier grades and curves than the original route through Ashland, and it became SP's main route in Oregon.

About the same time SP opened a line from Klamath Falls southeast to the Overland Route at Fernley, Nev. Some of the Modoc Line, as it is called, was new construction; other portions of it were the former 3-foot-gauge Nevada-California-Oregon Railway.

Construction of Shasta Dam between 1938 and 1942 required relocation of much of SP's line in the lower Sacramento River canyon. The Pit River bridge, which carries both railroad and highway traffic, was at the time of its construction the highest in the U. S. (433 feet). Subsequent filling of Shasta Lake brought the water level up to just below the girders.

Merger with Denver & Rio Grande Western

Southern Pacific and Santa Fe announced their merger proposal in May 1980, called it off later that year, and revived it in 1983. On December 23, 1983, Santa Fe Industries and Southern Pacific Company, the parent companies of the two railroads, were merged by Santa Fe Southern Pacific Corporation. The two railroads remained separate but went so far as to

205

paint and partway letter locomotives for the Southern Pacific & Santa Fe Railway (see page 41).

The Interstate Commerce Commission turned down the request for merger and the subsequent appeal, and ordered SFSP to divest itself of one railroad. Offers to buy SP came from Kansas City Southern; Rio Grande Industries, parent of the Denver & Rio Grande Western; Guilford Transportation Industries; and SP management. On August 9, 1988, the ICC approval sale of the SP to Rio Grande Industries. The sale was completed on October 13, 1988.

The name of the new system was Southern Pacific Lines. The identity and image of the Denver & Rio Grande Western (see page 100) are being replaced by those of SP, much as Delaware & Hudson and Soo Line are quickly becoming units of CP Rail System — and much like Cotton Belt has come to look like its parent, SP.

In 1991 SP sold its San Francisco-San Jose line and the commuter business it operated for the California Department of Transportation to San Francisco, San Mateo, and Santa Clara counties (retaining freight rights). The Peninsula Corridor Joint Powers Board assumed responsibility for funding and operating the service; Amtrak took over actual operation of the Peninsula commute trains on July 1, 1992.

Cotton Belt

The St. Louis Southwestern Railway (the Cotton Belt) is SP's principal subsidiary. It began as the 3-foot gauge Tyler Tap Railroad, opened in 1877 between Tyler, Tex., and a junction with the Texas & Pacific at Big Sandy. It was rechartered as the Texas & St. Louis Railway and extended to Texarkana and a connection with the St. Louis, Iron Mountain & Southern Railway in 1880. A year later it was extended west to Waco.

In 1881 Jay Gould purchased the Iron Mountain — he already had the T&P — returning the Texas & St. Louis to one-connection status. The T&StL decided to fulfill its name. In 1882 it reached Birds Point, Missouri, across the Mississippi River from Cairo, Illinois. There it connected by barge with the narrow gauge St. Louis & Cairo. By 1885 a continuous system of 3-foot gauge railroads reached from Toledo, Ohio, to Houston, Tex., with intentions of heading for Laredo and eventually Mexico City.

In 1886 the T&StL was reorganized as the St. Louis, Arkansas & Texas Railway. It converted its lines to standard gauge, built branches to Shreveport, Louisiana, and Fort Worth, Texas, in 1888, and entered bankruptcy in 1889. Jay Gould organized the St. Louis Southwestern Railway in 1891 and took over the StLA&T. The road gained access to Memphis, Tennessee; acquired trackage rights over Missouri Pacific from Thebes, Ill., to St. Louis in exchange for letting MP operate over SSW between Illmo, Mo., and Paragould, Ark.; and joined with MP in constructing a bridge over the Mississippi between Thebes and Illmo.

After World War I bridge traffic began to increase on the Cotton Belt. The Rock Island purchased a controlling interest in the road in 1925 and sold it almost immediately to Kansas City Southern. KCS proposed a regional system to include KCS, SSW, and the Missouri-Kansas-Texas, but the ICC refused approval. KCS lost interest in the Cotton Belt about the time Southern Pacific was looking for a connection to St. Louis from its Texas lines. SP applied for control and in 1932 took over.

In recent years Cotton Belt has been essentially a division of the SP, though its equipment is still lettered "Cotton Belt." In 1980 SSW acquired the former Rock Island line from St. Louis through Kansas City to Santa Rosa, N. M. (RI owned the line between Santa Rosa and Tucumcari, N. M., but it had long been leased to SP.) The St. Louis-Kansas City track was in poor condition and is out of service; SSW has trackage rights on Union Pacific's parallel ex-Missouri Pacific route. From Kansas City west the line is a fast freight route connecting with parent SP at Tucumcari.

SPCSL

Chicago, Missouri & Western Railway purchased Illinois Central Gulf's lines from Joliet to East St. Louis, Illinois, and from Springfield, Ill., to Kansas City on April 28, 1987, essentially resurrecting the old Alton Railroad. Less than a year later, on April 1, 1988, the CM&W entered bankruptcy. Southern Pacific purchased the East St. Louis-Joliet line (as far north as Godfrey it is owned jointly with Gateway Western) and operates it as SPCSL Corporation (Southern Pacific Chicago St. Louis). This most recent addition to SP's route map brings the road to Chicago for the first time in its 140-year history.

Other Subsidiaries

In 1907 SP and Santa Fe formed the jointly owned Northwestern Pacific Railroad, which consolidated several lines north of San Francisco. NWP built north through the redwood country and down the canyon of the Eel

River to Eureka, Calif. SP bought out Santa Fe's share in 1929, and sold the north end of the line in 1984.

SP had several subsidiary traction lines. The Portland, Eugene & Eastern served Oregon's Willamette Valley. The Interurban Electric Railway served the East Bay cities of Oakland, Berkeley, and Alameda, and for a short period connected them with San Francisco via the Bay Bridge. The Pacific Electric, largest interurban line in the U. S. blanketed the Los Angeles Basin. In addition, the Marin County suburban lines of Northwestern Pacific were electrified until the Golden Gate Bridge opened and buses replaced the train-and-ferry service. The last remnant of SP's electric lines, at least in name, is the Visalia Electric Railroad, a 30-mile short line at Exeter, Calif.

SP's empire also included a narrow gauge line, the former Carson & Colorado, which connected western Nevada with some of the emptiest parts of eastern California. The Laws-Keeler, Calif., segment of the line lasted long enough to be diesclized, but was shut down in 1960.

Address of general offices: 1 Market Plaza, San Francisco, CA 94105
Miles of road operated: 11,143
Reporting marks: SP, SPFE, SSW
Number of locomotives: 2,067
Number of freight cars: 37,936
Principal commodities carried: Food products, chemicals, lumber
Major yards: Colton, Calif.; Eugene, Ore.; Houston, Tex.; Kansas City, Kans. (Armourdale); Los Angeles, Calif. (Taylor); Roseville, Calif.
Principal shops: Denver, Colo. (Burnham)
Radio frequencies: 161.550, 160.320 (alternate, west of El Paso), 160.590 (alternate, east of El Paso), 160.290 (alternate, east of El Paso), 161.280 (Kansas City-St. Louis-Chicago)
Passenger routes:
Amtrak — Joliet, Ill.-St. Louis; Dallas Houston; New Orleans-El Paso-Los Angeles; Winnemucca, Nev.-Oakland, Calif.; Port Chicago-Martinez, Calif.; Portland, Ore.-Roseville, Calif.; Los Angeles-San Jose-Oakland
CalTrain — San Jose-Gilroy, Calif.
Historical and technical society: Southern Pacific Historical & Technical Society, 218 Norton, No. 6, Long Beach CA 90805
Recommended reading: *Blue Streak Merchandise*, by Fred W. Frai-

A fast New Orleans-Los Angeles double-stack train behind a trio of four-axle diesels winds through curves on Southern Pacific's Sunset Route at Tully, Arizona. Photo by Wesley Fox.

ley, published in 1991 by Kalmbach Publishing Co., 21027 Crossroads Circle, P. O. Box 1612, Waukesha, WI 53187 (ISBN 0-89024-130-9)
The Southern Pacific 1901-1985, by Don L. Hofsommer, published in 1986 by Texas A&M University Press, College Station, TX 77843-4354 (ISBN 0-89096-246-4)

SOUTHERN RAILWAY OF BRITISH COLUMBIA

Southern Railway of British Columbia had its beginnings in the British Columbia Electric Railway, a street and interurban system that served Vancouver and stretched 80 miles east to Chilliwack. Rail passenger operations ended in 1958. BCER was succeeded by British Columbia Hydro & Power Authority, which was owned by the province of British Columbia. In 1988 BC Hydro's rail operations were purchased from the province by Itel Rail Corporation and renamed Southern Railway of British Columbia.

Address of general offices: 5935 Glover Road, Langley, BC V3A 4B5
Miles of road operated: 75
Reporting marks: BCH, SRY

Number of locomotives: 19
Number of freight cars: 516
Principal commodities carried: Automobiles, forest products, food products
Shops: New Westminster, B. C.
Junctions with other railroads:
Burlington Northern: Huntingdon, B. C.; New Westminster, B. C.
Canadian National: Chilliwack, B. C.; New Westminster, B. C.
CP Rail: Abbotsford, B. C.; Huntingdon, B. C.; New Westminster, B. C.
Radio frequencies: 160.275, 160.515 (maintenance of way) 160.545 (road and yard), 160.695 (yard)
Map: See BC Rail, page 48

A British Columbia Hydro freight heads out the Fraser Valley Subdivision toward the BN interchange in 1982. The rear of the train is still on the Fraser River Bridge. Photo by John C. Illman.

SOUTH ORIENT RAILROAD

The South Orient began operation at the beginning of 1992 on a former Santa Fe line from San Angelo Junction, between Brownwood and Coleman, Texas, through San Angelo, Fort Stockton, and Alpine, to Presidio, Texas. The purchase of the line included a haulage agreement with Santa Fe between San Angelo Junction and Fort Worth, 163 miles. (In simplified terms, Santa Fe moves South Orient traffic between San Angelo Junction and Fort Worth, in effect extending the South Orient to Fort Worth, where it can interchange with other roads besides the Santa Fe.)

The South Orient line is part of the former Kansas City, Mexico & Orient Railway, which didn't become a Kansas City-to-Gulf of California railroad until 1961, by which time it was part of the Santa Fe in the U. S. and the Chihuahua Pacific Railway in Mexico.

The new trade agreements with Mexico are likely to result in an increase of traffic moving across the border. Three of the four major western railroads have direct connections with National Railways of Mexico: Santa Fe at El Paso, Texas; Union Pacific at Brownsville, Laredo, and El Paso; and Southern Pacific at six points from Brownsville, Texas, to Calexico, California. Burlington Northern, which has none, announced in May 1992 that it would beginning moving covered hopper cars of grain between Galveston, Texas, and Coatzacoalcos, southeast of Mexico City. In August 1992 BN announced a haulage agreement with the South Orient that in effect extends BN from Fort Worth to the international bridge between Presidio, Texas, and Ojinaga, Chihuahua.

Address of general offices: P. O. Box 232, San Angelo, TX 76902
Miles of road operated: 386
Reporting marks: SO
Number of locomotives: 5

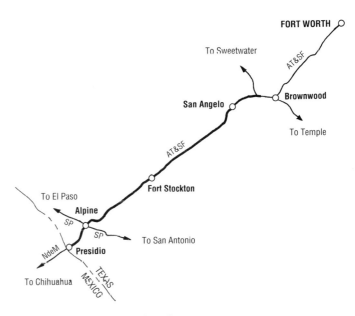

Junctions with other railroads:
Atchison, Topeka & Santa Fe: San Angelo Junction, Texas
National Railways of Mexico, Presidio, Texas
Southern Pacific: Alpine, Texas

THE SUPER SEVEN

About 90 percent of the ton-miles in American railroading are generated by seven railroads: Atchison, Topeka & Santa Fe; Burlington Northern; Conrail; CSX; Norfolk Southern; Southern Pacific Lines; and Union Pacific. They are the largest freight railroads in America by almost any measurement tool: route mileage, revenue, tonnage, or numbers of locomotives and cars. With one exception they are products of mergers within the past 25 years of railroads that were already large — and that exception, the Santa Fe, has tried to be the product of a recent merger (see page 41).

The Super Seven aren't the only big railroads on the continent. Canadian National Railways falls between BN and UP in size; CP Rail is between NS and SP; and National Railways of Mexico is between CSX and NS. Amtrak's route mileage exceeds BN's, largely on the rails of the Super Seven, but in principle that's like the trackage rights that are part of the Super Seven's route maps.

The statistics are from the Association of American Railroads' Analysis of Class I Railroads for 1989. The railroads are ranked by size in each category.

Route miles operated

BN	23,356
UP	21,882
CSX	19,565
NS	15,955
SP	15,023
CR	13,068
AT&SF	11,266

Revenue ton-miles (in thousands)

BN	232,527,257
UP	183,042,204
CSX	146,927,197
NS	100,111,004
SP	99,616,580
AT&SF	82,741,647
CR	82,125,064

Freight revenue (in thousands of dollars)

BN	4,479,951
UP	4,353,718
CSX	4,227,362
NS	3,580,008
CR	3,220,328
SP	2,553,753
AT&SF	2,155,240

Number of locomotives

CSX	3,220
UP	2,918
SP	2,428
CR	2,364
BN	2,309
NS	2,180
AT&SF	1,582

Number of freight cars

CSX	140,452
NS	114,438
UP	72,938
CR	70,660
BN	61,177
SP	53,546
AT&SF	38,357

What they carry

The AAR gives traffic statistics for 20 commodity groups: carloads originated by the railroad, gross freight revenue, and percentage of gross freight revenue. None is a perfect indicator of what each railroad carries. The first is probably the best, but doesn't reflect, for example, the carloads of auto parts that Grand Trunk Western picks up in and around Detroit and turns over to the Super Seven railroads at Chicago. The second is skewed by freight rates, which are based in part on the value of the commodity (the list of Standard Transportation Commodity Codes is both comprehensive and specific — for example, "Buffaloes, value for special purposes" and "Chautauqua or gospel tent outfits"). The third essentially answers the question, "What contributes the revenue?"

The major commodities are coal, grain, food and kindred products, chemicals, motor vehicles and equipment, forwarder and shipper association traffic ("intermodal"), and (consolidating three groups for convenience) wood and paper. Other commodities that produce significant numbers of carloads are included. The "railroad total" figure is for all commodities, not just the selected ones. For most railroads, the second largest commodity group is "All other."

Other Class 1 railroads originate significant amounts of certain commodities, occasionally more than some of the Super Seven.

Florida East Coast: Stone, gravel, and sand	106,713
Grand Trunk Western: Motor vehicles	151,341
Illinois Central: Coal	227,484
Chicago & North Western: Grain	143,256
Chicago & North Western: Ore	80,123
Soo Line: Grain	128,820

Carloads originated

AT&SF

Commodity	Value	Commodity	Value	Commodity	Value
Coal	86,123	Wood and paper	49,668	Motor vehicles	168,275
Grain	168,858	Motor vehicles	257,804	Intermodal	1,746
Food	95,243	Intermodal	6,905	Stone/clay/glass products	139,643
Chemicals	113,288	Metallic ores	123,708	Railroad total	3,134,263
Wood and paper	60,077	Metals and products	157,893	**SP**	
Motor vehicles	37,942	Railroad total	2,219,749	Coal	159,521
Intermodal	118,292	**CSX**		Grain	28,092
Railroad total	1,361,169	Coal	1,829,405	Food	52,354
BN		Grain	142,176	Chemicals	194,372
Coal	1,347,074	Food	91,715	Wood and paper	160,655
Grain	364,584	Chemicals	312,755	Motor vehicles	52,421
Food	138,461	Wood and paper	370,951	Intermodal	554
Chemicals	102,034	Motor vehicles	173,077	Metals and products	47,166
Wood and paper	249,238	Intermodal	34,501	Railroad total	1,288,785
Motor vehicles	64,969	Nonmetallic minerals	336,761	**UP**	
Intermodal	31,672	Stone/clay/glass products	107,254	Coal	295,668
Metallic ores	167,883	Railroad total	4,523,814	Grain	277,623
Railroad total	3,576,956	**NS**		Food	111,615
CR		Coal	1,260,947	Chemicals	373,858
Coal	367,560	Grain	129,095	Wood and paper	143,621
Grain	55,540	Food	49,623	Motor vehicles	114,018
Food	56,087	Chemicals	125,971	Intermodal	120
Chemicals	95,833	Wood and paper	253,460	Railroad total	2,428,893

TERMINAL RAILROAD ASSOCIATION OF ST. LOUIS

There were difficulties when the Eads Bridge was completed across the Mississippi River at St. Louis in 1874. The bridge company could not operate a railroad, and railroads chartered to operate in Missouri could not operate in Illinois and vice versa. Several railroad companies were chartered to resolve the situation.

In 1881 the bridge company, the terminal railroads in St. Louis, Missouri, and East St. Louis, Illinois, and the company that owned the tunnel

211

at the west end of the Eads Bridge all came under the control of Jay Gould. To forestall any possibility of the St. Louis gateway's being controlled by one railroad system, the major railroads serving St. Louis formed the Terminal Railroad Association in 1889. TRRA leased the Eads Bridge and the tunnel; built another bridge across the Mississippi, the Merchants Bridge; and built St. Louis Union Station, which was the largest in North America in terms of the number of tracks on one level.

By 1974 locomotives and cars had outgrown the century-old Eads Bridge. The rails were removed; then in 1989 TRRA transferred ownership of the bridge to the city of St. Louis and in return received the MacArthur Bridge. The Eads Bridge still carries highway traffic and will soon carry the light rail vehicles of a new transit system. Amtrak moved from Union Station to a small building nearby in 1978. Union Station and its trainshed have become a hotel, restaurant, and shopping complex.

TRRA is owned by the railroads marked with an asterisk in the list of connecting railroads below.

Address of general offices: 700 North Second Street, St. Louis, MO 63102

Miles of road operated: 205

Reporting marks: TRRA

Number of locomotives: 27

Major yards: Granite City, Ill.

Connects with:
Alton & Southern
Burlington Northern*
Chicago & North Western
Conrail
CSX*
Gateway Western
Illinois Central *
Manufacturers Railway
Norfolk Southern*
St. Louis Southwestern*
Southern Pacific
Union Pacific*
all within the St. Louis-East St. Louis Switching Districts

Radio frequencies: 160.500 (road), 160.650 (Madison Yard)

Historical and technical society: Terminal Railroad Association of St. Louis Historical & Technical Society, P. O. Box 1688, St. Louis, MO 63188-1688

SW9 1210 brings a transfer freight bound for Conrail past Willows tower in East St. Louis, Illinois, in October 1978. Photo by J. David Ingles.

TEXAS MEXICAN RAILWAY

In 1875 the Corpus Christi, San Diego & Rio Grande Narrow Gauge Railroad was chartered to build from the Gulf of Mexico at Corpus Christi, Texas, west across the southern tip of Texas to the Mexican border at Laredo. The road received its present name in 1881. It came under the control of National Railways of Mexico, but after 1902 NdeM's interest in the road was held by the Manufacturers Hanover Trust Co. of New York. In 1982 NdeM sold the railroad to a private Mexican firm.

Most of Tex-Mex's traffic is freight interchanged with NdeM at Laredo; its line extends to the center of the Rio Grande bridge between Laredo, Tex., and Nuevo Laredo, Tamaulipas. TM dieselized in 1939 with unique Whitcomb rigid-frame 8-wheel diesels; in 1946 the road built four similar units with a 1-D wheel arrangement.

In January 1986 the railroad restored passenger service between Corpus Christi and Laredo. The train, which ran seasonally, was withdrawn in 1989.

Address of general offices: P. O. Box 419, Laredo, TX 78040
Miles of road operated: 157
Reporting marks: TM
Number of locomotives: 18
Number of freight cars: 815
Principal commodities carried: Grain, chemicals, machinery
Shops: Laredo, Texas
Junctions with other railroads:
National Railways of Mexico: Laredo, Texas
Southern Pacific: Corpus Christi, Texas
Union Pacific: Corpus Christi, Texas; Laredo, Texas; Robstown, Texas
Radio frequencies: 161.130 (yard), 161.220 (road and dispatcher)

A Texas Mexican freight rolls across the south Texas plains toward Corpus Christi behind two GP38-2s and a GP38 in 1986. Photo by Jim Shaw.

TEXAS, OKLAHOMA & EASTERN RAILROAD and DE QUEEN & EASTERN RAILROAD

The Texas, Oklahoma & Eastern was incorporated in 1910 to provide rail service to Dierks sawmills in southeast Oklahoma. It opened in 1911 from Valliant, Oklahoma, to Bismarck (now Wright City) and in 1912 to Broken Bow. It built a number of branches (long since abandoned) north into the forests of the Ouachita Mountains.

The De Queen & Eastern was incorporated in 1900 as a 2-mile line to connect a Dierks Lumber & Coal Co. sawmill with the Kansas City Southern at De Queen, Arkansas. Within five years it had been extended east to company operations in a new town named Dierks. To connect the company's mills, the two roads were extended toward each other and met near the Arkansas-Oklahoma state line at West Line, Ark., on January 5, 1921.

In 1954 Dierks Forests, successor to the lumber and coal company, built a paper mill at Pine Bluff, Ark. The Missouri Pacific was interested in securing the traffic between Dierks' existing facilities and the new plant. MP's nearest track was at Nashville, Ark., 20 miles from Dierks. MP and De Queen & Eastern each built to Perkins, Ark., meeting on January 10, 1957. In 1969 Dierks Forests and its two railroads were purchased by the Weyerhaeuser Corporation.

Address of general offices: 412 E. Lockesburg, De Queen, AR 71832
Miles of road operated: 40 (TO&E), 46 (DQ&E)
Reporting marks: TOE, DQE
Number of locomotives: 9 (TO&E), 3 (DQ&E)

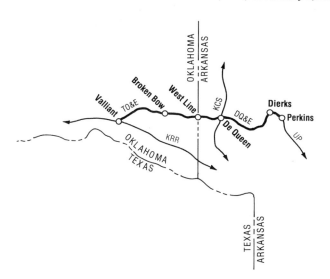

Texas, Oklahoma & Eastern GP35 D-22 and GP40 D-14 take empty wood-chip cars away from the Weyerhaeuser pulpboard mill at Valliant, Oklahoma, in 1983. The "D" prefix originally distinguished diesel locomotives from steam on the road's roster. Photo by Jim Shaw.

Number of freight cars: 2,458 (TO&E)
Principal commodities carried: Forest products
Shops: De Queen, Ark.
Junctions with other railroads:
TO&E
De Queen & Eastern: West Line, Ark.
Kiamichi Railroad: Valliant, Okla.

DQ&E
Kansas City Southern: De Queen, Ark.
Texas, Oklahoma & Eastern: West Line, Ark.
Union Pacific: Perkins, Ark.
Radio frequencies: 160.230 (road), 160.605 (yard), 160.785 (yard)
Recommended reading: "Rails through the Ouachita forests," by
J. Parker Lamb, in TRAINS Magazine, October 1990, pages 54-63

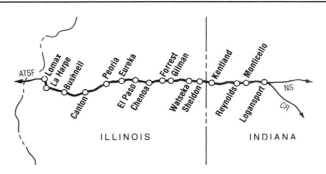

TOLEDO, PEORIA & WESTERN RAILWAY

The first Toledo, Peoria & Warsaw Railway was chartered in 1863. It was opened in 1868 from the Indiana-Illinois state line at what is now Effner through Peoria to Warsaw, Ill., on the Mississippi River. In 1880 the road was reorganized as the Toledo, Peoria & Western Railroad and leased to the Wabash, St. Louis & Pacific for a term of 49 years — the lease lasted only until 1884.

The Toledo, Peoria & Western Railway was chartered in 1887 to take over the railroad. In 1893 the Pennsylvania Railroad and a predecessor of the Chicago, Burlington & Quincy each acquired a large stock interest in the TP&W, which by then had been extended across the Mississippi to Keokuk, Iowa. In 1927 the TP&W made a connection with the Santa Fe at Lomax, Ill., over a 10-mile line from La Harpe, Ill.

In 1927 George P. McNear Jr. purchased the TP&W at foreclosure. He saw the road's potential as a bridge route bypassing the congestion of Chicago and St. Louis, and he began to improve its physical plant. In 1941 McN-

ear refused to go along with an industry-wide pay increase, proposing instead hourly wages and the elimination of inefficient practices. A bitter strike ensued, followed by government operation of the road during World War II and the 1947 murder of McNear. That year new management took over and the TP&W resumed operation after a 19-month work stoppage.

Another Toledo, Peoria & Western was incorporated in 1952, succeeding at least three previous Toledo, Peoria & Western companies. In 1960 the Santa Fe purchased the railroad and sold a half interest to the Pennsylvania Railroad. The TP&W formed a Chicago bypass for traffic moving between the Pennsylvania and the Santa Fe.

The formation of Conrail changed traffic patterns, and TP&W didn't fit into Conrail's plans. In 1976 TP&W bought the former Pennsylvania line from Effner east to Logansport, Ind., where it could interchange traf-

Toledo, Peoria & Western GP20 No. 2002, standing at East Peoria on April 29, 1990, illustrates the road's two-tone gray paint scheme, like that once used by the New York Central. Photo by Michael W. Blaszak.

fic with the Norfolk & Western. In 1979 the Pennsylvania Company, a subsidiary of Penn Central, sold its half interest in the TP&W back to the Santa Fe. Merger with Santa Fe took place on December 31, 1983.

In 1986 the Keokuk Junction Railway, a terminal railroad at Keokuk, Iowa, bought the westernmost 33 miles of the line, from La Harpe to Warsaw and Keokuk. On February 1, 1989, a group of investors purchased the Logansport-Lomax line from the Santa Fe, and yet another Toledo, Peoria & Western Railway began operating.

Address of general offices: 1661 Route 22 West, Bound Brook, NJ 08805

Miles of road operated: 287

Reporting marks: TPW

Number of locomotives: 20

Number of freight cars: 25

Principal commodities carried: Coal, grain, intermodal containers and trailers, auto parts, chemicals

Major yards: East Peoria, Ill.

Principal shops: East Peoria, Ill.

Junctions with other railroads:

Atchison, Topeka & Santa Fe: Fort Madison, Iowa

Bloomer Line: Chatsworth, Ill.

Burlington Northern: Bushnell, Ill.; Canton, Ill.

Chicago & North Western: Sommer, Ill.

Conrail: East Peoria, Ill.; Logansport, Ind.

CSX: Reynolds, Ind.; Watseka, Ill.

Illinois Central: Gilman, Ill.

Kankakee, Beaverville & Southern: Sheldon, Ill.; Webster, Ill.

Keokuk Junction: East Peoria, Ill.; La Harpe, Ill.

Norfolk Southern: East Peoria, Ill.

Peoria & Pekin Union: East Peoria, Ill.; Peoria, Ill.

Southern Pacific: Chenoa, Ill.,

Union Pacific: Watseka, Ill.

Radio frequencies: 161.400 (road), 161.310 (yard)

Historical and technical society: TP&W Historical Society, 615 Bullock Street, Eureka, IL 61530

TOURIST RAILROADS

Most railroads have a serious purpose — to carry coal to power plants or take people to work, for example. A few, though, operate primarily for the fun of it. They carry passengers, but for the experience of the ride itself. These are the tourist railroads and the operating railroad museums.

Railroad museums began to develop in the 1950s, when steam locomotives and streetcars were being replaced wholesale by diesels and buses. At first the museums were simply collections of cars and locomotives, but static display is unsatisfying for machines whose primary function is to move. The typical museum spiked down a few hundred feet of track and searched for something in the collection that would move — a four-wheel diesel switcher, perhaps, or a streetcar towing a flat car that carried a jury-rigged diesel engine and generator. Often this worked so well that the museum members extended the track, begged a castoff coach from the neighboring railroad, strung trolley wire, or sought a steam locomotive to restore.

Shortline railroads went through a similar progression: a car to carry passengers and an ad in the local newspaper saying "Train rides Saturday at 1:30 and 3:00" soon became a four-car train and a full-color brochure. Theme parks decided that a train running around the perimeter was a necessity. Even a few common-carrier railroads went after recreational passengers, among them the Denver & Rio Grande Western between Durango and Silverton, the White Pass & Yukon, and the Algoma Central.

Then railroad museums and tourist railroads began to spring up everywhere in a wide range of forms — from a small transplanted depot with one man's collection of railroadiana to big-city union stations with the platform area roofed over to display rolling stock; from a couple of gasoline-powered section cars on a half mile of track to a dinner train more elegant than most downtown restaurants. Today there are more than 350 railroad museums and tourist railroads across the United States and Canada. They provide the rail enthusiast an opportunity to experience railroading not only close up but also — since most are volunteer operations — hands on.

Recommended reading:
Guide to Tourist Railroads and Railroad Museums, by George H. Drury,

The Western Railway Museum at Rio Vista Junction, California, operates steam-powered trains and electric streetcars and interurbans. The steam locomotive is Western Pacific 94, which pulled the first passenger train through the Feather River Canyon in 1909; the electric car is Key System 182, which used to run across the San Francisco-Oakland Bay Bridge. Western Railway Museum photo by Dave Young.

published in 1990 by Kalmbach Publishing Co., 21027 Crossroads Circle, P. O. Box 1612, Waukesha, WI 53187 (ISBN 0-89024-103-1)
Steam Passenger Service Directory, c/o Locomotive & Railway Preservation, P. O. Box 599, Richmond, VT 05477
Addresses:
Association of Railway Museums, P. O. Box 3311, City of Industry, CA 91744-0311
TRAIN (Tourist Railway Association, INc.), P. O. Box 460537, Aurora, CO 80046-0537

TRI-RAIL (Tri-County Commuter Rail Authority)

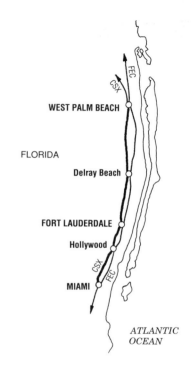

Tri-County Commuter Rail Authority began commuter service on 67 miles of CSX track (ex-Seaboard) between Miami and West Palm Beach, Florida, on January 9, 1989. The service was inaugurated because of construction on parallel highway I-95. Initially service was offered only during rush hours on weekdays, but when it was expanded to include midday and Saturday trains, ridership increased correspondingly. Sunday trains were added in September 1992.

Address of general offices: 305 South Andrews Avenue, Fort Lauderdale, FL 33301
Miles of road operated: 67
Number of locomotives: 7
Number of passenger cars: 21
Radio frequencies: 160.590, 161.100 (CSX frequencies)
Passenger routes: Miami-West Palm Beach, Fla.

Tri-Rail train 206, being pushed by locomotive 805, an F40PHL-2 built by Morrison-Knudsen, pauses at Delray Beach, Florida, on February 11, 1991. Photo by Michael W. Blaszak.

TTX COMPANY

By the mid-1950s a number of railroads had begun piggyback service — carrying highway truck trailers on flat cars. Most of the early services were single-railroad operations, and there were numerous variations in the equipment. Through service operating over two or more railroads came next. The Pennsylvania Railroad was a major piggyback operator with its fleet of TrucTrains, and its route structure made it the most likely railroad for other roads to team up with in offering through piggyback service. On November 9, 1955, Pennsy joined with the Norfolk & Western and the Rail-Trailer Company of Chicago in incorporating the Trailer Train Company to provide standardized piggyback cars for interchange service.

The key word is "standardized." Although a basic concept of the North American railroad network is standardization — track gauge, couplers, dimensions — the diversity within this standardization is incredible. Steam locomotives and freight and passenger cars were as much assembled as they were built, and each railroad had its favorite suppliers for the components. Sometimes the choice seemed to be based on what the railroad next door used — and the would be different, just to show individuality. The situation is more rational nowadays, when Electro-Motive basically lets you choose the color of your SD60 and Amtrak can get five different cars out of the same Superliner shell.

Trailer Train chose ACF Industries' new 35-foot, two-axle car (it was called the Adapto) and ordered 1,000 of them, but the company began operation on March 17, 1956, with 500 75-foot flat cars purchased from the Pennsy. No more was heard of two-axle piggyback cars until 1983, when Trailer Train introduced the 50-foot, two-axle Front Runner.

Trailer Train grew rapidly as other railroads bought into it, and its fleet of flat cars grew. Now the standard piggyback car is 89 feet long. TTX's fleet includes cars for containers, auto racks (the racks themselves

TTZX 86092, spotted at Rieth, Oregon for lumber loading, is a 60-foot center-beam flat car. Photo by Jeffrey L. Torretta.

TTUX 121061 is a "Front Runner" car, designed to carry a single trailer that must be lifted on and off. MODEL RAILROADER Magazine photo by Gordon Odegard.

are owned by the railroads), and special commodities. Each of the 47 reporting marks indicates a different type of car or different equipment, such as hitches, tie-downs, stake pockets, bulkheads, and chains with snubbers.

The company's name was changed to TTX on July 1, 1991. TTX is now owned by Atchison, Topeka & Santa Fe, Boston & Maine (Guilford Transportation Industries), Burlington Northern, Chicago & North Western, Conrail, CSX, Florida East Coast, Grand Trunk Western, Illinois Central, Kansas City Southern, Norfolk Southern, Soo Line (CP Rail System), Southern Pacific, and Union Pacific.

In January 1974 the company formed a subsidiary, American Rail Box Car Company, to operate a pool of free-running box cars. The subsidiary's name was subsequently changed to Railbox Company, and it has more than 13,000 box cars in service bearing ABOX and RBOX reporting marks. Similarly, in 1979 the Railgon company was formed to do the same for gondola cars. In early 1992 there were 1,175 GONX cars in service.

Address of general offices: 101 North Wacker Drive, Chicago, IL 60606

Reporting marks: TTX, ATTX through ZTTX (except TTTX and YTTX), TTAX through TTZX (except TTIX, TTTX, TTXX, and TTYX)

Number of freight cars: 83,932

Principal commodities carried: Containers, trailers, automobiles

Shops: Drayton Plains, Mich.; Jacksonville, Fla.; Mira Loma, Calif.; North Augusta, S. C.

PRIVATELY OWNED FREIGHT CARS

For more than a century railroads took an attitude toward freight customers that could be summarized as basic transportation: If floor, sides, ends, and perhaps a roof are sufficient protection for what you're shipping, we'll provide the car; if you want anything special, you provide the car. One reason was cost. A refrigerator car, the earliest kind of specialized car, cost twice as much as a box car because of its insulation and ice bunkers. Another reason was car utilization. A box car could carry a variety of ladings on its return trip; a refrigerator car was handicapped both by lessened capacity (the insulation and the ice bunkers took up space) and by dampness inside the car from the ice.

Special companies were formed to buy and manage fleets of refrigerator cars. Because of the seasonal nature of agriculture and the limited geographic extent of most railroads, a railroad would be likely to use refrigerator cars for only a month or two of the year. Since the companies transcended railroad boundaries, the cars could be moved where they were needed — to Maine for the potato harvest, to Florida for citrus fruit, to California for lettuce. Some refrigerator car companies were owned by railroads (Pacific Fruit Express and Merchants Despatch, for example); others were owned by shippers.

The ice-cooled refrigerator car was inefficient, and attempts to improve it included overhead ice bunkers and mechanical refrigeration. The car companies stayed with ice refrigeration, end bunkers, and wood car construction through World War II because of the expense of converting to mechanical refrigeration and because the wood served as part of the insulation. But wood cars loosened up with age, and gaps and cracks quickly negated any insulating advantage wood might have had. The growth of the frozen-food industry in the late 1940s forced the refrigerator car companies to convert to mechanical refrigeration (powered by a small diesel engine) and

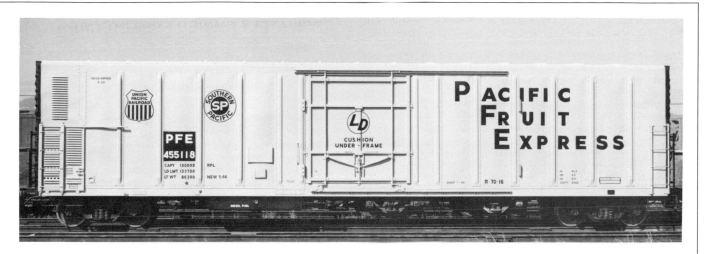

Pacific Fruit Express, owned by Southern Pacific and Union Pacific and dissolved in 1978 (SP now uses the name), had the largest fleet of refrigerator cars. Car 455118, built in 1966, had a diesel-powered refrigeration unit behind the louvers at the left end of the car. PFE bought its last refrigerator cars in 1970, and it was one of the few exceptions to the rule that private-owner reporting marks end with "X." PFE Photo.

better insulation. Within another two decades, the refrigerator car companies lost much of their perishable business to trucks — today many refrigerated trailers and containers move in piggyback trains.

Most tank cars are privately operated. The variety of features required for different commodities is staggering — glass linings for corrosive liquids, pressure-resistant fittings for gases, sloping bottoms for viscous commodities. That plus the need to keep the contents from contaminating the next load creates a car management situation that is the diametric opposite of that posed by the ordinary box car, which requires only a load going back in approximately the direction from which the car came. Some tank cars are owned by shippers; others are operated by companies that are subsidiaries of carbuilders (ACF Industries and General American Transportation, for example).

About half the covered hopper cars on American railroads are privately owned, usually by shippers or shippers' associations.

Recommended reading: *The Great Yellow Fleet*, by John H. White, published in 1986 by Golden West Books, P. O. Box 80250, San Marino, CA 91108 (ISBN 0-87095-091-6)

TUSCOLA & SAGINAW BAY RAILWAY

On October 1, 1977, the Tuscola & Saginaw Bay began operation on former Conrail lines radiating from Vassar, Michigan, southeast of Saginaw, to Harger, Munger, Colling, and Millington. The lines were former New York Central (ex-Michigan Central) routes; the Millington-Vassar-Munger track was part of the line from Detroit to Bay City.

In 1982 the railroad was designated to operate part of the former Ann Arbor, which had been purchased by the state of Michigan. Tuscola & Saginaw Bay received the middle portion of the AA, from Ann Arbor to Alma, plus a former New York Central line from Owosso, former operating headquarters of the AA, northeast 27 miles to Swan Creek. In 1983 the state transferred two more lines to the Tuscola & Saginaw Bay: the Alma-Thompsonville segment of the AA, which had been operated

Tuscola & Saginaw Bay GP35s gather at Cadillac, Michigan, in 1991. Two wear T&SB's yellow and black; No. 392 is still in Ann Arbor orange. Photo by Michael W. Blaszak.

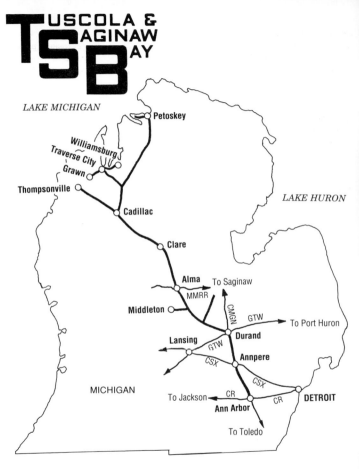

222

briefly by the Michigan Interstate Railway, then by the Michigan Northern Railway; and the Michigan Northern from Cadillac north to Petoskey, plus a branch to Traverse City, Grawn, and Williamsburg (the Grawn-Williamsburg portion is ex-Chesapeake & Ohio; the rest is ex-Pennsylvania Railroad).

In 1992 the T&SB leased the routes out of Vassar to the Huron & Eastern Railway (see page 127).

Address of general offices: P. O. Box 550, Owosso, MI 48867
Miles of road operated: 405
Reporting marks: TSBY

Number of locomotives: 11
Principal commodities carried: Grain, auto parts, molasses, coal
Shops: Cadillac and Owosso, Mich.
Junctions with other railroads:
Ann Arbor: Ann Arbor, Mich.
Central Michigan: Durand, Mich.
CSX: Ann Pere, Mich.
Grand Trunk Western: Durand, Mich.
Mid-Michigan: Alma, Mich.
Radio frequencies: 160.575, 161.100

UNION RAILROAD

The Union Railroad was incorporated in 1894 and opened in 1896. In 1937 it merged two railroads that were subsidiaries of Carnegie-Illinois Steel Corporation, the Monongahela Southern Railroad and the St. Clair Terminal Railroad. The Union Railroad serves a number of U. S. Steel mills and other customers in the Monongahela River Valley south of Pittsburgh, Pennsylvania. Most of Union's freight cars are gondolas for carrying steel in its various forms between plants and from plant to customer, and all its locomotives are switchers.

The railroad was owned by U. S. Steel until 1988, when it was acquired by Transtar, Inc. Blackstone Capital Partners owns a 51 percent interest in Transtar; USX, successor to U. S. Steel, owns 49 percent.
Address of general offices: P. O. Box 68, Monroeville, PA 15146
Miles of road operated: 33
Reporting marks: URR
Number of locomotives: 55
Number of freight cars: 262
Principal commodities carried: Steel products, iron ore, coal, coke
Major yards: North Bessemer, Monongahela Junction
Principal shops: Hall (Monroeville), Monongahela Junction
Junctions with other railroads:
Bessemer & Lake Erie: North Bessemer, Pa.

Conrail: Clairton, Duquesne Orchard & Swamp, Kenny Yard, and Munhall, Pa.
CSX: Dexter, Pa.; Port Perry, Pa.
McKeesport Connecting: Riverton, Pa.
Pittsburgh & Lake Erie: Union Junction, Pa.
Wheeling & Lake Erie: Clairton, Pa.; Mifflin Junction, Pa.
Radio frequencies: 160.260 (road), 160.500 (yard), 160.620 (yard)

Union Railroad SW1200 586 switches a pair of hot-metal cars at U. S. Steel's plant at Rankin, Pa., in 1981. Photo by Scott Hartley.

UNION PACIFIC RAILROAD

The Union Pacific was chartered by an act of Congress in 1862. The act provided subsidies and land grants to UP and to the Central Pacific, which was to build east from Sacramento, California, to meet the UP. Construction began in 1865, and the two roads met at Promontory, Utah, on May 10, 1869. Ceremonies and a golden spike celebrated the completion of the first railroad across North America.

The ensuing three decades were difficult for Union Pacific. Bad management, overextension, the effect of the Crédit Mobilier scandal, and the debt owed the federal government all took their toll. Affiliated or subsidiary lines were extended north from Ogden, Utah, to Butte, Montana (Utah & Northern), and northwest from Granger, Wyoming, to Portland, Oregon (Oregon Short Line), and in 1880 the UP merged the Kansas Pacific Railway, which had been opened from Kansas City, Kansas, to Denver, Colorado, in 1870, and the affiliated Denver Pacific, which connected Denver with the main line at Cheyenne. About that same time UP gained control of several railroads in Colorado that later became the Colorado & Southern Railway, and for a few years (until 1893) the UP system reached down into Texas.

In 1897 E. H. Harriman purchased the UP at a public auction and assembled a system that included Southern Pacific, Illinois Central, and Chicago & Alton. Harriman embarked on an improvement program that double tracked UP from Omaha west to Granger, Wyoming, and built a

A unit coal train rolls downhill through Utah's Echo Canyon east of Ogden. Photo by Wesley Fox.

new line over Sherman Hill between Cheyenne and Laramie, Wyoming.

In 1905 the Los Angeles & Salt Lake Railroad was completed between its namesake cities, but severe floods in several successive years in Nevada and western Utah destroyed much of the line in the Meadow Valley Canyon. The line was rebuilt and placed in service in 1912.

In 1912 UP was required to divest itself of its Southern Pacific stock, but close affiliation continued between the two railroads, aided by a 1924 agreement that permitted SP to control Central Pacific and required SP to solicit traffic to move via Ogden and the UP.

For the first three-quarters of the 20th century the map of the Union Pacific remained the same: Omaha to Ogden, Ogden to Los Angeles, Ogden to Butte, Granger, Wyo., to Portland (and on to Seattle, by trackage rights), with a branch to Spokane, and Kansas City through Denver to Cheyenne, plus branches. Chicago, the railroad center of the United States, was 500 miles east of the east end of the main line at Omaha (more precisely, at Council Bluffs, Iowa), but the Chicago & North Western's double-track route between Chicago and Omaha had been practically an eastern extension of the UP since before 1900. In 1955 UP suddenly shifted its streamliners to the Milwaukee Road east of Omaha, and in 1963 UP petitioned to merge the Rock Island, primarily for its Omaha-Chicago line. The Rock Island merger case dragged on for 12 years before the parties concerned gave up, and with the creation of Amtrak in 1971, the only passenger train through Omaha was on the Burlington Northern. By the late 1980s the C&NW was again UP's primary eastern connection, and UP now owns nearly 25 percent of the North Western.

On December 22, 1982, Union Pacific merged the Missouri Pacific and the Western Pacific, more than doubling in size. The name Pacific Rail Systems was used briefly to describe the combined railroads, but it did not catch on. WP was absorbed immediately, but MP was to remain separate in name and image. A year later yellow paint began to replace blue on Missouri Pacific locomotives, and not long after that "Union" replaced "Missouri" in the lettering diagrams. On paper Missouri Pacific remains a separate railroad.

In 1987 Union Pacific Railroad merged a number of its subsidiaries: Los Angeles & Salt Lake Railroad, Oregon Short Line Railroad, Oregon-Washington Railroad & Navigation Co., St. Joseph & Grand Island,

Spokane International (which operates a line from Spokane north to the Canadian border), Yakima Valley Transportation Co. (a traction line at Yakima, Wash.), Western Pacific Railroad, Sacramento Northern, and Tidewater Southern.

The Interstate Commerce Commission approved the purchase of the Missouri-Kansas-Texas by the Missouri Pacific Railroad on May 16, 1988. UP absorbed the Katy's operations on August 12, 1988.

Western Pacific, Missouri Pacific, Texas & Pacific, and Missouri-Kansas-Texas are described in depth in *The Historical Guide to North American Railroads*; brief histories follow.

Western Pacific

In 1900 the Gould railroads (Western Maryland, Wabash, Missouri Pacific, and Denver & Rio Grande) stretched from Baltimore to Ogden, Utah. The Southern Pacific, which reached east from California to Ogden, was a major source of traffic for the system — until E. H. Harriman gained control of the SP and all but merged it with his Union Pacific, which ran east from Ogden. At the same time there was considerable pressure for a second railroad east from northern California to break SP's monopoly.

The Western Pacific Railway was incorporated in 1903 with the backing of the Denver & Rio Grande to build a railroad from Salt Lake City to San Francisco.

The last spike was driven in 1909. The route was almost 150 miles longer than SP's route from Ogden, but it crossed the Sierra Nevada 2,000 feet lower and had easier grades. Operating revenue wasn't sufficient to cover the construction cost, and in 1915 WP entered bankruptcy, taking the Rio Grande along with it (Wabash and Western Maryland entered receivership about the same time).

In 1926 WP was acquired by interests affiliated with the Great Northern and the Northern Pacific. In 1931 it completed a line north to meet a line GN was constructing south from the Columbia River to form a second north-south route through Oregon and California, and it acquired several interurban lines in northern California. It remained an obscure railroad, however, until 1949 when it joined with the Rio Grande and the Chicago, Burlington & Quincy to operate the *California Zephyr*, a Chicago-San Francisco train scheduled and equipped for scenery rather than speed.

In 1960 both Southern Pacific and Santa Fe attempted to gain control

of WP. In 1963 an ICC examiner recommended Santa Fe control, but in 1966 the commission recommended that WP remain independent. In 1980 SP and Santa Fe were talking merger between themselves; Union Pacific merged Western Pacific on December 22, 1982.

Missouri Pacific

Ground was broken for the Pacific Railroad at St. Louis, Missouri, on July 4, 1851. The first four miles of the railroad were opened the next year, and its train was the first to operate west of the Mississippi River. The railroad reached Kansas City in 1865. In 1870 the railroad took a new name, Missouri Pacific Railroad, and was reorganized as the Missouri Pacific Railway in 1876.

Two early railroads formed the nucleus of the southern part of the Missouri Pacific. The St. Louis & Iron Mountain Railroad built south through De Soto and Poplar Bluff and reached the Arkansas state line in 1872. The Cairo & Fulton Railroad was chartered in 1854 to build a railroad from Birds Point, Mo., across the Mississippi River from Cairo, Illinois, to Fulton, Arkansas, near the Texas border. It reached a connection with the Texas & Pacific at Texarkana in 1873. In 1874 the Iron Mountain and the Cairo & Fulton were consolidated as the St. Louis, Iron Mountain & Southern Railway.

The International & Great Northern Railroad was chartered in 1873 to consolidate the Houston & Great Northern Railroad, a railroad between Houston and Palestine, Texas, and the International Railroad, which ran from Longview, where it connected with the Texas & Pacific, through Palestine to Hearne, with the intention of continuing to Laredo and Mexico City. The I&GN underwent reorganization in 1879 and soon after was leased to the Missouri, Kansas & Texas.

Jay Gould bought control of Missouri Pacific in 1879 and soon added to his portfolio the St. Louis, Iron Mountain & Southern; Missouri, Kansas & Texas; International & Great Northern; Texas & Pacific; Galveston, Houston & Henderson; and Wabash. He began an expansion program that extended MP to Omaha, Nebraska, and Pueblo, Colorado; I&GN to Laredo, Texas, on the Mexican border; SL&IM to Memphis, Tennessee, Lake Charles, Louisiana, and Fort Smith, Ark.; and T&P west to a connection with Southern Pacific at Sierra Blanca, Texas, 90 miles east of El Paso. Gould's empire fell apart in the late 1880s. MK&T became independent

and Wabash became part of the Pennsylvania Railroad system. In 1917 the Missouri Pacific Railroad was incorporated to consolidate the Missouri Pacific Railway and the St. Louis, Iron Mountain & Southern, which had entered receivership in 1915.

Gulf Coast Lines was a collection of railroads between New Orleans and Brownsville, Texas, which had been assembled by B. F. Yoakum when he was chairman of the board of the Rock Island and the Frisco. The principal component and parent of GCL was the New Orleans, Texas & Mexico; the biggest of the subsidiaries was the St. Louis, Brownsville & Mexico, a relative latecomer, opened in 1908 from Houston to Brownsville. The lines were cast off from the Frisco in 1913, at which time they acquired the Gulf Coast Lines name. In 1924 GCL purchased the International-Great Northern Railroad, the 1922 successor to the I&GN. In 1924 Missouri Pacific purchased control of NOT&M. By 1930 MP owned 92 percent of its stock.

MP owned half the common stock of the Denver & Rio Grande Western (Western Pacific had the other half). MP and WP lost their control when D&RGW was reorganized in 1947.

In 1967 MoPac acquired control of the Chicago & Eastern Illinois Railroad, which ran from Chicago to Evansville, Ind., Joppa, Ill., and St. Louis and Chaffee, Mo. In 1967 MoPac sold C&EI's Evansville line to the Louisville & Nashville, and in 1976 merged C&EI.

In 1968 MP purchased a half interest in Alton & Southern from the Aluminum Corporation of America (Alcoa); Chicago & North Western purchased the other half interest but sold it to St. Louis Southwestern (Cotton Belt). In 1976 MoPac merged the Texas & Pacific, with which it had been affiliated since the days of Jay Gould. The following year MP merged several smaller subsidiaries, among them the Fort Worth Belt and the Missouri-Illinois. That same year MP was reincorporated and became a wholly owned subsidiary of Missouri Pacific Corporation.

The creation of Burlington Northern in 1970 formalized long-established alliances, but Chicago, Burlington & Quincy's acquisition of Frisco stock in 1966 and the opening of merger discussions between BN and Frisco in 1977 in effect put BN in MoPac's back yard. Santa Fe and Union Pacific both considered MoPac as a merger partner in the early 1960s, and in 1966 MoPac purchased a large block of Santa Fe stock, filed an appli-

A 50-car unit soda-ash train prepares to leave La Grande, Oregon, on April 13, 1992. At the head of the train are a Dash 8-40C and two C30-7s; two 3000-h.p. helper units are being added to the rear for the climb west over the Blue Mountains. Photo by Jeffrey L. Torretta.

cation to control the Santa Fe, then withdrew the application a year or two later.

In January 1980 Union Pacific announced an agreement to acquire Missouri Pacific — then two weeks later made an offer for Western Pacific. The announcement constituted the first significant realignment of railroad alliances in the West since E. H. Harriman had put UP and Southern Pacific together 80 years before. On December 22, 1982, Union Pacific merged the Missouri Pacific.

Texas & Pacific

In 1871 Congress chartered the Texas Pacific Railroad to build from Marshall, Texas, to San Diego, Calif. The road soon changed its name to Texas & Pacific Railway and acquired a railroad already in operation between Shreveport, Louisiana, and Longview, Texas. By 1874 the T&P

was in operation from Shreveport to Dallas and from Marshall to Texarkana, and in July 1876 it reached Fort Worth, which remained the terminus of the road until 1880.

Westward construction resumed — Jay Gould joined the road's board of directors in 1880 — and in December 1881 the line met the Southern Pacific at Sierra Blanca, Texas, about 90 miles east of El Paso. By September 1882 the T&P had purchased and built a line east from Shreveport to New Orleans. The only additions to the road's map thereafter were a few branch lines, plus the lines of the Midland Valley and the Kansas, Oklahoma & Gulf, both acquired in 1964.

Between 1885 and 1924 the T&P was in and out of receivership. During its reorganization in 1923, Texas & Pacific issued preferred stock to Missouri Pacific in exchange for mortgage bonds. By 1930 MP owned all T&P's preferred stock and more than half its common stock. MP merged Texas & Pacific on October 15, 1976.

Missouri-Kansas-Texas

The Katy was born as the Union Pacific Railway, Southern Branch. (It had no corporate connection with the Union Pacific proper.) It was incorporated in 1865 to build south from Junction City, Kansas, along the Neosho River through Emporia and Parsons to New Orleans. The railroad received a land grant, and construction began in 1869. The road changed its name to Missouri, Kansas & Texas Railway the following year, and late in 1870 it reached the southern boundary of Kansas at Chetopa ahead of two rival lines, earning the right to build south through what is now Oklahoma.

By time it reached Dallas and Fort Worth in 1881, Jay Gould had gained control of the Katy and added to it the International & Great Northern. In 1888 Gould lost control of the Katy and the road regained independence. It emerged from receivership in 1891 and began a period of expansion. By 1915 the sprawling system had 3,865 miles of railroad that reached south from St. Louis, Hannibal, Kansas City, and Junction City to Galveston and San Antonio, east to Shreveport, and west into the Oklahoma panhandle.

In 1923 the Katy was reorganized as the Missouri-Kansas-Texas Railroad. World War II brought increased traffic to the Katy; oil moving north became an exception to Katy's customary southbound traffic pattern.

JOHN C. KENEFICK (1921-) was born in Buffalo, New York. He graduated from Princeton University in 1943, served in the U. S. Naval Reserves from 1943 to 1946, then worked a few months for the New York Central as a machinist's helper. He joined Union Pacific in 1947 as a draftsman and advanced to trainmaster. In 1952 he went to the Denver & Rio Grande Western and spent two years as foreman, roadmaster, and trainmaster. In 1954 he returned to the New York Central where he was successively a division superintendent, assistant general manager of NYC's eastern district, general manager of the New York district, general manager of transportation, and ultimately vice president of operations. When New York Central and Pennsylvania merged in 1968, he became PC's vice president of transportation.

Later that year he was named vice president-operations of Union Pacific. He became chief executive officer in 1970, president in 1971, and chairman in 1982. Kenefick retired in 1986. Anticipating that occasion he said, "W. M. Jeffers, a former president who retired in 1946 …

said on the occasion of his retirement that he would rather be president of the Union Pacific than president of the United States. I share Mr. Jeffers' views."

Kenefick was an operating man on an operating man's railroad. Speaking of the company airplane, he said, "You can't see the railroad from 30,000 feet in the air." You can from a business car, and seeing the railroad is necessary to understanding it. His views on track were similar: "The best way to the poorhouse — as some railroads discovered too late — is poor track maintenance." UP had some of the best track in the country.

He has served on the boards of banks, insurance companies, and hospitals, and his civic activities include a term as president of the Omaha Chamber of Commerce.

During a three month period in 1945 Katy's top three officers died. Dieselization helped the road briefly — it had not purchased new locomotives since 1925 — but Katy's diesel maintenance program was insufficient. Track deterioration that began during the war continued, and drought in the 1950s held traffic down. Suddenly in 1957 Katy was in the red. William N. Deramus III was brought in from the Chicago Great Western to become Katy's president. He rationalized the locomotive roster, abandoned the Junction City branch, trimmed the payroll, consolidated offices, and cut most of the road's passenger service.

Katy's decline resumed in a few years. In 1965 John W. Barriger III was brought in to save the railroad. He faced the same situation that he found on the Monon in the 1940s: almost complete deterioration of the physical plant and extremely low employee morale. He set to work rebuilding the track, purchasing new locomotives, and purchasing and leasing new freight cars. After a long period of economizing itself to death, Katy spent more than a year's gross receipts for new equipment.

A lean, rejuvenated Katy returned to profitability in 1971 under the leadership of Reginald Whitman. Upon the demise of the Rock Island in 1980 the Katy acquired RI's line from Abilene, Kan., south through Herington, Wichita, and El Reno, Okla., to Dallas through a subsidiary, the Oklahoma, Kansas & Texas Railway.

Much of Katy's business in the 1970s and 1980s consisted of unit trains of grain and coal moving south from connections. Since more than 70 percent of Katy's traffic was interline, the mergers taking place around Katy (Missouri Pacific into Union Pacific and Frisco into Burlington Northern) caused concern. The Katy's initial reaction to the UP-MP-WP merger was to protest it as unjustified. As a condition of that merger, Katy received trackage rights on UP and MP to Omaha, Council Bluffs, Lincoln, and Topeka.

In early 1985 the Katy announced that it was receptive to merger or sale, and in mid-1985 Union Pacific made a bid — which it soon withdrew, restructured, and resubmitted in mid-1986. Katy and UP already shared operations on several long routes through trackage rights on alternating stretches of each other's lines — indeed, by 1987, 939 miles (32 percent) of Katy's operation was on tracks of other roads, and other roads used 598 miles of Katy track. As a condition of the merger, the trackage rights between Kansas City and Omaha that Katy had used were granted to Kansas City Southern. The Interstate Commerce Commission approved the purchase of the Katy by the Missouri Pacific Railroad (a subsidiary of UP) on May 16, 1988. UP absorbed the Katy's operations on August 12, 1988.

Address of general offices: 1416 Dodge Street, Omaha, NE 68179
Miles of road operated: 21,882
Reporting marks: ARDP, ARMN, BKTY, CEI, CHTT, MI, MKT, MKTT, MP, OKKT, SI, TNM, TP, UP, UPFE, WP
Number of locomotives: 3,005
Number of freight cars: 72,103
Principal commodities carried: Farm products, soda ash and chemicals, forest products, foodstuffs, coal, automobiles and auto parts

Major yards: Fort Worth, Texas; Houston, Texas; Kansas City, Kan.; North Little Rock, Ark.; North Platte, Nebr.; Omaha; Pocatello, Idaho; Hinkle, Oreg.; Yermo, Calif.

Principal shops:
Locomotive: Fort Worth, Texas; North Little Rock, Ark.; North Platte, Nebr.; Salt Lake City, Utah
Car: DeSoto, Mo.; Palestine, Texas; Pocatello, Idaho; Portland, Oreg.

Radio frequencies: 160.740, others

Passenger routes: Amtrak — St. Louis-Kansas City; St. Louis-Fort Worth; Temple, Texas-San Antonio; Denver-Cheyenne-Ogden-Boise-Portland; Salt Lake City-Winnemucca, Nev.; Salt Lake City-Las Vegas-Barstow, Calif.

In addition, UP operates excursion trains several times a year, often with steam locomotives 844 (4-8-4) and 3985 (4-6-6-4).

Recommended reading: *Union Pacific*, by Maury Klein, published in 1987 (Volume I) and 1989 (Volume II) by Doubleday & Co., 245 Park Avenue, New York, NY 10167 (ISBN 0-385-17728-6 and 0-385-17735-6)

VERMONT RAILWAY and CLARENDON & PITTSFORD RAILROAD

The Rutland Railroad, chartered in 1843, had all the characteristics that railroad enthusiasts appreciate: a picturesque setting; a past that included bankruptcy, receivership, and control by other railroads (Central Vermont and New York Central); and a series of adversities, each worse than the one before — floods, labor troubles, loss of a connecting Great Lakes boat line, and various stockholder and bondholder proposals for salvation. The Rutland's lines extended from Bellows Falls, Vermont, and Chatham, New York, north through Rutland and Burlington, Vt., to Rouses Point, N. Y., then west to Ogdensburg, N. Y,

A strike shut down the Rutland in September 1961, and the railroad was officially abandoned two years later. Much of Vermont was left without rail service. There was still a need for it, so the state of Vermont purchased the railroad in 1963 and engaged Jay Wulfson to operate the portion

VERMONT RAILWAY

A Vermont Railway freight approaches the road's northern terminus, Burlington, on October 6, 1990. The consist includes several TankTrain cars, interconnected tank cars moved as a unit. Photo by Jim Shaw.

between White Creek, N. Y., west of Bennington, Vt., and Burlington. The Vermont Railway was incorporated in 1963 and began operation in January 1964.

Freed of the Rutland's worst problems, such as labor difficulties and the long tentacle across the Lake Champlain islands and the top of New York to Ogdensburg, VTR regained lost business and attracted new. The road bought many of the Rutland's box cars and acquired a large fleet of piggyback trailers. Soon more shippers were shipping and receiving tonnage on the VTR than had used the entire Rutland before the 1961 strike.

In 1972 VTR purchased the Clarendon & Pittsford Railroad, a short line between Rutland and the quarries of its owner, Vermont Marble Company, a few miles northwest. In December 1983 the Clarendon & Pittsford acquired Delaware & Hudson's 24-mile branch between Whitehall, N. Y., and Rutland.

Address of general offices: 1 Railway Lane, Burlington, VT 05401
Miles of road operated: 129 (VTR), 35 (CLP)
Reporting marks: VTR, CLP
Number of locomotives: 5 (VTR), 3 (CLP)

Number of freight cars: 12 (VTR), 12 (CLP)
Principal commodities carried: Grain, petroleum products, limestone, rock salt, marble, lumber, aggregates
Junctions with other railroads:
VTR
Central Vermont: Burlington, Vt.
Clarendon & Pittsford: Rutland, Vt.; Florence, Vt.
Green Mountain: Rutland, Vt.
Guilford Transportation Industries (Boston & Maine): White Creek, N. Y.
CLP
CP Rail System (Delaware & Hudson): Whitehall, N. Y.
Vermont Railway: Rutland, Vt.; Florence, Vt.
Radio frequencies: 161.010 (dispatcher), 160.710 (road and yard), 160.440 (road and yard)
Recommended reading: *The Rutland Road* (second edition), by Jim Shaughnessy, published in 1981 by Howell-North, P. O. Box 3051, La Jolla, CA 92038

VIA RAIL CANADA

During the first rocky years of Amtrak's existence, U. S. rail enthusiasts looked enviously at Canada's passenger trains. Canadian National had undergone a passenger service renaissance in the 1960s and offered service on most main routes and many branches. Even though CP Rail had trimmed many other trains, it still ran the Saint John-Montreal *Atlantic* *Limited* and the Montreal-Toronto-Vancouver *Canadian* — and ran them well. Running on Canada's first transcontinental railroad, CP's stainless-steel, domed *Canadian* was a national symbol.

VIA Rail Canada was created on January 12, 1977, as a subsidiary of Canadian National Railways. On June 1 of that year it assumed responsibility for marketing rail passenger service in Canada. On March 31, 1978, VIA acquired Canadian National's passenger equipment and took over management of CN rail passenger service. The next day, April 1, 1978, VIA became a separate crown corporation. On September 29 of that same year VIA took over CP Rail passenger service, acquired CP's pas-

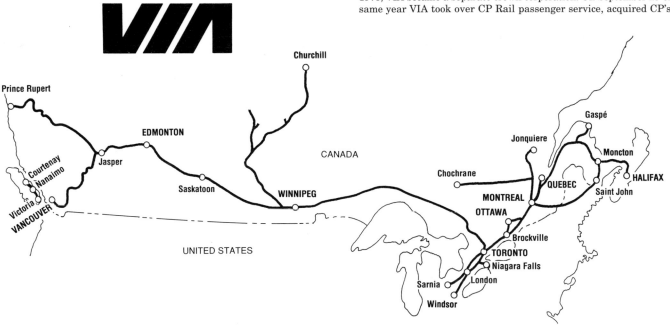

VIA purchased LRC trainsets to upgrade its service in the Quebec-Montreal-Toronto-Windsor corridor. The trains were VIA's first new rolling stock and introduced a new color scheme of light gray, yellow, and blue. Most of the LRC locomotives have been replaced by F40PH-2s, as on this train in Montreal on June 17, 1988. Photo by Michael W. Blaszak.

senger equipment, and assumed the employment of all CN and CP unionized and ground passenger-service staff.

VIA's first major change, in October 1978, was to eliminate the duplication of the *Canadian* and the *Super Continental*, former transcontinental flagships of CP and CN, respectively, east of Sudbury and Capreol, Ontario — both trains had Montreal and Toronto sections. VIA made the *Canadian* a Toronto-Vancouver train and the *Super Continental* a Montreal-Vancouver train. In the summer of 1979 the two trains swapped eastern terminals, and later that year they were combined between Winnipeg and Sudbury.

In October 1979 VIA discontinued CN's Montreal-Halifax *Scotian* and extended CP's Montreal-Saint John, New Brunswick, *Atlantic Limited* east to Halifax. The *Atlantic*, which cut across the middle of Maine, provided a much faster ride to the Maritimes than the *Ocean*, the remaining train on CN's all-Canada route. Business on the train increased dramatically, and VIA found itself operating a 12-car train where CP had run four. Indeed, between 1977 and 1980 VIA's ridership increased 41 percent, and VIA appeared to have a sunnier future than Amtrak, which was embroiled in some of its worst political battles.

But soon VIA suddenly found itself enduring what Amtrak had gone through. On November 15, 1981, Canadian transport minister Jean-Luc Pepin ordered the discontinuance or reduction of service on more than one-fifth of VIA's routes. The two principal trains discontinued were the *Atlantic* and the *Super Continental*. Local trains were inaugurated to maintain service on a few portions of the discontinued routes. The *Canadian* remained a Montreal-Vancouver train, but it was rerouted through Toronto, adding several hours to its schedule. Elsewhere in Canada branchline services were reduced from daily to triweekly or discontinued altogether. Pepin announced that the cuts would permit the purchase of LRC trainsets for service in the Maritimes and the West. VIA appeared to be concentrating its marketing efforts and its new equipment in the Quebec-Montreal-Toronto-Windsor corridor where the bulk of Canada's population lives.

Before long VIA restored some of its long-distance trains. By the end of 1985 the *Atlantic* returned to the Halifax-Montreal run; the *Ocean* had become a Moncton-Montreal train, connecting with the *Atlantic* at Moncton; the *Super Continental* had returned to the timetable as a Winnipeg-Vancouver train via the CN route; and the *Canadian* once again served Montreal and Toronto with separate trains east of Sudbury.

The restorations were only temporary. On January 15, 1990, new cuts ordered by transport minister Benoit Bouchard took effect. Among the trains axed were well-patronized overnight trains from Toronto to Montreal and to Cochrane, Ont., all service in Nova Scotia except the Halifax-Montreal *Ocean* and *Atlantic* (both of which became triweekly), numerous local trains, and the *Canadian*. Technically, the *Canadian* wasn't discontinued — the name was applied to a slow triweekly Toronto-Vancouver train on the Canadian National route, replacing the *Super Continental*. The outcry was fierce all across Canada.

VIA's trains were pulled by first-generation diesels until the early 1980s, when the corridor services were equipped with LRC diesels and

233

coaches (Light, Rapid, Comfortable — and in Quebec, Léger, Rapid, Confortable). In the late 1980s F40PH-2s arrived from GMD to take over the remaining trains (accompanied by B units or steam generator cars) and to pull the LRC trains — most of the LRC locomotives lasted less than a decade. The cars VIA inherited from CN and CP were built in the mid-1950s, and VIA has begun a rebuilding program that will adapt some, primarily the Budd-built ex-CP cars, for head-end power.

Address of general offices: 1801 McGill College Avenue, Suite 1300, Montreal, PQ, Canada H3A 2N4

Route-miles: 8,532

Number of locomotives: 91

Number of self-propelled passenger cars: 6

Number of passenger cars: 564

Passenger routes: (on CN lines except as noted)
Halifax, N. S.-Moncton, N. B.-Saint John, N. B.-Montreal (CP Saint John-Sherbrooke, Que.)
Halifax-Moncton-Matapedia, Que.-Montreal
Gaspé-Matapedia-Montreal
Quebec-Montreal
Montreal-Hervey-Jonquiere, Que.
Montreal-Hervey-Senneterre, Que.-Cochrane, Ont.
Montreal-Ottawa
Ottawa-Brockville, Ont.-Toronto (CP Smiths Falls-Brockville)
Montreal-Brockville-Toronto
Toronto-Stratford-London-Sarnia, Ont.
Toronto-Brantford-London-Windsor, Ont.
Toronto-Hamilton-Niagara Falls, Ont.
Toronto-Winnipeg-Saskatoon-Edmonton-Jasper-Vancouver
Sudbury-White River, Ont. (CP)
Winnipeg-The Pas-Thompson-Churchill, Man
The Pas-Lynn Lake, Man.
Jasper-Prince Rupert, B. C.
Victoria-Courtenay, B. C. (CP)

Recommended reading:
VIA Rail Canada: The First Five Years, by Tom Nelligan, published in 1982 by PTJ Publishing, Inc., P. O. Box 397, Park Forest, IL 60466 (ISBN 0-937658-08-1)
Not a Sentimental Journey, edited by Jo Davis, published in 1990 by Turnaround Decade Group, 23 James Street, Waterloo, ON, Canada N2J 2S8 (ISBN 0-921078-01-3)

VIRGINIA RAILWAY EXPRESS
(Northern Virginia Transportation Commission)
(Potomac and Rappahannock Transportation Commission)

The Northern Virginia Transportation Commission was established in 1964 to coordinate transportation in the Virginia suburbs of Washington, D. C. The commission did what it could with car pools and local bus systems, but the highways reached capacity. Rail commuter service was needed. In 1988 the Virginia legislature created the Potomac and Rappahannock Transportation Commission to extend transportation planning to outlying suburbs (more accurately, to cities that had become suburbs in the previous two decades).

The two agencies began planning commuter rail service to operate on the two lines that run south from Washington: 61 miles on the Richmond, Fredericksburg & Potomac (now CSX) to Fredericksburg, and 35 miles on the Southern (now Norfolk Southern) to Manassas Airport, a few miles beyond Manassas. The two routes use the same rails as far as AF Tower, just south of Alexandria.

The two commissions chose the name Virginia Railway Express and

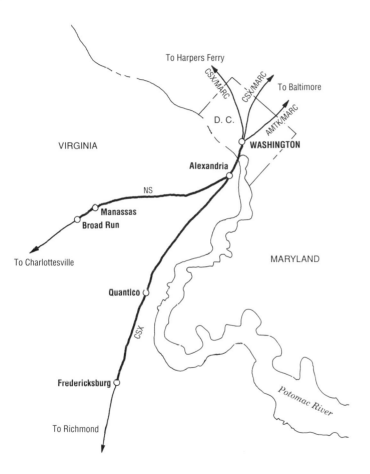

Virginia Railway Express's first outbound afternoon train arrives at Rolling Road station on the Manassas line on opening day, June 22, 1992. Photo by Alex Mayes.

in 1989 ordered 38 coaches from Mitsui & Co. USA and contracted with Amtrak to run the service. In 1990 they ordered 10 locomotives, rebuilt GP40s, from Morrison Knudsen.

The service was scheduled to start in 1991, but two matters delayed it. The use of Conrail track in Washington and over the Potomac River bridge brought up the issue of insurance (Amtrak trains had been using that track since 1971); an act of Congress was required to settle the matter. Mitsui subcontracted the cars to Mafersa, a carbuilder in Brazil, and labor problems and material shortages delayed delivery.

The service to Fredericksburg finally began on June 12, 1992, and service to Manassas began 10 days later. Initially trains were to operate only during morning and evening rush hours.

Address of general offices: 4350 North Fairfax Drive, Suite 720, Arlington, VA 22203

Miles of road operated: 82
Passenger routes:
Washington-Fredericksburg, Va. (CSX)
Washington-Broad Run/Manassas Airport, Va. (Norfolk Southern)

Number of locomotives: 10
Number of passenger cars: 59
Recommended reading: "Commuter trains in the Old Dominion," by Tracy Kirk Davis, in TRAINS Magazine, May 1992, pages 24-26

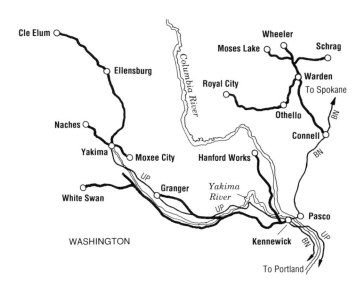

WASHINGTON CENTRAL RAILROAD

The last spike of the Northern Pacific Railway was driven on September 8, 1883, completing the country's first rail line across the northern tier of states. NP extended from Carlton, Minnesota, to Wallula Junction, Washington, then to Tacoma by way of the Oregon Railway & Navigation

Washington Central 301, a chop-nosed GP9, has four cars in tow at Ellensburg, Washington, on June 10, 1987. Photo by Jim Shaw.

Co. (now Union Pacific) to Portland and NP's own line north of there. In 1887 NP opened a line from Pasco, Wash., on the Columbia River, northwest over the Cascade Range to Tacoma. The new line cut off the long dogleg through Portland, and it became NP's main line.

Burlington Northern was created in 1970 by the merger of Northern Pacific; Great Northern; Spokane, Portland & Seattle; and Chicago, Burlington & Quincy. The new railroad had two routes from the Twin Cities to Puget Sound (plus bypasses, cutoffs, and alternates) and in a few years began to rationalize its map. The Great Northern route was a decade or so newer than NP's, had easier crossings of the Cascades and the Rockie, and between Spokane and Seattle was 67 miles shorter. If the NP line were cut, any Pasco-Seattle traffic could move via Vancouver, Washington, with the water-level route along the Columbia River more than compensating for the extra distance. The former NP route over the Cascades was an early candidate for spinning off.

In October 1986 Washington Central Railroad acquired 149 miles of the former Northern Pacific main line from SP&S Junction in Kennewick, across the Columbia River from Pasco, northwest to Cle Elum, plus branches to Granger, White Swan, Moxee City, and Naches. Two months later Washington Central acquired a cluster of former NP and Milwaukee Road lines in the wheat-growing area of central Washington, from Connell to Moses Lake, Royal City, Wheeler, and Schrag. Washington Central also operates the U. S. Government Railroad from Richland Junction to Hanford Works.

Address of general offices: 6 East Arlington, Yakima, WA 98901
Miles of road operated: 325
Reporting marks: WCRC
Number of locomotives: 9
Number of freight cars: 1,598
Principal commodities carried: Lumber, grain
Major yards: Yakima, Kennewick, and Warden, Wash.
Shops: Yakima, Wash.
Junctions with other railroads:
Burlington Northern: Connell and Pasco, Wash.
Union Pacific: Grandview, Kennewick, Sunnyside, and Yakima, Wash.
Radio frequencies: 161.295, 160.770, 160.440
Recommended reading: "In the path of the North Coast Limited," by Eric G. Nelson, in TRAINS Magazine, November 1987, pages 40-43

WHEELING & LAKE ERIE RAILWAY

The Wheeling & Lake Erie Rail Road was incorporated in 1871 to build from the Lake Erie ports of Sandusky and Toledo, Ohio, southeast through the coalfields of Ohio to Wheeling, West Virginia. The road got off to a slow, narrow gauge start; it took the backing of Jay Gould to convert it to standard gauge and get it to Wheeling in 1891. It gathered in a Cleveland-Zanesville railroad, the Cleveland, Canton & Southern, and continued to limp along, gathering strength only when Detroit's automobile industry burgeoned — factories along W&LE's line produced many automobile components.

In 1927 Nickel Plate, New York Central, and Baltimore & Ohio bought W&LE stock. The ICC ordered them to sell it, and the Van Sweringen brothers bought it and added it to what they already had. The Nickel Plate purchased control in 1947 and leased the road in 1949. To most observers the W&LE was gone, or at most was a railroad that existed only on paper. The lease passed to Norfolk & Western when it merged the Nickel Plate in 1964, and in 1988 N&W merged the Wheeling & Lake Erie.

It may be helpful to remember that railroads have four components: fixed plant (track, right of way, and buildings), rolling stock, human organization, and financial structure. The Nickel Plate leased the fixed plant and rolling stock of the W&LE and added the human organization to its payroll; the Norfolk & Western merged the financial structure, then dissolved it. When a railroad is reorganized, a new financial structure with a new name replaces the old one (usually "Railroad" replaces "Railway" or "and" replaces "&" in the name, or vice versa), but the physical plant, rolling stock, and human organization remain the same (except perhaps the man at the top).

High-nose GP35s still in Southern Railway paint but lettered for Wheeling & Lake Erie head up train MJD at Harmon, Ohio, on April 16, 1992. Photo by Michael W. Blaszak.

On May 17, 1990, Norfolk Southern Corporation, the holding company that owned the Norfolk & Western, sold to the Wheeling Acquisition Corporation a group of lines to be operated by a new Wheeling & Lake Erie Railway. The lines are the old Wheeling & Lake Erie east of Bellevue, Ohio, and what remained of the lines of the Akron, Canton & Youngstown Railway (N&W purchased the AC&Y in 1964 and dissolved it — its financial structure — in 1982). Included in the deal were the lease of the Pittsburgh & West Virginia Railway and trackage rights on Norfolk Southern between Chatfield and Parkertown, Ohio; later the new company acquired trackage rights on CSX from Connellsville, Pa., east to Hagerstown, Maryland.

Important sources of traffic on the new W&LE are coal mines northwest of Wheeling, the industrial area around Cleveland, and quarries at Cary, Flat Rock, and Parkertown. The lines had been profitable for N&W, but not as profitable as it would have liked. W&LE and P&WV had long been part of a Midwest-East Coast route assembled by a group of regional railroads to compete with the larger Eastern roads, but mergers had changed alliances, and N&W was moving its Midwest-East Coast traffic on the "old" N&W main line through Roanoke, Virginia. The new W&LE has the advantages of a regional railroad, including lower costs and being closer to its customers.

Address of general offices: 100 East First Street, Brewster, OH 44613

Miles of road operated: 751

Reporting marks: WE

Number of locomotives: 52

Number of freight cars: 1,697

Principal commodities carried: Coal, steel, aggregates and stone, chemicals, rubber

Shops: Brewster, Ohio

Radio frequencies: 161.250 (ex-NKP), 160.440 (ex-AC&Y), 160.665 (yard), 161.565 (yard)

Recommended reading: "Rebirth of the Wheeling," by Tracy Kirk Davis, in TRAINS Magazine, June 1990, pages 18B-20

WISCONSIN & CALUMET RAILROAD

The Wisconsin & Calumet Railroad operates the former Illinois Central line from Freeport, Ill., north through Monroe, Wis., to Madison, and former Milwaukee Road routes from Waukesha, Wis., through Milton Junction and Madison to Prairie du Chien; from Milton Junction through Janesville to Monroe; and from Janesville, Wis., southeast to Fox Lake, Ill., then by trackage rights on Metra and Belt Railway of Chicago to BRC's Clearing Yard in Chicago. All Wisconsin lines are owned by the state.

Several companies have operated the lines since they were cast off by IC and CMStP&P. Wisconsin & Calumet's predecessors deserve mention.

Chicago, Madison & Northern

The Freeport-Madison route was built by the Chicago, Madison & Northern Railroad, an Illinois Central subsidiary, as part of IC's expansion program of the late 1880s. Nearly a century later, in 1978, Illinois Central Gulf abandoned the line. A new company, the Chicago, Madison & Northern Railway, began operation in February 1978. In 1980 it extended its operations to the former Milwaukee Road line from Janesville west through Monroe to Mineral Point. For a short period the CM&N operated the state-owned former Milwaukee Road branch between Sparta and Viroqua, Wis.

Central Wisconsin

The Waukesha-Prairie du Chien route was built by the Milwaukee & Mississippi Rail Road between 1850 and 1857. It was purchased by the Milwaukee & St. Paul in 1868 and became part of the first Chicago-Milwaukee-St. Paul rail route. The line west of Madison was later part of Milwaukee Road's Chicago-Rapid City, South Dakota, route and retained secondary mainline status and passenger service until 1960. The line southeast from Janesville was built in 1900 as a shortcut for Chicago-Madison trains. The Janesville-Monroe line was built in 1877 and extended west in 1881 to connect with lines to Platteville and Mineral Point, Wis.

Milwaukee Road abandoned its Waukesha-Milton Junction line in 1978. To preserve rail access to an agricultural chemical plant at Whitewater, the line was purchased by the state of Wisconsin, which conveyed it to the city of Whitewater. Operation was begun by the Central Wisconsin

Wisconsin & Calumet 613, a GP7, spots a hopper car of coal at the University of Wisconsin heating plant in Madison on December 4, 1987. Photo by Paul Swanson.

Railroad in 1980. Upon the demise of the Chicago, Madison & Northern in 1982, the Central Wisconsin took over operation of its lines. Central Wisconsin established two subsidiaries to operate other ex-Milwaukee Road lines: In 1982 the Wisconsin & Western began working the Madison-Prairie du Chien line from Middleton, a few miles west of Madison, to Lone Rock; the Elkhorn & Walworth operated from Janesville to Elkhorn via Bardwell, and from Milton Junction northwest to Madison. Central Wisconsin's parent company entered bankruptcy at the end of 1984.

Wisconsin & Calumet

Wisconsin & Calumet began operation in January 1985 on the Freeport-Madison and Janesville-Monroe routes. It had authority to continue west of Monroe to Mineral Point, but Central Wisconsin had embargoed that line in 1984. It has since been dismantled. The Milwaukee Road ceased operating the Madison-Prairie du Chien line west of Lone Rock in 1980, but in 1986 Wisconsin & Calumet reopened it. Wisconsin & Calumet was operated by Chicago West Pullman Transportation Corporation until August 21, 1992, when it was purchased by Railroad Acquisition Corporation, owner of the Wisconsin & Southern Railroad.

Address of general offices: 203 South Pearl St., Janesville, WI 52545
Miles of road operated: 422
Reporting marks: WICT
Number of locomotives: 8
Number of freight cars: 359
Principal commodities carried: Sand, coal, grain
Shops: Janesville, Wis.
Radio frequencies: 160.215

Junctions with other railroads:
Belt Railway of Chicago: Chicago, Ill.
Burlington Northern: Crawford, Wis.
Chicago & North Western: Janesville, Wis.; Waukesha, Wis.
CP Rail System (Soo Line): Janesville, Wis.; Madison, Wis.
Wisconsin Central: Waukesha, Wis.
Recommended reading:
"Two days on the west end," by Paul Swanson, in TRAINS Magazine, July 1988, pages 24-29
"Third time charm?" by J. David Ingles, in TRAINS Magazine, July 1988, pages 30-31
Map: See Wisconsin & Southern, below

WISCONSIN & SOUTHERN RAILROAD

In 1978 the Milwaukee Road was considering abandonment of several branches that served the area northwest of Milwaukee, Wisconsin. The FSC Corporation of Pittsburgh, Pennsylvania, (which also operates the Upper Merion & Plymouth Railroad, a switching road at Conshohocken, Pa.) won the bidding to operate the lines, purchased them with state and federal aid, and organized the Wisconsin & Southern Railroad. The road began operation on July 1, 1980.

In 1988 the Wisconsin & Southern was purchased by the Railroad Acquisition Corporation, which is owned by William Gardner. On August 21, 1992, Railroad Acquisition Corp. purchased the Wisconsin & Calumet Railroad, and as this book went to press was negotiating for trackage rights to connect it with the Wisconsin & Southern.

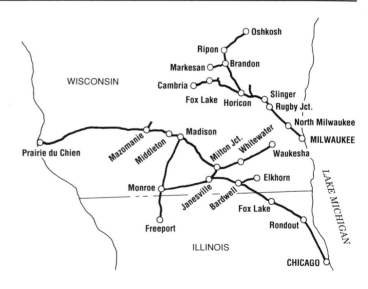

Address of general offices: P. O. Box A, Horicon, WI 53032
Miles of road operated: 148
Reporting marks: WSOR
Number of locomotives: 13
Number of freight cars: 550
Principal commodities carried: Canned goods, grain, agricultural lime, coal, industrial sand

Junctions with other railroads:
Chicago & North Western: Granville, Wis.
Fox River Valley: Germantown, Wis.
CP Rail System (Soo Line): North Milwaukee, Wis.
Wisconsin Central: Rugby Junction, Wis.; Slinger, Wis.
Radio frequencies: 160.575, 161.37

Wisconsin & Southern 4491, a rebuilt GP9, has a short freight in tow approaching Ripon, Wisconsin, on June 7, 1988. Photo by Jim Shaw.

WISCONSIN CENTRAL LTD.

The Wisconsin Central Railroad was incorporated in 1871 to build a line from Neenah, Wisconsin, northwest to Lake Superior at Ashland. It reached Ashland in 1877, then completed a line west to St. Paul in 1884 and a line south to Chicago in 1886. The road was leased by the Northern Pacific in 1890; the panic of 1893 and financial difficulties of both NP and WC ended that lease. WC flourished briefly at the beginning of the 20th century and completed a line northwest to Superior, Wis., in 1908.

In 1909 the Minneapolis, St. Paul & Sault Ste. Marie Railway (the Soo Line) leased the properties of the Wisconsin Central Railroad, then a 1,000-mile road extending from Chicago to St. Paul and Duluth, Minnesota, and

Rebuilt GP35s 4007 and 4009 bring a southbound Wisconsin Central freight under the Burlington Northern while on Duluth, Missabe & Iron Range rails at Saunders, Wisconsin, on June 25, 1989. Photo by Eric Hirsimaki.

Ashland, Wisconsin. In addition to gaining access to Chicago, Soo Line also obtained routes to the industrial Fox River Valley of Wisconsin and the iron ore deposits of northern Wisconsin. The lease ended in 1932, but Soo Line continued to operate the road. Except for tiny "WC" letters on some Soo Line locomotives and cars, Wisconsin Central became a paper railroad. It was merged by the Soo Line in 1961.

When Soo Line purchased the Milwaukee Road in 1985, it acquired a double-track Chicago-Twin Cities line that was 50 miles shorter than its own single-track route. Soo Line consolidated its operations on the former Milwaukee route. It briefly tried operating its light-density lines in Michi-

gan and Wisconsin as Lake States Transportation Division (not to be confused with Michigan's Lake State Railway, which is the former Detroit & Mackinac Railway), but was unable to change work rules to cut costs on those lines. The Milwaukee Road's dowry included accumulations of debt and deferred maintenance. Soo Line found itself short of cash and offered the Lake States lines for sale.

A company headed by Edward A. Burkhardt and Thomas F. Power bought the lines in 1987. The company's name was Wisconsin Central Ltd., and the map of the new railroad looked much like the map of the old Wisconsin Central: the Chicago-Twin Cities main line; branches from Neenah to Manitowoc and to Argonne; from Spencer, Wis., north to Ashland (in two pieces); and from Owen to Superior (mostly as trackage rights on Soo Line). Along with the old WC came former Milwaukee Road branches from Milwaukee to Green Bay and from New Lisbon to Tomahawk; nearly all the original (1883) Soo Line route from St. Paul to Sault Ste. Marie, Ontario; and two pieces of the former Duluth, South Shore & Atlantic main line.

Soo Line was scheduled to transfer the property on September 11, 1987, and Wisconsin Central had worked out precise plans for an orderly transfer of operations, but on that very day the Interstate Commerce Commission decreed a 45-day delay so it could study the matter. After a storm of protest, the ICC reduced the stay to 30 days, and Wisconsin Central Ltd. began operation on October 11, 1987.

In August 1989 WC purchased the 5-mile Munising Junction-Munising portion of the Lake Superior & Ishpeming, which had long been isolated from the rest of the LS&I. In July 1992 WC purchased 98 miles of Chicago & North Western track between Cameron and Superior, Wis., giving it a second route to Superior. Part of its original purchase agreement was that if WC acquired its own rails to Superior, Soo Line would have to sell and WC would have to buy the Ladysmith-Superior line, on which WC had trackage rights. WC did so, then combined the best of the two lines: the former Soo Line from Ladysmith to Gordon, Wis., and the former C&NW from Gordon to Superior.

As this book goes to press in fall 1992, WC is negotiating the purchase of the Green Bay & Western and the Fox River Valley through a new subsidiary, Fox Valley & Western.

Address of general offices: P. O. Box 5062, Rosemont, IL 60017-5062
Miles of road operated: 2,068
Reporting marks: WC
Number of locomotives: 1148
Number of freight cars: 5,170
Principal commodities carried: Paper, pulpwood, chemicals
Major yards: North Fond du Lac, Wis.; Stevens Point, Wis.
Principal shops: North Fond du Lac, Wis.; Stevens Point, Wis.
Radio frequencies: 160.785 (road, North Fond du Lac-Stevens Point, Milwaukee-Hilbert-Argonne), 160.260 (yard), 161.295 (road, other than lines noted)

Historical and technical society: Soo Line Historical & Technical Society, 3410 Kasten Court, Middleton, WI 53562
Recommended reading: "The Wisconsin Central Story," by Otto Dobnick, in TRAINS Magazine, September 1990, pages 32-47, and October 1990, pages 40-53.

EDWARD A BURKHARDT (1938-   ) was born in New York. He graduated from Yale University in 1960 and went to work for the Wabash, holding a succession of positions in the operating department. In 1967 he moved from the Norfolk & Western, successor to the Wabash, to the Chicago & North Western as assistant to the general manager. He was assistant vice president, transportation, from 1969 to 1977, vice president, marketing, from 1977 to 1980, and became vice president, transportation, in 1980. He held that post until he left to organize the Wisconsin Central in 1987.

Burkhardt married Sandra Schwaegel in 1967. He is a director of the Lake Superior Museum of Transportation in Duluth and the John W. Barriger III National Railroad library in St. Louis. Burkhardt was a backer of C&NW's steam program — exhibition trips and excursions pulled by C&NW 1385, a Ten-Wheeler on loan from the Mid-Continent Railway Museum.

NORTH AMERICAN RAIL TRANSIT SYSTEMS

The spectrum of fixed-guideway transportation systems stretches from Burlington Northern and Union Pacific, which are railroads, to roller coasters and airport people movers, which are not. The line that separates BN and UP from the things that aren't railroads lies somewhere below the commuter authorities; rail transit straddles the line.

The test question for railroads, is "Does it interchange carload freight with other railroads?" The commuter authorities, which took over a portion of the railroads' business, can be included by changing "does" to "could." But a number of the commuter authorities are also in the transit business, and rail transit is for the most part steel wheel on steel rail.

Rail transit operations share several characteristics:
• passenger-only traffic in electric self-propelled cars, drawing power from overhead wire or a third rail
• cars built to other than AAR standard dimensions
• track not connected to the regular railroad network (not counting connections used only for delivery of new rolling stock)
• track in, over, and under public streets
• fare payment by cash, token, or magnetic card
• operation every so many minutes rather than according to published timetables (or so the riders perceive).
A few of these characteristics can be found on one or more railroads in this book, but the combination constitutes "rail transit."

Rail transit is the fastest-growing sector of the railroad industry. At the end of the 1960s streetcars and rapid transit systems (subways and elevateds) could be found in only a handful of North American cities. There had been little rapid transit construction in decades. A fair number of streetcar systems endured into the late 1940s, but World War II had worn them out, and in 1947 new buses looked even more modern than they had before the war. Besides, the transit companies quickly recognized that it cost far less to run buses on city-maintained streets than to maintain their own rails and trolley wires. A few streetcar lines survived beyond the mid-1950s because they ran on private rights of way or in subways or tunnels that couldn't be converted to bus operation.

Postwar urban planners encouraged automobiles with freeways and parking lots, but the utopian dream of driving effortlessly from home to office to store never came true: The parking lots filled fast, and traffic became slower and slower until the freeways looked like parking lots. Little by little rail transit began to experience a renaissance. Cities like Boston and Chicago that already had rail transit undertook a few tentative extensions and discovered they were successful. Then several cities, among them Atlanta, San Francisco, and Washington, D. C., built "heavy rail" subway systems. ("Heavy rail" has tracks completely separated from other traffic, station platforms at car-floor level, and, usually, third-rail current distribution. Such a system is sometimes referred to as a "Metro" — from the French chemin de fer métropolitaine, metropolitan railway.)

Then came the great transit compromise of the 1970s, "light rail," characterized primarily by tracks in the street or highway median for at least part of the route; secondary characteristics are low-level station platforms and overhead wire current distribution — but the distinction between light and heavy is not a precise one. Edmonton, Alberta, opened the first such system in North America in 1978. It runs partly in subway and partly on private right of way adjacent to a Canadian National Railways line. In 1981 systems opened in Calgary, Alberta, and San Diego, California. They shared two features: downtown street running and, like Edmonton, a standard, stock, German-built articulated light rail vehicle.

The aerospace industry is probably responsible for the term "Light Rail Vehicle" (LRV), which means "new streetcar." Several light rail systems have discovered that current technology is surprisingly compatible with that of 75 years ago and share their rails with historic streetcars. Several light rail lines have used the right of way of streetcar and interurban systems dismantled decades before. Indeed, the whole light rail phenomenon is a rare example of a technology disappearing almost completely, then returning in substantially the same form, for substantially the same purpose.

Atlanta, Georgia: Metropolitan Atlanta Rapid Transit Authority's heavy rail subway system began operation in 1979. MARTA's original two lines

A Massachusetts Bay Transportation Authority Orange Line train stops at Massachusetts Avenue station in Boston on November 28, 1987. Third-rail current distribution and station platforms at car floor level typify heavy rail transit. Photo by William D. Middleton.

have since been extended, and further extensions are under construction. The north-south line runs right to the terminal building at Hartsfield International Airport, second busiest in the U. S.

Route miles: 34   Stations: 30   Cars: 240

Baltimore, Maryland: The first section of Baltimore's heavy rail Metro from Charles Center to Reisterstown Plaza, opened November 21, 1983. The line was extended 6 miles northwest to Owings Mills in 1987, largely in the media strip of I-795, and an extension to Johns Hopkins Hospital is under construction. On May 17, 1992, regular service began on the first segment of Baltimore's Central Light Rail Line, from Camden Yards, next to the MARC (ex-Baltimore & Ohio) station to Timonium. North of downtown Baltimore the tracks are on Conrail right of way, the one-time Northern Central. Conrail freight trains operate on the line at night. The line is to be extended to the south on former Baltimore & Annapolis right of way. Both lines are operated by the Mass Transit Administration, an agency of the Maryland Department of Transportation.

Heavy rail route miles: 14   Stations: 12   Cars: 100
Light rail route miles: 22   Stations: 18   Cars: 35

Boston, Massachusetts: In addition to its railroad commuter services, Massachusetts Bay Transportation Authority operates the Boston subway system. Four separate lines intersect in downtown Boston. Three lines use high-platform third-rail equipment; the fourth, which runs through the oldest subway in the U. S., uses LRVs. Several lines occupy former railroad rights of way; others run in streets or median strips.

Heavy rail route miles: 42   Stations: 56   Cars: 411
Light rail route miles: 35   Stations: 27   Cars: 222

Buffalo, New York: Niagara Frontier Transit Metro System opened the first portion of its light rail line in October 1984 and the remainder in May 1985. Most of the line is in a subway.

Light rail route miles: 6   Stations: 14   Cars: 26

Calgary, Alberta: The first line of Calgary's light-rail system was opened in 1981 by the City of Calgary Transportation Department. It operates

A four-car "L" train bound for Ravenswood rounds the curve into Sedgwick station on Chicago's North Side on June 26, 1987. Photo by William D. Middleton.

German-built LRVs on the streets downtown and on private right of way parallel to a Canadian Pacific line south of downtown. Since 1981 two other routes have opened.
Route miles: 17   Stations: 26   Cars: 83

Chicago, Illinois: The Chicago Transit Authority operates six heavy rail routes in Chicago. Two routes are partly in subway, and much of the recently built part of the system is in the median strip of expressways. A notable part of the system is the elevated loop that defines downtown Chicago. The cars draw current from third rail, except on the Skokie Swift line, which uses catenary. An extension to O'Hare airport opened in 1984; a 9-mile line to Midway Airport is scheduled to open in 1993.
Route miles: 89   Stations: 140   Cars: 1,900

Cleveland, Ohio: Greater Cleveland Regional Transit Authority operates two lines: an overhead wire heavy rail route between 155th Street in the eastern part of the city and the airport on the west, and a light rail route, the former Shaker Heights Rapid Transit line, from downtown Cleveland (the station is the former Cleveland Union Terminal) to Shaker Heights. The dissimilar cars of the two routes share track and stations east of downtown.
Heavy rail route miles: 19   Stations: 18   Cars: 60
Light rail route miles: 13   Stations: 29   Cars: 48

Dallas, Texas: In February 1992 Dallas Area Rapid Transit began construction of a light rail system that is scheduled to open in 1996.
Route miles: 20   Stations: 21

Edmonton, Alberta: In 1978 Edmonton Transit opened a light rail line running east and west through the city. A short extension across the Saskatchewan River was opened in 1992.
Route miles: 7   Stations: 10   Cars: 37

Fort Worth, Texas: In 1963 Leonard's department store opened a subway between the basement of its store and a parking lot some distance away. Rolling stock consisted of five extensively rebuilt ex-Washington, D. C., PCC cars. In 1967 the store and the subway were purchased by the Tandy Corporation. The cars have been rebuilt again so that almost nothing remains of the original cars, and the line continues to operate, carrying good loads — and rides are free, as they have been since the beginning.
Route miles: 1   Stations: 5   Cars: 8

Guadalajara, Mexico: Sistema de Tren Electric Urbano opened a north-south light rail line in 1989 using a subway that had been built for trolley buses, and in 1991 began construction of an east-west line.
Route miles: 10   Stations: 19   Cars: 16

Los Angeles, California: Los Angeles County Transportation Commission opened a light rail line, the Blue Line, from downtown Los Angeles to Long Beach in July 1990. The heavy rail Red Line is due to open in early 1993.
Heavy rail route miles: 5   Stations: 5   Cars: 30
Light rail route miles: 22   Stations: 21   Cars: 54

Mexico City, Mexico: The first portion of Mexico City's subway system (Metro) opened in 1970, and it has expanded several times since then. Like the Montreal subway, it uses rubber-tired trains. It is operated by the Sistema de Transporte Colectivo, which also operates a new light rail line from Pantitlan to La Paz. The Sistema de Transportes Electricos operates a light rail line (the last remnant of the city's streetcar system) to Xochimilco and Tlalpan from the Taxqueña Metro terminal.

The rubber-tire transit technology used by the Montreal and Mexico City systems was pioneered by the French. It requires wide running rails, guide rails (which are also the electrical conductors), and supplemental steel running rails for emergency use. A nine-car train approaches Taxqueña terminal of Line 2 of the Mexico City Metro on August 4, 1976. Photo by William D. Middleton.

Metro route miles: 88   Stations: 74   Cars: 2,260
STC light rail route miles: 11   Cars: 120
STE light rail route miles: 8   Stations: 16   Cars: 13

Miami, Florida: Dade County Transportation Administration opened a heavy rail system in early 1984. The cars are identical to those of the Baltimore Metro. The system connects with a 2-mile people mover that serves downtown Miami.
Route miles: 21   Stations: Cars: 136

Monterrey, Mexico: Mexico's third largest city opened a rail transit line, Metrorrey, on April 25, 1991. The cars on the line are considered light rail vehicles, but the entire right of way is elevated, and station platforms are at car floor level.
Route miles: 11   Stations: 18   Cars: 25

Montreal, Quebec: In addition to the commuter services formerly operated by CP Rail and Canadian National, Montreal Urban Community Transit Commission operates the Montreal Metro. The first section opened in 1966. The system has several routes, entirely underground, operated with rubber-tired equipment.
Route miles: 40   Stations: 62   Cars: 792

Newark, New Jersey: NJ Transit operates a single subway route, the Newark City Subway, with PCC cars from the basement of the Amtrak-NJ Transit station in Newark. From the upper level of the station, Port Authority Trans Hudson Corporation operates heavy rail trains to two terminals in Manhattan: the World Trade Center and (via the NJ Transit terminal at Hoboken, N. J.) West 33rd Street and Sixth Avenue. The line is the successor to a joint Hudson & Manhattan Railroad-Pennsylvania Railroad operation.
NJT route miles: 5   Stations: 11   Cars: 24
PATH route miles: 14   Stations: 13   Cars: 342

New Orleans, Louisiana: Regional Transit Authority operates the last conventional streetcars in regular revenue service in North America. The

5'2½" gauge line along St. Charles Street is considered the oldest street railway in continuous operation in the world. The line was rebuilt in 1990; rehabilitation of the cars, built in 1923 and 1924, should be complete in 1994. RTA opened a standard-gauge 1½-mile line along the riverfront in 1990.

Route miles: 8	Cars: 41

New York, New York: New York City Transit Authority, a division of Metropolitan Transportation Authority, operates the New York subway system, by far the most extensive in the country. Another MTA division, the Staten Island Rapid Transit Operating Authority, runs heavy rail trains on Staten Island on a line that was once part of the Baltimore & Ohio. Port Authority Trans-Hudson subway trains run between two Manhattan terminals and Hoboken, Jersey City, and Newark, N. J. — see the listing for Newark, above.

NYCTA

Track miles: 714	Stations: 469	Cars: 5,950

SIRTOA

Route miles: 14	Stations: 22	Cars: 64

Philadelphia, Pennsylvania: In addition to rail commuter service, Southeastern Pennsylvania Transportation Authority operates two heavy rail transit routes, the north-south Broad Street subway (standard gauge) and the east-west Market-Frankford subway and elevated (5'2¼" gauge), and many streetcar routes, several of which operate through part of the Market Street subway. The Market-Frankford line connects at its west end, 69th Street Terminal in Upper Darby, with the 5'2¼"-gauge streetcar routes and the standard-gauge Norristown line of the former Philadelphia Suburban Transportation Co. (Red Arrow), now also operated by SEPTA. In 1969 the Port Authority Transit Corporation of Pennsylvania and New Jersey (PATCO) opened a line from Camden, N. J., to Lindenwold, N. J., where it connects with NJ Transit and Amtrak trains to Atlantic City. The line serves as an extension of the Philadelphia-Camden line that was opened in 1936.

SEPTA (ex-Philadelphia Transportation Co.)

Heavy rail route miles: 25	Stations: 53	Cars: 356

Several light rail lines in Philadelphia run through part of the Market Street Subway. Southeastern Pennsylvania Tranportation Authority car 9006, built by Kawasaki, has just emerged from the subway at 40th and Woodlawn on May 8, 1988, and will continue to Darby on street trackage. Photo by William D. Middleton.

Light rail route miles: 24	Stations: 8	Cars: 115

SEPTA (ex-Red Arrow)

Heavy rail route miles: 13	Stations: 22	Cars: 19
Light rail route miles: 12	Stations: 49	Cars: 29

PATCO

Route miles: 15	Stations: 13	Cars: 121

Pittsburgh, Pennsylvania: The Port Authority of Allegheny County operates several light rail lines that run through a recently opened downtown subway that has four stations, cross the Monongahela River on a former Pennsylvania Railroad bridge, pass through the South Hills Tunnel, and diverge to Library, Drake, South Hills Village, and Mount Lebanon.

Route miles: 24	Cars: 68

Portland, Oregon: Tri-County Metropolitan Transit District opened a light rail line from downtown Portland east to Gresham in September 1986. It is known as MAX — Metropolitan Area eXpress. Part of the line is on the roadbed of a Portland Traction Co. line that ceased passenger service in 1958. Portland Vintage Trolley operates old-style streetcars on the same line between downtown and Lloyd Center.

Route miles: 15   Cars: 26

Sacramento, California: Sacramento opened its North line in March 1987 and its East line in September of that year. Part of the North line is built on an abandoned section of freeway; the East line parallels a Southern Pacific branch. The system's LRVs run on city streets through downtown.

Route miles: 18   Stations: 27   Cars: 36

St. Louis, Missouri: A light rail system is under construction to run from Lambert-St. Louis International Airport east to downtown St. Louis, through an abandoned railroad tunnel, and across the Mississippi River on the Eads Bridge to East St. Louis, Illinois. It is scheduled to open in July 1993.

Route miles: 18   Stations: 20   Cars.

San Diego, California: In 1981 San Diego Trolley, an agency of the city of San Diego, began operation between the Amtrak station in San Diego and the Mexican border at San Ysidro, a mile from downtown Tijuana, Baja California. The light rail line was built by the Metropolitan Transit Development Board along the former San Diego & Arizona Eastern right of way. Passenger counts on the bright red German-built cars quickly outstripped projections, requiring that the single-track portion of the line be double-tracked. A second route east to El Cajon was opened in 1989. Extensions totaling 6 miles are under construction.

Route miles: 35   Stations: 35   Cars: 71

San Francisco, California: The San Francisco Municipal Railway (Muni) is best known for its cable cars, which operate on three routes. The Muni has five light rail lines which come together in the upper level of the subway under Market Street; three of the lines meet at their outer ends. The lower level of the subway is occupied by the 5'6"-gauge heavy rail trains of the Bay Area Rapid Transit District. They operate south to Daly City and east under San Francisco Bay to Oakland, where lines diverge to Hayward, Walnut Creek, and Richmond. BART opened its East Bay lines in 1972 and the line to San Francisco in 1974. It is building extensions to San Francisco International Airport and to Dublin and Pleasanton.

Muni

Light rail route miles: 23	Stations: 9	Cars: 128
Cable car route miles: 9		Cars: 37

BART

Heavy rail route miles: 73	Stations: 34	Cars: 447

San Jose, California: Santa Clara County Transportation Agency opened a light rail line through downtown San Jose in December 1987. In 1991 the line was extended north and south.

Light rail route miles: 21   Stations: Cars:

Seattle, Washington: In May 1982 Seattle Metro completed and put into service a short trolley line in the tourist district along the waterfront using 1927-vintage streetcars from Melbourne, Australia.

Route miles: 2   Stations: 2   Cars: 4

A Toronto Transit Commission ICTS train approaches the Ellesmere station on May 17, 1988. The system uses linear induction motor technology. Photo by William D. Middleton.

Toronto, Ontario: Toronto Transit Commission operates a number of light rail lines and two heavy rail subway lines, one east-west and the other a north-south U-shaped route, with conventional high-platform, third-rail cars. It also operates a short Intermediate Capacity Transit System (ICTS) that uses linear induction motors.

Heavy rail route miles: 36 Stations: 58 Cars: 622
ICTS route miles: 4 Stations: 6 Cars: 24
Light rail route miles: 46 Cars: 170

Vancouver, British Columbia: BC Transit opened its Skytrain line from Vancouver to New Westminster in 1985. It is an Intermediate Capacity Transit System using linear induction motors and fully automatic operation. Most of the line is on a former British Columbia Electric Railway right of way; a short portion in downtown Vancouver is in a former CP Rail tunnel. It has since been extended south across the Fraser River.

Route miles: 16 Stations: 17 Cars: 130

Washington, D. C.: Washington Metropolitan Area Transit Authority opened the first 4 miles of its first subway in March 1976 and experienced a unique phenomenon, at least until its lines were extended out of downtown: a noontime peak period instead of morning and evening peaks as people used the Metro to go to lunch. Its heavy rail lines now extend into nearby Maryland and across the Potomac River to Arlington, Virginia, and Washington National Airport, and it continues to extend them. It connects with Amtrak trains at Union Station and New Carrollton, Md.

Route miles: 103 Stations: 83 Cars: 660

Recommended reading:

From Bullets to Bart, by William D. Middleton, published in 1989 by Central Electric Railfans' Association, P. O. Box 503, Chicago, IL 60690 (ISBN 0-915348-27-4)

Light Rail Annual and User's Guide, edited by Richard Kunz, published in 1992 by Interurban Press, P. O. Box 6444, Glendale, CA 91225

A Washington Metro Orange Line train bound for New Carrollton, Maryland, passes John F. Kennedy Stadium in Washington on October 27, 1979. Photo by William D. Middleton.

REPORTING MARKS OF RAILROADS

Railroad cars are identified by two to four letters (reporting marks) to indicate owner, and one to six digits. The reporting marks are usually the initials of the name of the owner, such as BN for Burlington Northern and ATSF for Atchison, Topeka & Santa Fe. Private owners — companies that are not railroads — have reporting marks that end in X. A few railroads still indicate the "and" in their name with an ampersand on their cars, but it is omitted in paperwork. Some railroads and private car owners have more than one set of initials to indicate cars that have special equipment or are assigned to special service. For example, each set of Trailer Train reporting marks indicates a different configuration of things like tie-down devices, auto racks, and end bulkheads. Most of Algoma Central's cars are lettered "AC," but one series lettered "ACIS" is to be used only in international service between Canada and the U. S.

When railroads merge, old reporting marks do not disappear immediately. It takes time to reletter and renumber freight cars, and most cars do not receive a new identity until they are shopped for one reason or another. I have given previous names in parentheses.

This list includes reporting marks for all railroads with cars in interchange service according to the April 1992 issue of The Official Railway Equipment Register. I have omitted private car owners and refrigerator-car affiliates of railroads, and for the sake of brevity in the list I have omitted terms like "Railroad," "Co.," "Inc.," and "Corp." Although Missouri Pacific and its subsidiaries are still listed separately from Union Pacific in The Official Railway Equipment Register, I have shown them as Union Pacific. Information on most of the short lines in the list can be found in Edward A. Lewis's *American Shortline Railway Guide.*

AA	Ann Arbor
AC	Algoma Central
ACIS	Algoma Central
ACJR	Ashtabula Carson Jefferson
ACL	CSX (Atlantic Coast Line)
ACWR	Aberdeen, Carolina & Western
ACY	Norfolk Southern (Akron, Canton & Youngstown)
ADN	Ashley, Drew & Northern
AG	Abbeville Grimes
AGLF	Atlantic & Gulf
AHW	Ahnapee & Western
ALM	Arkansas Louisiana & Mississippi
ALQS	Aliquippa & Southern
AM	Arkansas & Missouri
AMC	Amador Central
AMTK	Amtrak
AN	Apalachicola Northern

ANR	Angelina & Neches River
APA	Apache
AR	Aberdeen & Rockfish
ARR	Alaska Railroad
ASAB	Atlanta & St. Andrews Bay
ATLT	AT&L Railroad
ATSF	Atchison, Topeka & Santa Fe
ATW	Atlantic & Western
AVL	Aroostook Valley
AWP	CSX (Atlanta & West Point)
AWW	Algers, Winslow & Western
AZER	Arizona Eastern
BA	Conrail (Boston & Albany)
BAR	Bangor & Aroostook
BB	Buckingham Branch
BCH	Southern Railway of British Columbia (BC Hydro)
BCIT	BC Rail
BCK	Conrail (Buffalo Creek)
BCLR	Bay Colony
BCNE	Canadian National
BCOL	BC Rail
BFRR	Buffalo Ridge
BKTY	Union Pacific (Missouri-Kansas-Texas)
BLE	Bessemer & Lake Erie
BM	Guilford Transportation Industries (Boston & Maine)
BMS	Berlin Mills Ry.
BN	Burlington Northern
BO	CSX (Baltimore & Ohio)
BPRR	Buffalo & Pittsburgh
BS	Birmingham Southern
BVRY	Brandywine Valley
BXN	Bauxite & Northern
CAGY	Columbus & Greenville
CBQ	Burlington Northern (Chicago, Burlington & Quincy)
CBRY	Copper Basin
CBYN	Crosbyton Railway

CC	Chicago, Central & Pacific
CCR	Tennrail (Corinth & Counce)
CCT	Central California Traction
CEI	Union Pacific (Chicago & Eastern Illinois)
CERA	Central Railroad of Indianapolis
CFWR	Caney Fork & Western
CG	Norfolk Southern (Central of Georgia)
CGW	Chicago & North Western (Chicago Great Western)
CHP	National Railways of Mexico (Chihuahua Pacific)
CHTT	Union Pacific (Chicago Heights Terminal Transfer)
CHW	Norfolk Southern (Chesapeake Western)
CI	Cambria & Indiana
CIC	Cedar Rapids & Iowa City
CIM	Chicago & Illinois Midland
CIRR	Chattahoochee Industrial
CIW	Illinois Central (Chicago & Illinois Western)
CLC	Columbia & Cowlitz
CLP	Clarendon & Pittsford
CMNW	Gateway Western (Chicago, Missouri & Western)
CN	Canadian National
CNA	Canadian National
CNIS	Canadian National
CNJ	Conrail (Central of New Jersey)
CNQ	Canadian National
CNW	Chicago & North Western
CO	CSX (Chesapeake & Ohio)
COER	Crab Orchard & Egyptian
COP	City of Prineville
CP	CP Rail
CPAA	CP Rail
CPI	CP Rail
CPT	CP Rail
CR	Conrail
CRI	Conrail (Chicago River & Indiana)
CRL	Chicago Rail Link
CRLE	Coe Rail

CRR	CSX (Clinchfield)	FCP	National Railways of Mexico (Ferrocarril del Pacifico)
CS	Burlington Northern (Colorado & Southern)	FDDM	Chicago & North Western (Fort Dodge, Des Moines & Southern)
CSL	Chicago Short Line	FEC	Florida East Coast
CSS	Chicago SouthShore & South Bend	FMID	Florida Midland
CSXT	CSX Transportation	FMRC	Farmrail
CTIE	Kansas City Southern	FP	Fordyce & Princeton
CTML	Cairo Terminal	FRDN	Hartford & Slocomb (Ferdinand Railroad)
CTN	Canton Railroad	FRVR	Fox River Valley
CUVA	Cuyahoga Valley	FSR	Fort Smith Railroad
CV	Central Vermont	FUS	National Railways of Mexico (Ferrocarriles Unidos del Sureste)
CVC	Canadian National (Central Vermont)	FWD	Burlington Northern (Fort Worth & Denver)
CW	Colorado & Wyoming	FWRC	Florida West Coast
CWP	Chicago, West Pullman & Southern	GA	CSX (Georgia Railroad)
DCLR	Delaware Coast Line	GBW	Green Bay & Western
DH	CP Rail System (Delaware & Hudson)	GC	Georgia Central
DHNY	CP Rail System (Delaware & Hudson)	GCRC	Golden Cat Railroad
DLW	Conrail (Delaware, Lackawanna & Western)	GETY	Gettysburg Railroad
DM	Lake State (Detroit & Mackinac)	GF	Norfolk Southern (Georgia & Florida)
DMIR	Duluth, Missabe & Iron Range	GLSR	Gloster Southern
DNE	Duluth & Northeastern	GMO	Illinois Central Gulf (Gulf, Mobile & Ohio)
DRGW	Southern Pacific Lines (Denver & Rio Grande Western)	GMRC	Green Mountain
DSRC	Dakota Southern	GMSR	SouthRail (Gulf & Mississippi)
DTI	Grand Trunk Western (Detroit, Toledo & Ironton)	GN	Burlington Northern (Great Northern)
DTS	Grand Trunk Western (Detroit & Toledo Shore Line)	GNA	Graysonia, Nashville & Ashdown
DVS	Delta Valley & Southern	GNRR	Georgia Northeastern
DWC	Duluth, Winnipeg & Pacific	GNWR	Genesee & Wyoming
EACH	East Camden & Highland	GRN	Greenville & Northern
EIRC	Eastern Illinois	GRR	Georgetown RR
EJE	Elgin, Joliet & Eastern	GSOR	Indiana Hi-Rail
EL	Conrail (Erie Lackawanna)	GSWR	Georgia Southwestern
ELS	Escanaba & Lake Superior	GTRA	Golden Triangle
EN	CP Rail System (Esquimalt & Nanaimo)	GTW	Grand Trunk Western
ERIE	Conrail (Erie)	GVSR	Galveston Railroad
ESHR	Eastern Shore	GWR	Great Western
ETRY	East Tennessee	GWWR	Gateway Western
FCM	National Railways of Mexico (Ferrocarril Mexicano)	HE	Hollis & Eastern

HESR	Huron & Eastern		MB	Meridian & Bigbee
HS	Hartford & Slocomb		MCSA	Moscow, Camden & San Augustine
IAIS	Iowa Interstate		MDR	MidLouisiana Rail
IATR	Iowa Traction		MDW	Minnesota, Dakota & Western
IC	Illinois Central		MEC	Guilford Transportation Industries (Maine Central)
ICG	Illinois Central (Illinois Central Gulf)		MI	Union Pacific (Missouri Illinois)
IHB	Indiana Harbor Belt		MILW	CP Rail System (Soo Line [Milwaukee Road])
IHRC	Indiana Hi-Rail Corp.		MISS	Mississippian Railway
INRD	Indiana Rail Road		MJ	Manufacturers' Junction Ry.
IOCR	Indiana & Ohio Central		MKC	McKeesport Connecting
IORY	Indiana & Ohio Railway		MKT	Union Pacific (Missouri-Kansas-Texas)
ITC	Norfolk Southern (Illinois Terminal)		MKTT	Union Pacific (Missouri-Kansas-Texas)
JEFW	Jefferson Warrior		MMID	Maryland Midland
JSRC	Jackson & Southern		MMRR	Mid-Michigan
KBSR	Kankakee, Beaverville & Southern			
KCS	Kansas City Southern			
KCT	Kansas City Terminal			
KJRY	Keokuk Junction			
KRR	Kiamichi Railroad			
KWT	K.W.T. Railway			
KYLE	Kyle Railroad			
LC	Lancaster & Chester			
LEF	Lake Erie, Franklin & Clarion			
LN	CSX (Louisville & Nashville)			
LNAC	Hartford & Slocomb (Louisville, New Albany & Corydon)			
LNW	Louisiana & North West			
LPN	Longview, Portland & Northern			
LRS	Laurinburg & Southern			
LRWN	Little Rock & Western			
LSI	Lake Superior & Ishpeming			
LT	Lake Terminal			
LV	Conrail (Lehigh Valley)			
LVAL	Lackawanna Valley			
LVRC	Lamoille Valley			
MAA	Magma Arizona			
MACO	McCormick, Ashland City & Nashville			

MNNR	Minnesota Commercial
MNS	CP Rail System (Soo Line [Minneapolis, Northfield & Southern])
MNVA	MNVA Railroad
MON	CSX (Monon)
MP	Union Pacific (Missouri Pacific)
MPA	Maryland & Pennsylvania
MR	McCloud Railway
MRL	Montana Rail Link
MRR	Mid Atlantic
MRS	Manufacturers Railway
MSDR	Mississippi Delta
MSE	Mississippi Export RR
MSRC	MidSouth
MSTL	Chicago & North Western (Minneapolis & St. Louis)
MSV	Mississippi & Skuna Valley
MTR	Pittsburgh & Lake Erie (Montour)
MTW	Tomahawk Railway (Marinette, Tomahawk & Western)
NAR	Canadian National (Northern Alberta)
NBNR	Nicolet Badger Northern
NC	CSX (Nashville, Chattanooga & St. Louis)
NDM	National Railways of Mexico
NHVT	New Hampshire & Vermont
NJ	CP Rail System (Napierville Junction)
NKP	Norfolk Southern (Nickel Plate)
NLG	MidLouisiana
NOKL	Northwestern Oklahoma
NOPB	New Orleans Public Belt
NP	Burlington Northern (Northern Pacific)
NS	Norfolk Southern
NSL	St. Lawrence & Raquette River (Norwood & St. Lawrence)
NSR	Newburgh & South Shore
NTR	Natchez Trace RR
NW	Norfolk Southern (Norfolk & Western)
NYC	Conrail (New York Central)
OAR	Old Augusta Railroad
OCE	Oregon, California & Eastern

OHCR	Ohio Central
OKKT	Union Pacific (Oklahoma, Kansas & Texas)
OLB	Omaha, Lincoln & Beatrice
OLY	Olympic Railroad
ONT	Ontario Northland
ONTA	Ontario Northland
OPE	Oregon, Pacific & Eastern
OTVR	Otter Tail Valley
PAE	Conrail (Peoria & Eastern)
PAL	Paducah & Louisville
PBNE	Philadelphia, Bethlehem & New England
PBR	Patapsco & Back Rivers
PC	Conrail (Penn Central)
PCA	Conrail (Penn Central)
PCN	Point Comfort & Northern
PGE	BC Rail (Pacific Great Eastern)
PHD	Port Huron & Detroit
PICK	Pickens Railroad
PLE	Pittsburgh & Lake Erie
PPU	Peoria & Pekin Union Railway
PRR	Conrail (Pennsylvania)
PS	Pittsburgh & Shawmut
PW	Providence & Worcester
QC	CP Rail System (Quebec Central)
RDG	Conrail (Reading)
RFP	CSX (Richmond, Fredericksburg & Potomac)
RJCM	R. J. Corman Railroad, Memphis Line
RMRR	Rocky Mountain Railcar & Railroad
RS	Roberval & Saguenay
RSR	Rochester & Southern
RSS	Rockdale, Sandow & Southern
SAL	CSX (Seaboard Air Line)
SAN	Sandersville RR
SB	South Buffalo Ry.
SBC	National Railways of Mexico (Sonora-Baja California)
SBD	CSX (Seaboard System)

SCFE	South Central Florida		TP	Union Pacific (Texas & Pacific)
SCL	CSX (Seaboard Coast Line)		TPW	Toledo, Peoria & Western
SCTR	South Central Tennessee		TSE	Texas South-Eastern
SGLR	Seminole Gulf		TSRD	Twin State Railroad
SH	Steelton & Highspire		TSRR	Tennessee Southern
SI	Union Pacific (Spokane International)		TTIS	Transkentucky Transportation Railroad
SLC	San Luis Central		TWRY	Tradewater Railway
SLR	St. Lawrence & Atlantic		UMP	Upper Merion & Plymouth
SLSF	Burlington Northern (St. Louis-San Francisco)		UP	Union Pacific
SM	St. Marys Railroad		URR	Union Railroad
SMRR	Sisseton Milbank Railroad		VCY	Ventura County
SOM	Somerset Railroad		VGN	Norfolk Southern (Virginian)
SOO	CP Rail System (Soo Line)		VTR	Vermont Ry.
SOU	Norfolk Southern (Southern Railway)		WA	CSX (Western Ry. of Alabama)
SP	Southern Pacific		WAB	Norfolk Southern (Wabash)
SPS	Burlington Northern (Spokane, Portland & Seattle)		WC	Wisconsin Central
SR	SouthRail		WCRC	Washington Central
SRN	Sabine River & Northern		WCTR	WCTU Railway
SSW	Southern Pacific (St. Louis Southwestern)		WE	Wheeling & Lake Erie
STE	Stockton Terminal & Eastern		WGRR	Willamina & Grand Ronde
STMA	St. Maries River		WICT	Wisconsin & Calumet
SWGR	Seagraves, Whiteface & Lubbock		WLO	Waterloo Railroad
TASD	Terminal Ry. Alabama State Docks		WM	CSX (Western Maryland)
TBER	Terre Haute, Brazil & Eastern		WNFR	Winifrede Railroad
TCWR	Twin Cities & Western		WP	Union Pacific (Western Pacific)
THB	CP Rail (Toronto, Hamilton & Buffalo)		WRRC	Western Rail Road
TM	Texas Mexican		WSOR	Wisconsin & Southern
TN	Texas & Northern		WW	Winchester & Western
TNM	Union Pacific (Texas-New Mexico)		YS	Youngstown & Southern
TOE	Texas, Oklahoma & Eastern			

FREIGHT LOCOMOTIVES

Fifty years ago the common lament among rail enthusiasts was that diesel locomotives all looked alike. They didn't, of course — imagine a line-up that includes a DL109, an Erie-built, an early VO660, a 44-tonner, and a BL2. Today's rail enthusiasts can say the same more truthfully about today's freight diesels. They come from only two locomotive builders, General Motors and General Electric; they ride on either two four-wheel trucks or two six-wheel trucks; and they have a limited number of body configurations — conventional hood or full-width cowl; low short hood, wide short hood, high short hood (not many of those left), or no short hood. They can be distinguished from each other by the number and size of louvers, fans, and other protrusions. They are even more alike under the sheet metal than they are outwardly.

General Motors

General Motors Locomotive Group, formerly GM's Electro-Motive Division, has three model series, GP, SD, and MP. The letters denote, respectively, four-axle road-switchers, six-axle road-switchers, and four-axle switchers — and those terms refer to configuration rather than intended service. The cab of a road-switcher is set back from the front of the locomotive, behind a short hood or nose. A switcher has its cab at the rear.

Some explanation and some history is necessary. In steam days there were road engines, which had lead trucks and pilots ("cowcatchers"), and switchers, which lacked lead trucks and had footboards instead of pilots. Footboards were where the brakeman rode during switching maneuvers. Diesel locomotives were well established before it was recognized that the steps behind the footboard were a safer place to ride; soon riding on the footboards was prohibited, and eventually footboards were eliminated.

Until 1938 diesel locomotives were also either road engines or switchers. Road engines had full-width streamlined bodies and trucks suitable for high-speed running; switchers were definitely not streamlined — they had a boxy hood covering the diesel engine and the generator, walkways on each side of the hood, and a cab at the rear — plus footboards at each end and trucks intended for low-speed operation. Between 1938 and 1947 Electro-Motive stretched its 1000-h.p. switcher and substituted road trucks to

Footboards used to be required on switchers. Photo by Jim Shaughnessy.

Boston & Maine 1561 is a GP7. The position of the brakeman illustrates why footboards became unnecessary. Photo by Ted Shrady.

make road engines, which it termed road-switchers, mostly for Great Northern. In 1941 Electro-Motive placed the machinery of the 1350-h.p. FT (the road freight diesel it introduced in 1939) in switcher carbodies for the Illinois Central. Production of the four models (NW3, NW4, NW5, and TR1) totaled 26 units, not many compared with the E-series passenger locomotives, F-series freight locomotives, and SW- and NW-series switchers, which EMD was turning out by hundreds.

American Locomotive Company (Alco) was more successful with its stretched 1000-h.p. switcher, the RS1 of 1941, possibly because of War Production Board orders that restricted EMD to building road locomotives and Alco to building switchers during World War II. Alco introduced its RS2 in 1946, and Baldwin its DRS44-15 in 1947. Both were 1500-h.p. road-switchers, equal in horsepower to contemporary freight engines. In response

to the competition, Electro-Motive brought out the BL2 in 1948. It was a 1500-h.p. semi-cab unit, an F3 with the corners chiseled away and footboards on each end. It was more successful than the stretched switchers — 59 units against 1,807 F3s, 510 E7s, and 1,143 NW2s.

In late 1949 EMD introduced a general-purpose locomotive, the 1500-h.p. GP7. Its hood construction permitted much easier access for maintenance than the BL2's truss-type carbody; it offered the crew a good view both forward and back; the controls could be arranged so either end was front, according to the buyer's preference; and it cost less than the BL2. The GP7 sold well: 2,729 units versus 4,225 F7s and FP7s. Its successor, the 1750-h.p. GP9, sold 4,257 units, totally eclipsing the equivalent stream-lined units, the F9 and FP9. By the time the GP18 was introduced in 1959, the GP (or Geep) was a road freight unit rather than a road-switcher, and "hood unit" began to replace "road-switcher" as a descriptive term. The low short hood introduced toward the end of GP9 production became standard — railroads rarely wanted a steam generator anymore — and the Geep became a one-direction locomotive, like the BL2 and the Fs.

The Geep continued to evolve. EMD increased the power of the 16-cylinder, 45-degree-vee engine first by turbocharging it (and continued to offer a normally aspirated version for work that didn't demand high horsepower and for railroads that wanted to avoid turbocharger maintenance), then by increasing the bore, then by increasing the stroke. The most recent GP models, introduced in 1985, are the GP60, which has a 3800-h.p., turbocharged, 16-cylinder engine, and GP 59 — 3000 h.p., 12 turbocharged cylinders.

The SD7 (SD for Special Duty) came along in 1952, a six-axle, six-motor version of the GP7. It was intended for heavy hauling at low speeds. The two additional axles allowed extra weight for adhesion (and indeed provided some of it); two additional motors for the electricity produced by the generator reduced the risk of burning out a motor. The evolution of the SD has paralleled that of the GP. The two differ in the frame and trucks; the engine and generator are the same. As horsepower increased, the SD evolved into a fast mainline freight locomotive. Through most of the 1970s and 1980s the turbocharged 3000-h.p. SD40 and SD40-2 were virtually every railroad's standard mainline freight locomotive. For lighter duties the normally aspirated 2000-h.p. GP38 and GP38-2 were equally favored.

EMD switchers underwent a similar evolution. In the late 1930s Elec-

Norfolk Southern 4608 is a GP59 built in 1989. There are family resemblances to the GP7. EMD photo.

tro-Motive offered a choice of two engines (8 cylinders and 600 h.p. or 12 cylinders and 900 h.p.) and cast or welded frame. The model designations, which indicated horsepower and frame, were SC, SW, NC, and NW. The 900-h.p. unit soon proved capable of 1000 h.p. but kept the "N" designation; by 1940 only the welded frame was offered. In 1949 the 1000-h.p. NW2 was replaced in EMD's catalog by the 1000-h.p. SW7 — "SW" had come to mean switcher rather than 600 h.p., welded frame. Within a few years the model designations included the horsepower.

By 1970 the distinction between a switcher and a light road-switcher was not a sharp one. A GP7 replaced in road service by a GP40 was just about as good a switcher as an SW1500 and could handle over-the-road duties that the SW1500 couldn't. EMD recognized this, too, and in 1974 replaced the its SW1500 with the multipurpose MP15, which had the same 12-cylinder, 1500-h.p. engine but a longer frame and road trucks instead of switcher trucks. It soon acquired two variants: the MP15AC, which had the AC electrical system used on most road engines, and the MP15T, which

Burlington Northern 7016 is an SD40-2, one of the most plentiful of EMD models — BN alone has more than 800. The hood and the cab are similar to those of the GP59. Photo by Charles W. McDonald.

Universal, derived from GE's 1956 line of export diesels; 25 for the horse-power, B for two-axle trucks). Electro-Motive had just introduced the 2400-h.p. SD24, but not until late 1963 would EMD offer a 2500-h.p. four-axle unit. In 1963 GE overtook Alco as the No. 2 locomotive builder in the U. S., and in 1983 built more locomotives than EMD. GE has maintained the No. 1 position since then.

GE's line of U-boats evolved just as EMD's diesels did. Horsepower was increased to 2800 in late 1965, and by 1969 GE was able to get 3600 horsepower out of the same 16-cylinder, 45-degree-vee engine. In 1968 GE introduced the 2250-h.p. U23B and U23C, which have a 12-cylinder version of the same engine; and in 1963 brought out the 1800 h.p. U18B, which has an 8-cylinder engine. The six-axle U25C was introduced in 1963; the only four-axle unit without a corresponding "C" model was the U18B.

In 1972 EMD introduced its "Dash 2" line. Changes to the locomotives were internal, chiefly a modular electrical system, which could be repaired had an 8-cylinder turbocharged engine. No MP15s have been built since 1987, and EMD's current catalog doesn't include a switcher. There is not much market for a switcher today. Unit trains and run-through freights have reduced the amount of switching to be done, and the price difference is not worth the restrictions on utilization imposed by the switcher.

Historically, Electro-Motive's home was La Grange, Illinois, a suburb southwest of Chicago. In 1988 most locomotive production was moved from La Grange to the London, Ontario, plant of Electro-Motive's Canadian subsidiary, General Motors Diesel Division.

General Electric

In 1940 General Electric, which built electric locomotives and a line of industrial diesels at its plant is in Erie, Pennsylvania, teamed up with American Locomotive Company to produce and market road diesels. That partnership was dissolved in 1953 and GE began to develop its own line. In 1959 GE introduced a 2500-h.p. four-axle road-switcher, the U25B (U for

Golden Triangle G-1 is an MP15AC. The model is the culmination of the line of switchers Electro-Motive introduced in 1935. Photo by David Hurt.

Soo Line 6060 is an SD60M built in 1989. It has the full-width nose and safety cab that EMD started offering in 1988. Photo by Fred Radek.

by replacing modular assemblies. Rather than establish new models, EMD appended "-2" to existing designations. In 1976 GE announced a similar wave of internal changes and new model designations: the U30B would be replaced by the B30-7, the U36C by the C36 7, and so on. The "Dash 7" was initially for 1977.

The 3000-h.p. U30C and its successor, the C30-7, were GE's best selling six-axle units, just as were EMD's SD40 and SD40-2. The U23B and the B23-7 sold well but didn't achieve the market penetration of EMD's GP38 and GP38-2, their closest equivalents.

The next new models appeared in 1984 with "-8" suffixes. The primary feature of the "Dash 8" line was microprocessor control; it was accompanied by significant changes in appearance: a more angular nose, a hump behind the cab for the equipment blower and the dynamic brakes, and protruding radiators at the rear. In 1988 the model designations were changed again, concurrent with an increase in horsepower. The B39-8, for example, gave way to the Dash 8-40B. (A few roads have stuck with the old format for the name, considering "Dash" to be simply makeweight, and besides, the model designation already has a dash or a hyphen or a minus sign.)

Rock Island 253 is a U28B built in 1966. It illustrates the characteristic shape of GE units from 1959 to 1984. Photo by Louis A. Marre.

Differences and similarities

Both EMD and GE use 12- and 16-cylinder 45-degree-vee prime movers. EMD's is a two-stroke-cycle engine; GE's is four-cycle. In 1988 both builders began to offer the full-width nose and accompanying "safety," "comfort," or "Canadian" cab that Montreal Locomotive Works introduced in 1973. It is the biggest change in locomotive appearance since the low nose appeared in the late 1950s. The most reliable novice-level spotting features are probably the radiator configuration and the sound the units make. EMD units make a much smoother noise than the GE's, which make a chugging sound — perhaps best transcribed as "phlap-phlap-phlap."

Rebuilders

The average diesel locomotive is ready for a major overhaul in 15 years. Low-mileage locomotives, such as switchers, last longer; high-mileage units wear out faster. Conrail, for instance, has a large number of switchers built

Conrail 6611, a C32-8, illustrates the look of General Electric's Dash 8 line. The most obvious distinguishing feature is the dynamic brake and equipment blower hump behind the cab. Photo by Joseph R. Snopek.

in the 1950s; so do Grand Trunk Western and Soo Line. These switching locomotives aren't used in high-mileage, high-speed service; they simply continue to do the jobs for which they were purchased. (Electric locomotives in low-mileage service last even longer than diesels. For a case in point, see page 168.)

Most locomotive components can be replaced readily. Often a new or an upgraded version of the part is used, making the locomotive a bit more powerful or efficient. By the time a locomotive is scrapped, it's quite possible that the frame is the only major original component.

There's a point where repair becomes rebuilding. Until the late 1980s rebuilding offered tax advantages — if the cost of the rebuilding was at least half the original purchase price of the locomotive, the locomotive could be considered new for accounting purposes. A number of railroads undertook extensive locomotive rebuilding programs. Some did the work in their own shops; others contracted it out to firms specializing in locomotive rebuilding such as Morrison Knudsen.

Recommended reading:

The Second Diesel Spotter's Guide, by Jerry A. Pinkepank, published in 1973 by Kalmbach Publishing Co., 21027 Crossroads Circle, P. O. Box 1612, Waukesha, WI 53187 (ISBN 0-89024-026-4)

The Contemporary Diesel Spotter's Guide, by Louis A. Marre and Jerry A. Pinkepank, published in 1989 by Kalmbach Publishing Co., 21027 Crossroads Circle, P. O. Box 1612, Waukesha, WI 53187 (ISBN 0-89024-088-4)

Diesel Locomotive Rosters: U. S., Canada, Mexico, by Charles W. McDonald, published in 1992 by Kalmbach Publishing Co., 21027 Crossroads Circle, P. O. Box 1612, Waukesha, WI 53187 (ISBN 0-89024-112-0)

THE FUTURE OF NORTH AMERICAN RAILROADING

In 1945 Edward Hungerford wrote *A Railroad for Tomorrow*, a look forward at 1960. A number of the things he foresaw have come to pass. His single nationalized railroad exists for long-distance passenger travel, if not for freight, and its headquarters are in Washington Union Station. Hungerford predicted that freight railroading would concentrate on long distance service on main lines, and CTC and single track would replace double track in many places. A number of minor items have come true: a passenger station in New York connected to New York Central's line down the west side of Manhattan, the Pullman Company out of the business of operating sleeping cars, the bankruptcy of the Milwaukee Road (that was a fairly safe prediction), Illinois Central spinning off its Chicago-Omaha route, one- and two-car diesel passenger trains serving New England (the Budd RDC got its start on the Boston & Albany and flourished on the Boston & Maine and New Haven in the 1950s), a new passenger station at Syracuse on New York Central's freight bypass, and a new passenger station in New Orleans (which opened about five years before Hungerford predicted).

Other things he mentioned are soon to happen, such as electrification from New Haven to Boston and rail transit over the Eads Bridge and through the tunnel in St. Louis. But Hungerford's crystal ball had cloudy spots. His United States Railroad of 1960 had approximately 50,000 locomotives in service: 10,000 diesel, 10,000 electric, and 30,000 steam; the actual figure for that year for the entire U. S. was about 29,000 locomotives, more than 28,000 of which were diesel. The hero of the book takes a plane from Washington to Seattle, "a matter of a brief fifteen or sixteen hours, and there were sleeping arrangements that delighted him."

What lies ahead for North American railroads through the 1990s? I can offer little experience or skill at clairvoyance, but if nothing else, the following predictions may give us a good laugh a decade or more hence.

Nationalization

Everywhere else in the world the government runs the trains, as it does the postal service, the telephones, the highways, and the airlines.

The U. S. was practically the last stand of private-enterprise transportation, but by 1971 it was far from universal: urban transit had become the responsibility of city and regional government, and the federal government was a strong financial supporter of air, water, and highway transportation.

In 1971 the railroads of the United States took a big step toward nationalization with the establishment of Amtrak. In 1976 the federal government took over several bankrupt railroads to form Conrail — another step in the same direction. Something happened to Conrail in the early 1980s: it turned into a well-run, efficient, profitable railroad. In 1987 it went back into the hands of private investors. The situation is changing elsewhere. Japan has recently privatized its rail system, and several other countries are doing so.

Intercity passenger railroads

When Amtrak was established, many persons in the rail industry and in government believed Amtrak's mission was the orderly termination of rail passenger service. That was indeed the net effect in many places on May 1, 1971, but in other places Amtrak's advertisements were the first passenger-train advertising in decades. People began to ride passenger trains again.

Amtrak's first decade was difficult as it struggled to keep secondhand cars and locomotives running, attract and retain passengers, persuade railroads to keep Amtrak trains on time, and justify its existence to the federal government. The last was the hardest. After creating and funding Amtrak, the government changed direction and set out to dismantle it.

Amtrak survived the battles and achieved a stable existence. Each year it covers a greater portion of its costs, and it has been able to obtain private financing for new cars and locomotives. Its traffic and revenue held up well during the recession of the early 1990s while airlines lost money and declared bankruptcy. During most of the year Amtrak trains operate at capacity.

What lies ahead? New cars and locomotives are on order to equip the remaining triweekly trains to run daily, and Amtrak is testing prototype sleeping and dining cars to replace Heritage Fleet cars on trains east of Chicago. Until it receives new cars, though, Amtrak is unable to add new long-distance routes to its map. Short-haul routes, which usually require only coaches and cafe cars, are easier to add, and the legislation that cre-

No longer the fastest train in the world — French National Railways has a second generation Train à Grande Vitesse that is faster that the original TGVs that run southeast from Paris, but both generations can (and do) run on ordinary lines as well as the specially constructed high-speed routes. Photo by Y. Broncard.

ated Amtrak provided for states to fund Amtrak trains — "403(b) trains," and they are noted as such in Amtrak's timetable.

Amtrak acquired the Northeast Corridor route between Boston, New York, and Washington in 1976 and completely rebuilt the line. It is electrified from Washington to New Haven, Connecticut. The New York, New Haven & Hartford intended to extend the electrification to Boston, but finances never permitted it. Amtrak has begun the project. The electrification will eliminate the need to change engines at New Haven — the engine change is often blamed for delays, but the delays result as much from switching to combine trains from Boston and Springfield for the trip to Washington — and will permit higher speeds along the shore east of New Haven, because electric locomotives accelerate faster than diesels.

High-speed trains

The development of sleek, exotic-looking high-speed trains in Japan, France, and Germany hasn't gone unnoticed in North America. State and regional commissions and associations have studied them and recommended that high-speed train systems be built to serve several metropolitan corridors. That's as far as it has gone. The major problem is finance.

Technology is another problem. The monorail was the train of the future in the 1950s. After a few years the monorail was succeeded by the air-cushion vehicle. Now tomorrow's train uses magnetic levitation. The Japanese, French, and German trains use existing railroad technology and still don't push its limits. The French and German trains run part of their trips on new, high-speed right of way and the rest on existing lines. Japan's bullet

A GO Transit train accelerates through the maze of tracks west of Toronto Union Station in a scene of exemplary urban railroading in an exemplary city. Photo by William D. Middleton.

trains are standard gauge, like those in France and Germany, but the rest of the country's rail system is 3'6" gauge. What of previous trains of the future? The monorail has found a place in the sun shuttling people at Disneyland and Walt Disney World; air-cushion vehicles, Hovercrafts, ply the English Channel; and magnetic levitation remains experimental.

The development of high-speed passenger trains in North America will probably be incremental. For example, let's say a maglev train is proposed to run from Chicago to St. Paul and Minneapolis in less than 3 hours. The first fruits of that proposal will probably not be batallions of bulldozers creating a new railroad across Wisconsin. More likely, we'll see a second 8-hour train on Amtrak's Chicago-Twin Cities route — far less glamorous and far less exotic, but immediately achievable and far less expensive.

Urban railroading

Commuter service — local trains scheduled to take people to work in the morning and home in the evening — began to disappear after World War II. One of the causes was, paradoxically, the growth of the suburbs. When suburbs were small towns, people lived close enough to the station to walk to and from the trains. When the suburbs expanded into what had been fields and pastures, the trip to the station required a car, so why not drive all the way into the city? The convenience outweighed the problems of traffic and parking.

By the mid-1980s only eight metropolitan areas in North America had rail commuter service: Boston, New York, Philadelphia, Washington, Chicago, San Francisco, Montreal, and Toronto. Detroit and Pittsburgh had lost their commuter service in the early 1980s, and Milwaukee and Cleveland each had a single train that lasted into the 1970s.

The trains may have been discontinued, but the right of way they used is probably still in place, more often that not with tracks on it that are still used by freight trains. In Milwaukee, for example, virtually unused rail lines parallel most of the freeways into the city. Passenger trains could also operate on those lines and carry some of the people who are in cars moving at 10 miles per hour on the freeway .

Numerous barriers to such service will have to be removed. In most cases they aren't physical barriers but matters of jurisdiction. Commuter services cross city, county, and sometimes even state lines. Regional transportation administrations are often the solution.

Some of the commuter trains will be of conventional "steam railroad" configuration, diesel locomotives and single-level or bilevel coaches, which can run on existing tracks. Others will be light rail vehicles, which require more extensive construction, usually complete rebuilding of the track and erection of overhead wires.

Transit is a growth industry which stimulates urban growth. Most business and commercial activity requires and creates concentrations of people, and rail transit is the best way to move large numbers of people. The urban growth that transit creates can be seen most vividly from the CN Tower in Toronto. The view to the north across the city is punctuated by groups of tall buildings clustered around the stations of the subway system Toronto began building in the early 1950s.

Most new transit systems and commuter railroads have been successful. Indeed, the common experience is that about 6 hours after the ribbon-cutting that inaugurates the service, ridership is outstripping the projections for several years in the future.

A crane erects catenary poles at Matawan on the North Jersey Coast route in 1981 as part of NJ Transit's electrification project. Photo by Don Wood.

Electrification

Railroads have studied electrification of high-density main lines for decades, and a few railroads have even erected short stretches of overhead wire (less than a mile), ostensibly to see how it stands up to winter weather (a phone call to Norwegian State Railways would have accomplished the same end). Electrification is characterized by low operating costs and high construction costs. Electric locomotives are simpler machines than diesels, and they last longer. They are cleaner, quieter, require less maintenance, and don't need fuel facilities.

The right of way used by the San Diego Trolley is also used for power transmission lines. Photo by William D. Middleton.

The expensive part of electrification is erecting the overhead wires and the current distribution network. Electrification also requires that a substantial stretch of railroad be electrified. A short stretch of electric operation makes no sense for long-distance trains; the electrified line has to be long enough that the economies of electric operation will more than balance the cost of changing back to diesel power at the end of the electric district. The New Haven electrified its main line from New York to New Haven, where its main line divided for Boston and Springfield. New Haven was a crew change point and the farthest point served by commuter trains to New York. The New Haven also electrified its yards and branch lines west of New Haven, eliminating the need for steam locomotive service facilities in that district.

Until 1930 the Pennsylvania Railroad's electrification around Philadelphia was solely for commuter trains. Through trains continued to use steam locomotives, and the railroad had to keep all its facilities in place for servicing steam power. Pennsy's electrification didn't make complete sense until it extended the full length of the road's New York-Washington line. Harrisburg was a logical point for the western terminal of the electrification;

Pennsy's routes that blanketed the area from New York to Washington came together there. The Pennsylvania long wanted to electrify its line between Harrisburg and Pittsburgh, but PRR's finances wouldn't stretch that far.

The 1950s saw a number of railroads eliminate electric operation, usually short stretches of line through tunnels or over heavy mountain grades. However, in the past two decades there has been a little progress in electrification. Power companies have built several electrified mine-mouth-to-power-plant railroads in the western U. S. They are isolated from other railroads, so diesel fuel would have to be trucked in, uneconomic compared with electricity fresh from the power plant. National Railways of Mexico rebuilt and electrified its main line from Mexico City to Querétaro. BC Rail constructed a new line to serve coal mines in a remote area of British Columbia and chose electric operation.

During the last decade two commuter railroads have quietly undertaken electrification projects. The Long Island Rail Road extended its third rail to Huntington and Ronkonkoma, permitting direct trains between New York and those points (LIRR runs only M.U. cars, not locomotive-hauled trains, into Penn Station).

NJ Transit inherited two electrified routes, the former Pennsylvania line from New York to Trenton (owned by Amtrak) and its branch to South Amboy (owned by NJ Transit), and the former Lackawanna suburban electrification from Hoboken to Montclair, Dover, and Gladstone.

The Pennsy electrification was 11,000-volt, 25-hertz AC; the Lackawanna was 3,000-volt DC. NJ Transit extended the wires from South Amboy to Long Branch in several stages, eliminating the engine change for New York-Long Branch trains.

The Lackawanna electrification dated from 1930, and the cars, though well maintained, were ripe for replacement. NJ Transit chose to install a new system, 25,000-volt, 60-hertz AC, for eventual compatibility with the ex-Pennsylvania Railroad routes. (At present Amtrak's Northeast Corridor route is 12,000-volt, 25-hertz from Washington to New York and 12,000-volt, 60-hertz north of New York. The voltage is Amtrak's figure. Some sources give the voltage as 11,000 volts; other, 12,500. Except to an electrical engineer the difference is academic.)

With a good portion of its routes under wire, it is likely that NJ Transit will extend electrification to other lines. The most likely candidate is the Raritan Valley route (ex-Central Railroad of New Jersey), which runs for several miles on electrified track. The arrival of the Amtrak electrification in Boston may spur Massachusetts Bay Transportation Authority to electrify some of its routes out of South Station — at least the Boston-Attleboro-Providence route, which will be under wires for the whole distance. On several Metra routes out of Chicago, train frequency could justify electrification, but the right of way belongs to Burlington Northern and Chicago & North Western. Most commuter authorities have purchased diesel locomotives recently; don't expect electrification until those diesels wear out or oil prices increase.

It will take a combination of factors to make freight railroads electrify: heavy traffic, frequent trains, rising oil prices, and partnership with an electric utility, possibly using the railroad right of way for power distribution lines.

One other factor may override the others. In southern California there is talk of cleaning up the air, starting with diesel locomotives (which contribute only a minuscule part of the exhaust emissions that turn the sky gray, but politically they are an easier target than cars and trucks).

In many respects, today's railroad scene is the most vibrant since World War II. Deregulation has given the railroads freedom in tailoring the services they offer and the prices they charge. The large railroads are doing what they do best, carrying freight long distances, and new regional railroads and short lines are turning a profit at business in areas previously thought unprofitable. The railroads are glad to be free of the details of running passenger service, and the agencies that run passenger trains are gratified by passenger counts that increase each year. Railroad technology becomes more sophisticated each year, but at the same time it retains compatibility with previous technology.

The railroad scene is never static. Watch for changing trains.

WHERE TO WATCH TRAINS

Train-watching requires trains, but where do you find them? Around home it's easy — you know where and when you can find a train. Where are the best places, the Top Ten, worth a trip or at least stopping if you're nearby? The qualifications for Top Ten include lots of trains (at least one per hour), a variety of types of trains, more than one railroad, and an interesting setting. Some train-watching places are compact. You can stand in the park at Conrail's Horse Shoe Curve in Pennsylvania or sit on the station platform at Downers Grove, Illinois, and see everything. Other train-watching places stretch over several miles or several hundred miles. In the list below they are arranged from northeast to southwest, more or less, rather than ranked by quality. That's a matter of preference — if you like Burlington Northern and mountain scenery, Bowie, Maryland, won't be your No. 1 train-watching place.

TRAINS Magazine has a monthly feature, Trains Hot Spots, that documents good places to see and photograph trains. Also scan the advertisements in TRAINS for railfan guides to different areas — some are cited below.

Northeast Corridor

Practically anywhere from New Haven, Connecticut, to Washington, D. C., you can be assured of several trains an hour, between Amtrak and the commuter train operators (Metro-North, NJ Transit, SEPTA, and MARC). The only stretch of the line not served by commuter trains as this book goes to press in fall 1992 is between Wilmington, Delaware, and Perryville, Maryland. Several places along the line have received special mention by rail enthusiasts: New Haven (TRAINS, April 1990, page 66); Elizabeth, New Jersey (TRAINS, July 1989, page 60); Princeton Junction, N. J.; Frankford Junction in Philadelphia (TRAINS, November 1991, page 72); and Bowie, Maryland.

Dorval, Quebec

For 16 miles between Lachine and Dorion, west of Montreal, the principal transcontinental routes of Canadian National and CP Rail run on parallel lines that are as little as 100 feet apart. VIA Rail Canada's Montreal-Toronto and Montreal-Ottawa trains run on the CN and Mon-treal Urban Community Transportation Commission trains run on CP. (TRAINS, November 1989, page 76)

Horse Shoe Curve

In 1848 J. Edgar Thomson surveyed the Pennsylvania Railroad's line from Harrisburg to Pittsburgh so it followed the Juniata River as far west as Altoona, then climbed over the Alleghenies quickly, concentrating the problems of mountain railroading in one area. To gain altitude yet keep the grade from becoming too steep, west of Altoona Thomson took the line up one side of the valley of Burgoon Run, then crossed to the other side in a sharp curve that reversed the direction of the line. The traffic on the line soon required four tracks. It was the busiest stretch of mountain railroad in the world for a long time. It's Conrail's line now, reduced to three tracks and not so busy as it was when Pennsy

Two Conrail SD40s drift downgrade around Horse Shoe Curve after assisting a westbound freight up the grade. Photo by Wesley Fox.

ran dozens of passenger trains each way, but it remains busy and impressive.

To reach the curve, follow 40th Street west from downtown Altoona. The way is well signed, and a park inside the curve affords a good view of the action. (TRAINS, March 1989, page 54; *Horseshoe Heritage*, by Dan Cupper, published by Withers Publishing, 528 Dunkle School Road, Halifax, PA 17032)

Chicago

Chicago is America's railroad capital, and train-watching opportunities abound. For a mixture of commuter and freight trains, the best routes are Burlington Northern's three-track Chicago-Aurora main line and Chicago & North Western's line to Geneva — Metra calls it the West Line. The BN line also carries two Amtrak trains, the *California Zephyr* and the *Illinois Zephyr*. (*Train Watcher's Guide to Chicago*, com-

During peak hours Burlington Northern dispatches commuter trains west from Chicago on two tracks and sometimes all three. At Harlem Avenue an express behind an E9 on the center trak is overtaking a local pulled by a Metra F40PH-2 on June 13, 1989. Photo by Mike Kiriazis.

piled and published by John Szwajkart, P. O. Box 163, Brookfield, IL 60513)

Chicago Union Station is almost totally underground. The best view of the action is from the headquarters of the Twentieth Century Railroad Club, 329 West 18th Street — open Saturdays, 12-5; $3 for nonmembers. (TRAINS, April 1990, page 60)

Fort Worth, Texas

In downtown Fort Worth the Santa Fe and Union Pacific (ex-Texas & Pacific and ex-Missouri-Kansas-Texas) cross at a junction controlled by an interlocking tower called Tower 55. The junction includes a multiple-track crossing and connecting tracks in all four quadrants. Most trains through Fort Worth pass the tower; in addition to Santa Fe and UP, Burlington Northern gets into the act, and Southern Pacific has track through the area, a vestige of the days when it operated passenger trains. The tower is south of the Amtrak station and southwest of the intersection of I-30 and I-35W. An access road north off Vickery Boulevard just west of I-35W leads to the tower. (TRAINS, February 1985, pages 36-43; *Dallas/Fort Worth Railfan Guide*, by David Moore, 1829 Skyline, Sherman, TX 75090)

Fremont, Nebraska, to Laramie, Wyoming

Interstate Highway 80 will whisk you across Nebraska without much in the way of visual stimulation, but most of the way from Fremont west across the state line to Cheyenne, parallel U. S. Highway 30 is within sight of the Union Pacific main line — the route it laid down in the 1860s on its way to meet the Central Pacific in Utah. Between Cheyenne and Laramie it climbs over Sherman Hill on a line that has been relocated and rebuilt many times to ease the grade. It is a busy railroad. (*Sherman Hill*, by Donald K. Park II, published by Parkrail, 1025 Oxford, Apt. L-138, Fort Collins, CO 80525)

Bill, Wyoming

For the ultimate in coal railroading, visit the hamlet of Bill in the Powder River Basin north of Douglas, Wyoming. Its remoteness is compensated for by the frequency of Burlington Northern and Chicago & North Western unit coal trains. (TRAINS, September 1992, page 64; also *Powder River Coal*, by Donald K. Park II, published by Parkrail, 1025 Oxford, Apt. L-138, Fort Collins, CO 80525)

Union Pacific's line over Sherman Hill between Cheyenne and Laramie, Wyoming, climbs to 8,015 feet. Photo by Wesley Fox.

Denver to Pueblo, Colorado

Nearer civilization is the 115-mile line from Denver south to Pueblo, Colorado, operated jointly by Santa Fe and Southern Pacific (formerly Denver & Rio Grande Western), with Burlington Northern as a tenant primarily for unit coal trains. The line is part double track and part single. It was originally two railroads which crossed and recrossed each other. In 1918 the Rio Grande and the Santa Fe agreed to operate their lines as a pair of one-way railroads and built connecting tracks to maintain right-hand running. The line ascends south from Denver and north from Colorado Springs to the summit at Palmer Lake. Much of the line between Denver and Colorado Springs (scenically the more interesting part) is paralleled by older highways; I-25 is nearby. (TRAINS, April 1989, page 60; also *Colorado's Joint Line*, by Donald K. Park II, published by Parkrail, 1025 Oxford, Apt. L-138, Fort Collins, CO 80525)

Essex, Montana

Essex is a small town on the southern boundary of Glacier National Park. It is the base for helper engines that assist eastbound freight trains climbing Marias Pass on Burlington Northern's ex-Great Northern transcontinental main line. Except for Amtrak's *Empire Builder*, which stops in Essex, the action is all BN — but the magnificent scenery

An eastbound Santa Fe freight rounds the curve just west of the summit of Cajon Pass in October 1981. Photo by Wesley Fox.

and the hospitality of the Izaak Walton Inn at Essex more than make up for that. (TRAINS, December 1989, page 84)

Cajon Pass, California

Santa Fe's double-track main line from the east reaches the Los Angeles Basin by way of Cajon Pass north of San Bernardino. The north side of the pass is relatively easy going through high desert; the south side of the pass is steep, with grades from 2.2 to 3 percent. As if Santa Fe weren't enough, Union Pacific has trackage rights on Santa Fe — and in the 1960s Southern Pacific built a parallel line over the pass as part of its Colton-Palmdale Cutoff. Amtrak's *Southwest Chief* traverses the pass in darkness, but the *Desert Wind* does it in both directions in the early afternoon. (TRAINS, September 1974, pages 20-37; *Cajon Field Guide*, by Jason Paul Kazarian, Box 476, Ridgecrest, CA 93556-0476)

Organized train-watching (and other activities)

There are several nationwide rail enthusiast organizations of a general nature offering such activities as local meetings, national conventions, field trips, and rail excursions. Write for information to:
• National Railway Historical Society, P. O. Box 58153, Philadelphia, PA 19102
• Railway & Locomotive Historical Society, Box 1418, Westford, MA 01886
• The Railroad Enthusiasts, Inc., c/o John Reading, 102 Dean Road, Brookline, MA 02146
• Canadian Railroad Historical Association, 120 Rue St. Pierre, St. Constant, PQ, Canada J5A 2G9
• Upper Canada Railway Society, P. O. Box 122, Station A, Toronto ON, Canada M5W 1A2

Safety

A railroad is the only dangerous industry that does not have a chain link fence around it. Do not trespass on railroad property. Remember that trains can move at any time on any track; they can move quietly; and they are bigger than you. Be alert to the character of the neighborhood when you choose a train-watching spot. There are places — and not just in the cities — where a person standing alone carrying an expensive camera (or a cheap camera) is in personal danger.

GLOSSARY

Abandon: to cease operating all or part of a route or service, especially with the intent of never resuming it again.

Affiliate: a company effectively controlled by another or associated with others under common ownership or control.

American Short Line Railroad Association: a trade association of railroads and suppliers that provides legislative, management, and traffic assistance to short lines (see page 18).

Association of American Railroads (AAR): the coordinating and research agency of the United States railroad industry. It is not a government agency but rather an organization to which railroads belong, much as local businesses belong to a chamber of commerce (see page 36).

Bankrupt: declared legally insolvent (unable to pay debts as they fall due) and with assets taken over by judicial process to be distributed among creditors.

Bridge route, bridge traffic: Bridge traffic is freight received from one railroad to be moved by a second railroad for delivery to a third. A bridge route is a railroad with more bridge traffic than traffic originating or terminating on line.

Broad gauge: any track gauge greater than 4'8½". The Erie Railroad was built with a gauge of 6 feet; contemporary examples include BART (5'6"); Toronto Transit Commission (4'10"); and SEPTA (5'2¼"). Elsewhere in the world gauges greater than standard are found in Spain, Portugal, India (5'6"); Ireland and New South Wales, Australia (5'3"); and Russia (5').

Capitalization: the total par value or stated value of the capital of a company. Overcapitalization means the value of the stocks and bonds exceeds the value of the physical properties of the railroad; conservative capitalization means the two values are close.

Centralized Traffic Control (CTC): a traffic control system whereby train movements are directed through remote control of switches and signals from a central control panel. The trains operate on the authority of signal indications instead of the authority of a timetable and train orders.

Charter: an instrument in writing from a state or country granting or guaranteeing rights, franchises, and privileges to a corporation. Obtaining a charter is a necessary part of incorporation.

Class 1 Railroad: a railroad with average annual gross revenue of $250 million or more for three or more consecutive years.

Class 2 Railroad: a railroad with average annual gross revenue between $20 and $250 million.

Class 3 railroad: a railroad with average annual gross revenue under $20 million.

COFC: Container on Flat Car — see Piggyback.

Bay Area Rapid Transit's track gauge of 5'6" was chosen to provide greater stability at high speeds and under windy conditions (the cars are quite light, about 31 tons). BART also uses a non-standard voltage, 1000 volts. A five-car train, led by one of the new cars that can run either at the end of the train or in the middle, accelerates south from Balboa Park Station in San Francisco on May 30, 1991. Photo by William D. Middleton.

The Manitou & Pike's Peak Railway in Colorado is the highest cog railroad in the world and one of only two cog railroads in North America — the other ascends Mount Washington in New Hampshire. In 1949 steam locomotives were still commonplace on the line; Swiss-built diesel cars now climb Pike's Peak. Photo by A. C. Kalmbach.

Cog railroad: a railroad that uses toothed wheels on the locomotive meshing with a rack between the running rails for traction. Much steeper grades are possible than on an ordinary railroad. The term "rack railroad" is synonymous.

Common carrier: a transportation company that offers — indeed, must offer — its services to all customers, as differentiated from a contract carrier, which carries goods for one shipper. The difference is like that between two buses, one signed "Main Street;" the other, "Charter."

Commuter service: passenger service that takes people to and from work. Characteristics include morning and evening peak periods, fares with multiple-ride discounts, the same riders Monday through Friday, and luggage consisting mostly of briefcases.

Company-owned railroad: a railroad whose stock is held by a another

Crews guide 100-pound continuous welded rail into postion on the Norfolk Southern on December 11, 1972. Photo by Wharton Separk III.

company rather than by individuals.

Consolidation: the unification of two or more corporations by dissolution of existing ones and creation of a single new corporation.

Continuous welded rail (CWR): rail laid in lengths of 1,500 feet or so, rather than 39-foot pieces bolted together. It doesn't buckle, because the track structure resists thermal expansion and contraction, and the elasticity of the steel forces dimensional changes to occur in the cross section of the rail rather than in its length.

Control: ownership by a railroad or by those sympathetic to its interests of enough of the securities of a second road to control its traffic policies.

Controlling interest: sufficient stock ownership in a corporation to exert control over policy.

Coupler: the device that fastens cars and locomotives together.

CTC: see Centralized Traffic Control.

Degree: a measure of the sharpness of a curve. It is the angle through

Today CTC panels include video displays, but the basic principle is unchanged: The dispatcher controls switches and signals from a control panel that may be miles from the track itself. Union Pacific photo.

The coupler is one of the basic elements of railroading. Photo by Jim Shaughnessy.

which the track turns in 100 feet of track. The number of degrees is equal to 5,729 divided by the radius of the curve in feet.

Embargo: an order issued by a common carrier or public regulatory agency that prohibits the acceptance of some or all kinds of freight for transportation on the carrier's lines or between specified points or areas because of traffic congestion, labor difficulties, or other reasons.

Ex: in this book, "formerly" or "formerly belonging to."

Federal Railroad Administration (FRA): the agency of the U. S. Department of Transportation that deals with transportation policy as it affects railroads.

Financial interest: ownership of enough securities of a second road, short of control, to influence its traffic policies.

Foreclosure: a legal proceeding that bars or extinguishes a mortgagor's right of redeeming a mortgaged estate. In domestic terms, you mortgage your house as security on a loan for its purchase. If you fail to keep up payments, the mortgagee — the bank — can foreclose, which means the bank gets the house and you no longer have it. It's the same with a loan for construction of a railroad.

Gauge: the distance between the running rails of track.

Grade: the inclination or slope of the track. It is usually measured as a percent (the tangent of the angle of inclination) — for example, a rise of 2 feet in 100 feet of track is 2 percent. Occasionally it is expressed as "1 in n," where n is the number of feet in which the track rises 1 foot. Both measures are ratios — 1 in 50 is the same as 2 percent. The steepest mainline grade in North America is 4.7 percent on a Norfolk Southern (ex-Southern Railway) line near Saluda, North Carolina. The usual maximum for a main line in mountainous territory is about 2 percent.

Haulage: movement of one railroad's traffic by a second road between specific points under the terms of a contract. The hauling road exercises no control over the traffic, is not shown in the route for the traffic, and does not get a division of the revenue.

Head-end power (HEP): electricity from either a locomotive's main generator or an auxiliary generator for heating, lighting, and cooling passenger cars in lieu of steam heat and generators on the passenger-car axles.

The grade is distinctly visible as a Southern Railway passenger train starts up Saluda Grade at Melrose, North Carolina, with steam locomotives fore and aft. Photo by E. H. Bennett Jr.

Holding company: a company that owns other companies for purposes of control. The charter of one such company empowered it to acquire, hold, and dispose of stocks, bonds, and securities issued by corporations and government, state, and local authorities — in other words, do everything but coin money and administer the sacraments.

ICC: Interstate Commerce Commission, below (also see page 136)

Incentive per diem: To alleviate a shortage of box cars in the mid-1970s, the railroad industry encouraged the railroads to put new cars into service by offering an incentive payment — basically almost double the daily rental for new box cars in good condition. Investors teamed up with short lines to take advantage of incentive payments, accounting regulations, and tax laws; shortline box cars blossomed forth. Then the recession of 1978 hit, followed by truck deregulation. The box cars were soon idle and eventually many of them were sold to other railroads.

Incorporate: to form into a corporation recognized by law as an entity.

Industrial railroad: a railroad owned and operated by an industry to move cars within a factory, plant, or mill and to and from a common-carrier interchange; in colloquial terms, a railroad behind a chain-link fence. Industrial railroads are usually not common carriers.

Interchange: a junction of two railroads where cars are transferred from one road to another.

Intercity passenger service: as distinguished from commuter service, the passengers don't make the trip every day, tickets are for single trips, and the luggage contains clothing, not the newspaper and work to do at home. Intercity passenger trains usually include reclining-seat coaches and, for night trips, sleeping cars, and offer food and beverage service.

Intermodal: traffic moving by more than one mode on its trip from shipper to receiver. The term is most frequently used for piggyback or trailer-on-flat-car traffic, but includes containers transferred from seagoing ships to special rail cars.

Interstate Commerce Commission (ICC): the agency of the federal government that carries out the provisions of the Interstate Commerce Act and other laws regulating interstate transportation (see page 136).

Interurban: an electric railroad running between cities, often of lighter

The Illinois Terminal Railroad, which connected Peoria, Danville, and Springfield with St. Louis was one of the longest-lived interurbans: Passenger service and electric operation ended in 1958; Norfolk & Western purchased the road in 1981. A one-car IT train approaches the passenger shelter at Gardena, near Morton, Illinois, on March 16, 1953. Photo by Paul Stringham.

Colorado & Southern No. 8, a narrow gauge 2-6-0 at the head of a short passenger train, awaits departure time on three-rail, dual-gauge track in Denver Union Station some time in the late 1930s. Photo by L. C. McClure.

construction than "steam" railroads and often operating in the streets of cities and towns instead of on private right of way. Interurbans had their rise and fall during the first four decades of the twentieth century.

Joint operation: operation of two railroads as one unit under two separate boards of directors.

Lease: the handing over of the property of a railroad in return for a specified yearly payment. The railroad must be returned in as good condition as when it was handed over. The most prevalent form of lease calls for the guarantee of the interest and principal of outstanding bonds of the lessor and a guaranteed percentage on the stock. The lessor company continues to exist and to retain ownership of its railroad property.

Line-haul railroad: a railroad that performs point-to-point service, as distinguished from a switching or terminal railroad. For line-haul railroads, interline revenue is usually some portion of the through rate.

Load limit: the maximum load that may be moved over a line. It depends on the construction and condition of track and bridges as well as other factors. Also the maximum weight that may be carried by a freight car. Wheels, axles, and bearings are the limiting elements in determining the load limit of a car.

Merger: the issuing of additional securities by a major company in payment for the securities of a minor company whose corporate existence is then ended; absorption by a corporation of one or more others. In precise terms, Northern Pacific, Great Northern, and Burlington were not merged with each other to form Burlington Northern but were merged *by* Burlington Northern. Sometimes a new name is involved: Seaboard Air Line merged Atlantic Coast Line and simultaneously adopted a new name, Seaboard Coast Line.

Mixed train: a train carrying both freight and passengers, the latter either in passenger cars or in the caboose, and usually running on a slow schedule.

Narrow gauge: any track gauge less than 4'8½" (standard gauge). The most common North American narrow gauge was 3 feet, and the largest concentration of it was in Colorado. Two isolated portions remain in existence carrying tourists: Cumbres & Toltec and Durango & Silverton. Some 3-foot-gauge track remains in common-carrier service in Mexico, primarily in Yucatan. Canadian National's lines in Newfoundland (abandoned in 1988) were 3'6" gauge, the British colonial track gauge. Elsewhere in the world the most prevalent narrow gauges are 3'6" and 1 meter (39.37").

Operating contract: operation of a minor road in return for a payment to the major road for the service rendered. The minor company continues to exist and retains ownership of its property.

Operating ratio: the ratio of operating expenses to revenue from operations. A railroad with an operating ratio of 80 or lower is doing nicely; a railroad that has an operating ratio over 100 is in trouble or soon will be.

Overhead traffic: same as Bridge traffic, above.

Percent: the measure of slope or inclination of track — see Grade, above.

Piggyback service: the transportation of highway truck trailers and containers on flatcars.

Pooling agreement: Under a pooling agreement railroads are operated separately but all income is divided arbitrarily, irrespective of traffic carried.

Manufacturer, date, and weight can be found on the web of the rail. This is 112-pound rail produced in 1934 by Bethlehem Steel Company at its Steelton, Pa., plant. Photo by Tom Nelligan.

Pound (rail): The unit of measure of rail size is weight per yard — a 3-foot length of 112-pound rail, for example, weighs 112 pounds.

Proprietary company: a corporation owning all or a controlling portion of the shares of another.

Purchase: payment of cash outright for all the property of a railroad, which may divide such proceeds as it wishes among its owners and then cease to exist as a corporation.

Push-pull: a mode of operation, usually of commuter trains. In one direction the train operates conventionally, but in the other direction the train runs with the locomotive pushing. The car at the opposite end from the locomotive has a control cab for the engineer.

Receiver, receivership: a person appointed by a court to manage a corporation during a period of reorganization — receivership — in an effort to avoid bankruptcy.

Regional railroad: a railroad bigger than a short line but smaller than a major railroad, usually a Class 2 railroad.

Reorganization: the rehabilitation of the finances of a business concern under procedures prescribed by federal bankruptcy legislation.

Right of way: the track, roadbed, and property along the track owned by the railroad.

Route mile: a mile of railroad line without regard to the number of tracks on that line. For example, the Soo Line route from Chicago to

Milwaukee is 85 route miles. The line is double track, so it includes 170 track miles for main track alone, not counting sidings and spurs.

Short line: a railroad with less than 100 miles of mainline track. There is no official or legal definition of the term; this is the criterion used by the railroad industry and the American Short Line Railroad Association.

Shorthaul: to move traffic a shorter distance than the maximum possible for a given railroad between two points. For example, Burlington Northern can be said to shorthaul itself if it turns over Seattle-Chicago traffic to Wisconsin Central at St. Paul rather than take it all the way to Chicago on its own rails.

Staggers Act: The Staggers Rail Act, named for Rep. Harley O. Staggers of West Virginia, was signed into law by President Jimmy Carter on October 14, 1980. It was massive deregulation of the railroads, including provisions to raise any rate that falls below 160 percent of out-of-pocket costs (later 180 percent) and to enter into contracts with shippers to set price and service, both without ICC approval.

Standard gauge: a track gauge of 4'8½".

Steam railroad: a term still used by regulatory bodies to differentiate ordinary railroads from "electric railways" — interurbans and streetcar companies.

Subsidiary: a company wholly controlled by another that owns more

An Amtrak San Diegan rolls south through Sorrento Canyon on July 28, 1989, with an ex-Metroliner control coach on the head end (another is two cars back in the train) and two F40PH's pushing. Photo by William D. Middleton.

The weight of a freight car rests on the truck bolster. The ends of the bolster rest on springs that transmit the weight to the truck sideframe. The sideframe holds the journal bearings, which transmit the load to the axles. Photo by Jim Shaughnessy.

than half its voting stock.

Switching district: an area within which a shipper located on one railroad has equal access to other railroads, either through a terminal or switching railroad or through reciprocal switching agreements among the line-haul railroads.

Switching railroad or
Terminal railroad: a railroad whose business is not point-to-point transportation but rather pickup and delivery service for a connecting line-haul road. Switching and terminal companies usually receive a flat per-car amount for their services.

Tie: the crosswise member of the track structure, usually made of wood or concrete, to which the rails are fastened.

Truck trailers ride on flatcars on a Conrail TOFC train at Spencer, Massachusetts, in 1980. Photo by Scott Hartley.

TOFC: Trailer on Flat Car — commonly called "piggyback."
Track gauge: the distance between running rails.
Track mile: a mile of track — see Route mile.
Trackage rights: rights granted by a railroad to another to operate on the tracks of the first, usually for a rental fee or a toll and usually without rights to service customers along that line.
Transit: short-distance, high-density passenger service usually characterized by electric propulsion, fare payment by token, magnetic card, or cash, and operation under, above, and on streets.
Trolley: a streetcar, an electric-powered rail vehicle drawing current from an overhead wire. The term "trolley" is often used nowadays to mean a bus gussied up to look like an old streetcar or a cable car.
Truck: the wheel-axle-frame assembly under each end of a car or locomotive.
Unit train: a train carrying a single bulk commodity, usually coal or grain, from shipper to consignee without any switching or classification en route.
USRA: United States Railroad Administration, the federal agency that took over operation of almost all U. S. railroads during World War I.

INDEX

The index lists the first appearance of subjects within each entry. Boldface type indicates the primary entry for each subject. Present-day railroads and previous companies with the same name are distinguished as "new" and "old."

A

UPDATE

This book was compiled and produced in summer 1992. It is a snapshot of the railroad industry at that time, but the railroad industry wouldn't hold still for the picture. Here are the significant changes that took place just before press time.

Metrolink

Southern California Regional Rail Authority began rail commuter service on October 26, 1992, the most extensive commuter service to be introduced at one time in North America. Its locale, the city that "invented" the urban freeway, is especially significant. Metrolink's initial routes are:

• Moorpark to Los Angeles, 47 miles, on Southern Pacific's Coast Line. The line already hosts Amtrak's *Coast Starlight* and two Santa Barbara-San Diego trains. From 1981 to 1983 California Department of Transportation sponsored commuter service on the route between Oxnard and Los Angeles, 67 miles.

• Santa Clarita to Los Angeles, 35 miles, on SP's Mojave-Saugus-Los Angeles route. The line has lacked passenger service since the inception of Amtrak in 1971.

• Pomona to Los Angeles, 57 miles, on SP's main line from the east. The service is scheduled to be extended to San Bernardino in 1994.

Amtrak operates the service, which uses the Metrolink name. The initial batch of rolling stock consists of 17 F59PHs built by General Motors at London, Ontario, and 70 Bombardier double-deck coaches like those used in Toronto and Miami.

Two more routes are projected to open in 1993: Riverside to Los Angeles, 57 miles, on Union Pacific rails, and San Juan Capistrano to Los Angeles, 58 miles, on Santa Fe's Surf Line, already used by Amtrak and a train sponsored by Orange County Transportation Authority. Other routes further in the future are Riverside to Los Angeles via Fullerton (currently the route of Amtrak's *Desert Wind*), San Bernardino-Riverside-Santa Ana-Irvine on Santa Fe, Hemet to Riverside (40 miles), and Redlands to San Bernardino (8 miles).

Kansas City Southern and MidSouth

Rail enthusiasts sometimes get together to play a hypothetical gamed called "Merger." Everyone sits in a circle, and someone starts by saying, "If Southern Pacific had gone after the Chicago & Eastern Illinois in 1954 ...," and everyone parcels out the other railroads, much as the Interstate Commerce Commission did in the original edition of the game in the 1920s. Toward the end of the evening someone asks, "What about Kansas City Southern?" It usually winds up as part of the Santa Fe (the ICC gave it to Union Pacific).

Until now Kansas City Southern (page 139) hasn't been a player in the real game of Merger that the railroads have been playing, but since the mid-1950s it has seen its neighbors absorbed into larger systems. None of the larger railroads has shown much interest in the KCS. Union Pacific already goes everywhere KCS goes; Burlington Northern already reaches the Mississippi River and the Gulf of Mexico at several points; and so does Southern Pacific. Besides, KCS lies crosswise to the traffic flow of UP, BN, and SP. That may be the reason KCS is still independent: It is a north-south railroad in an east-west country. The one exception to that on its map is a line from Shreveport, Louisiana, west to Dallas, Texas.

KCS finally entered the real, for-keeps merger game on September 21, 1992, when it announced it was acquiring MidSouth Rail Corporation (page 162), whose main line runs from Shreveport east to Meridian, Mississippi, essentially extending KCS's east-west route.

Pittsburgh & Lake Erie

On September 11, 1992, P&LE (page 186) ceased operation. The railroad was sold to a CSX subsidiary, Three Rivers Railway, which began operation September 15. P&LE's parent company retained the shops, locomotives, cars, ownership of the Youngstown & Southern, and half-ownership of the Pittsburgh, Chartiers & Youghiogheny and the Lake Erie & Eastern.